Predictive Policing and Artificial Intelligence

This edited text draws together the insights of numerous worldwide eminent academics to evaluate the condition of predictive policing and artificial intelligence (AI) as interlocked policy areas. Predictive and AI technologies are growing in prominence and at an unprecedented rate. Powerful digital crime mapping tools are being used to identify crime hotspots in real-time, as pattern-matching and search algorithms are sorting through huge police databases populated by growing volumes of data in an effort to identify people liable to experience (or commit) crime, places likely to host it, and variables associated with its solvability. Facial and vehicle recognition cameras are locating criminals as they move, while police services develop strategies informed by machine learning and other kinds of predictive analytics. Many of these innovations are features of modern policing in the UK, the US and Australia, among other jurisdictions.

AI promises to reduce unnecessary labour, speed up various forms of police work, encourage police forces to more efficiently apportion their resources, and enable police officers to prevent crime and protect people from a variety of future harms. However, the promises of predictive and AI technologies and innovations do not always match reality. They often have significant weaknesses, come at a considerable cost and require challenging trade-offs to be made. Focusing on the UK, the US and Australia, this book explores themes of choice architecture, decision-making, human rights, accountability and the rule of law, as well as future uses of AI and predictive technologies in various policing contexts. The text contributes to ongoing debates on the benefits and biases of predictive algorithms, big data sets, machine learning systems, and broader policing strategies and challenges.

Written in a clear and direct style, this book will appeal to students and scholars of policing, criminology, crime science, sociology, computer science, cognitive psychology and all those interested in the emergence of AI as a feature of contemporary policing.

John L.M. McDaniel teaches and researches within the University of Wolverhampton Department of Social Science, Inclusion and Public Protection and is an active member of the University's Law Research Centre. He focuses on issues of police accountability, corruption, human rights, and international cooperation and security.

Ken G. Pease is a Professor in Policing at the University of Derby. He has written numerous books on policing, psychology and crime science.

Routledge Frontiers of Criminal Justice

For more information about this series, please visit: www.routledge.com/
Routledge-Frontiers-of-Criminal-Justice/book-series/RFCJ

Predictive Policing and Artificial Intelligence

Edited by John L.M. McDaniel and Ken G. Pease

Routledge
Taylor & Francis Group

LONDON AND NEW YORK

First published 2021
by Routledge
2 Park Square, Milton Park, Abingdon, Oxon OX14 4RN

and by Routledge
52 Vanderbilt Avenue, New York, NY 10017

Routledge is an imprint of the Taylor & Francis Group, an informa business

British Library Cataloguing-in-Publication Data
A catalogue record for this book is available from the British Library

Library of Congress Cataloging-in-Publication Data
A catalog record has been requested for this book

ISBN: 9780367210984 (hbk)
ISBN: 978-0-367-70136-9 (pbk)
ISBN: 9780429265365 (ebk)

Typeset in Bembo
by Newgen Publishing UK

For Ponniah and Balasoundari Jeyendran

Contents

Illustrations

Figures

Tables

Foreword

This landmark volume documents what is known about the present practices of policing, predictive analytics and artificial intelligence in some of the major democracies of the West. In order that it not be lost to all but the domain expert, the task here is to make things plain for the non-specialist reader. For fifty years, the police institution has been in a process of continuous organizational change due to the transformative capacities of increasingly powerful networked surveillance, information and communications technologies. In the 21st century digital computing has made possible the alienation of human thought, or an approximation of thought. All of a sudden, the idiosyncrasies, the weaknesses and powers, the vagaries and vicissitudes of human thinking have been found embedded in machines that contain incalculable amounts of information, and thereby have increasingly become arbiters of human fate.

As this book goes to press, the effects of technologically mediated thinking – 'artificial intelligence' or AI – on policework have never been more politically charged. The way techno-policing is imagined veers between utopia and dystopia, but this is no surprise because beliefs about technological advance in general also tend to oscillate between these extremes. On the one hand there are developers who sell technological solutions to police services and the academic researchers thirsty for research grants. On the other are a range of social activists, researchers and non-governmental organizations challenging the hegemony of the underlying system, often in clearly dystopian terms and always with suspicion about the interaction between the techno-solutions and the problems they purportedly aim to solve. This toxic pendulum of imaginings describes the conditions in which impersonal historical forces play out, notwithstanding humans' attempts to be masters of their own destiny.

Research on policing and artificial intelligence provides crucial insights into the emergence of the general pattern of Technopoly, wherein all the problems of social, cultural and economic life are brought under the aegis of technology. Looking at the effects of AI on society by focusing on the empirical reality expressed in policing organization is highly revealing. The police métier has evolved as a set of institutional practices of tracking, surveillance, keeping watch, and unending vigilance, and it remains ready to apply force, up to and including fatal force, in pursuit of police organizational goals of reproducing social order, making crime, managing risk and governing insecurity.

As this volume shows, there are two analytically distinct practices, policing territory and suspect populations – 'hot spots' and 'hot people'. On the basis of already existing policing practice, mediated thinking routines have been embedded as algorithms that patrol and analyse available data and generate proactive police tasking. Officers' decisions to stop-and-search an individual at a particular location and time, for instance, are the product of institutional thinking embedded in the information and communications processing systems that manage the police intelligence division-of-labour 'in real time'. In this scenario, standardized deterrence is the logic and imagined outcome underlying the application of the police métier.

Policework has become subject to efficiency, effectiveness and economy measures that focus officer attention on accountability metrics. A choice architecture shapes and channels officers' discretionary action into pre-destined routines, often assuming an enforcement role is primary. The depressing reality on the ground is that this fosters distrust, especially in communities suffering multiple social deprivation. Under the influence of technology developers with commercial and other interests, police organization has become subject to dehumanized decision-making on the grounds that human decision-making is biased. The difficulty is, ever since the invention of the personal computer, transparency has been reduced to something visible on a screen and very few people understand how those images are created. Screen icons that organize an unambiguous access to programs and data create a façade of transparency all the more difficult to discern because digital information processing has colonized the life world. Digital computers direct the activities of police patrol, and police agents' notions of 'reasonable suspicion' are the creation of data mining and algorithmic calculation that even experts cannot adequately explain. Information displayed on the screens is taken as transparently revealing the accountable truth.

Epistemic anxieties about crime and insecurity are imported into the machinery of police artificial intelligence and take the form of detectable patterns of correlation displayed on screens. This is the basis upon which lies police accountability, in both the sense of the ability to give an account and to take a count. Real responsibility is distributed widely across the police division-of-labour, and both decision-making and knowledge production are shared between humans connected by automated systems of mediated communication. Interactions between police and public are subject to multiple points of surveillance. In fact, surveillance is now 'ambient', meaning it is an unquestioned background factor at all times. Police have cameras and so does the public they interact with. Police dressed as 'crime fighters' enact routines defined by intelligence systems that unite humans and digital machines in a logic that defines police priorities and proportionate use-of-force. It is therefore unsurprising to find that people in low-income communities segregated along the lines of race and ethnicity view police as a hostile occupation force. Observing this, some researchers in the field have attempted to re-engineer policework away from enforcement metrics and towards metrics concerning community safety and social harm. Many would give up national security for human security. Readers of this volume will learn about the tremendous difficulties there are in shifting the police métier away from the enforcement emphasis and deterrence thinking.

This is an extremely difficult area to do empirical work in and there is an absolute need for this book. Readers will find that the perniciousness of AI in policing is rather more complex than the commonly held techno-imaginaries inherited from science fiction suggest. Humans program the machines which are deployed to train humans in order to perform machine-assisted tasks. The research presented here helps explain the indeterminacies that result in a world of fully mediated communication and information processing, breaking through a good deal of the secrecy and confusion surrounding police technology.

Citizens in democracies ought to be concerned about the influence of large corporations (IBM, Motorola, Microsoft, to name the most obvious), or companies backed by venture capital like PredPol, or (even worse) companies backed by covert government funding like Palantir because they provide the technological underpinnings of police organization and, as the respected policing scholar David Bayley once put it, police is to government as the edge is to the knife.

In a culture where we seek authorization in technology, find satisfactions in technology and take orders from technology there is danger keenly expressed in police technology above all others. Police organizations, in common with other major social institutions (for example in insurance and finance, news and entertainment, medicine and health) suffer from a surplus of information generated by technology which, in turn and paradoxically, requires new technological tools in order to cope. Technological fascination has become the source of direction and purpose for society and the individuals that comprise it. The information technologies that we play and work with every day – our smartphones and tablets – are the nearly perfect basis for technological totalitarianism. Computerized information processing establishes sovereignty over all areas of human experience because technology 'thinks' better, faster and more exactly than humans can. It follows that some people have a 'knowledge monopoly' in these domains, and celebrity Technopolists have been granted (undeserved) prestige, authority, and influence over human affairs. They elevate information to a metaphysical status and their power rests on ownership and control of the instruments of its possession. The belief that machine-thinking is superior to lax, ambiguous and complex human thinking and judgment has much in common with the principles of scientific management espoused by Frederick Taylor in an earlier time. Taylorization has become Uberization, and this becomes unpleasantly visible in policework because it so often concerns social conflict. The values of efficiency, precision and objectivity are encoded into machine-thinking. The value of social justice is not. *Homo sapiens* yearns for understanding and transcendence and *Homo digitalis* works for system-defined interests.

Sociologists of science and technology have long known that humankind is experiencing an unprecedented breakneck-speed technological transformation of culture. Like any other revolutionary period, our current time has the feeling of a natural cataclysm, which affects everyone whether they welcome it or not. Watching the interactions between police and public in different jurisdictions provides a metric to measure the intensity of the social change. From the point of view of the individual, history does seem inevitable in that we are all born into a stream of change which carries us along. Between a past that none can alter and an uncertain future there is the present fleeting moment in which one is free to act in ways that may affect future history. What we do in the present constructs our legacy. We might not be able to precisely determine what that will be, but we can try to make it a better one. The task is difficult but it would be impossible were it not for the efforts of researchers asking the difficult questions and seeking answers.

Professor James Sheptycki
York University, Toronto, Canada

Contributors

Harith Alani is a professor at the Knowledge Media institute, The Open University, where he heads a Social Data Science group. Professor Alani published around 150 scientific papers in various leading journals and conferences, and recently was research track co-chair at The Web Conference (WWW 2017) and at the Extended Semantic Web Conference (ESWC 2017). He is the co-ordinator of COMRADES (2016–2019), a € 2M European H2020 project to research and develop a collaborative platform for supporting communities during crises. He is also the PI of H2020 TRIVALENT, which is developing novel methods for the tracking and detection of online radicalization.

Alexander Babuta is a Research Fellow at the Royal United Services Institute. His research covers a range of areas relating to national security, digital policing and emerging technologies. He is Co-Director of the Observatory for Monitoring Data-Driven Approaches to COVID-19, a SPRITE+ Expert Fellow (Security, Privacy, Identity and Trust Engagement Network), and a Member of the Essex Centre for Data Analytics Data Ethics Committee.

Mark Britton is a Police Inspector for the Isle of Man Constabulary. He is currently the Information Manager for the Constabulary. He is the lead officer for the introduction of Body Worn Video for the Constabulary.

Janet Chan is Professor at UNSW Law and co-leader of the Data Justice Research Network at the Allens Hub for Technology, Law and Innovation. She is internationally recognised for her contributions to policing research, especially her work on police culture, police reform, and the use of information technology in policing. Her major publications in this field include *Changing Police Culture* and *Fair Cop: Learning the Art of Policing*. In recent years she has published (with Lyria Bennett Moses) articles and chapters on big data and algorithms in *Theoretical Criminology*, *British Journal of Criminology*, *Policing & Society* and a number of edited books. She is currently leader of an Australian Research Council funded project on using big data for social policy and a co-investigator in a Canadian SSHRC funded project on conceptions of police intelligence (led by Carrie Sanders). Janet was elected Fellow of the Academy of Social Sciences in Australia in 2002 and received the Australian and New Zealand Society of Criminology Distinguished Criminologist Award in 2015.

I. Glenn Cohen is the James A. Attwood and Leslie Williams Professor of Law at Harvard Law School. He is one of the world's leading experts on the intersection of bioethics (sometimes also called 'medical ethics') and the law. His research interests relate to big data, health information technologies, mobile health, reproduction/reproductive technology, research ethics, organ transplantation, rationing in law and medicine, and health policy.

Miriam Fernandez is a Senior Research Fellow at the Knowledge Media Institute (KMi), Open University. Before joining KMi, she was research associate at Universidad Autonoma de Madrid, Spain and software engineer (intern) at Google Zurich, Switzerland. Her research is at the intersection of the Web Science (WS) and Semantic Web communities (SW), where she has contributed with more than 100 peer-reviewed articles. She has extensive expertise in leading EU and national projects and frequently participates in organising committees and editorial boards of the top SW and WS conferences, recently being program co-chair of the International (ISWC 2017) and Extended (ESWC 2019) Semantic Web Conferences.

Jamie Grace is a Senior Lecturer in Law in the Department of Law and Criminology at Sheffield Hallam University. Jamie is also vice-Chair of the West Midlands Police and Crime Commissioner's Independent Data Analytics Ethics Committee. Jamie's co-authored research on the legalities of the algorithmic analysis of police intelligence led to a model regulatory framework for algorithmic decision-making in UK policing (known as 'ALGO-CARE'), that has been promoted for use by the National Police Chiefs' Council. 'ALGO-CARE' was cited favourably in a report on artificial intelligence by the Lords Select Committee on Artificial Intelligence in April 2018. Jamie's evidence to a separate Parliamentary inquiry on algorithmic decision-making in the UK public sector was cited in the final inquiry report in May 2018.

Harry Graver is a graduate of Yale University and Harvard Law School. His writing has been featured in the Harvard Law Review, UC Davis Law Review, Wall Street Journal, and other publications.

Melissa Hamilton is a Reader in Law & Criminal Justice and Impact Lead at the University of Surrey School of Law. She researches on issues related to risk assessment practices, domestic and sexual violence, trauma responses in victims of assault, sentencing, and corrections. Prior to taking up her academic posts, she worked as a police officer and corrections officer in Florida and as a lawyer in Texas. She has a JD in Law and a PhD in Sociology from the University of Texas at Austin.

Rick Muir is Director of the Police Foundation, the UK's independent policing think tank. Prior to that he was the Associate Director for Public Service Reform at the Institute for Public Policy Research (IPPR). He has a D Phil in Politics from the University of Oxford. He is a Visiting Professor at Northumbria University.

Marion Oswald is Vice-Chancellor's Senior Fellow in Law at Northumbria University. She researches the interaction between law and digital technology and has a particular interest in the use of information and innovative technology by criminal justice bodies and the wider public sector. She is a solicitor (non-practicing), an Associate Fellow of the Royal United Services Institute, and chairs the West Midlands Police & Crime Commissioner and West Midlands Police data ethics committee. She is PI and Director of the AHRC-funded 'Observatory for the Monitoring of Data-Driven Approaches to Covid-19'.

Pamela Richards leads the vision for the research *theme "Developing Expertise in individuals and teams"* at the University of Central Lancashire. Pam supervises doctoral students in the UK and worldwide in the area of decision-making (including military/fire & technical complex water rescues and elite sport). Her research focuses on the development and operationalisation of shared mental models and team decision-making, in high pressurised naturalistic settings.

Debbie Roberts is the Foundation of Nursing Studies Professor of Practice Learning at Bangor University. Debbie has published widely in the field of nurse education and is particularly interested in practice learning. Her previous work has explored the role of immersive learning in facilitating empathy amongst nursing and occupational therapy students; her current projects include exploring the links between environment and the organisation of nursing care and exploring the use of artificial odours in immersive learning.

Michael Rowe is Professor of Criminology at Northumbria University. He has an international reputation for his research and publications in the field of policing, paying particular attention to policing culture and reforms, race and racism, police culture, and the policing of domestic violence. Other interests include on-line victimisation and offender desistance. He has published seven books on policing, crime, race and related issues.

Aaron Shapiro is Assistant Professor of Technology Studies at the University of North Carolina at Chapel Hill. He received his PhD from the Annenberg School for Communication at the University of Pennsylvania. His research on predictive policing was published in Surveillance & Society and Nature, and his work on media technologies, inequality and urban geography has been published in Media, Culture & Society, Space & Culture and New Media & Society.

Manuel A. Utset, Jr. is the William & Catherine Van Der Creek Professor and Associate Dean for Juris Master Programs at Florida State University College of Law. His research focuses on applying behavioural law and economics to criminal law, corporate law and financial regulation. He has written extensively on self-control problems and repeated criminal misconduct, on the relationship between engineering principles and the law, and on complexity and financial bubbles and crises.

Introduction

John L.M. McDaniel and Ken G. Pease

The policing landscape is changing. Systems and technologies labelled as 'predictive' and 'artificial intelligence' (AI) are growing in prominence and at an unprecedented rate. Powerful digital crime mapping tools are being used to identify crime hotspots in real-time; pattern-matching and search algorithms are sorting through huge police databases filled with hitherto unimaginable volumes of data; routine form-filling and data entry processes are being assisted by automated predictive text software; and facial and vehicle recognition cameras are locating suspects as they move. These are just some of the technologies being utilised by police services around the world today. Search algorithms and recognition technologies, among others, can potentially reduce unnecessary labour, speed up various forms of police work, encourage police forces to more efficiently apportion their resources, and most importantly hold the promise of enabling police officers to prevent crime and protect people from a variety of future harms. However, new predictive and AI technologies may come at a price, not only as a financial cost to a police force but as a consequence of making trade-offs to accommodate them. This book attempts to shed light on some of the wider organisational and societal costs involved, their origins and their implications for modern policing.

The text will introduce the reader to the ideas of predictive policing and AI as they have developed in the public policing context. Although there are significant overlaps with developments in the private and plural policing spaces, our focus is predominantly on the use, or potential use, of these technologies and systems by modern police services. It is important also to note that while AI can form an integral part of predictive policing systems both are distinct concepts and can be applied very differently in context. Although they both centre on the use of algorithms, they are not interdependent. Within this introductory chapter, we will introduce the non-specialist to the concepts by tracing the development of predictive policing from hand-crafted algorithms through to the use of machine learning processes which are commonly described as AI. We will address the use of AI in other policing contexts separately. If readers are looking for a purely mathematical description of AI algorithms and predictive policing formulae, they will need to explore the sources that we cite. We try to avoid an overly technical review so that the introduction and the overall text remain accessible.

Throughout the edited collection, the chapters focus almost exclusively on police services in the UK, US and Australia. This is due largely to the rapid growth of new systems and technologies in these jurisdictions, as well as their shared linguistic and common law heritage which allows comparisons to be drawn. Another reason is that, although police services in places such as China, South Korea and Spain use variations of the systems described in the chapters and in a myriad of ways, much of the academic research available today emanates from the former. This is due, in part, to a longstanding interest in the development of AI technologies within universities and laboratories in the UK, US and Australia, including not least the seminal work of McCarthy et al. (1955) and Turing (1950). Similarly, the use of predictive algorithms in crime and policing has long been spearheaded by pioneers such as Kelling (1974), Pease (Pease et al., 1974; Pease et al., 1977) and Sherman (1983; Sherman and Weisburd, 1995) who have helped to create a relatively strong tradition of predictive experimentation and modelling across the three jurisdictions. We do not wish to ascribe specific developments to any particular place, person or time, partly because the academic subjects of predictive policing and AI have never been clearly delineated. What they are and what should legitimately fall within them is not an easy question to answer. The purpose of this edited collection is to bring some of the key issues and realities into sharp focus.

Two extremes

In an attempt to clear some ground at the outset, it may be instructive to address some easy misconceptions and myths surrounding predictive policing and AI. The first concerns the prominent discourse of positivity that surrounds them. They are readily associated, in some media reporting and academic circles, with superior quality, objectivity, efficiency and cost effectiveness (Brantingham et al., 2017). Predictive and AI technologies, so the positive narrative goes, can greatly increase the capacity of the police to detect and investigate crime (Perrot, 2017). The combination of computer science and mathematics can process data on their behalf, thereby freeing up police officers to focus on 'real' police work while pointing them towards the most likely suspects and the most reliable and effective evidence (Deloitte, 2018). It can enable them to do more with less resources and reduce crime rates through 'smart policing'. Not only can new technologies potentially improve quality across all areas of police work, they can reportedly beat mankind hands down when it comes to predicting events, so much so that statistical forecasting should be preferred to professional judgment in a variety of circumstances (Mohler et al., 2015; Ariel, 2019). The judgment of police officers in comparison is frequently characterised as inferior, resting heavily upon hunches, guess-work, opinions, whims, emotions, habits, anecdotes and stereotypes (Law Society, 2019). Algorithmic and AI systems are portrayed as being more objective (and therefore morally superior), accurate and efficient because they do not suffer from human weaknesses. More broadly, the general status quo has been depicted as unacceptable. Crime rates are too high, policing is ineffective and discriminatory, and the criminal justice system is seen as opaque and unfair (Stevenson, 2018). Billions of pounds (and dollars) are spent annually to prop up this apparently outdated system, some of which should be redirected towards technologies that can do a better job.

In the UK, national bodies such as Her Majesty's Inspectorate of Constabulary (HMIC) have called upon police forces "to harness the power of technology – particularly artificial intelligence" in order to exploit their full potential (2018: 33). The national inspectorate even lamented that "the lack of progress is frustrating, because there is real potential for technology, such as artificial intelligence (AI) … to make the police more effective and efficient" (Ibid: 34). It is frequently argued that if high-risk people and places can be identified, and crimes forecasted, then we, as a society, have a moral obligation to capitalise on such methods (Babuta et al., 2018). By augmenting or replacing various aspects of police work with prediction tools and AI systems, the public could enjoy more effective policing for less money, a reduced likelihood that innocent people will get caught up in the criminal justice system and a greater likelihood that criminals will be caught and prosecuted. In the US, *Time* magazine even named one predictive policing tool as one of the 50 best inventions of 2011 (alongside a malaria vaccine and Apple's Siri).

A positive discourse around AI is not unique to policing. AI systems are developing rapidly within many different professions. Within the field of healthcare, AI is being used in medical imaging to identify cancer, to detect and track the outbreak of infectious diseases, to identify effective treatments in clinical trials, to risk assess the likelihood of being diagnosed with kidney disease or cancer, to help people to speak and walk, and to optimise demand management and resource allocation within organisational systems. In the automotive industry, cars are being trained to self-drive, and aerial vehicles designed to fly autonomously (to deliver packages and to find people in disaster zones) using AI. Online, people are using AI-powered search systems like Google to navigate websites; spam filters are organising email inboxes; image recognition systems are automatically tagging photos on Facebook and Instagram; speech recognition allows users to interact with inter-connected virtual assistants like Alexa and Siri; and recommender systems are helping them to choose what to watch next on Netflix or buy on Amazon. Considerations of 'cities of the future' even frequently revolve around AI-enabled private household appliances that can function autonomously and interact with a broader public infrastructure, referred to colloquially as the 'Internet of Things' (Joh, 2019). AI is often presented as having a ubiquitous quality which allows it to make most aspects of human life better, including policing.

We have just outlined one extreme. The opposite terminus concerns a panoply of negative qualities associated with predictive policing and AI. Serious concerns abound about data privacy and the accountability of complex and opaque predictive systems (Shapiro, 2017). Being able to scrutinise machine learning systems, some of which are so complex that they are colloquially referred to as 'black box' systems is a key concern (Ferguson, 2017b). Critics contend that predictive policing and AI technologies can be harmful in reality, that they can even do more harm than good in many contexts (Moravec, 2019). Pre-existing biases and social inequalities can be entrenched during the design and operation of new technologies, and inherently biased systems may reinforce societal inequalities if they are used carelessly or if automated decision-making processes are adopted. Some sceptics argue that the use of predictive and AI technologies in policing is so dangerous that they should be abandoned in their entirety (Liberty, 2019). Partly as a result of the negative factors associated with AI, surveys in the UK have shown that although the public has a 'very limited awareness' of how AI tools work, people tend to have an "unduly negative view" of them (HLSC, 2018: 23). There is frequent mention of the negative portrayal of AI in Hollywood movies as a key reason for this.

We hope that once the reader reaches the end of the text, they will have abandoned such perspectives if they were previously held. We do not believe that reasonable people should take deeply entrenched positions on predictive policing or AI in general. These discourses are arguably too simplistic. The intersection of policing, prediction-generation and AI is far more complex and disparate. Many of the systems and technologies that fall under the rubrics of predictive policing and AI are used in specific ways for particular purposes and raise their own unique set of problems. Predictive policing and AI is not a single immutable thing. They are relatively loose concepts that refer to numerous different systems, processes and ideas. Predictive policing is an umbrella term that captures a range of different techniques and processes (including various AI systems), while the term 'AI' does not refer to one specific technology. It too is an umbrella term covering a range of different techniques and processes, which can be used to generate predictions or employed in different ways (not least logistics and identification tasks).

One of the reasons we embarked on this edited collection was to challenge readers to think about these discourses. When people think carefully about the different techniques used in predictive policing and the array of circumstances in which AI can be used, their attitudes, both positive and negative, should change from technology to technology and situation to situation. Surveys already show that when members of the public are asked to think about individual technologies in isolation their views can change (Royal Society, 2017). We also want readers to consider whether the terms 'predictive policing' and 'AI' should even be applied to many of the processes that they are currently associated with. The constituent systems and technologies can be so distinct and complex that a cursory understanding of how they work should raise questions about whether these descriptors should be used at all. Simply because a new system can outperform a police officer trying to carry out the same function does not necessarily mean that it should be described as an AI. A digital calculator programmed to add together every number entered into it (which can be described as a very basic algorithm) could outperform humans doing similar calculations by hand, but it does not mean that it qualifies as an AI system. Nor does it mean that the technology is superior to all police officers in general terms simply because the calculator has outperformed them in one relatively simple task. It just means that one particular technology, whether a digital calculator or a more advanced AI system, proved to be useful in one specific task within a particular environment.

Inordinately positive views appear to have permeated police organisations, the commercial entities developing predictive and AI technologies and, indeed, academia. From narrow pilot studies, inflated assessments about the general performance of predictive and AI technologies have been made (Berk et al., 2009; Russell and Norvig, 2014). Inflated assessments of performance are confined not only to commercial AI developers who sell technologies to police services in a highly lucrative and competitive market but scientists and academics have also been accused of exaggerating findings as they chase research funding, downplaying the peculiar nature and narrowness of their particular models (Richards et al., 2016; Nagendran et al., 2020). Similarly, researchers could find that an algorithm "can forecast well" and lead to "usefully accurate" forecasts of criminal behaviour during one particular analysis (Berk and Bleich, 2014: 79), but such findings may subsequently be reinterpreted by academics or commentators who want to expand an algorithm's repertoire of applications to serve other interests (without testing). In other words, instead of clarifying that discoveries relate only to one or two forms of behaviour, are particular to the specific area from which the data sets were drawn, and may be of dubious quality, it is not unusual for hyperbole to be misrepresented as fact. Ideally, rigorous testing of hypotheses under a range of different conditions, including randomised controlled trials, should be required before a new finding becomes part of the established canon, but this does not appear to represent the current reality in these fields. Substantive peer review of claims and regulatory approval to use systems in particular ways rarely feature at the nexus of policing, prediction and AI. Computer scientists, cognitive psychologists, mathematicians, behavioural scientists and even accountants seem remarkably capable of taking a view on the wholesale reform of policing by way of AI without presenting evidence of quality studies or possessing an intricate understanding of the subject as it is experienced by police officers and civilians on the ground.

Among the ideological proponents are various government bodies, computer scientists and commercial enterprises, while the critics often count lawyers, social scientists and NGOs among their ranks. The former are usually engaged in the development or procurement of systems, whereas the latter frequently claim to represent the people subjected to them. The emerging (and confused) struggle is perhaps well reflected in a recent report by the House of Lords (HLSC, 2018: 5–6) which states that the UK "is right to embrace"

AI, yet acknowledged that the "hopes and fears presently associated with AI are out of kilter with reality". One way of redressing this situation would be for stakeholders to avoid lauding particular innovations as proof that predictive policing or AI processes work in a general sense, and focus only on those applications for which they have been rigorously tested. Similarly, individual occurrences should not be jumped upon as proof that predictive and AI technologies are always dangerous. Distinct systems should be treated as independent and complex, each with its own code, biases and uses. Each predictive or AI system used by a police force is simply one tool in the policing toolbox, and they are frequently 'dual-use'. They are capable of being used to protect or discriminate, for the public good or for private interests, or for policing or non-policing purposes.

We would not expect people to take an ideological standpoint on whether digital cameras, as a concept, should exist. Rather, we would expect people to take issue with the materials used to make it (if they are hazardous), how it was made (labour rights), how it was used (privacy and safety), the quality of the snapshot (if the software produces an accurate picture, resembling real life), how it was sold to consumers (marketing and mis-selling), the returns policy (the ability to challenge all of these processes and to receive a remedy) and how all relevant processes are evaluated, among other ongoing concerns. We are not saying that predictive and AI systems are directly comparable to digital cameras (it as a metaphor), only that these are the types of issues that would ordinarily be probed. Quite unlike a digital camera (which can be developed, constructed and utilised in millions of different configurations), there is no one recognisable construct or brand that epitomises predictive policing or AI in policing. The fields contain an array of remarkably different products and processes, and each one raises a long list of concerns and considerations.

A challenging environment for police forces

Police forces are more than capable of incorporating new technologies and systems in specific ways, limiting their use to particular purposes and setting standards of performance and accountability. A tapestry of rules and regulations already surrounds the use of digital cameras, smartphones, personal computers, the compilation of case files and the processing of digital information, among other technologies, in a variety of policing contexts. Therefore we should not immediately discount the ability of police services, parliament, government bodies and civil society to work together to build a sensible architecture around predictive and AI policing systems. However, a variety of external pressures can cause police forces to eschew historical antecedents. Projections suggest that police services across the UK will be hundreds of millions of pounds in deficit by 2021 (National Audit Office, 2016). Years of austerity mean that the wider criminal justice system is faced with an "avalanche of problems" from the inability to gather and present crucial evidence within shorter timeframes to a growing shortage of solicitors and socio-economic barriers to legal aid (Law Society, 2019: 14). Complicating the landscape further is the fact that a broader shift from policing as a reactive, crime-fighting role to more of a victim-focused, risk-based, preventative role is taking place in various crime areas. Addressing these problems through cost-effective and scalable technologies carries a particular attraction. Police forces may even consider the procurement of such technologies to be necessary to carry out their basic functions and to maintain the rule of law with the limited resources available to them (Ibid).

Not only are police services attracted to the promise of innovative predictive and AI technologies but they also have broad appeal across the political spectrum. British governments have provided millions of pounds of funding to police services to implement digital transformation projects in recent years. Public support is also palpable. The promise of drastically reduced crime rates, increased public safety, better value for money and smart-on-crime policies ticks many boxes. These factors arguably create quite strong incentives for police services to develop and employ digital technologies within remarkably short timeframes. Their allure is such that some police services have even procured them with little or no competitive bidding or evidence that they work in practice (Stevenson, 2018; Valentine, 2019). The culture of positive discourse around predictive and AI technologies in policy-making circles allied to the financial and external pressures to use them to 'fix' policing has created a challenging, and potentially toxic, environment. Stakeholders and the public should be cognisant of these incentives and pressures as they proceed, for they may serve to drown out the critics. In this vein of thought, we endeavour in the next two sections to introduce the reader to predictive policing and AI as two distinct, yet overlapping, features of modern policing, each with their own unique processes and issues. Generating greater clarity around what they represent is surely a step in the right direction.

What is predictive policing?

Predictive policing is a relatively new concept that involves the application of analytical techniques to data for the purposes of generating statistical predictions about events so that something can be done about them in advance. It is tempting to discuss factors such as crime and harm prevention in a description of predictive policing, but it arguably has more general qualities. Predictions can concern offenders, victims, police behaviour and organisational efficiencies among an array of other applications. Calculating the risk that X may lead to Y in any policing context and doing something about X or Y could be construed as predictive policing. Commentators have even pointed out that predictive policing is a misnomer since a prediction is usually subjective, relies upon intuition, often involves a right or wrong outcome and is nonreproducible, whereas a process that is objective, scientific and reproducible and comes with an associated probability is better described as a 'forecast' (Perry et al., 2013). Although much of what happens in this field would be better described as forecasting, it is predictive policing rather than forecast policing that has become the more popular term (Ratcliffe, 2019). What we do know is that there should be two key parts to predictive policing in practice: 1) generating a prediction, and 2) carrying out some type of policing intervention, investigation or activity as a result (Perry et al., 2013).

The 'predictive' part

The first part of predictive policing, the predictive part, is rooted in concepts that are situated largely within criminology (often environmental criminology), crime science and, more recently, computer science. Taking the relevance of each one in turn, criminology recognises that the behaviours of some criminals are patterned. Studies have shown that criminal behaviour can happen in particular ways, often through identifiable sequences and decisions that are repeated across time and place. These patterns allow researchers to forecast a likelihood of future offending in a variety of contexts. This should not alarm the non-specialist. Studying trends and patterns in previous human behaviour for the purposes of forecasting future occurrences is quite standard. It is common convention that insurance companies estimate the cost of insuring drivers on the basis of their driving history (whether they have a 'no claims bonus'), where they live (the frequency of thefts in the area), their age and their gender among other factors. The premium that insurers charge is commensurate to the calculated risk of an individual crashing or having their car stolen in the future. Using the aggregated data of previously and currently insured drivers, they determine where people with some features in common fall on a scale from high to low risk and charge their customers accordingly.

Forecasting criminal behaviour can follow a similar process. In 1928, the sociologist Ernest Burgess (1928) examined data from thousands of prisoners in Illinois to deduce whether there was a pattern to those who would later go on to violate the terms of their parole. His study found significant correlations between offences, time served in prison and negative behaviours including alcohol abuse and homelessness, among other factors. Simply by attaching a score of zero for each negative factor or one for each positive factor (such as their behaviour in prison), Burgess generated an overall score for each prisoner. Those who had a higher score were deemed to be least likely to breach the terms of their parole, whereas those with lower scores (more negative behaviours) were at the greatest risk of being returned to prison. Realising that the Burgess scale was more accurate than the toss of a coin (the majority of the high-risk prisoners in his study subsequently violated the terms of their parole, whereas a majority of the low risk prisoners did not), some parole boards in Illinois began to use the mathematical formula to inform their decisions. Although academics would later take issue with the wisdom of reducing human behaviours down to ones and zeros, and equating what are quite disparate factors, Burgess's formula generated predictions about future criminal behaviour, and was one of the earliest forms of what we now refer to as 'behavioural science' or 'behavioural insights' in criminal justice.

Although the Burgess scale was developed almost a century ago, researchers began to pay serious attention to the development of mathematical formulae in criminal justice only in more recent decades. Rather than focus on hand-crafted formulae, as Burgess had done in the 1920s, researchers seem to have been attracted by and large to the potential of automated algorithms at the nexus of criminal justice and computer science. An algorithm is simply a sequence of instructions established to solve a particular task, and an automated one is capable of being implemented by a machine, usually a digital computer (Russell and Norvig, 2014). Various criminologists found that negative factors present in a person's criminal or behavioural history appeared to increase the risk of some categories of people engaging in crime or becoming a victim of crime in future. Negative factors ranged from adverse childhood experiences (ACEs), such as emotional, physical and sexual abuse; to witnessing serious violence at an early age; parental conflict; being a victim of violence; low educational attainment; substance abuse; being affiliated to a gang; and, of course, having a criminal record and previously committing violent acts (especially at a young age) (Donnelly and Ward, 2015). These occurrences could combine in different permutations to elevate the likelihood of future offending or victimisation. Soothill et al. (2002), for example, found correlations between convictions for kidnapping and subsequent convictions for murder, while Francis et al. (2004) determined that the past five years of an offender's history could be particularly informative when predicting the quality and type of offending that would occur in the next five year period. Of course, such findings did not prove that these formulae could be applied to the population at large, it just meant that notable patterns were found in the criminal histories of the offenders in the researchers' respective samples.

In more recent years, an array of mathematical measurements have been developed for the purposes of estimating a single number which reflects the likelihood of a person being involved in crime, whether as an offender or victim. The process of assessing the likelihood of someone committing an offence or being a victim of crime using a single numerical score is usually known as an 'individual risk assessment'. The same kind of score is occasionally called a 'recidivism score' when the process involves a known offender but the former is broadly used to capture both first-time offenders and recidivists. The scores are generated predominantly from individuals' criminal and personal histories and can involve other variables such as a questionnaire completed by the offender. Examples in the UK of risk assessment formulae include a tool for assessing domestic abuse, stalking, harassment and honour-based violence known as DASH (Robinson et al., 2016), a harm assessment risk tool (HART) which is used for pre-trial custodial decisions (Oswald et al., 2018) and an estimator of a prisoner's risk of violence in prison (Viper) (HMIP, 2020).

Today, risk scoring systems are being used by some police services and criminal justice agencies to identify, prioritise and classify high-risk offenders and victims. Prioritisation usually takes the form of a rank-ordered list so that officials can identity the riskiest people, from greatest to lowest risk. This approach can be found in the HART tool used in Durham (England), the Strategic Subjects List used by the Chicago Police Department, and the Chronic Violent Crime Offender Bulletins used by the Los Angeles Police Department (LAPD) among others. Rank-ordered lists for serious violent crime are commonly referred to as 'heat lists', while those people who are predicted to be at the highest risk of offending or victimisation are colloquially referred to as 'hot people' (Ferguson, 2017a). The relatively small proportion of offenders at the top of heat lists are usually considered to be responsible for a significantly large volume of crime (Sherman, 2007; Kennedy, 2019). Another popular technique involves the classification of offenders and victims according to their risk score or their association with particular characteristics and variables. Individuals who share some characteristics have been grouped together using labels such as 'drunkard', 'conman' and 'professional fringe violator' to aid decision-making (see Lombroso, 1911; Burgess, 1928; Gibbons and Garrity, 1962). Even though the use of such categories and rank-ordered lists invariably ignores key individual differences among the people concerned, they have been used in practice by custody officers to determine whether individuals should be diverted away from the criminal justice system, by judges to determine how severe sentences should be, and by offender management systems to determine the type of prison that offenders should be held in and the facilities that they can avail of (Ferguson, 2017a). In some cases, risk scores must be provided to judges before individuals are sentenced, if they are available (in parts of Kentucky and Pennsylvania, US, for instance).

Environmental criminology and crime science

Burgess's formula and lists of 'hot people' are concerned primarily with the calculation of predictions of future offending or victimisation largely on the basis of people's histories, characteristics and behaviours. Understanding the backgrounds and motivations of offenders and victims is a key concern of criminologists. The approach that we have outlined thus far is predominantly people-focused. However, an emerging and increasingly distinct offshoot of criminology is not so readily concerned with the criminal or the victim but with the immediate location where crime takes place and how the environment can influence various crimes and cause some places to become criminogenic. The examination of crime primarily from a place-based perspective has become known as 'environmental criminology' (Jeffrey, 1971) or crime science. Environmental criminology and crime science are concerned almost exclusively with the characteristics of the criminal event ('the crime') rather than the biological, developmental and social factors that shape the beliefs and characteristics of criminal offenders ('the criminal'), which it largely leaves to criminology and psychology to address (Pease, 2004; Wortley and Townsley, 2017). By focusing on the place-based or spatial aspect of crime, on the basis that the environment or situation provides the opportunity for the act to occur, analysts collect data on crime, look for patterns, seek to explain them in terms of environmental influences, and subsequently attempt to reduce crime by modifying, relocating or redesigning features of the environment, including street furniture, road networks, car parks, footpaths, vehicles, residential and commercial buildings, nightclubs, and smartphones, among others (Jeffrey, 1971; Newman, 1972; Clarke, 1980; Brantingham and Brantingham, 1981; Ekblom, 2017; Monchuk et al., 2018; Dakin et al., 2020).

The key concern of crime scientists, more particularly, is with the 'near causes of crime' (or situational causes) that can be modified quickly to deter criminals without much concern for the 'distant' (or dispositional) causes of criminality, such as any adverse childhood experiences the offender may have experienced (Clarke, 2017). It requires devising immediate and practical strategies to prevent a crime from occurring, 'not to cure offenders or reform society' (Wortley and Townsley, 2017: 2). Changing the 'near causes', if possible, is believed to be more likely to succeed in reducing crime from occurring in the short-term because the link between cause and effect is more direct. Clarke uses the example of a speed bump to illustrate the concept. He explains that

> if traffic engineers want to stop speeding on a stretch of road, they do not need to mount detailed studies of the causes of speeding. All they need do is introduce speed bumps and, as long as they do this carefully with full awareness of other nearby routes that drivers might take instead, speeding will be reduced.
>
> (Clarke, 2017: 289)

In practice, it can include 'target hardening' vulnerable properties by adding new security measures and working with urban planners to redesign street networks to make it more difficult for individuals to offend, increase the risks attending criminality and lessen the rewards. Since it is considerably difficult to identify the direct causes of crime, crime scientists are explicitly encouraged to devise immediate interventions to disrupt crimes from occurring on the basis of hypotheses about correlations between concentrations of crime and environmental features. Pilot interventions can be attempted quickly and without evidence that they will work as long as they have been risk assessed and are tied to a rigorous evaluation of treatment and control groups to test whether they work in reality. Such processes now commonly fall under the rubric of 'situational crime prevention'.

Research conducted within this field has found that, when looked at spatially or from a place-based perspective, a significant degree of crime is patterned. Routine activity theory, for example, is a popular heuristic device for understanding the confluence of people, place and time that can lead to the occurrence of crime in various contexts. The rule of thumb is such that if a motivated offender, a suitable and convenient target, and the absence of an authority figure or guardian cross in space and time (an 'opportunity'), the risk of crime can increase substantially (Cohen and Felson, 1979). The presence of these factors are treated as key principles in the offender's reasoning process or logic. Clarke and Cornish (1985) subsequently used this reasoning process, involving the weighing up of costs and benefits and probabilities of success, to depict offenders as rational agents capable of choosing who or what to target, when to commit an offence and the best strategy to pursue in doing so (known as 'rational choice theory').

A simple way of thinking about a place-based approach is to consider any individual's range of routine daily activities (their 'activity patterns'). Many adults have a 9 to 5 job, eat lunch at the same time every day, interact with the same people in similar ways, and engage in the same routines before and after their working day. Offenders and victims are often no different. Studies have found that repeat offenders are more likely to undertake short trips from their home locality or primary place of business rather than longer trips due partly to their familiarity with the former and the discomfort of upsetting the day-to-day routines of their own lives (this is commonly referred to as 'distance decay') (Rengert et al., 1999; Rossmo, 1999). Many crimes that occur in close spatial and temporal proximity, although the *modus operandi* may be inconsistent, have been found to be related as a result. These findings have led to the popular usage of techniques such as geo-profiling to narrow down the range of places a suspect, such as a recidivist burglar, might live (taking account of the fact that a burglar is unlikely to commit crimes on the street that they live) (Rossmo, 1999; Rossmo and Rombouts, 2017).

Studies have found that many crimes committed within any particular geographical area are usually attributable to a very small number of repeat offenders, and committed against a relatively small number of repeat victims (Pease and Farrell, 2017). The 'flag and boost' concept, for example, illustrates how the successful commission of a burglary within a neighbourhood of similar looking houses can encourage an offender to target neighbouring houses since they are likely to have a common layout, comparable security systems (likely to be of poor quality) and shared networks of roads and back alleys that provide good cover. The initial successes then 'flag' the vulnerability of the victims and the broader area for other criminals, encouraging them to commit similar-type crimes, thereby 'boosting' the likelihood of re-victimisation and crime rates (Tseloni and Pease, 2004; Pease and Farrell, 2017). Research by Bowers et al. (2004) indicates that properties within 400 metres of a burgled household can be at a significantly elevated risk of victimisation for up to two months after the initial event.

Individuals who are targeted numerous times are often referred to as 'repeat victims', while those who get targeted soon afterwards because of their proximity to repeat victims are referred to as 'near-repeat victims' (Pease, 1998; Tseloni and Pease, 2004). The risk profiles of repeat and near-repeat victims are highest immediately after the crime and reduce over time (as new security measures are introduced) and space (from neighbourhood to neighbourhood). This ripple-like effect of place-based crimes, which can be visualised using techniques such as 'risk terrain modelling', has been compared to the seismic waves of an earthquake as they move outward from the centre. These occurrences have even been described as communicable, contagious and infectious, akin to the transmission of viruses.

Similar patterns have been found in the outward spread of violence caused by gang-related shootings, as retaliation causes violence to cascade (Caplan et al., 2011; Green et al., 2017). Temporal correlations have been found between weekends and evenings in cases of domestic violence within households (when the structured working day becomes unstructured); reports of anti-social behaviour can increase around schools once the school day finishes at 3pm, and sports games in stadiums can attract significant volumes of violence, anti-social behaviour, pickpocketing and car thefts around venues before and after a game (Vulliamy et al., 2018). Adverse weather conditions can even lead to fewer thefts, burglaries and incidents of violence, disturbing the patterns of offenders (Cohn, 1990). The key from a crime science perspective is that these patterns and ripples serve as a predictor of future victimisation and, more particularly, create a window of opportunity for crime events to be risk assessed within a relatively narrow timeframe and geographic area so that preventative action can potentially take place.

Another, way of looking at place-based crime is to examine where high volumes of particular crimes cluster together. Using aggregated data about where crimes are reported, researchers and analysts can determine whether particular crimes are clustered within specific geographical areas. Those areas that record a significant volume of crime within a relatively short time frame, in comparison to others, are referred to colloquially as 'hot spots', and the process is commonly referred to as 'crime mapping' (Bowers et al., 2004; Ferguson, 2017a). A popular rule of thumb is that 20 per cent of places within major towns and cities tend to experience about 80 per cent of the crime, which is referred to as the Pareto principle in other disciplines (Johnson, 2017). More acute studies have shown that a majority of street robberies, shootings and even calls for service from the public tend to occur on a very small number of urban streets in practice, usually less than 10 per cent of them (Sherman and Weisburd, 1995; Braga et al., 2011). Traditionally, these crime hotspots could be visualised using push pins or colours on a printed map on police station noticeboards (like Jake Maple's famed 'charts of the future' depicting crime in the New York subway system) but they are now typically generated using Geographical Information System (GIS) computer programmes which are capable of processing information and updating maps in real time using AI.

The various theories and concepts studied in criminology and crime science show that there is a degree of consistency in how some people, though not all, behave when a particular set of conditions are present. The theoretical basis of much of the research in the field of predictive policing centres on the empirical phenomenon that repeat offenders and victims of crime are at a higher risk of crime, at least temporarily, because of spatial and non-spatial factors (Law Society, 2019). Although researchers, and police officers, will invariably lack a complete understanding of all of the factors in play, some features are prominent enough within crime occurrences across time and space for the patterns to be recognised and for predictive modelling to take place. Researchers can rarely, if ever, be absolutely certain that crimes will occur, or when, but if modelling shows a particularly high-risk then perhaps something can be done to prevent them from happening, no matter how blunt the intervention or the prediction. Human researchers and police officers, however, are not the only game in town.

Artificial intelligence

Information processing is crucial to police forces, partly because it allows them to identify, predict and control uncertainty to various degrees (Manning, 2018). The traditional predictive processes outlined above usually involved researchers painstakingly poring over crime-related data to develop hand-crafted formulae that could generate risk scores about people and places. AI has the potential to do this work on their behalf, rapidly, more efficiently and at significant scale. Although there is currently no commonly accepted definition of artificial intelligence, it refers to the ability of digital technologies to apply mathematical reasoning processes to large datasets for the purpose of producing outcomes that are comparable to, or surpass, one or more forms of human intelligence (Russell and Norvig, 2014). The evolution of these technologies has been quite recent, occurring long after Burgess developed his risk scoring algorithm by hand.

In the early days of AI research, a premium was paid to developing information processing technologies that could imitate human thinking and problem solving techniques (Minsky, 1961; McCarthy, 1968). Turing (1950) developed his famous 'Turing Test' that established relevant standards to assess AI technologies according to their fidelity to human qualities of perception, reasoning and behaviour and, more particularly, their ability to imitate them. One test involved examining whether a computer could answer questions in a manner that could convince a human interrogator that the written responses had come from a human (and not the computer). This would involve the computer being able to store what it knew or heard; to be able to use the stored information to reason, answer questions and draw new conclusions; to possess natural language processing to enable it to communicate fluently and successfully with a human in the relevant language; and to be able to adapt to new circumstances and detect and extrapolate patterns. If the program's input-output behaviours corresponded to human behaviours, then it was considered to possess human-level AI (HLAI) or human-level machine intelligence (HLMI). Other tests included demonstrating the ability to perceive objects using some form of computer vision, and to be able to manipulate objects and use robotic hardware to move about (like a human). It was in this vein of thought that McCarthy (1955: 13) organised a famous two-month workshop at Dartmouth College in the summer of 1956 so that a carefully selected group of scientists could work together to study "the conjecture that every aspect of learning or any other feature of intelligence can in principle be so precisely described that a machine can be made to simulate it."

Although the 'thinking humanly' school led to major advancements such as the use of rule-based expert systems that were generally coded by hand and were capable of automating various forms of expert decision-making processes (Simon, 1969; Bostrom, 2017), the development of AI in more recent years has moved beyond attempts to simply imitate human thinking and action. Many computer scientists are now focused on the development of machines that can analyse data to extrapolate patterns and draw conclusions irrespective of whether they follow patterns of logic associated with human thought processes. Russell and Norvig (2014: 3), for example, use the analogy of flight to remind computer scientists that the Wright brothers succeeded in their quest for artificial flight when they stopped trying to imitate birds (to "fly so exactly like pigeons that they can fool even other pigeons"), and focussed instead on aerodynamics, physics, engineering and synthetic designs. Many AI technologies which have been developed in recent years are similarly celebrated because of their ability to think *unlike* humans, i.e. to disregard the thought steps of human experts. One of the central features of this school of thought is known as 'machine learning'.

The term 'machine learning' is inspired by the step-by-step reinforcement processes that children use to learn from experience (reflecting a form of human intelligence) but extant machine learning technologies are capable of analysing and interrogating huge volumes of data, learning new rules through processes of trial and error and inventing algorithms in ways that far exceed the capability of child-like or human thinking. Unlike the hand-coded rule-based algorithms that Burgess and others established using defined sets of variables, machine learning algorithms can, in principle, be given access to a large volume of data and set loose, tasked only to identify patterns without being told how to do it. They can use what they learn to form their own rules and create new functionality. Machine learning systems are often referred to as non-parametric, as the parameters that define the input–output transformation do not need to be comprehensively defined in advance but can potentially be derived organically from the data (Law Society, 2019).

To help machine learning code avoid the production of nonsensical rules or intractable problems, many are 'taught' or trained by humans using positive feedback ('rewards') for correct pattern associations and inferences. Feedback is usually more concerned with the relevancy and accuracy of the outcome, than the process the programme used to get there. If, for example, a machine learning programme is fed data in the form of x-ray images, a supervising technician can reward it for correctly identifying a lung cancer diagnosis or bone fracture without knowing exactly how it reached those conclusions. The programme could then begin to use organic rules to diagnose similar patterns wherever it encountered them, and to continue generating new rules as it uncovered new patterns and received more feedback. The feedback could cause a machine learning algorithm to change so much that the new rules and variables it develops may render it entirely different, in look and function, to the form that it originally took. Machine learning algorithms are celebrated precisely because of this unpredictability. One of the things that separates current machine learning algorithms from human thinking is that the algorithmic process often bears no comparison to human-like deductive reasoning.

The mathematics underpinning machine learning algorithms can come in various different forms. The Bayesian method (using Bayes' theorem) is particularly popular at present. It uses probabilities and decision theory to represent and reason with uncertain knowledge (Pearl, 1988). Another technique used by many contemporary algorithms is known as 'random forests', which usually consists of an ensemble of tree-structured classifiers (Breiman, 2001). In an attempt to explain both techniques, which can be used in tandem, to the non-specialist (among whom we count ourselves), we will sketch the following example. A random forest may comprise of numerous decision trees that contain data and variables concerning offender characteristics, behaviours and outcomes. One of the trees could be much like a simple classification tree that a person might draw by hand. To determine whether someone was at high-risk of offending, the first branch could ask a question like: was the person convicted of a criminal offence before the age of 18? If the answer is no, the node could point to 'no risk'. If, however, the answer were to be yes, the node could point to another branch which asks: did they spend longer than two months in prison? A negative answer could again lead to a conclusion of no risk but a positive answer could lead to further extending branches, and so on along the frontier, causing redundant paths to be closed and relevant nodes to be expanded, until one or more outcomes are reached. As each node is passed and a new branch is opened the risk may heighten. By using a multitude of such trees, an algorithm can attempt to calculate how closely an individual's profile relates to the behavioural patterns associated with historical offenders with similar characteristics (or a composite of them across a time range) and generate a risk score. This is just a simplistic and hypothetical decision tree used for illustrative purposes. Random forests are not usually as rudimentary as this.

Random forests typically grow an ensemble of trees that contain more random selections of data, variables and features. They may use random split selections, random weights and random outputs that make little sense to an observer (Breiman, 2001). Each forest may also contain tens of thousands of nodes, rendering them practically incomprehensible to humans. The algorithm, however, can carry out an action sequence across the trees to test and assess whether and to what extent new profiles relate to the data trees within milliseconds (and update the system as new feedback is received). Since it is unlikely that an individual's profile will perfectly match the profile of one historical offender or any particular classification or data tree, Bayes' theorem is often used to calculate correlations in percentage terms at each node to determine which way to go (Berk and Bleich, 2014). The algorithm could even ask each tree to cast a unit 'vote' on the question being asked using Bayes' theorem. The algorithm could then generate a pooled prediction in percentage terms based on the similarity or popularity score across the forest. If the prediction is eventually proved accurate or inaccurate, feeding the outcome back to the algorithm can allow it to grow new nodes, branches, trees, values or salient variables and generate random vectors in an attempt to ensure more accurate scores in future (Breiman, 2001). It is through this process that machine learning algorithms are considered to learn, create and think. Random forests that work in this way are reportedly the best performing machine learning technique in criminal justice behavioural forecasting at present (Berk and Bleich, 2014). They are also particularly attractive to users because the randomness is believed to reduce bias (Breiman, 2001).

Random forests are not the only type of algorithm used in the predictive policing space. Another kind of machine learning algorithm relies on artificial 'neural networks', which are algorithms that are designed to work outside of rule-based decision trees (Hinton, 1992). Consisting of layers of interconnected nodes or 'neurons' that can receive and transmit data, a neural network or 'net' can be fed lots of unlabelled or uncategorised data, usually with the objective of identifying hidden statistical patterns in the input (HLSC, 2018). Similar to other machine learning techniques, the weights, values and thresholds applied by the networks of nodes can change as the algorithm receives new data and feedback on its outputs. The addition of new variables and values and the changing or discarding of older ones allows the network to bootstrap its computational structures and to engineer new algorithms (Bostrom, 2017). The use of many layers of nodes to process data has led to the term 'deep learning' being applied to neural nets.

The text to this point illustrates just some of the techniques used by machine learning systems that have been found to be effective predictive tools (Breiman, 2001). Whether a pattern concerns an association between adverse childhood experiences and violence or similarities in abnormal medical images, if relevant data is fed to the algorithms they are often capable of spotting patterns and generating a prediction. However, it is important to note that if an algorithm has been trained with a particular output or goal in mind, such as predicting a likelihood that an individual will commit a violent offence in the short-term or identifying abnormal medical images, this is all that the algorithm will usually be capable of doing. Since extant algorithms can only perform a single or a minimal range of functions that could possibly be described as 'intelligent', computer scientists refer to this as 'narrow' intelligence or 'Artificial Narrow Intelligence' (ANI) (HLSC, 2018). If an algorithm was capable of performing a more universal range of intelligent functions within real environments, akin to the full intellectual capabilities of humans, it could be said to have 'Artificial General Intelligence' (AGI). On the other hand, if it could greatly surpass the best current human minds in virtually all general cognitive domains of interest, it could be said to have Artificial Super Intelligence (ASI) (Bostrom, 2017). We are nowhere near the latter two domains at present. The current iteration of algorithms in the policing space are firmly in the category of ANI. They are generally restricted to the defined environment in which they work, and with significant human supervision.

Arguments abound about whether the types of machine learning techniques used in predictive policing should be considered 'intelligent', even as the narrow variety, in the first instance. Some commentators argue that they are simply good at processing large volumes of data, pattern recognition and basic math at scale. The concept of human-like intelligence is considerably complex and may not be so flexible that it can be applied to computer programmes that can carry out no more than one task. Although Amazon's Alexa or Apple's Siri may be able to trick the interrogator in Turing's imitation test, there are many who argue that the Turing test does not constitute an appropriate or useful criterion for human-level AI (Nilsson, 2005). This debate may not matter much to the computer programmer who describes a one-dimensional computer programme as intelligent in order to generate interest, but it may matter a great deal to a police officer who might assume that such a programme is more 'intelligent' than it is in a context where real human rights and lives are at stake. To assume that an equivalence exists between artificial and human intelligence (i.e. artificial intelligence = human intelligence), where no real equivalence exists, could result in major errors in decision-making.

Sleepwalking into foreseeable problems seems somewhat needless since police forces are not in the business of developing AGI or ASI. What they are primarily concerned about in 2020 extends largely to data matching technologies that can sort and interrogate data. Once information is entered into a database, whether in the form of case files, scanned documents, photos, DNA profiles, digital video footage, phone transcripts, folders of emails, browser histories or social media posts, police forces seem to be particularly interested in algorithms that can search and make matches (or approximations) across multiple databases. Searching for and matching names, dates, specific keywords, phrases, licence plate numbers, faces, behaviours, sounds and other variables is currently one of the most prized, and perhaps most rudimentary, of AI-related qualities. Such programmes, if they worked well, would enable police officers to identify people, places and things that are relevant to the work of the police, or at least a likelihood that they are relevant. This means that it should not matter greatly if they are called pattern recognition technologies or prioritisation algorithms (or whatever) rather than intelligent systems. Attaching the label of intelligence so readily may serve only to mislead police officers, at least in the present climate. We would recommend caution when applying the label of 'artificial intelligence' to many predictive technologies currently used by police services as a result.

The 'policing' part

If the predictive part of 'predictive policing' seems complex, comprising a collection of different techniques ranging from hand-crafted algorithms to machine learning systems, which are designed to produce outcomes ranging from individual risk assessments to geo-profiling, the policing part is arguably even more perplexing. The policing part is tricky partly because there has been so little consistency. Police services occasionally pilot new initiatives with a view to addressing substantive crime problems yet regularly fail to subject them to robust evaluation and often discard them prematurely, not because they are ineffective but because of competing demands on their resources which police leaders may treat as more important (Goldstein, 1979). Police officers and their wider organisations typically operate on short time-scales, and are invariably attracted to immediate solutions to pressing issues (Francis et al., 2004). In many cases, little more than a superficial analysis of problems is carried out followed by a rush to implement a response (Weisburd and Braga, 2019). This rushed response occasionally involves creative measures but usually revolves around traditional and localised forms of policing that officers are comfortable with, such as new patrol patterns (Eck et al., 2017).

Another major factor that clouds the policing part is the reality that many crime problems may be solved only through a multi-agency approach. If an individual is assessed to be at high-risk of future offending or victimisation, some of the ways of reducing the risk can involve voluntary participation in a drug treatment centre, anger management counselling, enrolment in educational programmes or child behavioural development if the individual is still young. The police, in such cases, typically rely on psychologists, medical professionals and other stakeholders to deliver interventions. Moreover, the evidence that any one intervention will work for a particular individual (or even that they work in general) may not be very strong. Similarly, if the problem is with a particular place (i.e. a crime hotspot), some of the ways of reducing risk may be to improve the quality of housing or to create better outdoor amenities for young people. This type of approach may require a 'public health' whole-systems ideology, bringing together all relevant agencies in a systematic manner, with requisite resources at their disposal. However, the evidence that a defined amount of effort will lead to a specific amount of gain for each participant in such endeavours rarely exists. Realising sustained cooperation between relevant agencies to achieve particular goals in the long-term, and how, is something that many societies have yet to figure out. Partner agencies are often as guilty as police services of conducting superficial analyses of problems and rushing through short-lived initiatives. Furthermore, crime is often treated as a problem that belongs squarely to the police, and partner agencies can therefore "resist bending their own professional priorities and budgets to police officers who call on them for help" (Skogan, 2019: 34).The net result is that few police services and local governments in the UK, US and Australia can point to serious and holistic strategies that have dramatically reduced rates of crime and violence on a long-term basis in recent years.

One key feature that links together the short-term approaches of police organisations and potential partner agencies is the issue of uncertainty, and it harks back to the predictive part.Taking place-based predictions as an example, if a house burglary is reported today, the police will not know with certainty if the same house or a neighbouring property will be targeted tomorrow. The research by Bowers et al. (2004) tells us only that the risk of victimisation may be elevated by up to two months. Even digital hotspot maps, which may appear to the user to be the most innocent and straight-forward of technologies, may not be very helpful. As Johnson (2017) conveys, hotspot maps are an interesting way of bringing spatial data to life, enabling police leaders to visualise patterns that are almost impossible to communicate in other ways, but they can be misleading by implying that the risk of crime is the same at all locations within the hotspot at particular times. In reality, streets and households even within the same hotspot can experience radically different forms of crime, and crime rates can fluctuate from street to street and house to house because of short-term phenomena such as repeat and near repeat victimisation, among other occurrences (Ibid).The hotspot map itself does not provide sufficient fine grain detail to enable police officers to know where exactly to intervene, when and how. The same applies to findings that burglaries can spike after pay-day, domestic abuse can increase at the weekend, and violence can increase when schools are closed during the summer holidays. It does not tell police officers exactly where to be and at what precise time. Operationally, such insights are of limited use.

Many of the hand-crafted formulae we discussed earlier were not deduced at scale but identified by disparate teams of psychologists, political scientists, public policy scholars and even epidemiologists who were engaged in relatively small pilot studies. Many did not involve expensive software packages but relied on Excel spreadsheets, Microsoft Office and rudimentary geographic information systems such as ArcGIS (Perry et al., 2013). The information they relied upon was often drawn from police records, intelligence logs and crime surveys which were reflective of short time periods and inevitably piecemeal in nature. Some of the most popular theories in criminology are little more than simple heuristics or rules of thumb.

Decades ago police officers were not incapable of relying on local knowledge to predict where and when drug pushers, gang members and domestic abusers could be found in the midst of offending either. The benefit of previous experience could give them an extraordinary insight into who was fighting with whom, who was most likely to have committed particular offences, the kinds of offences that were taking place but were not being reported to the police, and what was going to happen next (Manning, 2003; Kennedy, 2019). The abilities of some extant predictive algorithms do not extend far beyond the intuition of experienced police officers in times past.

Moving from the hand-crafted variety to the possible employment of AI technologies in these endeavours, if police forces think that AI represents some kind of magic bullet that readily addresses the flaws of human-made predictive algorithms, they would be sorely mistaken. Extant AI programmes can carry out analyses at great scale but they too contain weaknesses and can amplify rather than reduce deficiencies. To say that one *can* produce a statistical probability of future offending or victimisation does not mean that they will necessarily produce a good one. What various AI algorithms are good at doing is generating an inference with a significant margin for error. Their predictions are often little more than an educated guess and they frequently rely heavily on stereotypes or classifications to do so (Ferguson, 2017a).

Simply because crime statistics might, for example, show that young people commit more crimes than older people, men more than women, poor more than rich, it should not mean that a generalised police suspicion must fall on the people in these categories, or on those who fall within more than one category (i.e. young, poor men). Yet many AI classification technologies are designed to do this very thing; they are designed to discriminate, to tell the difference between people, places and features. However, allocating people to loosely structured typologies or categorisations is messy and ambiguous, and does not transfer neatly to real-life. It is well established that an array of different factors and life events can cause some individuals to discontinue various forms of criminal activity (Francis et al., 2004). Algorithms, though, may only be capable of attaching a simplistic weighting to a variable such as age (young people are more likely to commit crime and 'age out' of crime as they get older), which reflects nothing substantive of the individual. Aggregate or group-level patterns are not the same as individual-level predictions. As a result, algorithms may remain blind to specific contexts and be entirely unsuited to pre-judging the direction of travel of a particular individual at a defined moment in time. Much statistical modelling is created using historical data on specific populations within particular time frames. The patterns and relationships identified in historic populations may not apply in the same way to future populations living in different social contexts and geographic regions

(Babuta and Oswald, 2020). Attitudes to past offences, such as drug offences and hate crime, may also have changed during the lifetimes of offenders meaning that different weights could and should be attached. The law evolves over time and, when laws change, practitioners are expected to work through principled analysis rather than simply relying upon past cases (Law Society, 2019). Since most predictive and machine learning systems are trained on past data and are incapable of human-level principled analysis in a comparable fashion, reliance on them can lead to stagnation and conservative outcomes that hold the evolution of justice "anchored in the past" (Ibid: 23).

Perhaps most importantly, the generation of statistical predictions usually says nothing of causation and the most appropriate forms of intervention to employ. By crunching data on historical crime records and policing activities, algorithms may draw known correlations between high-risk areas and population density, high unemployment, low cost housing, abandoned buildings, poorly lit roads, off-licences, small convenience stores and schools, for example, but they usually provide no substantive guidance or clarity on the question of 'how' underlying factors should be addressed. As Berk and Bleich (2014: 82) explain: "the primary goal of forecasting is not explanation"; algorithms and machine learning systems typically deal in correlation and not causality. Explanations and interventions that attempt to turn a high-risk person or place into a low risk one are generally left to police forces and partner agencies to devise. Not only is the police force left with little guidance about what to do, it is faced with the reality that the partial forecasts that are produced by extant algorithmic and AI systems are open to a wide range of interpretations and, depending on which technique is used, they may differ significantly in their projections. In other words, predictive and AI technologies may bring with them more uncertainty.

What police forces should already know is that devising policing strategies and action on the basis of a correlation, without attempting to understand causation, might work but it could also be considerably dangerous at both the individual and community levels. It might work because of the previous successes of crime science. Situational crime prevention initiatives such as speed bumps to prevent speeding, the installation of signs to remind cyclists how best to lock their bikes, or even attaching a sticker of 'watching eyes' to a bicycle rack have been shown to deter would-be offenders and avoid crimes taking place and arrests being made in the first instance (Sidebottom et al., 2009; Nettle et al., 2012; Roach et al., 2016). In some cases, crime scientists may not even know why some measures worked, only that they did (for reasons that lie within behavioural psychology and criminology). To draw an analogy, it was not unusual for doctors in the 20th century to prescribe medicines such as aspirin to treat a range of different ailments without fully understanding their mechanisms of action, only that they were confident that they would work (see Chapter 4).

Nevertheless, proceeding without attempting to understand causation could be hugely damaging. Picking the most dangerous people and places identified by algorithms and subjecting them to intense surveillance, routine searches and frequent home visits without some clear evidence that such interventions are the most appropriate ways to address high risk scores could lead to increased disproportionality in policing, the abuse of police powers, greater social control of particular parts of the population, and rising inequality, poverty and other forms of structural violence. The use of stop and search powers, tasers, firearms and police fines generally correlate to where police officers are sent. Dispatching police officers towards people and places with a heightened sense of danger or purpose because of a high-risk score may only increase such occurrences (Ferguson, 2017a; Eck, 2019). Unfortunately, police history is littered with examples of police organisations barrelling ahead with these kinds of strategies, preferring to adopt an attitude that they will learn from their mistakes rather than proceeding cautiously with academic research in tow. For these reasons, place-based policing strategies in high-crime areas are frequently associated with police oppression. Fixating upon or ignoring correlations between high-crime areas, deprivation and ethnicity has also led to numerous findings of racial discrimination (Ferguson, 2017a).

The capabilities of AI technologies mean that they could also be used in new and intrusive ways by the police. For example, algorithmic tools could be used to monitor all social media posts and online activities from a hotspot in order to predict criminality, potentially undermining human rights norms. Communication data from smart phone apps could be monitored to reveal the location of individuals within a hotspot, as well as the nature of their social interactions and communications. A combination of different technologies (like CCTV and Wi-Fi sensors) could potentially detect the formation of large groups, track their direction of travel, assess their mood on the basis of messages exchanged and posted online, and use network analysis to identify ringleaders. Small autonomous surveillance drones could even be tasked to monitor crowds as they move. Such methods could serve to quell dissent and inhibit free speech, acting in the interests of crime control over and above social equality and due process.

Treating predictive and machine learning policing algorithms as simple technical solutions to what are complex problems that require political debate, non confrontational interactions and long-term inter agency interventions could lead to the kind of rapid unravelling of community trust, support, cooperation and civil liberties that neighbourhoods have witnessed in the past. Predictive technologies are a useful way of raising awareness about risk in a pre-crime space but they do not, at present, unlock the problem of fully understanding and addressing the factors that cause patterns of crime and harm. Police officers and members of the public may instinctively desire easy answers to complex problems and want to be told that deep and knotty issues of criminality, inequality and race can be resolved by a few AI-informed police patrols or home visits but policing rarely proves to be this simple (taking these approaches can be dangerous for all involved). Policing continues to be defined by a series of complex puzzles for which very few police forces have developed satisfactory solutions. Extant predictive and AI algorithms have not been designed to solve the kinds of thorny problems to which we refer. Many of them do little other than turn human behaviours and places that they cannot fully understand into crude data points and statistics. Human life is too important and policing too complex to be reduced to a game of chess or for people to be treated as faceless pawns with limited value (some AI systems have proved to be very good at chess). Good strategic decisions are usually not attributable to one source, even if that source is a high-performing AI. Tetlock and Gardner (2016) argue that some of the best decisions that people make are derived from their human abilities to gather evidence from a variety of sources, to think probabilistically, to act as part of a team, to learn lessons from previous attempts, to be open to changing course if a strategy does not work out, and to be able to put all of this together to decide upon a course of action quite quickly. Although AI systems may be quite good at executing this kind of sequence (or algorithm), humans are also highly capable of making well-considered and predictive judgements without the use of powerful computers. Some humans are exceptionally good at it (Ibid). These human skills and the types of countervailing outputs that they might produce should not be disregarded.

AI in policing

The application of AI technologies is not restricted to the field of predictive policing. Emerging AI technologies are central to digital systems that can potentially recognise people by the way they look, walk, speak, write and type. AI systems that contain computer vision capabilities and rules to identify relevant patterns are now capable of identifying people (with some margin of error) by their faces (based on eye shape, colour and distance between eyes, among other features); their gait (i.e. walking or running movements); the way they speak (by recognising patterns in their pronunciation, intonation, syntax and accent); gauging their mood on the basis of their facial expressions; their writing style (by patterns in sentence structure, phrasing and spelling for instance); and even by 'reading' their lips where conversations are inaudible (Quijano-Sanchez, 2018; Joh, 2019). Other forms of 'smart' recognition systems include technologies that can identify vehicle registration plates, knives and the sound of gunshots. The accuracy of recognition systems, particularly facial recognition technologies, have increased dramatically in the past five years, frequently beating human recognition capabilities in head-to-head tests (Brundage et al., 2018). It is important to note, however, that they are still capable of error. Facial recognition technologies, in particular, tend to be high on sensitivity (spotting correlations) but low on specificity (being able to reject weak correlations) at present. One facial recognition technology used by a police service in the UK reportedly generated 'false positives' almost 90 per cent of the time (The Guardian, 2018).

In comparison, humans can only retain a relatively limited amount of information and, in the case of digital footage, cannot constantly monitor multiple screens all of the time. Much CCTV goes unwatched or crime-related occurrences are missed due to human error, and humans do not always recognise a face that they have seen before. AI computer systems can potentially maintain constant vigilance, analyse material rapidly, consistently identify known patterns and edit a selection of relevant clips for human operators to review. Moreover, once identified, a networked AI system connected to a web of cameras and other sensors can potentially locate and track the movements of suspects, objects, witnesses and other persons of interest in real-time or use existing recordings to trace their movements and activities hours or days into the past. These capabilities are hugely valuable to police services, completing tasks far more quickly than humans could, and at significant scale.

AI systems can also help police officers with more mundane data inputs. Systems can use natural language processing to transcribe speech to text, translate from one language to another, speed up data entry through auto-complete and predictive text functions, undertake the mass digitisation of case files, and populate numerous linked databases from individual inputs. Huge libraries of digital data can be organised in a matter of seconds, and the information most salient for decision makers can be highlighted and flagged. For instance, an algorithm trained on relevant legal rules could rapidly identify information of relevance for disclosure purposes when it could take an entire team of humans thousands of hours to do the same work. This is particularly attractive to police officers who have a legal duty to pursue all reasonable lines of inquiry, leading both towards and away from a conviction. Reports suggest that, in reality, investigating officers will only utilise a limited amount of 'digital trail' data, if at all, due to the difficulty of collating and interpreting the vast stores of data that make up an individual's digital footprint. As one chief constable recently observed, AI may be 'the only way' that police services can deal with the volumes of digital evidence currently being produced (Deloitte, 2018: 13).

Search algorithms can be hugely beneficial in practice too, allowing officers to manually enter characteristics and personal information, such as an alias, an age range, a suspect's height, a location or even a particular *modus operandi* into a search engine. Many types of information processing, from the automation of form-filling to file retrieval, can arguably be undertaken by machine learning systems without controversy, unexpected side effects or impacting on fundamental rights in various contexts (Law Society, 2019). Arranged in a human rights-compliant and consensual manner, some AI technologies could contribute to fewer failed cases and renewed public confidence that good investigative police work is occurring (Joh, 2018). They could even be used to help police officers learn within virtual reality training environments and real-time settings with the aid of a virtual personal assistant. AI technologies of varying sorts could ultimately transform and speed up parts of the policing economy. Our concern, and that of our contributors, is that while some predictive and AI technologies may have the potential to effect change for the better, others may effect a significant turn for the worse. We all worry about the latter. Much depends on how they are designed and used in practice.

Structure of book

The chapter contributors address an array of different, yet often overlapping issues affecting predictive policing and AI. The text focuses in particular on problems concerning bias, big data, police accountability and human rights. The text is divided broadly along these lines. A chapter by Chan is the first entry, serving to draw together the respective areas by conceptualising the development of a number of competing 'sociotechnical imaginaries' around AI. She illustrates, in Chapter 1, how these imaginaries establish different visions of desirable futures, ranging from unduly optimistic and uniformly positive to 'resistant imaginaries'. They are, the chapter argues, transforming as new ideas are introduced and critical debates are opening up in societies. This discussion serves as a conceptual springboard to the two substantive sections of the text (bias and big data in Part I and police accountability and human rights in Part II).

Part I: Bias and big data

The first part of the edited collection contains chapters that are concerned *inter alia* with a variety of biases which permeate big data sets, predictive algorithms, machine learning systems and the decision-making of the people who use them. Hamilton in Chapter 2 focuses on the biases associated with offender-based predictive policing, and the use of risk assessments and data analytics to identify 'hot people'. She addresses a number of individual risk assessment tools in use in the UK and North America, outlining the breadth of techniques in use at present. They include: the Strategic Subject List (SSL) in use in Chicago; the Violent Offender Identification Directive (VOID) tool in upstate New York; the Ontario Domestic Assault Risk Assessment (ODARA); and the DASH and HART instruments in the UK. New forms of predictive experimentation and their implications for crime control are examined.

In Chapter 3, McDaniel and Pease draw upon Thaler and Sunstein's (2008) concept of 'choice architecture' to examine how biases in the development and use of AI can play a significant role in influencing the way police officers make decisions in practice. The chapter examines the choice architecture surrounding AI and predictive technologies and the peculiar possibility of AI acting as a choice architect largely because of the presence of biases. The discussion is considerably conceptual in nature so a more contextual approach is taken in the two chapters that follow. In Chapter 4, Cohen and Graver take two professions – police officers and doctors – and place their experiences with big data and AI in dialogue. The authors observe that both professions are grappling with a lot of the same moral, social and legal questions and choices around big data, predictive analytics and AI. These include: bias, the exercise of individual discretion, role disruption, privacy, data ownership, consent, trade secrets, liability and the adequacy of existing regulatory regimes. In Chapter 5, Fernandez and Alani undertake a literature review of various algorithms and systems that are being used by police organisations, social media platforms and governments, among others, to analyse, detect and predict the spread of extremist ideas and radicalisation online. These include AI-infused tools that analyse the language used in online posts and tweets, and broader communication flows. Their chapter uncovers a number of key issues that have not yet been fully addressed in the field, ranging from the issue of irreproducibility to the tendency of AI practitioners to largely eschew existing theories and studies of radicalisation from the social and cognitive sciences. Finally, Part I is rounded off by Utset, who in Chapter 6 rises to the challenge of reconciling predictive policing, AI and the criminal law around inchoate offences. Inchoate offences can be integral to predictive policing strategies since many of them are built to address criminal acts which have not yet been committed or completed. His chapter addresses some of the social and legal costs associated with biased and uncertain predictive algorithms, and the potential costs and benefits of using 'focussed deterrence' and crime prevention strategies, among others.

Key themes that permeate the chapters in Part I include the presence of biases within machine learning inputs; cognitive weaknesses in police officers (and other humans more generally); and broader biases in academic research and public discourse around predictive and AI technologies. The former, for example, concerns the widely acknowledged reality that police-recorded statistics and associated data on crime do not reflect the full extent of criminality and harm within a police area, but rather represent some complex interaction between criminality, policing strategies, the extent to which civilians communicate with the police, and how police officers choose to interpret occurrences and exercise their discretion. For instance, some place-based studies have shown that while drug offences may occur across a broad geographical area, drug arrests may be more likely to occur in those areas that patrol officers are frequently sent to (this can result in a disproportionate number of arrests in urban areas and areas of high deprivation, for example) (Lum and Isaac, 2016).

The result is that the use of stop and search powers and arrest rates, among other occurrences, correlate to where and how most police officers are deployed or direct their own activities; they are poor proxies for the true rates of disorder, violence and crime. Furthermore, in recent decades police-recorded crime statistics have been subjected to manipulation and gaming in several jurisdictions, which frequently involves police officers and administrators describing and charging serious offences as more minor ones, or not recording them at all, in an attempt to artificially deflate crime statistics and make police areas appear safer than they are. Mistakes are also plentiful. Records and data sets held by police forces can be disparate, fragmented, inaccurate, outdated and imperfectly sourced; it is not unusual for digital data to be incorrectly and incompletely recorded numerous times a day across whole police areas (Valentine, 2019). All of these issues mean that police data, which is frequently used by machine learning systems and as training data for predictive algorithms, can reflect a multitude of systematic biases and errors, including biases associated with race (Ferguson, 2017a; Rowe, 2020).

A major aspect addressed by contributors such as Fernandez and Alani, and Cohen and Graver in Part I is the complex relationship between police services, third party technology companies and big data. One of the most exciting new frontiers around predictive and AI technologies, at least for behavioural and data scientists, is the drawing of behavioural insights about people from their interactions with digital and online technologies (Sanders and Sheptycki, 2017). Technology companies, particularly those that maintain social media sites online, now record vast volumes of digital data on a daily basis as a result of people's frequent interactions with computer and communication technologies. Users interactions can be mined for patterns and insights about how they think and behave. Statistical and probabilistic patterns and insights can potentially be drawn from the words and phrases users post online, the profiles they comment on, the photos they like, and the people in the photos they are 'tagged' in, among other possibilities (Schaffer, 2013). Machine learning algorithms are particularly attractive in this space because not only can they interrogate vast libraries of information in milliseconds, far exceeding the capability of humans, but people are continually changing the way that they communicate and interact online (sometimes in order to evade detection).

The analysis and sorting of friendship connections and associate networks that surround users of social media sites such as Facebook, Twitter, Instagram, Tencent and eBay can be undertaken to assess closeness, proximity and interdependency in a whole host of different contexts (Ariel, 2019). Insights may relate to a person's interests, politics or, potentially, criminal behaviours (Law Society, 2019). As Hamilton outlines in Chapter 2, young people use social media as a major form of direct and indirect communication, and since young age is a consistently strong predictor of violent offences, these techniques can have a predictive policing application. Techniques such as 'social network analysis' now commonly fall under the rubric of 'social media intelligence' (SOCMINT). However, such approaches were not designed for policing, they were predominantly designed for and are still used by many technology companies for commercial purposes.

Many 'tech' companies carry out data mining of what people search for, what they view and when, their social media posts, the things they 'like', and their purchases, among other activities, for the purposes of consumer data collection.

The insights are used to inform new products and attract advertisers. Not only are these companies interested in social media activities but the companies that provide financial and online shopping services also record data on individual, group and population behaviours for the same reasons. Advertisers, for instance, may want to target particular advertisements (for example, running clothes for sale on Amazon) and at specific times (when a person usually returns from their run, according to their Fitbit or previous transactions) in order to ensure the most likely chance of a purchase. For these purposes, data scientists and machine learning algorithms are frequently tasked with developing profiles of consumers, often by placing them in categories or 'buckets' which provide some estimation of their likelihood to act in particular ways, purchase particular items or be interested in specific products (Taylor et al., 2011; Fuchs, 2017). Predatory, personalised advertisements may even enable a seller to adjust the prices shown online according to when people are most likely to buy products or what a person might be willing to pay on the basis of previous behaviours (HLSC, 2018). Other companies, such as those in the communications industry, also record huge volumes of data as mobile phones constantly interact with wireless technologies and networks as they, or their owner (by proxy), travel through an environment. These digital trails can be used to map out where people have been, whose devices they interacted with, and what their routines are, among other insights.

It is these advances in the computer and data sciences, allied to the changes in how people interact with digital and online technologies (leading to the collection and analysis of huge troves of digital data) that is now commonly referred to as 'big data'. The extent of ongoing commercial endeavours in this area has led to the big data economy being described as 'the greatest laboratory ever for consumer research' (O'Neil, 2016: 75). It should be unsurprising at this stage to learn that machine learning systems have moved to the forefront of these endeavours, since they are capable of mining huge volumes of data, sorting and interrogating data rapidly, and distilling patterns into predictive analytics. The policing applications are many, from the identification of previously unknown co-offenders to the analysis of financial transactions to develop insights into fraud and money laundering. However, as we outlined in our section on AI earlier, just because correlations can be found between particular kinds of behaviours, characteristics and activities, it doesn't mean that such correlations are true in all cases. In many cases, predictions can be very wrong. One of the key differences between policing and the commercial interests of big tech companies is that being wrong doesn't matter so much in advertising. An array of complex issues arise when these techniques are employed in a policing context, such as the risk assessment of particular people (see Chapter 2 by Hamilton), prioritisation (see Chapter 3 by McDaniel and Pease), decisions to stop and search (see Chapter 4 by Cohen and Graver), counter-extremism strategies (see Chapter 5 by Fernandez and Alani) and crime disruption interventions (see Chapter 6 by Utset). The contributors introduce the reader to an elaborate web of interconnected issues at the nexus of policing, predictions, big data and AI, with a variety of biases at its centre.

Part II: Police accountability and human rights

The adequacy of extant regulatory regimes and various modes of accountability are examined in particular depth in the second half of the text. Shapiro, in Chapter 7, traces ideas of police accountability from the early introduction of police technologies through to CompStat and the development of more advanced predictive tools. His chapter considers the emerging arguments about whether accountability is a rationale in favour of predictive policing or a charge against it in different contexts, delineating concepts of public accountability, supervisory accountability and algorithmic accountability. He addresses, for example, key differences between secretive vendors of predictive policing technologies and those vendors developing tools which are more ethically-oriented. Drawing upon empirical research conducted in the US, there is a particular focus on one vendor, Hunchlab, which was set up initially to be ethically-minded.

Chapter 8, in turn, focuses more broadly on the oversight and governance of a number of different machine learning algorithms that are presently being used to aid police decision-making in the UK. In the chapter, Babuta and Oswald pay particular attention to the impact that these technologies are having on individual rights and the administrative law principles governing public sector decision-making. They argue that in the absence of adequate safeguards, rights to privacy, a fair trial, assembly and expression could be jeopardised in various contexts. They recommend the introduction of numerous mechanisms of accountability, not least the incorporation of ALGOCARE and an expansion of the role of police and data inspectorates, among other local and national bodies. Austerity is located as a key driver for various policy decisions in the fields of predictive policing and AI, leading them to label some extant machine learning systems as 'Austerity AI'.

Continuing the discussion on human rights, Grace (in Chapter 9) examines a number of recent findings by the European Court of Human Rights and the UK Information Commissioner's office which criticise various legal frameworks and forms of police data gathering and retention practices within the predictive policing space. He recommends the establishment of a new statutory authorisation process for predictive and AI tools to enhance their democratic quality, and the increased use of bespoke ethics committees to guide their development.

The text then shines a spotlight on some of the issues raised, within the contexts of domestic abuse and sex offences particularly. In Chapter 10, Rowe and Muir caution that the excessive analysis of the digital devices of victims represents a significant intrusion into their private lives and may discourage them from coming forward to report domestic violence and sex offences. The chapter also considers broader problems of accountability, from the role of private firms in the development of predictive and AI tools to the limited possibilities of judicial review.

Finally, the last chapter uses a number of vignettes to address some of the inherent complexities of police training and learning. In Chapter 11, Richards, Roberts and Britton consider different ways that synthetic and naturalistic learning environments can be enhanced through AI, involving the use of virtual reality and Body Worn Camera technologies, among others. They argue that the embedding of AI and other technologies into training environments could help police officers to assess their behaviour, enhance individual and collective decision-making, and better prepare themselves for future occurrences.

This set of chapters is linked together by a number of themes, one of which is an inherent contradiction at the intersection of predictive policing and AI. On the one hand, many predictive policing technologies have the capacity to generate relatively high levels of police accountability in theory. An algorithm is, after all, a sequence of instructions and actions. It should mean that police organisations can point to these sequences, and the quantifiable outputs they generate, as a rationale for some of the decisions they make and activities they undertake (the quality of the calculation aside). This can be a significant improvement on current approaches to police policy-making and prioritisation, which can involve police leaders relying upon anecdotes, opinions, fads and the whims of political representatives to guide their strategies (McDaniel, 2018; Law Society, 2019). Although the interventions that police forces subsequently choose to engage in may be controversial, algorithms can provide a cleaner rationale for police officers to optimise patrol time in crime hotspots in particular ways (Pease and Tseloni, 2014), or to intervene in the lives of victims, offenders and suspects. To rely heavily on predictive algorithms, police leaders would, in a sense, be holding their feet to the fire, leaving them with little room to fudge statements about policy and priority. Police chiefs have always been choice architects. The trouble is that they can be idiosyncratic and inconsistent. If predictions point them in inconvenient or uncomfortable directions, it becomes harder for them to ignore the thornier problems that they might otherwise have preferred to leave untended.

The nub is that this kind of accountability relies to a significant extent upon transparency. Police accountability, as a general concept, demands transparency in relevant contexts because it involves a capacity to require and access relatively fulsome information and accounts from an explanatory and cooperative police service (Marshall, 1965). The modern concept of police accountability is intrinsically concerned with the establishment and functioning of multiple processes through which police policies, strategies, practices, acts and omissions can be questioned and contextualised (Walsh, 2009). These processes cannot work without a high level of transparency. People cannot subject police officers and their organisations to much scrutiny if they cannot look beyond the police station reception or study or seek to understand police activities and the environmental factors that influence them in real life (Patten Commission, 1999).

Civilians, academics, reporters and non-governmental organisations should not have to spend their time scouring for information or submitting Freedom of Information (FOI) requests to find out what police services are up to; such information should ideally be made available to the public openly, willingly and systematically (unless it is specifically not in the public interest to make some information available) so that people may judge the quality of policing for themselves (Ibid). Even though police forces may strongly wish that police errors, misbehaviours, derelictions of duty and controversial occurrences are not made public, they have a responsibility to divulge the choices that they make and the strategies they pursue so that they can be understood, debated and remedied where appropriate. These processes are fundamental ingredients for the proper functioning of the police in liberal democratic societies (Walsh, 1998).

Unfortunately, very few predictive and AI technologies are what we would call transparent. The complexity of 'black box' machine learning systems, for instance, means that members of the public and vulnerable communities may find it impossible to understand and challenge system errors (Valentine, 2019). This could serve to restrict the choices open to individuals, limit opportunities for appeal, and worsen power imbalances between police forces and citizens, and between the rich and poor who are less able to fund legal challenges. Appeals may require the production of quite strong evidence that an algorithm is wrong, even though a machine learning system may have relied on little more than weak correlations and 'best guesses' to generate a prediction in the first instance. Complainants who have impairments may be particularly affected. When legal remedies become harder to access, civil liberties are placed in jeopardy.

It is because of the complexities of various algorithms and the potential for misinterpretation and abuse that police forces should be highly sensitive to the need for transparency and accountability in this space. The commercial entities that they do business with are not subject to the same architecture of police accountability. As a result, police forces and individual officers should compensate by being particularly transparent in how they, at least, interpret algorithm outputs and apply them in practice. Regrettably, the chapters show that this has not proven to be the case across the UK, US and Australia. The uncertainty and complexity of many algorithms and machine learning systems means that there is still much room for fudging in reality. Without knowing when exactly to intervene, how to intervene or whether partner agencies can be encouraged to participate, police leaders remain somewhat free to implement assumptive strategies and innovations which often have a short shelf life. It is difficult to hold police officers to account for organisational strategies that revolve around untested and short-lived assumptions about what works.

Not only are predictive and AI technologies generally surrounded by a fog of uncertainty but some police organisations have even signed non-disclosure agreements (NDAs) that serve to hide the contents of algorithms from the public in order to protect the proprietary technologies and competitive advantages of the commercial enterprises they are in partnership with (Ferguson, 2017a; Joh, 2019). Some police services, like Durham Constabulary and West Midlands Police in the UK, either alone or in a consortium with other agencies are striving to develop their own tools in-house, but many of the systems in use around the world are commercially owned. This makes it even harder for civilians and researchers to determine just how biased and error-prone various predictive and AI technologies are, and whether they are being used by police officers in problematic ways. Some police forces appear to be complicit in maintaining and generating secrecy and confusion. The authors tackle these problems head-on.

References

Ariel, B. (2019). Technology in Policing. In: Weisburd, D. and Braga, A.A (eds), *Police innovation: Contrasting perspectives*. Cambridge: Cambridge University Press, pp. 314–336.

Babuta, A. and Oswald, M. (2020). Machine learning predictive algorithms and the policing of future crimes: Governance and oversight. In: McDaniel J.L.M and Pease K.G. (eds), *Predictive policing and artificial intelligence*, Oxford: Routledge.

Babuta, A., Oswald, M. and Rinik, C. (2018). *Machine learning algorithms and police decision-making: Legal, ethical and regulatory challenges*. London: Royal United Services Institute (RUSI).

Bennett Moses, L. and Chan, J. (2018). Algorithmic prediction in policing: assumptions, evaluation, and accountability, *Policing and Society*, 28(7), pp. 806–822.

Berk, R. and Bleich, J. (2014). Forecasts of violence to inform sentencing decisions. *Journal of Quantitative Criminology*, 30, 79–96.

Berk, R.A. et al. (2009). Forecasting murder in a population of probationers and parolees: A high stakes application of statistical learning. *Journal of the Royal Statistical Society*, 172(1), 191–211.

Bostrom, N. (2017). *Superintelligence: Paths, dangers, strategies*. Oxford: OUP.

Bowers, K.J., Johnson, S.D. and Pease, K. (2004). Prospective Hot-Spotting. *British Journal of Criminology*, 44(5), pp. 641–658.

Braga, A.A., Hureau, D.M. and Papachristos, A.V. (2011). The relevance of micro places to citywide robbery trends: A longitudinal analysis of robbery incidents at street corners and block faces in Boston. *Journal of Research in Crime and Delinquency*, 48(1), pp. 7–32.

Brantingham, P.J. and Brantingham, P.L. (eds) (1981). *Environmental criminology*. Beverly Hills, CA: Sage.

Brantingham, P.J., Brantingham, P.L., and Andresen, M.A. (2017). The geometry of crime and crime pattern theory. In: Wortley, R. and Townsley, M. (eds), *Environmental criminology and crime analysis, 2nd edition*, Abingdon, Oxon: Routledge, pp. 98–114.

Breiman, L. (2001). Random Forests. *Machine Learning*, 45, pp. 5–32.

Brundage, M. et al. (2018). *The malicious use of artificial intelligence: Forecasting, prevention and mitigation*. Future of Humanity Institute, University of Oxford.

Burgess, E.M. (1928). Factors determining success or failure on parole. In: Bruce A.A., Harno A.J., Burgess E.W. and Landesco E.W. (eds), *The working of the indeterminate sentence law and the parole system in Illinois.* State Board of Parole, Springfield, pp. 205–249.

Caplan, J.M., Kennedy, L.W. and Miller, J. (2011). Risk terrain modeling: Brokering criminological theory and GIS methods for crime forecasting. *Justice Quarterly*, 28(2), pp. 360–381.

Clarke, R.V. and Cornish, D.B. (1985). Modeling offenders' decisions: A framework for research and policy. *Crime and Justice*, 6, pp. 147–185.

Clarke, Ronald V. (2017). Situational Crime Prevention. In: Wortley, R. and Townsley, M. (eds), *Environmental criminology and crime analysis, 2nd edition*, Abingdon, Oxon: Routledge, pp. 286–303.

Cohen, L.E and Felson, M. (1979). Social change and crime rate trends: A routine activity approach. *American Sociological Review*, 44(4), pp. 588–608.

Cohn, E. (1990). Weather and crime. *The British Journal of Criminology*, 30(1), pp. 51–64.

Cornish, D.B. (1994). The procedural analysis of offending and its relevance for situational prevention. In: R.V. Clarke (ed), *Crime prevention studies*, New York: Criminal Justice Press, Vol. 3, p. 151–196.

Dakin, K., Xie, W., Parkinson, S., Khan, S., Monchuk, L. and Pease, K. (2020). Built environment attributes and crime: An automated machine learning approach. *Crime Science*, 9(1).

Deloitte. (2018). Policing 4.0: Deciding the future of policing in the UK.

Donnelly, P.D and Ward, C.L. (eds) (2015). *Oxford Textbook of Violence Prevention: Epidemiology, Evidence and Policy*, Oxford: Oxford University Press.

Eck, J., Lee, Y. and Corsaro, N. (2017). Adding more police is unlikely to reduce crime: A meta-analysis of police agency size and crime research. *Translational Criminology*, Spring 2017, 14–16.

Ekblom, P. (2017). Designing products against crime. In: Wortley, R. and Townsley, M. (eds), *Environmental criminology and crime analysis*, 2nd edition, Abingdon, Oxon: Routledge, p. 304–333.

Ethics Committee West Midlands Police and Crime Commissioner. (2019b). Notes of meeting held Wednesday 24 July 2019, 10am–2pm, Lloyd House, Colmore Circus Queensway, Birmingham, B4 6NQ (Chaired by Marion Oswald).

Ethics Committee West Midlands Police and Crime Commissioner. (2019a). Notes of meeting held Wednesday 03 April 2019, 10:00–14:00 hrs, Lloyd House, Colmore Circus Queensway, Birmingham, B4 6NQ (Chaired by Marion Oswald).

Ferguson, A.G. (2017a). *The Rise of big data policing: Surveillance, race and the future of law enforcement.* New York: New York University Press.

Ferguson, A.G. (2017b). Policing predictive policing. *Washington University Law Review*, 94(5), p. 1109.

Francis, B., Soothill, K. Fligelstone, R. (2004). Identifying patterns and pathways of offending behaviour. *European Journal of Criminology*, 1(1), pp. 47–87.

Fuchs, C. (2017). *Social media: A critical introduction, 2nd edition*, London: Sage.

Gibbons, D. and Garrity, D. (1962). Definition and analysis of certain criminal types. *The Journal of Criminal Law, Criminology, and Police Science*, 53(1), pp. 27–35.

Goldstein, H. (1979). Improving policing: A problem-oriented approach. *Crime and Delinquency*, 25(2), pp. 236–258.

The Guardian. (2018). Welsh police wrongly identify thousands as potential criminals. Available at: www.theguardian.com/uk-news/2018/may/05/welsh-police-wrongly-identify-thousands-as-potential-criminals [accessed 1 February 2019].

Green, B., Horel, T., and Papachristos, A.V. (2017). Modeling contagion through social networks to explain and predict gunshot violence in Chicago, 2006–2014. *JAMA Intern Medicine*, 177(3), 326–333.

Hinton, G.E. (1992). How neural networks learn from experience. *Scientific American*, 267(3), pp. 144–151.

HMIC. (2018). *State of policing: The annual assessment of policing in England and Wales.* London: Her Majesty's Chief Inspector of Constabulary.

HMIP. (2020). Report on an unannounced inspection of HMP & YOI Doncaster. Canary Wharf, London: HM Chief Inspector of Prisons, 9–20 September 2019.

House of Commons Science and Technology Committee. (2018). Algorithms in decision-making, Fourth Report of Session 2017–19, 23 May 2018.

House of Lords Select Committee (HLSC) on Artificial Intelligence. (2018). AI in the UK: ready, willing and able? Report of Session 2017-19, HL Paper 100.

Hymas, C. (2019). Police use AI to avoid having to mount investigations into crimes unlikely to be solved. *The Telegraph*, 5 June 2019.

Jeffrey, C.R. (1971). *Crime prevention through environmental design.* Beverly Hills, CA: Sage.

Joh, E.E. (2018). Artificial Intelligence and Policing: First Questions (April 25, 2018). 41 Seattle Univ. L. Rev. 1139 (2018).

Joh, E.E. (2019). Policing the smart city. *International Journal of Law in Context*, 15(2), pp. 177–182.

Johnson, S.D. and Bowers, K.J. (2004). The burglary as a clue to the future: The beginnings of prospective hot-spotting. *The European Journal of Criminology*, 1, pp. 237–255.

Johnson, S.D. (2017). Crime mapping and spatial analysis. In: Wortley, R. and Townsley, M. (eds), *Environmental criminology and crime analysis, 2nd Edition*, Abingdon, Oxon: Routledge, pp. 199–223.

Kelling, G. et al. (1974). Kansas City Preventive Patrol Strategy.

Kennedy, D.M. (2019). Policing and the lessons of focused deterrence. In: David Weisburd and Anthony A. Braga (eds), *Police innovation: Contrasting perspectives, 2nd Edition*, Cambridge: Cambridge University Press, pp. 205–221.

Law Society. (2019). Algorithms in the criminal justice system. *The Law Society Commission on the Use of Algorithms in the Justice System*, June 2019.

Liberty. (2019). Policing by Machine: Predictive policing and the threat to our rights. *Liberty*, January 2019.

Lombroso C. (1911). Crime: Its Causes and Remedies. Boston: Little, Brown and Co.

Lum, K. and Isaac, W. (2016). To predict and serve? *In Detail*, October 2016, pp. 14–19.

Manning, P.K. (2003). *Policing contingencies.* Chicago: University of Chicago Press.

Manning, P.K (2004). Police technology: Crime analysis. *Criminal Justice Matters*, 58, pp. 26–27.

Manning, P.K. (2018). Technology, law and policing. In: den Boer, M. (ed.), *Comparative policing from a legal perspective.* Cheltenham, UK: Edward Elgar. pp. 290–305.

Marshall, G. (1965). *Police and Government: The Status and Accountability of the English Constable.* London: Methuen.

McCarthy, J. (1968). Programs with Common Sense. In: Minksy, M. (ed.), *Semantic information processing.* Cambridge: MIT Press, pp. 403–418.

McCarthy, J., Minsky, M.L., Rochester, N. and Shannon, C.E. (1955). A Proposal for the Dartmouth Summer Research Project on Artificial Intelligence. In: *AI Magazine* (2006), 27(4), pp. 12–14.

McDaniel, J.L.M. (2017). Rethinking the law and politics of democratic police account-ability. *The Police Journal: Theory, Practice and Principles*, 91(1), 22–43.

McDaniel, J.L.M., Moss, K. and Pease, K. (eds) (2020). *Policing and mental health: theory, policy and practice*. Abingdon: Routledge.

Minsky, M. (1961). A selected descriptor-indexed bibliography to the literature on arti-ficial intelligence. *IRE Transactions on Human Factors in Electronics*, vol. HFE-2, no. 1, pp. 39–55.

Mohler, G., Short, M. B., Malinowski, S., Johnson, M., Tita, G.E., Bertozzi, A.L. , and Brantingham, P.J. (2015). Randomized controlled field trials of predictive policing. *Journal of the American Statistical Association*, 110, pp. 1399–1411.

Monchuk, L., Pease, K. and Armitage, R. (2018). Is it just a guessing game? The appli-cation of crime prevention through environmental design (CPTED) to predict burg-lary. *Journal of Planning Practice and Research*, 33(4), pp. 426–440.

Moravec, E.R. (2019). Do algorithms have a place in policing? *The Atlantic*, September 5, 2019.

Nagendran, M. et al. (2020). Artificial intelligence versus clinicians: systematic review of design, reporting standards, and claims of deep learning studies, *BMJ*, 368(689), doi: 10.1136/bmj.m689.

National Audit Office. (2016). Efficiency in the Criminal Justice System. (Comptroller General 2016).

Nettle, D., Nott, K. and Bateson, M. (2012). 'Cycle thieves, we are watching you': Impact of a simple Signage intervention against bicycle theft. *PLoS ONE*.

Newman, O. (1972). *Defensible space: Crime prevention through urban design*. New York: Macmillan.

Nilsson, N.J. (2005). Human-level artificial intelligence? Be serious! *AI Magazine*, Winter, pp. 68–75.

O'Neil, C. (2016). *Weapons of math destruction: How big data increases inequality and threatens democracy*. New York: Crown.

Oswald, M., Grace, J., Urwin, S. and Barnes, G.C. (2018). Algorithmic risk assessment policing models: lessons from the Durham Hart model and 'experimental' propor-tionality. *Information and Communications Technology Law*, 27(2), pp. 223–3350.

Patten Commission. (1999). A New Beginning: Policing in Northern Ireland (The Report of the Independent Commission on Policing for Northern Ireland 1999).

Pearl, J. (1988). Probabilistic reasoning in intelligence systems: Networks of plausible inference. Burlington, Mass: Morgan Kaufmann.

Pease, K. (1998). Repeat victimisation: Taking stock. *Crime Detection and Prevention Series*, Paper 90. Home Office: London.

Pease, K. (2004). Crime science. *Criminal Justice Matters*, 58, p. 4–5.

Pease, K., Ireson, J. and Thorpe, J. (1974). Additivity assumptions in the measurement of delinquency. *British Journal of Criminology*, 14, 256–263.

Pease, K., Ireson, J., Billingham, S. and Thorpe, J. (1977). The development of a scale of offence seriousness. *International Journal of Criminology and Penology*, 5, 17–29.

Pease, K. and Farrell, G. (2017). Repeat Victimisation. In: Wortley, R. and Townsley, M. (eds), *Environmental criminology and crime analysis, 2nd edition*, Abingdon, Oxon: Routledge, pp. 180–198.

Pease, K. and Tseloni, A. (2014). Using modeling to predict and prevent victimization. Springer International Publishing.

Perrot, P. (2017). What about AI in criminal intelligence? From predictive policing to AI perspectives. *European Police Science and Research Bulletin*, 16, 65–76.

Perry, W.L, McInnis, B., Price, C.C., Smith, S.C. and Hollywood, J.S, (2013). *Predictive policing: The role of crime forecasting in law enforcement operations*. Santa Monica: RAND Safety and Justice Program.

Quijano-Sanchez, L., Liberatore, F., Camacho-Collados, J. and Camacho-Collados, M. (2018). Applying automatic text-based detection of deceptive language to police reports: Extracting behavioral patterns from a multi-step classification model to understand how we lie to the police. *Knowledge-Based Systems*, 149(1), p.155–168.

Rengert, G.F., Piquero, A.R. and Jones, P.R. (1999). Distance decay re-examined. *Criminology*, 37(2), 427–446.

Ratcliffe, J. (2019). Predictive policing. In: David Weisburd and Anthony A. Braga (eds), *Police innovation: Contrasting perspectives, 2nd Edition*, Cmbridge: Cambridge University Press, pp. 347–363.

Rich, M.L. (2016). Machine learning, automated suspicion algorithms, and the Fourth Amendment. *University of Pennsylvania Law Review*, 164(4), pp. 871–929.

Roach, J., Weir, K., Phillips, P., Gaskell, K., and Walton, M. (2016). Nudging down theft from insecure vehicles. A pilot study. *International Journal of Police Science and Management*, 19(1), pp. 31–38.

Robinson, A.L., Myhill, A., Wire, J., Roberts, J. and Tilley, N. (2016). *Risk-led policing of domestic abuse and the DASH risk model*. London: College of Policing.

Rossmo, D.K. (1999). *Geographic profiling*. Washington, DC: CRC Press LLC.

Rossmo, D.K. and Rombouts, S. (2017). Geographic profiling. In: Wortley, R. and Townsley, M. (eds), *Environmental criminology and crime analysis, 2nd edition*, Abingdon, Oxon: Routledge, pp. 162–179.

Royal Society. (2017). Machine learning: the power and promise of computers that learn by example, The Royal Society, April 2017.

Rowe, R. and Muir, R. (2020). Big data policing: Governing the machine? In: McDaniel J.L.M and Pease K.G. (eds), *Predictive policing and artificial intelligence*, Routledge, Oxford.

Russell, S. and Norvig, P. (2014). *Artificial Intelligence: A Modern Approach, 3rd Edition*. Harlow: Pearson Education Limited.

Sanders, C. and Sheptycki, J. (2017). Policing, crime and 'big data'; towards a critique of the moral economy of stochastic governance. *Crime Law and Social Change*, 68(1), pp. 1–15.

Saunders, J., Hunt, P. and Hollywood, J.S. (2016). Predictions put into practice: A quasi-experimental evaluation of Chicago's predictive policing pilot. *Journal of Experimental Criminology*, 12(3), pp. 347–371.

Schaffer, N. (2013). *Maximize your social: one-stop guide to building a social media strategy for marketing and business success*. Hoboken, New Jersey: Wiley.

Shapiro, A. (2017). Reform predictive policing, *Nature*, 541, pp. 458–460.

Sherman, L.W. (1983). Reducing police gun use: Critical events, administrative policy and organizational change. In: Punch, M. (ed.), Control in the Police organization, Cambridge, Massachusetts: M.I.T. Press.

Sherman, L.W. and Weisburd, D.L. (1995). General deterrent effects of police patrol in crime "hot spots": A randomized, controlled trial. *Justice Quarterly*, 12(4), pp. 625–648.

Sherman, L.W. (2007). The power few: experimental criminology and the reduction of harm. *Journal of Experimental Criminology*, 3, pp. 299–321.

Sidebottom, A., Thorpe, A. and Johnson S.D. (2009). Using targeted publicity to reduce opportunities for bicycle theft: A demonstration and replication. *European Journal of Criminology*, 6(3), pp. 267–286.

Simon, H.A. (1969). *The sciences of the artificial*. Cambridge, MA: MIT Press.

Skogan, W. (2019). Community Policing. In: Weisburd, D. and Braga, A.A (eds), *Police innovation: Contrasting perspectives*. Cambridge: Cambridge University Press, pp. 27–42.

Soothill, K., Francis, B., Ackerley, E. and Fligelstone, R. (2002). *Murder and serious sexual assault: What criminal histories can reveal about future serious offending* (Police Research Series Paper 144), London: Home Office.

Stevenson, M. (2018). Assessing risk assessment in action. *Minnesota Law Review*, 58, pp. 303–378.

Taylor, D.G., Lewin, J.E. and Strutton, D. (2011). Friends, fans, and followers: Do ads work on social networks. *Journal of Advertising Research*, 51(1), pp. 258–275.

Tetlock, P.E. and Gardner, D. (2016). *Superforecasting: The art and science of prediction*. London: Random House.

Townsley, M. and Pease, K. (2002). Hot Spots and Cold Comfort: The Importance of Having a Working Thermometer. In: N. Tilley (ed.), *Analysis for crime prevention* (Crime Prevention Studies Vol. 13). Monsey, NY: Criminal Justice Press.

Tseloni, A. and Pease, K. (2004). Repeat personal victimization. 'Boosts' or 'Flags'? *British Journal of Criminology*, 43(1), pp. 196–212.

Turing, A. (1950). Computing machinery and intelligence. *Mind*, 59(236), pp. 433–60.

Valentine, S. (2019). Impoverished algorithms: Misguided governments, flawed technologies and social control. *Fordham Urban Law Journal*, pp. 364–405.

Vulliamy P. et al. (2018). Temporal and geographic patterns of stab injuries in young people: a retrospective cohort study from a UK major trauma centre. *British Medical Journal*, Open, 8:e023114.

Walsh D.P.J. (2009). *Human Rights and policing in Ireland*. Dublin: Clarus Press.

Walsh, D.P.J. (1998). *The Irish Police: A legal and constitutional perspective*. Dublin: Roundhall, Sweet and Maxwell.

West Midlands Police National Analytics Solution Project Team, Response to the Alan Turing Institute and IDEPP, West Midlands Police, pp. 1–4.

Wiener, N. (1948). *Cybernetics: Or control and communication in the animal and the machine*. New York & Paris: John Wiley & Sons.

Wortley, R. and Townsley, M. (eds) (2017). *Environmental criminology and crime analysis, 2nd Edition*. Abingdon, Oxon: Routledge.

Part I

Bias and Big Data

Chapter 1

The future of AI in policing
Exploring the sociotechnical imaginaries

Janet Chan

Introduction

Artificial intelligence (AI) is a generic term that covers a variety of related computational techniques such as machine learning, speech recognition, machine vision, national language processing, expert systems and various tools for planning and optimisation, used for problem solving and performance of tasks that normally require human intelligence (Walsh et al., 2019). Through advances in modern technology, the use of AI for services to human society is no longer a distant future in the realm of science fiction. According to the majority of AI experts, there's a 50 per cent chance that 2062 is the year when we would have created machines as intelligent as we are (Walsh, 2018). The promises of AI in making human decisions smarter, more efficient and more rational are extremely attractive in an environment where information has become increasingly complex, voluminous and fast changing. What, then, is the future of AI in policing? There is, unfortunately, no clear answer to this question that we can look up in the literature or in government publications. This is partly because AI is still a relatively new technology, even though it is being developed rapidly and its applications are growing exponentially. It is safe to say, though, that the future of AI depends on how societies *see* AI technology and its relevance to society in general, and to policing in particular. And this is what this chapter is trying to examine.

The chapter is structured as follows. Section 1 introduces the concept of "sociotechnical imaginaries" which underpins the analysis presented in this chapter. Section 2 discusses in general the benefits and risks of AI, while Section 3 examines more closely four co-existing sociotechnical imaginaries connected with the use of AI in policing, focusing on the case of predictive policing. The final section suggests how society should approach the advent of AI.

1. Sociotechnical imaginaries

Throughout this chapter, I will be using the concept of "sociotechnical imaginaries" as popularised by the Science and Technology Studies scholar

Sheila Jasanoff (2015a). Jasanoff defines sociotechnical imaginaries as "collect-ively held, institutionally stabilized, and publicly performed visions of desirable futures, animated by shared understandings of forms of social life and social order attainable through, and supportive of, advances in science and technology" (2015a: 4). Even though this definition seems to privilege visions that are "desir-able", the concept is not confined to utopian visions of technology; in fact, as in most forms of technologies, there are inevitably dystopian visions foreseen by segments, sometimes substantial segments, of the population. The existence of "resistant imaginaries" is part of the framework. It should also be pointed out that this definition does not assume that there is only one dominant vision that is "collectively held", there are likely to be multiple visions co-existing in soci-eties. The definition also is not premised on visions being unchanging in time or space; rather, it allows for a process of transformation where new ideas are introduced, embedded in social practice or resisted, leading to their expansion or removal. In this formulation, "[i]maginaries operate as both glue and solvent, able—when widely disseminated and effectively performed—to preserve con-tinuity across the sharpest ruptures of innovation or, in reverse, to upend firm worlds and make them anew" (2015a: 29).

The concept of social imaginaries has been in existence for some time. Jasanoff (2015a: 5–8) has traced the genealogies of "imagination as a social practice" to the works of Durkheim and Weber, anthropologists such as Evans-Pritchard and Mary Douglas, Benedict Anderson's work on imagined communities, and Charles Taylor's use of the term "social imaginaries". She notes a "startling, almost inexplicable omission" from the classic accounts of social imaginaries—"a detailed investigation of modernity's two most salient forces: science and technology" (2015a: 8). Jasanoff sees sociotechnical imaginaries as occupying "the theoretically underdeveloped space between the idealistic collective imaginations identified by social and political theorists and the hybrid but politically neutered networks or assemblages with which STS scholars often describe reality":

> Our definition pulls together the normativity of the imagination with the materiality of networks ... Unlike mere ideas and fashions, sociotechnical imaginaries are collective, durable, capable of being performed; yet they are also temporally situated and culturally particular. ... [T]hese imaginaries are at once products of and instruments of the co-production of science, tech-nology, and society in modernity.
>
> (2015a: 19)

To recognise or identify sociotechnical imaginaries about AI in policing, I have drawn on published academic literature, available government documents and other online resources in order to examine the language used to frame and visualise the use of AI in society and in policing.

2. The benefits and risks of AI for society

The report by Walsh et al. (2019) is drawn on heavily in this section as it provides the most recent survey of the applications of AI to society and represents the sociotechnical imaginaries of the top Australian researchers in humanities, social sciences, science, technology and engineering.[1] The report appears to maintain a relatively "balanced" sociotechnical imaginary of AI; in other words, it lays out equally the benefits as well as the risks of AI for society.

Definition of AI

Walsh et al. (2019: 14) are careful to define what AI is and is not, noting however that there is not consensus among AI researchers on a universal definition. AI is "not a specific technology" but "a collection of interrelated technologies used to solve problems and perform tasks that, when humans do them, requires thinking". The "components of AI" include machine learning, as well as a range of techniques including natural language processing, speech recognition, computer vision and automated reasoning (see Figure 1.1). Walsh et al. (2019: 15) claim that AI is superior to simpler technologies "in its ability to

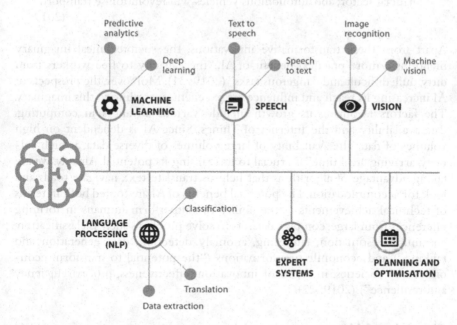

Figure 1.1 Components of AI, reproduced with permission from ACOLA (2019).

Source: Walsh, T., Levy, N., Bell, G., Elliott, A., Maclaurin, J., Mareels, I.M.Y., Wood, F.M. (2019) *The effective and ethical development of artificial intelligence: An opportunity to improve our wellbeing.* Report for the Australian Council of Learned Academies, www.acola.org.

handle problems involving complex features such as ambiguity, multiple and sometimes conflicting objectives, and uncertainty" and in many cases, its "ability to learn and improve over time".

The benefits of AI

Walsh et al. give numerous examples of the potential benefits of AI for a variety of sectors in society, including manufacturing, health, communication, transportation and financial applications:

> New techniques of machine learning are spurring unprecedented developments in AI applications. Next-generation robotics promise to transform our manufacturing, infrastructure and agriculture sectors; advances in natural language processing are revolutionising the way clinicians interpret the results of diagnostic tests and treat patients; chatbots and automated assistants are ushering in a new world of communication, analytics and customer service; unmanned autonomous vehicles are changing our capacities for defence, security and emergency response; intelligent financial technologies are establishing a more accountable, transparent and risk-aware financial sector; and autonomous vehicles will revolutionise transport.
>
> (2019: 4)

Apart from these transformative innovations, the sociotechnical imaginary mentions a more practical benefit of AI, "the capacity to free workers from dirty, dull, difficult and dangerous tasks" (2019: 31). Moreover, the prospects of AI increasing its reach and influence are excellent, according to this imaginary. The factors favouring its growth include various advances in computing, data availability and the Internet of Things. Since AI is dependent on high volumes of data, the availability of large volumes of diverse data, at high velocity, arriving "real time" is crucial to its realising its potential. Already, we are taking advantage of algorithms that help us translate text, navigate roads and look for accommodation. The potential benefits of AI are touted both in terms of technical achievements ("the ability to outperform humans in forming inferences from large, complex datasets to solve problems such as classification, continuous estimation, clustering, anomaly detection, data generation and ranking") and economic transformations ("the potential to transform economies and societies, in terms of innovation, effectiveness, process efficiency and resilience") (2019: 22).

The risks of AI

Walsh et al.'s (2019) sociotechnical imaginary of AI is not totally rosy. The risks of AI are not papered over but discussed in great detail. In this way, the "resistant imaginary" coexists with the utopian one:

It is well known, for example, that smart facial recognition technologies have often been inaccurate and can replicate the underlying biases of the human-encoded data they rely upon; that AI relies on data that can and has been exploited for ethically dubious purposes, leading to social injustice and inequality; and that while the impact of AI is often described as 'revolutionary' and 'impending', there is no guarantee that AI technologies such as autonomous vehicles will have their intended effects, or even that their uptake in society will be inevitable or seamless.

(2019: 4)

This recognition of potential problems is quickly followed by a sociotechnical imaginary that normalises these issues variously as temporary "teething problems of a new technology" or a "risk associated with all technological developments", adding that "AI technologies could in fact be applied to oppose this misuse" (2019: 4).

The risks or downsides of AI are discussed in terms of its current technical limitations, including the risks of *errors*, the risk of *data-driven biases* and the problem of *trust*. These risks are discussed in more detail below.

Technical limitations

The report points out that AI, in spite of its widely circulated achievements, is not without problems. For example, there are risks of errors in current facial recognition systems. The report cites the case of a Chinese businesswoman incorrectly identified as having jaywalked when her face on a bus advertisement was captured by the facial recognition system as it went through an intersection (Shen, 2018, cited in Walsh et al., 2019: 23). Machine learning (ML) algorithms are also singled out for their limited capability:

ML systems will often break in strange ways, do not provide meaningful explanations, and struggle to transfer to a new domain.

(Walsh et al., 2019: 15–16)

A good example is the apparently superhuman achievements of AlphaZero when trained to play games like Go and Chess; however, this skill is not easily converted to playing a game of poker or reading x-rays (2019: 15–16). The report suggests that the "narrow focus" of machine learning systems will "likely be the case for many years" (2019: 15–16). Machine learning also suffers from the problem of intelligibility: "It can be difficult – even for an expert – to understand how a ML system produces its results (the so-called 'black box' problem)" (2019: 34–35).

Natural language processing (NLP), in spite of its impressive achievements and improvements over the years, is, according to the report, still work in progress:

NLP still has limitations as demonstrated by the Winograd Schema Challenge, a test of machine intelligence. The Winograd Schema tasks computer programs with answering carefully tailored questions that require common sense reasoning to solve. The results from the first annual Winograd Schema Challenge ranged from the low 30th percentile in answering correctly to the high 50s, suggesting that further research is required to develop systems that can handle such tests. Notably, human subjects were asked the same questions and scored much higher, with an overall average of approximately 90 percent.

(2019: 34–35)

Data-driven biases

The report devotes a great deal of space to what might be called a "resistant imaginary" of AI. Most of this discussion related to the "risk of amplifying discrimination and bias, and problems of fairness" that stem from the use of aggregated data (Walsh et al., 2019: 175). The report distinguishes between algorithmic bias and bias in the input data. In relation to the latter, the report cites research on biases in human decisions, as a result of "various failures of reasoning" and negative emotions such as fear (2019: 176). However, algorithms designed to reduce bias may not be effective because of the risks of *intrinsic* as well as *extrinsic* bias:

> Intrinsic bias is built-in in the development of the AI system or results from inputs causing permanent change in the system's structure and rules of operation. … Extrinsic bias derives from a system's inputs in a way that does not effect a permanent change in the system's internal structure and rules of operation. The output of such systems might be inaccurate or unfair but the system remains 'rational' in that new evidence is capable of correcting the fault.
>
> (2019: 178–9)

Where intrinsic biases can come from a range of sources, including developers who are biased, technological constraints, programming errors or historical biases, extrinsic biases can originate from unrepresentative, skewed or erroneous data, hence perpetuating historical biases. This problem with biased data can limit the usefulness of NLP algorithms:

> Most of the advances in NLP over the past decade have been achieved with specific tasks and datasets, which are driven by ever larger datasets. However, NLP is only as good as the data set underlying it. If not appropriately trained, NLP models can accentuate bias in underlying datasets, leading to systems that work better for users who are overrepresented in the training data. Further, NLP is currently unable to distinguish between

data or language that is irrelevant and damaging. This can create inherent inequities in the ability of different populations to benefit from AI; it can also actively disadvantage populations. To alleviate such biases, there generally needs to be explicit knowledge of the existence of the bias, with training data then used to mitigate the bias.

(2019: 35–36)

Trust

The report uses the language of "trust" to formulate this type of risk in AI systems. While being dependent on any form of technology makes its user vulnerable, the complexity of AI makes it more important to understand the dynamics of trust. For users to trust AI, the report suggests, there are at least four considerations: whether the technology has been proven to work reliably and securely, whether it is useable, whether its purpose is beneficial and visible, and whether it is designed in a way that the users feel they have control (Walsh et al., 2019: 182). Major errors such as an autonomous vehicle killing a cyclist or scandals such as the use of Facebook data by Cambridge Analytica to interfere with electoral processes understandably create distrust in some instances of AI technologies or technology providers (2019: 183).

Another important factor is the "explainability" of the technology. This issue is discussed in another source of "resistant imaginary" by Castelvecchi (2016: 21) when discussing "deep learning", where neural networks are trained on "vast archives of big data". The problem with such algorithms is that they raise questions such as "[e]xactly how is the machine finding those worthwhile signals …? And how can anyone be sure that it's right? How far should people be willing to trust deep learning?" (2016). The ability of such neural networks to learn was what made them attractive in the first place, but the computer scientists who created these networks are having difficulties understanding them: even if the machine makes predictions that are "very accurate", the prediction does not identify why, thus creating dilemmas for users who need to make decisions on the basis of the prediction (Castelvecchi, 2016). This difficulty is summarised as follows:

> "The problem is that the knowledge gets baked into the network, rather than into us," says Michael Tyka, a biophysicist and programmer at Google in Seattle, Washington. "Have we really understood anything? Not really — the network has."

(Castelvecchi, 2016)

3. Using AI in policing

The use of technology in policing in Western democracies has had a long history (Manning, 2014; Chan, 2003). The sociotechnical imaginaries shared by police organisations were uniformly positive: technology was going to bring increased effectiveness and efficiency to policing, resulting in safer communities and lower crime rates. The use of AI in policing is likely to invoke the same vision of 'smarter' policing, bringing better security to a world where crime is increasingly complex and organised. There are numerous ways in which AI could play an important role in policing: from the automation of crime reporting and other police administrative tasks, the use of autonomous vehicles for mobile patrols and emergency responses, speech and image recognition software for investigative purposes, to machine learning to predict the times/places of crime occurrence and identify suspects. Given the discretionary powers vested in police actions (including the use of coercive force), not surprisingly, two contradictory imaginaries have emerged in relation to the use of AI in policing: on the one hand, technology developers and police managers are convinced that AI would help the 'smarter' policing vision; on the other hand, independent researchers and human rights activists are putting forward an alternative vision where the benefits of AI for policing are questioned and its risks seriously considered.

A good example of how these opposing imaginaries are being played out is in the case of predictive policing. It is a good example because predictive policing technology has already been adopted by many police organisations, and the debate about its pros and cons is more developed, whereas the use of autonomous vehicles and image/speech recognition software for policing has not been as widely examined. Predictive policing has often been likened to the 2002 movie *Minority Report* or PreCrime policing where psychics ('precogs') have foreknowledge of where and when crime will happen, so that crime can be stopped before it is committed. The reality is a little different. There are no psychics, but some kind of predictive software that will identify 'hot spots' where police will deploy more patrol cars to deter crime.

The underlying model of predictive policing is represented in Figure 1.2 (reproduced from Perry et al., 2013: 128). The report points out that predictive policing is "not fundamentally about making crime-related predictions" but about implementing a prediction-led policing business process, which consists of a cycle of activities and decision points: data collection, analysis, police operations, criminal response, and then back to data collection. At each stage of the cycle, choices are made with regard to: the types of data to collect, the duration and frequency of data collection and update, the types of analytical tools to employ, the dependent variables to focus on, the types of police operations to deploy, how and when to evaluate the success of interventions, and what changes in interventions should be implemented following the evaluation (see Bennett Moses and Chan, 2018).

Without going into the technical details of the techniques used in predictive policing, we can broadly classify them into four categories:

(i)   classical statistical techniques, using processes such as "regression, data mining, time-series analysis, and seasonality adjustments";

The Prediction-Led Policing Business Process

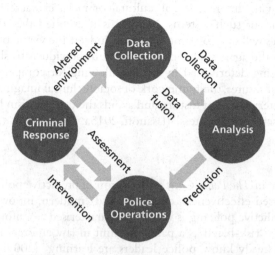

Figure 1.2 The prediction-led policing business process (from Perry et al., 2013). Copyright RAND included with permission in Bennett Moses and Chan (2018).

(ii) simple methods such as using checklists and indexes;
(iii) complex applications that require sophisticated computer programmes and large volumes of data; and
(iv) tailored methods that use existing techniques to provide visualisation of data to support predictive policing.

(Perry et al., 2013: 18)

To understand some of the sociotechnical imaginaries related to predictive policing, I refer to four exemplars of how predictive policing has been described and analysed. The first is what might be called a *utopian* view, as represented by Beck and McCue's (2009) vision and Perry et al.'s (2013) description of the 'myths' of predictive policing. The second is a *social science* view, exemplified by Bennett Moses and Chan (2018) where we examined the assumptions underlying predictive policing models, the results of systematic evaluation, and issues of accountability. The third is a view from *data scientists*, as drawn from an article by D'Alessandro et al. (2017) where they discussed the ethics of data science in predictions. The final one is a view from *civil rights community groups*, as represented by "A Shared Statement of Civil Rights Concerns" (see ACLU, 2016). The second to fourth views might be regarded as examples of resistant sociotechnical imaginaries. This analysis is designed to compare and highlight different discourses in visions between groups as 'ideal types'. It is not assumed that all members of each group would share the same vision as the exemplars chosen: for example, it is highly likely that social scientists and data scientists are not unanimous in their critique of predictive policing, just as it is possible that communities with different social, cultural or racial characteristics hold conflicting views about such systems. Neither is it assumed that these sociotechnical imaginaries will stay constant over time. Indeed, the virtue of the framework is to reaffirm the agency of social groups and individuals to shape technology, instead of being determined by it: "by allowing for competition among different visions of futures, the framework of sociotechnical imaginaries restores some of the indeterminacy of history and avoids the determinism built into grand narratives of scientific progress" (Jasanoff, 2015a: 23).

A utopian view

Beck and McCue's article in *The Police Chief* sells a vision of predictive policing that will result in increased effectiveness, efficiency, and "modern, innovative policing" (2009: 19). Predictive policing is variously characterised as "information based", "fact-based", "risk-based", "a paradigm shift in law enforcement" and "what big retailers already know, police leaders are learning" (2009: 19–23). This sociotechnical imaginary promises "doing more with less" and "significantly improving policing outcomes through information-based tactics, strategy and policy" (2009: 19).

Perry et al. (2013: xix) have summarised some of the "myths" in connection with predictive policing, which they regard as "hyperbole". For example, some accounts of predictive policing make it sound as if the computer can foretell the future" or that predictive policing "is a crystal ball", when the software is only capable of predicting the *risks* of future crime, and the predictions are "only as good as the underlying data used" (2013: xix). Another myth is that the computer "will do everything for you" when humans are an essential element of predictive policing. The third myth is that predictive policing programs require the use of expensive software and powerful computers, when less sophisticated software and "simple heuristics" could work well, especially for small police departments. The final myth is that "accurate predictions automatically lead to major crime reductions", when prediction is only one element of the process.

Although Beck and McCue (2009) does not promote the myth of predictive policing as a crystal ball, the utopian view it promotes does not discuss the quality of the data, nor does it emphasise the need for humans to make the process works.

A social science view

Bennett Moses and Chan's (2018) article represents a typical sociotechnical imaginary of predictive policing constructed by social scientists.[2] It examines the assumptions, evaluation and accountability issues connected with this type of prediction-led policing process.

Assumptions

The authors argue that predictive policing models rely on at least ten assumptions for it to be successful, but not all of these assumptions are valid or can be satisfied. I will not go into all ten assumptions but here are some examples. The data used by the predictive policing software can be limited or inaccurate because of a variety of problems such as under-reporting, classification differences, discretionary decisions and historical biases. Another consideration is the range of variables being used for prediction: some variables are routinely collected but some are routinely omitted. The omission of relevant variables will affect the accuracy of the model. We also pointed out that algorithms and analytics are not necessarily neutral. Bias and discrimination can creep in even if we exclude sensitive variables such as race from the models. Finally, it is not safe to assume that police officers would necessarily implement intervention strategies perfectly. Much will depend on the level of trust the police have in the predictive system. Often officers have local knowledge that is not captured by the data.

Evaluation

The next question the article looks at is whether predictive policing has led to reduction in crime. Predictive policing has been credited with substantial reductions in crime in some police agencies. For example, the PredPol website reports the drop in particular categories of crime in particular jurisdictions employing its software. Media and other sources also report percentage reductions in crime. However, these claims were often made without evidence or references to published evaluations. The authors' literature review found that very few formal evaluations of predictive policing have been conducted. They could only find two systematic evaluations. One was published in 2014 and it relates to the Shreveport Police Department in Louisiana (Hunt et al., 2014). The other was published in 2015 and it relates to the Los Angeles Police Department (Mohler et al., 2015). The Shreveport predictive policing experiment compared three districts that used a predictive policing strategy with three control group districts that continued with existing policing strategy. The evaluation found no statistically significant difference in crime rates between the experimental and the control districts. One of the explanations was that there were variations in the level of implementation of the predictive strategy between districts and over time. The Los Angeles predictive policing trial was carried out in three divisions of the LAPD (Mohler et al., 2015). It uses a randomised controlled experiment to compare the impact of the Predpol predictions with those produced by human crime analysts. The evaluation reports that the PredPol tool led to an average 7.4% reduction in crime volume, much higher than the control group.

Given the contradictory findings of the two evaluations, the authors suggest that further rigorous studies in different areas using different predictive tools are required to come to a more definitive conclusion as to whether predictive policing actually reduces crime. They note that two of the authors of the LAPD evaluation Mohler and Brantingham were co-founders of PredPol and five of the seven authors hold stock in PredPol. In their view, the independence of the evaluation is also a very important issue as it affects the credibility of the findings.

Accountability

Finally, the article raises two issues in relation to accountability in predictive policing. The first issue relates to the challenges of multi-agent responsibility for deployment decisions. Let's say that a senior police officer is asked to explain why police patrols were deployed in a particular way. Since it is the software that makes such decisions, the officer would have to say something like "The computer said so". This, they suggest, is "outsourcing" accountability to the software (2018: 817). The second issue relates to the challenges of digging deeper for an explanation. This requires a level of transparency and an understanding of how the data is collected or altered, the algorithms and processes that are used on the data (the "source code"), as well as the assumptions and biases underlying the analysis. The article suggests that this kind of full transparency and comprehensibility is usually not possible in predictive policing. Software may be subject to commercial-in-confidence provisions in licensing contracts. Even where the source code is available, there may be emergent properties of the algorithm (particularly in the case of machine learning) that cannot be anticipated. The authors suggest that a more fruitful alternative to transparency is to have proper evaluations of the software, not only for effectiveness in reducing (rather than displacing) crime, but also for differential impact on historically disadvantaged communities. This would enable some form of accountability so that decision-makers can describe the benefits of using the software, even though they can't explain exactly how the program brings those benefits. It allows the decision-maker to justify the use of this software and that it is effective and non-stigmatising.

A data science view

A recent article written by D'Alessandro et al. (2017) represents another example of "resistant imaginary"; it points out specifically issues of discrimination that machine-learning systems can introduce. Predictive policing is one of the case studies they presented. The authors identify several sources of discrimination. The first source of discrimination relates to *data issues* – rephrasing the age-old saying in computer science, "garbage in, garbage out", the authors see "discrimination in, discrimination out" as one of the data issues (2017: 125–126). This means that if there were systemic biases against a certain group in the data, then the prediction based on this data will be biased. Another data issue is sample bias: i.e. when certain groups are over- or under-represented in the data – either problem can affect the accuracy of the model.

The second source of discrimination relates to *model misspecification* – for example, in predictive policing, one of the objectives may be to reduce violent crime, but data on violent crime may be sparse. To increase the model's ability to predict, the analyst might decide to include less serious crimes in the model. However, if there is no correlation between violent crime and an attribute like race, but there is a correlation of less serious crime with race, then the inclusion of less serious crime in the model will end up discriminating against race.

The third source of discrimination relates to *process failure* – the authors suggest that the data scientist should be vigilant about the process of evaluating models. They should test algorithms for potential discriminatory behaviour, they should make sure that the system does not result in inappropriate feedback loops, and they should also involve human experts in the process.

In summary, the authors state that "[predictive policing's] potential for socially destructive disparate impact, target variable misspecification coupled with a negatively reinforcing feedback loop could lead to a self-perpetuating system that continuously targets poorer and more minority concentrated communities" (2017: 132). The authors advocate that data scientists should be:

> intentional about modeling and reducing discriminatory outcomes. Without doing so, their efforts will result in perpetuating any systemic discrimination that may exist, but under a misleading veil of data-driven objectivity.
>
> (2017: 120)

A civil rights community view

Apart from the concerns raised by criminologists and data scientists, in the United States at least, community organisations are starting to make their voices heard (see ACLU, 2016). 'A Shared Statement of Civil Rights Concerns' dated 31 August 2016, signed by 17 US organisations such as the American Civil Liberties Union, Data & Society Research Institute and the Electronic Frontier Foundation, expresses reservations about six aspects of predictive policing and demands action to address these concerns. The statement does not call for a blanket ban on predictive policing but for the building of more transparent, community-based and fair systems that are subject to informed public debate, independent evaluation and continuous monitoring as to their racial impact. Details of their concerns and demands are as follows:

- *A lack of transparency about predictive policing systems prevents a meaningful, well-informed public debate.* The signatories demand "a thorough and well-informed public debate, and rigorous, independent, expert assessment of the statistical validity and operational impact of any new system … before any new system can be deployed at scale" and "continuous assessment as long as the system is in use".

- *Predictive policing systems ignore community needs.* The signatories wanted the measurement and tracking of "all uses of coercive authority and the demographics of the people involved".
- *Predictive policing systems threaten to undermine the constitutional rights of individuals.* The "rights of due process and equal protection" must not be eroded.
- *Predictive technologies are primarily being used to intensify enforcement, rather than to meet human needs.* The statement advocates a return to providing services and "partnerships across sectors and at every level of government" in order to find "effective and legitimate long-term solutions to ensuring public safety".
- *Police could use predictive tools to anticipate which officers might engage in misconduct, but most departments have not done so.*
- *Predictive policing systems are failing to monitor their racial impact.* The statement calls for regular auditing and monitoring of the impact of predictive policing on different communities, and for any disparities to be addressed.

This statement reflects a similar trend for civil rights and community organisations to voice their concerns about pretrial risk assessment in the US (see Leadership Conference on Civil & Human Rights, 2018).

This section has examined the co-existing sociotechnical imaginaries of one application of AI to policing—predictive policing—from a utopian view to the views of social scientists, data scientists and civil rights communities. My focus has been on the resistant imaginaries, as these are mindful of the injustices and errors that an imperfect predictive policing system can produce. Absent in this discussion are the views of police officers who might be implementing these systems "on the ground". As a postscript, I note a report in the Los Angeles Times in July 2019 (Puente, 2019) that "numerous" police departments are "dumping [predictive policing] software because it did not help them reduce crime and essentially provided information already being gathered by officers patrolling the streets.". The departments mentioned include the Palo Alto police, the Mountain View police in California and the police in Rio Rancho, New Mexico. A more representative view will need to await a more systematic analysis of police organisations that have introduced such systems into their operations.

Conclusion

Leading AI scientist Toby Walsh has predicted that *Homo sapiens* will eventually be replaced by *Homo digitalis*, a digital form of our current species: "*Homo digitalis* will be far smarter than *Homo sapiens*" and we "will live both in our brains and in the larger digital space" (2018: loc 292). The choices we make will determine how we build this digital future. The question for us is: do we want to use the power of our new-found intelligence to bring about a world that is "fair, just and beautiful", or do we want to "allow it to be full of inequality, injustice and suffering" (2018: loc 292)? These choices will not always be easy and some will require courage.

In this chapter I have examined that the future of AI in policing through the lens of sociotechnical imaginaries, which "makes possible a study of alternative futures (Jasanoff, 2015b: 339). But we need to recognise that "imagining the future is political", and "political action is also profoundly imaginative" (2015b: 338). My analysis has barely scratched the surface of what sociotechnical imaginaries can offer: much more research is required to understand where imaginaries originate, how they become embedded in collective consciousness or resisted by social groups, and the conditions under which they are extended (or removed) (Jasanoff, 2015a, 2015b).

The future of AI is what we make of it. Even though we would no longer allow pharmaceutical companies to sell drugs to treat human health conditions without some rigorous scientific tests, as a society we have so far given little scrutiny to the new technology that has become part of our everyday life. This may be because we are eager to take advantage of the benefits of technology or because we are ignorant of the risks. As Crawford and Calo (2016: 313) point out:

> Artificial intelligence presents a cultural shift as much as a technical one. This is similar to technological inflection points of the past, such as the introduction of the printing press or the railways. Autonomous systems are changing workplaces, streets and schools. We need to ensure that those changes are beneficial, before they are built further into the infrastructure of everyday life.

Until the downsides of technology start to impact on our lives, it is all too easy to shrug and say, so what? We may be able to afford to adopt that kind of attitude individually, but society as a whole must be more vigilant about the public good.

Crawford and Calo (2016: 312) nominate three current responses to concerns about AI: deploy and comply, ethical design and thought experiments, but suggest that "[n]one is individually or collectively sufficient". They advocate a "social-system analysis" that engages with the community and examines the social, political and other impact of AI in a holistic way. Social scientists are experts in evaluation research which, if done properly and independently, is interested not only in what works but also what doesn't work, who is affected, why, how, and what can be done.

The analysis in this chapter suggests that there are many things we can do as citizens of a democracy to ensure that AI is a force for good. First of all, we should educate ourselves and become aware of the benefits and risks of AI. Secondly, we should insist on having independent evaluations of the impact of AI where such systems are being introduced. Thirdly, we should promote ethical design and transparency of AI processes wherever possible. Finally, we should resist and contest unduly optimistic visions that gloss over the potential harmful effects of technological change. We should be the master, not the slave, of AI.

Notes

1   Walsh et al. (2019) is published by the Australian Council of Learned Academies [ACOLA], which "combines the strengths of the four Australian Learned Academies": Humanities, Science, Social Sciences, and Technology and Engineering. For a series of excellent discussion of the social implications of AI, see AI Now Institute (2016, 2017, 2018).
2   There is now a growing body of academic literature (e.g. Ferguson, 2017, Brayne, 2017, Lum and Isaac, 2016) as well as online reports (e.g. Shapiro, 2017, Rieland, 2018) on predictive policing. These will not be analysed separately in this chapter.

References

ACLU (American Civil Liberties Union). (2016). Predictive policing today: A shared statement of civil rights concerns, 31 August 2016, available from www.aclu.org/other/statement-concern-about-predictive-policing-aclu-and-16-civil-rights-privacy-racial-justice [accessed 1 February 2019].

AI Now Institute. (2016). *AI Now 2016 Report: The social and economic implications of Artificial Intelligence technologies in the near-term.* https://ainowinstitute.org/AI_Now_2016_Report.pdf [accessed 5 February 2019].

AI Now Institute. (2017). *AI Now 2017 Report.* https://ainowinstitute.org/AI_Now_2017_Report.pdf [accessed 6 February 2019].

AI Now Institute. (2018). *AI Now 2018 Report.* https://ainowinstitute.org/AI_Now_2018_Report.pdf [accessed 7 February 2019].

Beck, C. and McCue C. (2009). Predictive policing: What can we learn from Wal-Mart and Amazon about fighting crime in a recession? *The Police Chief*, November 2009.

Bennett Moses, L. and Chan, J. (2018). Algorithmic prediction in policing: assumptions, evaluation, and accountability. *Policing and Society*, 28(7), pp. 806–822. DOI:10.1080/10439463.2016.1253695. Available at: https://doi.org/10.1080/10439463.2016.1253695.

Brayne, S. (2017). Big data surveillance: The case of policing. *American Sociological Review*, 82(5), pp. 977–1008.

Castelvecchi, D. (2016). The black box of AI. Feature News. *Nature*, 538, pp. 21–23.

Chan, J. (2003). Police and new technologies. In: T. Newburn (ed.), *Handbook of Policing*, pp. 655–679.

Crawford, K. and Calo, R. (2016). There is a blind spot in AI research. Comment. *Nature*, 538, pp. 311–313.

d'Alessandro B., O'Neil C., and LaGatta T. (2017). Conscientious classification: a data scientist's guide to discrimination aware classification. *Big Data*, 5(2), pp. 120–134. DOI: 10.1089/big.2016.0048.

Ferguson, A.G. (2017). *The rise of big data policing: Surveillance, race, and the future of law enforcement*. New York: NYU Press.

Hunt, P., Saunders, J. and Hollywood, J.S. (2014). *Evaluation of the Shreveport predictive policing experiment*. Santa Monica, CA: RAND.

Jasanoff, S. (2015a). Future imperfect: Science, technology, and the imaginations of modernity. In: Jasanoff, S and Kim, S–H (eds), *Dreamscapes of Modernity: Sociotechnical Imaginaries and the Fabrication of Power*. Chicago: University of Chicago Press, pp. 1–33.

Jasanoff, S. (2015b). Imagined and invented worlds. In: Jasanoff, S. and Kim, S–H. (eds), *Dreamscapes of Modernity: Sociotechnical Imaginaries and the Fabrication of Power*. Chicago: University of Chicago Press, pp. 321–341.

The Leadership Conference on Civil & Human Rights. (2018). More than 100 civil rights, digital justice, and community-based organisations raise concerns about pre-trial risk assessment, 30 July 2018, available at https://civilrights.org/2018/07/30/more-than-100-civil-rights-digital-justice-and-community-based-organizations-raise-concerns-about-pretrial-risk-assessment/ [accessed 7 February 2019].

Lum, K. and Issac, W. (2016). To predict and serve? *Significance*, October 2016, available at significancemagazine.com [accessed 1 December 2018].

Manning, P.K. (2014). Information technology and police work. In: G. Bruinsma and D. Weisburd, (eds.), *Encyclopedia of Criminology and Criminal Justice*, pp. 2501–2513. New York: Springer.

Mohler, G.O., et al. (2015). Randomized controlled field trials of predictive policing. *Journal of the American Statistical Association*, 110(512), 1399–1411.

Perry, W.L., et al. (2013). *Predictive policing: the role of crime forecasting in law enforcement operations*. Santa Monica, CA: RAND.

Puente, M. (2019). LAPD pioneered predictive crime with data. Many police don't think it works. *Los Angeles Times*, 3 July 2019.

Rieland, R. (2018). Artificial intelligence is now used to predict crime. But is it biased? *Smithsonian.com*, 5 March 2018. Available at: www.smithsonianmag.com/innovation/artificial-intelligence-is-now-used-predict-crime-is-it-biased-180968337/ [accessed 1 December 2018].

Shapiro, A. (2017). Reform predictive policing. *Nature*, 541, pp. 458–460.

Shen, X. (2018). Facial recognition camera catches top businesswoman "jaywalking" because her face was on a bus. *Abacus News*. Available at: www. abacusnews.com/digital-life/facial-recognition-camera-catches-top-businesswoman-jaywalking-because-her-face-was bus/article/2174508 [accessed 8 February 2019].

Walsh, T. (2018). *2062: The world that AI made*. Carlton, VIC: La Trobe University Press with Black Inc.

Walsh, T., Levy, N., Bell, G., Elliott, A., Maclaurin, J., Mareels, I.M.Y. and Wood, F.M (2019). The effective and ethical development of artificial intelligence: An opportunity to improve our wellbeing. Report for the Australian Council of Learned Academies, www.acola.org.

Chapter 2

Predictive policing through risk assessment

Melissa Hamilton

Introduction

The emergence of big data, advancements in technologies and interest in experimentation have coalesced to usher in a new wave of crime control in the form of predictive policing. Intended as a progressive initiative, predictive policing refers to "the application of analytical techniques—particularly quantitative techniques—to identify likely targets for police intervention and prevent crime or solve past crimes by making statistical predictions" (Perry et al., 2013: xiii). One author finds that definition too broad and has suggested an alternative.

> [Predictive policing means] the use of historical data to create a forecast of areas of criminality or crime hot spots, or high-risk offender characteristic profiles that will be one component of police resource allocation decisions. The resources will be allocated with the expectation that, with targeted deployment, criminal activity can be prevented, reduced, or disrupted.
>
> (Ratcliffe, 2019: 349)

This reform requires "datification" in which social activity and human behaviours are turned into data points to be tracked, analysed and managed (Dencik et al., 2018: 7). Policing through data fits under the umbrella of intelligence-led policing, whereby objective information guides decisions in police operations (Vestby and Vestby, 2019).

Three main types of predictive policing exist: forecasting hot spots, in terms of where crime is likely to flourish; predicting victimization; and predicting who is likely to be offenders. This chapter is mainly concerned with the latter, predicting 'hot people'. Predictive policing in the form of identifying likely individuals who will offend is a more recent endeavour than the identification of hot spots (Babuta, Oswald and Rinik, 2018). Much less is known about predicting who will offend. Further, far more policing resources are concerned with criminals than predicting who will be victims.

Certainly, individual risk prediction occurs in other areas of criminal justice decisions (e.g. pretrial bail, sentencing or parole). A major difference is that those other decision points are primarily about managing known offenders according to their risk level. At a high gradient of analysis, the ideal is to efficiently harness resources by diverting low risk offenders while saving precious cell space and intensive rehabilitative programming for high-risk offenders. In policing, though, individual risk relates to predictions of both known and unknown (potential) offenders. Plus, predictive policing concerns properly managing offenders, but it is also strongly about managing policing personnel resources (Shapiro, 2017). Resource management may include insight into where and when to deploy officers, whether to send specialised units (e.g. tactical teams, bomb squads, hostage negotiators), what level of response is reasonable in terms of force, and the type and amount of intervention that is most suitable to the predicted risk.

This chapter will review the expected advantages of offender-based predictive policing. Describing a selection of predictive tools in use will provide context for how recent efforts are taking shape and the variety of ways that policing agencies are experimenting with predictive technologies. Despite the potential benefits of predictive policing models, awareness of potential critical issues with them is important in order to manage unwanted consequences. One such issue is that, despite using scientific methods as a foundation for predictive policing, biases can still plague these tools. Various sources for how different biases may become imbedded into predictive policing models for assessing individual risk are discussed. Finally, the chapter offers some insights into the future, both near and far, of offender-based predictive policing. Overall, predictive policing will likely evolve quite quickly by drawing on emerging offerings from big data in social media and social network analysis to revolutionise crime prevention and pre-emption.

Projected benefits of predictive policing with individual risk

Predictive policing is a more recent evolution of a broader proactive policing movement that began in the 1980s and 1990s as a novel strategy to stem the then-rising crime rates (Weisburd et al., 2019). The theory was that pre-emptive, knowledge-based policing may yield greater gains than what was being achieved by a traditional, reactionary policing style (Bennett Moses and Chan, 2018). Manning (2018) contends that while the *structure* of policing in democratic societies has remained largely unchanged in the last century, policing *practices* have undergone significant shifts in recent years due to employing algorithmic technologies. In more recent years with extreme budget cuts, algorithm-led practices are also a response to such austerity measures (Ratcliffe and Kikuchi, 2019).

An algorithm simply provides "automated instructions to process data and produce outputs" (Dencik et al., 2018: 7). An algorithm, then, provides an equation that drives the predictions. These algorithms are generally developed by researchers who study large datasets to determine which factors are statistically associated with offending. For example, common risk factors for future offending are young age, being male, having a criminal history and associating with criminal friends. Overall, algorithmic predictions operate as evidence-based practices in relying upon scientific findings. More simply, predictive policing is criminal profiling using data and computer technology (Selbst, 2017). Importantly, models may need updating as follow-on studies may show that predictive factors change as environmental, cultural and individual links to criminal offending shift over time or place.

Predictive policing offers multiple advantages. Predictive policing methods promise to provide value to the public:

> With a more precise focus, there is less inadvertent collateral damage to civilians unconnected to criminality, we benefit from improved efficiency within our criminal justice services, there is greater objectivity, and there may even be increased public trust and law enforcement legitimacy when people see the police are focused on the right people at the right places.
>
> (Ratcliffe, 2019: 348)

Advance knowledge allows law enforcement officials to optimise their limited resources toward forecasting crimes (Brantingham, 2018) and thus permit the agency to operate more effectively (Perry et al., 2013). Where police actions are perceived as more objective in relying upon scientific study, these decisions may thereby be more defensible to both citizens and to courts.

The general methodology for creating an algorithmic predictive tool can be summarily explained. The developers of a tool statistically analyse historical data to isolate those factors that predict (e.g. correlate with) their outcome of interest (e.g. being involved in gun violence, homicide, or committing any new offense). Developers select significant factors and weight them, as some factors are more highly predictive than others. The selection and weighting create the resulting algorithmic equation on which the predictive model is based.

The algorithms underlying predictive tools often identify personal and social connections within individuals and across people that relate to criminal offending (Babuta, Oswald and Rinik, 2018). Algorithmic processing can locate *patterns* in social behaviour that humans are not capable of cognitively replicating. This is the basis of the pre-emptive ideal. "[T]he promise of the pattern is thus to serve as a basis for the extrapolation of possible criminal futures and to render those futures actionable for prevention programmes" (Kaufmann, Egbert and Leese, 2019: 674). In addition, predictive models single out which sociodemographic characteristics are related to committing crimes (Meijer and Wessels, 2019).

The goal of drawing on algorithmic tools to identify riskier individuals is justified as a large number of crimes are committed by a small number of people who are repeat offenders. Estimates are that, overall, six per cent of the population commit sixty per cent of crimes (Ratcliffe and Kikuchi, 2019). People often develop routines in their day-to-day activities, and criminal engagement may simply become a part of certain individuals' lifestyles (Perry et al., 2013). Thus, the ability to isolate the riskiest and thus focus resources on them serves to effectively protect the public from future harms. This focus also reduces unnecessary contacts with civilians by police that less informed and thus poorly targeted missions cause, which otherwise may lead to questioning police legitimacy and expertise (Papachristos and Sierra-Arévalo, 2018).

Another advantage of the predictive algorithm is its ability to reduce human biases (Babuta, Oswald and Rinik, 2018). Human decision-making is replete with implicit and explicit biases. Humans can act out of prejudice. Their decisions can be affected by being tired, angry or distracted. Unlike a person, though, an algorithm cannot harbour animus or be diverted by such distractions. Humans, as well, may not cognitively be capable of processing as many data points that a computer algorithm can efficiently handle. To illustrate an advantage for an algorithm, an initiative in Philadelphia aimed to triage repeat gun offenders using an algorithm that calculates a harm score based on past offenses with a time decay adjustment. Results indicated that this algorithmic method identified dangerous gun offenders better than human analysts (Ratcliffe and Kikuchi, 2019).

A side benefit of the automation offered by an algorithmic tool is the recordkeeping required (i.e. to score the inputs) to retrieve an output. These records mean that more information will be available to officers and serve to bolster big data for future studies to improve the algorithmic models. As some of the real-world examples of predictive policing programs that follow will attest, an intended consequence of the predictive policing turn is to improve communications about relevant facts and circumstances among officers within a police department and, in some cases, across agencies. Further, the recordkeeping that algorithms necessitate may bring greater accountability of decisions informed by predictive models.

The potential value here is not just in protecting the public by pre-empting crime. Several of the risk assessment tools may be useful for officer safety. For example, tools designed specifically to predict the threat of gang members or of domestic violence perpetrators may inform officers on the importance of greater precaution than they may otherwise take in responding to calls for assistance involving specific suspects. Domestic violence calls are, in particular, among the most confounding and dangerous encounters for the police (Campbell, Gill and Ballucci, 2018). Prior knowledge about the risk profile of the suspect assists officers in quickly adapting their response style as a result.

Examples of predictive policing tools with individual risk

The experimental nature of predictive policing may be a primary asset in this venture. Tools to assess individual risk that are in use today vary in their focus, goals and methods. Representative examples herein are meant to provide a sense of the breadth and possibilities of predictive policing. Several will highlight the public and private partnerships, as well as the technology and criminal justice collaborations that often characterise predictive policing programs. To begin, law enforcement agencies have tended to choose violent offenders as appropriate targets of their efforts due to the disproportionate harm violence causes victims and communities.

Chicago police manage a program called the Strategic Subject List (SSL). The SSL was developed by the Illinois Institute of Technology and funded by the US Department of Justice through a Bureau of Justice Assistance grant program (Richardson, Schultz and Crawford, 2019). The SSL uses a computerised tool to identify and rank individuals for their risk specifically of being involved (as a perpetrator or victim) in a shooting or a homicide (Richardson, Schultz and Crawford, 2019). The algorithm produces a threat score from one (very low risk) to 500 (very high risk) for each person arrested (Ferguson, 2017b). The SSL produces what has been colloquially referred to as the "heat list" or a "virtual most wanted list" (Ferguson, 2018: 505, 520). When an officer encounters a scored person, his or her relative risk via the score is available on the officer's dashboard computer (Ferguson, 2017a). The algorithm's predictors include prior gun violence victimization, prior violent victimization, prior arrests for unlawful use of a weapon, prior arrests for violence, age at last arrest and an indicator of whether the individual's criminal activity is increasing or decreasing (Chicago Police Department, 2019). An official statement of the Chicago Police Department claims that the program does not use race, gender, or place of residence (Chicago Police Department, 2019). Confirming that testing new datasets may require a change in model, researchers removed factors relating to gang affiliation and drug arrests from the original algorithm once they discovered these factors were no longer found to have statistical significance (Sheehey, 2019).

The SSL is designed to guide decisions for an intervention. A score of 250 (range 1–500) indicates the individual deserves heightened attention (Sheehey, 2019). Such attention comes in the form of Customs Notifications in which a police officer, social worker and a community leader personally contact individuals to notify them of their having been flagged and to warn that any future criminal offending will yield more severe consequences (Sheehey, 2019.). Overall, the SSL's focused deterrence "approach seeks a reduction in harm from specific, identified individuals by increasing the certainty, swiftness and severity of police interdiction and punishment, and communicating consequences directly to individuals while simultaneously providing motivations to desist from crime" (Ratcliff and Kikuchi, 2019: 61).

The Violent Offender Identification Directive (VOID) tool was developed in an upstate New York jurisdiction. VOID provides a means for which the department can produce a top ten list of those in crisis of potentially being involved in gun violence (Wheeler, Worden and Silver, 2019). Such a list is developed from a combination of an algorithmic risk score and intelligence from police professionals. As with the SSL in Chicago, the top ten list predicts either those likely to be shooters or victims of firearm assaults. Factors in the algorithm concern such data points as criminal history, prior victimizations, previous police interactions, history as a missing person, previous involvement in gun violence, known gang membership and disorderly conduct in jail (Wheeler, Worden and Silver, 2019).

Similarly, the Kansas City No Violence Alliance (KC NoVA) developed a tool to isolate individuals most likely to engage in violence. The city's tool is rather unique, though, compared to the foregoing in using social network analysis software. The data officers feed in derive from information recorded in officers' field contacts, traffic stop reports, and criminal history records (Bannon, 2017). The software then creates a web of these social alliances: known offenders, their criminal associates and the associates of the associates (Ferguson, 2017b). The goal is a targeted response that is pre-emptive in nature for those most likely to be *influencers* of criminal behaviour in others (Bannon, 2017). Officials contact the riskiest to warn them and those in their social networks that criminal activities beget punitive consequences and to offer relevant social services to pre-empt offending (Ferguson, 2017b).

Two of the tools designed specifically for domestic violence offending are briefly noted. The Ontario Domestic Assault Risk Assessment (ODARA) is a 13-item tool created for frontline officers to assess the risk of males who are known to have previously committed domestic violence (Jung and Buro, 2017). The ODARA factors include criminal history events, type of offending, the presence of children in the relationship and victim circumstances (Jung and Bero, 2017). Police in the UK use the Domestic Abuse, Stalking and Harassment and Honour-Based Violence (DASH) instrument. DASH ranks risk based on predictive items regarding current situation, children/dependents, domestic violence history and characteristics of the abuser (Almond, McManus, Brian and Merrington, 2017).

The Metropolitan Police (2019) in London maintain a Gangs Violence Matrix that assesses identified gang members in London for the risk of perpetrating or being victimised by violence. The algorithm ranks individuals on a colourised scale of red, amber or green (highest risk to lowest). The harm score is based on arrests, convictions and intelligence on violence/weapons access. Amnesty International (2018) suggests that matrix scores are supplemented with data from social media intelligence. London police officials contend that the tool allows the department to prioritise resources and interventions. Critics, though, argue that it amounts to an intelligence-led stop and frisk instrument (Amnesty International, 2018).

Some tools are designed to apply to other types of offending in addition to violence. The Durham Constabulary in England (a police force), collaborating with statisticians from the University of Cambridge, developed the Harm Assessment Risk Tool (HART) (Oswald et al., 2018). The purpose is to yield risk predictions within a diversionary program. The policy is that any arrested offender who scores as moderate risk is eligible to be diverted from prosecution into an appropriate community service option. HART contains over two dozen predictors, most of which assess various aspects of criminal history, plus age, gender and postal code (Nilsson, 2019).

The Avon and Somerset police force in England has significantly broadened the predictive policing endeavour in several ways. This agency has created multiple assessment instruments to assess such risks as general reoffending, perpetrating a serious domestic assault or sexual assault, committing burglary or stalking and harassing (Liberty, 2019). The tool, called Qlik Sense, is exceptional in linking more than ten police databases with emergency call logs and data on recorded crimes in the area (Kearns and Muir, 2019). The software enables officials to triage responses by outputting a score indicating the likelihood of reoffending from zero to 100 (Dencik et al., 2018). Another novelty is that the software allows an officer the ability to search all the databases at once.

A new initiative in England is attempting to take predictive policing far further. Using the name National Analytics Solution (NAS), a consortium of police agencies in England are collectively engaged in developing "a new shared, central data and analytics capability" (Police Transformation Fund, 2019: 8). Their mission statement concisely conceptualises the promise of predictive policing. "Aiming to put information at the heart of the law enforcement mission, the project seeks to derive greater value from the wealth of data that exists at the local and national level to help meet the challenges of law enforcement in the 21st century" (Police Transformation Fund, 2019: 7). Like the KC NoVA, the intent is to use social network analysis to identify individuals who are *influencers* of crime (Police Transformation Fund, 2019). This project team recognises that many first offenders are pressured to engage in criminal activity. Further, influencers are often engaged in co-offending with multiple other people (West Midlands Police, 2017). Hence, triggering early intervention with these influencers may pre-empt many criminal careers (West Midlands Police, 2017). The NAS is among the most comprehensive amongst the examples mentioned herein by using 32 predictors (out of over 1,300 indicators initially identified) (Police Transformation Fund, 2019). Similar to the Avon and Somerset police project, the NAS merges datasets across departments within the same city. Yet the NAS goes further by merging datasets not only among departments within the same jurisdiction (e.g. social services, education, emergency services), but across multiple policing agencies. The NAS also draws upon private sector databases and open source outlets (Police Transformation Fund, 2019).

Contentious issues with individual risk prediction

The hype of predictive policing models because of the allure of their techno-logical marvels has received a lot of media attention (Ferguson, 2017b). Yet what they can produce in reality is less certain (Perry et al., 2013; Bennett Moses and Chan, 2018). Several concerns have been raised. A risk assessment program may lead to police behaving more aggressively with those identified as high risk (Ferguson, 2017). A high-risk attribution, to the extent it begets punitive responses, acts like a status offense in which the person is punished for his status and not for any action on his part. The designation of high risk can thereby be stigmatizing to individuals, resulting in a self-fulfilling prophecy in which they then act as expected (Meijer and Wessels, 2019). Even in the absence of actual offending, risk prediction here means that police responses are based on hypothetical future offending. This is akin to pre-empting the pre-crime as in the film *Minority Report*, with all sorts of ethical issues attached (Hamilton, 2015).

At least some of the tools may cause mission creep, pushing police agencies into non-law enforcement activities, such as linking high-risk individuals to relevant social services (Feeley, 2018). It is not clear, though, that such a conse-quence is necessarily bad. Police officers are governmental officials and in this broader vein have responsibilities to improve the community. Still, a related issue that does appear more problematic is the potential for net widening. To the extent officers use predictive policing tools to engage with more individ-uals and with greater frequency, it is possible that more community members will be pulled within the orbit of law enforcement. In this way, the net of the law enforcement web snags more people into its formal social control grasp. This reach may not always be beneficial. In the context of predictive policing operating by feeding on big data and contributing to more big data, greater numbers of individuals may end up being identified in policing records. Even if the interactions do not amount to official actions (e.g. arrests), these links may be viewed by others as suggesting criminal activity and thus reify the high-risk label.

The increasing reliance upon big data has attracted new criticisms. The guise of science and the enigmatic nature of the algorithm should not lure officials into allowing such outcomes to completely override decisions that necessarily call for human discretion (Babuta, Oswald and Rinik, 2018). The appetite of the algorithms to learn on ever-increasing sources of data and to use social networks means more privacy invasions to feed these algorithms (Degeling and Berendt, 2018; Meijer and Wessels, 2019). This appetite also serves to more deeply entrench the law enforcement norm of surveillance in new and broader ways by increasing the virtual police presence (Brennan-Marquez, 2018). The practice amounts to technology-enhanced profiling, though bearing all of the negative connotations that exist with criminal profiling biases based on sociodemographic traits (Meijer and Wessels, 2019).

There is also a concern with the lack of transparency, particularly with respect to identifying potential biases. "Few predictive policing vendors are fully transparent about how their systems operate, what specific data is used in each jurisdiction that deploys the technology, or what accountability measures the vendor employs in each jurisdiction to address potential inaccuracy, bias, or evidence of misconduct" (Richardson, Schultz and Crawford, 2019: 198). Consequently, agencies are urged to be more transparent through various methods, including these: (a) publicly acknowledging the predictive systems they use; (b) allow for opportunities for agency representatives with the algorithm developer to engage in discussion with interested members of the public; and (c) making at least parts of the algorithm available as open source so that data scientists can test and potentially improve it (Shapiro, 2017). Such reforms might reveal, and help alleviate, the impact of potential biases that may otherwise become imbedded in the algorithms, as discussed next.

Entry points for biases in predictive policing algorithms

The use of algorithms (even those created through machine-learning) does not, as one might assume, necessarily mean that predictive policing tools operate fairly in practice in terms of the outcomes they produce. The algorithms can be, and generally are in practice, biased. Several types of bias are prevalent in predictive policing algorithms.

Label bias

The tools generally attempt to predict committing a crime. Yet the measurement of crime is innately biased. This means that that the predictive outcome of 'crime' is mislabelled. There is simply no practical or theoretical way to measure crime *per se*. Thus, tool developers must resort to using proxies thereto. By definition, any proxy measure will be fundamentally inaccurate. Proxies for crime in criminal justice tools generally vary, but common ones include probation or parole failures, technical violations, arrests or convictions. These, though, are more representative of official *responses* to potential antisociality than of offenders' actual behaviours. As none of these are synonymous with actual crimes committed, the resulting inaccuracies create noise in the algorithms.

Proxies for crime convey multiple types of overlapping errors and gaps. For various reasons, not all crimes are known. Victims may not identify what was done as crimes in the first place. Not all crimes are reported and thus not recorded (Brantingham, 2018). Even if reported, officers may not respond to record them. Then, even if officers respond, they may not take a report. This may be due to some type of internal bias. For instance, when a member of a targeted social group purports to be a victim of a crime, implicit bias on the part of an officer may lead to cognitively minimizing the event's significance, with the officer discouraging the victim from filing a report (Brantingham, 2018).

Even when officers respond and make arrests, this action is still a proxy for crime. An arrest is not equivalent to a crime occurring or that the arrestee committed it. The action of an arrest is one of the least procedurally protected interactions between police and the citizenry (Eaglin, 2017). As a result, the arrest may be inaccurate. Police may arrest the wrong suspect, or may arrest for behaviour that turns out not to be criminal at all, once a full investigation has been completed. Charges may be brought against the wrong defendant, or may not align with the actual behaviour in which the defendant engaged. The fact that many such cases do not proceed to conviction gives rise to doubt about whether a crime occurred at all, or whether an error was made by system actors themselves (Klingele, 2019).

In addition, arrest statistics may reflect bad data because of poor recording practices. For example, it was revealed that the Los Angeles Police Department misrecorded 14,000 serious assaults as minor offenses between 2005 and 2012 (Richardson, Schultz and Crawford, 2019). In the United Kingdom, an oversight agency found significant lapses in police not recording significant numbers of violent crimes that were reported to them (British Broadcasting Corporation, 2019).

Crime as studied by these tools may also be biased where they are based on dirty data, which signifies data that are tainted because of corrupt, racially biased or otherwise illegal police practices (Richardson, Schultz and Crawford, 2019). Police may be acting out of implicit or explicit biases when making arrests. Bias occurs when a member of a targeted social group is suspected of committing a crime, but his liability is maximised as a result, which may mean an arrest is more likely (Brantingham, 2018). Then there are too many case studies of law enforcement agencies overpolicing minority neighbourhoods, leading to disproportionate arrests of minorities, while underpolicing upper income neighbourhoods, which artificially decreases arrests there. These practices lead to the algorithm overestimating risk for minorities while at the same time underestimating the risk of the powerful (Corbett-Davies and Goel, 2018).

The label of crime by using official statistics is also biased when police intentionally engage in practices such as those exemplified in the popular television series The Wire by 'juking the stats' (Richardson, Schultz and Crawford, 2019). Police may, for instance, intentionally undercount crimes in order to make it appear that their communities are safer (Brantingham, 2018). Even convictions are biased accounts of crime. Those convicted of crimes may have been factually innocent. Alternatively, convictions may simply replicate the bias patterns in arrests or discriminatory decisions by prosecutors or juries.

The attempt by proponents of algorithmic tools to discount these types of biases merely amounts to tech-washing or math-washing of racially based police practices (Burrington, 2015). Colloquially, the underlying data are not raw; these data are already cooked (Sheehey, 2019). Importantly, there is no evidence that tool developers validate the accuracy of the official data on which their predictive policing algorithms learn (Richardson, Schultz and Crawford, 2019).

Feature selection

Bias may be embedded within the collection of predictive factors scored by the algorithm. Crime is a complex issue. Faced with a multifaceted, real-world scenario in which crimes occur, tool developers must select from a multitude of possible predictors. Despite how many dozens of factors the final algorithm scores, it cannot possibly present a complete picture of the circumstances in which crimes occur. The choice of predictors, known as feature selection, is thereby an inherently reductionist exercise (Favaretto, De Clercq and Elger, 2019). Simply put, every tool oversimplifies crime (Veale, 2019). The point is that developers introduce bias by choosing which factors to test in the first place, and again by narrowing to a smaller number of predictors to incorporate into their final algorithms (Favaretto et al., 2019).

Omitted variable bias occurs when an instrument excludes a variable that is correlated with both an existing predictor and the outcome (here, offending). The fact that tools as they exist today contain relatively few variables (and most of which depend on criminal history measures) means that a plethora of relevant data is ignored. As an illustration, it may be that prior arrests for violence as a predictor of future violent offending are both correlated with the neighbourhood of residence. Hence, if the model excludes home locale, then it would exemplify omitted variable bias, thereby weakening the algorithm's predictive ability. The situation only enhances the probability of significant numbers of false positives (wrongly predicting individuals who will offend) and/or false negatives (failing to predict who will offend).

Sample bias

Ideally, the sample on which an algorithm is trained is sufficiently representative of the population on which the tool will be used in a real-world setting. In criminal justice, this often means that the sample should reflect roughly equivalent percentages of the larger population on sociodemographic factors, such as race, ethnicity, gender, age and class. A failure of representativeness exemplifies sample bias. Because of the general lack of transparency in predictive policing tools, it is not known how representative the testing dataset may be. On the one hand, unlike the experience with prediction tools in other criminal justice decision points, which are often based on external sample data (Hamilton, 2019a), predictive policing tools often appear to be learned on local datasets (Liberty, 2019). This suggests the potential for bias presenting through non-representative data is not as strong. On the other hand, the evidence suggests that the predictive policing models have mostly been normed on individuals who were already known by police because they were represented in official criminal justice records. As individuals with previous police contacts may differ in risk-relevant ways from those not already known to police, the resulting algorithm will better predict offending in the former group versus the latter.

Sample bias is also likely to exist to some degree because model developers do not generally comply with some best practice standards in empirical research. Typically, tool development does not use independent, random samples. Instead, test samples are often dependent samples (e.g. individuals arrested by the same police force) and convenience samples (the data were accessible).

Risk algorithms learn on historical data. The training data may incorporate information reflecting (and reifying) pre-existing discriminatory decisions (Joh, 2018). A significant source of bias derives from a disproportionately heavy reliance upon criminal history measures as predictors (recall such predictors as prior arrests, prior gun violence). Clearly, criminal history information in the historical data may represent discriminatory practices by victims, police and prosecutors based on sociodemographic characteristics (e.g. race/ethnic affiliation, gender, immigration status). For example, prosecutorial policies that impose a disproportionate burden on minorities may also introduce bias into the training data. Initiatives such as no drop policies to deter a particular problem (e.g. gun violence, knife crimes, street-level drug dealing) may increase conviction rates for minorities to a greater degree than non-minorities. If unchecked, the resulting algorithms would thereby learn that such sociodemographic traits are predictive of offending.

Equally important, the mere recitation by tool developers that their models do not include race or gender is rather misleading. Even where those factors are not explicitly listed, the algorithms will learn on factors that are proxies to sociodemographic characteristics. Recall that some of the predictive policing tools incorporate events relating to involvement in gun violence (as victims or perpetrators). To the extent that minorities and men are more likely to have been victims or perpetrators of gun violence, that factor (involvement in gun violence) will serve as a proxy to minority race and male gender.

Another issue with gender should be highlighted here. Offender-based risk tools have tended to learn on convenience samples of individuals known to police as arrestees or considered to be potential future criminals. Males are simply arrested or identified as suspects far more often than females across jurisdictions and time frames. As a result, a significant majority of the conveni ence samples used are learned on males. Risk factors therein thus are often more relevant to males, such that meaningful risk factors that are more culturally sensitive to female populations may be omitted. A risk assessment process that presumes that risk tools are somehow universal, generic or culturally neutral will result in misestimation. Importantly, research indicates that a woman's likelihood of offending is impacted to a greater extent by such experiences as parental stress, personal relationship problems, prior and effects of trauma (Hamilton, 2019c). Women are also highly likely to be influenced to commit crimes by others, often their (male) intimate partners. Failure to include such gender-sensitive, risk-relevant attributes will mean the tool will perform more weakly for females.

Feedback loop

Biases, once embedded in an algorithm, can become further entrenched. Algorithms may suffer from a feedback loop in which biases are amplified over time. Biased predictions create additional inequalities from which the algorithm learns and then skews future predictions even more (New and Castro, 2018). As an example, where a jurisdiction uses a biased algorithm, higher risk predictions may mean that minorities are arrested more often, and thus are seen as more dangerous, thereby magnifying the likelihood of minority arrests in the future.

Bias may be exacerbated when the training data are produced by the same actors as those who will use those predictive tools (Veale, 2019). A predictable scenario is when police target a certain neighbourhood such that the arrest rates of area residents thereby increase. This arrest data is then used to inform an algorithm. In turn, the algorithm predicts higher risk of recidivism for this neighbourhood's residents, leading to a high rate rearrests, and thereby entrenching overpolicing practices. The results can thereby become circular. The algorithm's prediction of an individual's being subject to overpolicing is itself predicted by a past history of people like him being overpoliced (Hamilton, 2019b).

These issues of bias are particularly problematic as little is known about the extent to which they exist. Observers contend that the predictive policing scheme is too secretive, with tool developers and users failing to acknowledge potential avenues for bias or inaccuracies, or how they might (if at all) remediate them (Richardson, Schultz and Crawford, 2019). Despite these issues, there are many reasons to find promise in predictive policing tools in identifying individuals who are at high risk of committing a future crime.

Future prospects for predictive policing

Predictive policing in the form of individual risk assessment is likely only to broaden and solidify within organizational practices. The values are difficult to deny, particularly in the age of exponential technological transformation. To date, predictive policing tools have been hampered by a reliance on data points that are readily available in police databases. These have valuable, though limited, contributions to forecasting future offending. To improve models, data specialists must seek alternative sources of data to inform on many other factors that research likely will identify as predicting criminal offenders. Future investigations could fruitfully go beyond the current framework of principally using interactions with police (e.g. arrests, field contacts) and the offender's age. The next big growth area may be to further exploit datasets to locate a myriad of personal and social connections to offending patterns. Relationships of interest may be of co-perpetrators, perpetrator/victim dyads and potential future accomplices. Algorithms could be trained to make broader social connections amongst various datapoints. Thus, if Individual A (the focus of analysis) was arrested with B, then the records of B could be mined to determine B's co-offenders and so on to establish potentially unknown collaborators of A. Then, algorithms can find common links in formal and informal reports across officers and departments to visualise broader network pathways to offending, such as anticipated by the National Analytics Solution in England.

Understanding social connections to crime is particularly salient in certain types of offenses, such as those connected to gang membership, drug trafficking and gun violence. In an entirely different realm, footage from body worn police cameras may offer a new source of data. This might require extensive personnel resources to review them, though it is also probable that an algorithm can be trained to identify individuals through facial recognition programs and to then create typologies of behavioural profiles and relationship dynamics.

To date, predictive policing focused on social connections has thereby been mostly oriented around street crimes. It might be worthwhile to expand such efforts to organised crime operating at a different level, those which cause significant harms while posing unique challenges to police. Social network analysis might be fruitful in uncovering co-offending operations in more white collar-like crime syndicates, such as identity fraud, sophisticated online scams, securities fraud, and environmental crime. Emphasizing how tracking social ties can reveal insights into pre-empting crime might also target multi-offender syndicates operating somewhere between street-level and white collar levels, such as with human trafficking, child pornography distribution and prescription drug sale scams.

Broader social network analysis than what is currently being done is on the horizon. For example, the current state of social network analysis in crime has been described as "rudimentary" (Faust and Tita, 2019: 117). The basic framework for social network analysis is to identify actors or groups of actors and their ties in a network (Faust and Tita, 2019). Ties may be based on kinship, friendship, rivalries or opportunistic liaisons. Social network analysis focuses on how people interact in a social world and the effects that these relationships have on criminal offending (Papachristos and Sierra-Arévalo, 2018). Attention must be paid to indications of whether certain social networks, or parts of them, are temporally long-term, suggesting stability in criminal activities. Alternatively, co-offending may be more transitory such that over-emphasis on past conspiracies may be misplaced, and unfortunately mask the creation of newer collectives (Faust and Tita, 2019).

Social network analysis is also served by understanding that individuals involved in criminal networks play various roles. Individuals may at times be perpetrators, while at others find themselves victimised by either those operating within the same network, those hovering on the outskirts of the network or rivals. Communications can be old-style, such as face-to-face or by mail, email and phone calls. Newer forms are through social media posts or evidence of following or otherwise tracking other people's communications or online or offline movements. Social network analysis should also pay heed to communicative messaging through non-explicit, but symbolic means, such as the use of strategic acts of violent retaliation, acts that serve as threats, or gestures symbolising openness to cooperative criminality. In other words, researchers can push social network analysis beyond the mere identification of personal contacts. Gathering and collating information from direct and indirect communications may have value in deciphering offending and co-offending patterns. Exploration may be valuable in digging deeper to decipher the meaning of short-form texting, tweeting or use of emojis to convey plans and intent.

Thus, a transformative turn for the future is to more intensely exploit social media networks. A few policing agencies have begun to explore open-source data and to liaise with social media companies for (ethical) access to their rich troves of data. Social media offers many advantages to social network analysis, such as scalability and real-time information for computer programs to scour. As previously suggested, algorithms are a proficient asset in detecting complex patterns in offending within individuals and across individuals. Further, algorithms may be able to decipher how such patterns change over time, geography, social groupings and other variable contexts.

The use of open-source and private databases of social communications for predictive tools offers the 6Vs, referring to their relevant benefits and challenges (Williams, Burnap and Sloan, 2017):

(1) *Volume* offers an ever-growing trove of social information made available in every moment on technology platforms.
(2) *Variety* regards the multiple forms, differing densities, and levels of formalities in online data that offer mixed-methods researchers (quantitative and qualitative) many opportunities for analyses.
(3) *Velocity* is about the increasing speeds at which online data are generated, shared, and morphed. The connection to real-time processing promises to allow police faster responses to better pre-empt criminal activity. This advantage may be particularly suitable for responding whereby the contagion effect of the online world has fostered flash mobs, riots, and other quickly coordinated violent or destructive outbursts.
(4) *Veracity* identifies the challenge that these data are not self-authenticating in that it may not be evidently clear their quality or truthfulness. Checks and balances thus must be incorporated to verify the credibility of leads as reasonable.
(5) *Virtue* concerns the ethics of researchers using this data. Still, to the extent that users agreed in the sites' terms of service that their information may be shared, privacy concerns are reduced.

(6) *Value* represents the fusion of the foregoing five V-themes in terms of big data and technological advancements harnessing the benefits of the volume, velocity, and variety of the data points as long as veracity is established in a virtuous (ethical) way.

Some police forces anticipate using social media to inform risk assessment tools in the near future (Police Transformation Fund, 2019). Social network efforts by the National Analytics Solution in the UK appear at the forefront in capitalizing on the 6Vs while reducing attendant risks. An issue that has traditionally plagued police forces is the lack of cooperation and sharing of communication between agencies. Too many instances have occurred of criminals evading identification (e.g. serial killers, serial rapists or other repeat offenders) by exploiting communication loopholes by offending in new areas covered by different police agencies. Cross-jurisdictional communications in real-time fostered by technological transformations may remedy such gaps.

Technology firms appear ready to assist in gathering relevant data to feed such efforts. For example, Oracle currently offers what it terms 'Social-Enabled Policing' (Oracle, 2015). The company touts its ability to engage big data to fuse information points from traditional sources, social networks, and open source intelligence to provide "valuable and actionable intelligence to the police officers; be it to prevent a threat, detect a threat, or mitigate a threat" (Oracle, 2015: 8). The intersection between, on the one hand, the connectedness of youth on social media as a major form of direct and indirect communication with their peers and, on the other hand, young age being a consistently strong predictor of violent and property offending means that incorporating social media data into social network analyses holds great promise. Here, online messaging is indicative of offline criminality, which is useful for police predictions of individual risk (Williams, Burnap and Sloan, 2017). The advantages of mining online platforms are clear here as well in that a significant percentage of crimes today are cyber-enabled (Kearns and Muir, 2019).

Indeed, the velocity element of cyberspace data uniquely provides an avenue to assess a dimension of risk that other data points or methodologies are rarely able to gauge. Risk has multiple dimensions for predicting future offending. These include such aspects of probability, severity, frequency, duration and imminence. The latter dimension is of note here in that the real-time aspect of social media and internet-based communications carries the ability to better assess whether an individual is at a crisis point in that their crimes are likely imminent. Risk assessment in criminal justice generally has traditionally been better at assessing the probability and severity of future offending. The likelihood that the predicted offense may be far in the future could still be relevant when risk assessment informs a decision concerning the long-term management of offenders, such as in sentencing or whether to grant parole. Contrastingly, in a policing context, it is far more important to gauge the short term, temporal aspect of the potential future crime. Thus, a police action to intervene may be more justifiable when the evidence suggests an individual's criminal offending is close-at-hand. The ability to utilise cyber-data in social network analysis for crime prevention is thereby another conceivably promising innovation, along with others mentioned herein.

Conclusions

The evidence-based practices movement has taken over criminal justice in a variety of ways. The framework is to draw on research from the behavioural sciences and from big data to determine which factors predict likely perpetrators and their criminal offending. Predictive policing is not just about using traditional enforcement tools such as stop-and-searches or arrest. Predictive policing can instead be pre-emptive in other formal and informal ways, allowing officers to tailor interventions according to the individual's level of risk and needs through civil remedies or community-based services. Further, by targeting individuals at a heightened likelihood of offending, police forces may more efficiently manage their own personnel and other resources accordingly.

Offender-based predictive policing is at a relatively early stage. Predictive policing has its proponents and its detractors. Despite significant challenges predictive policing face, such as with biases penetrating algorithms, it is clear that the future of policing techniques will be heavily driven by data and advancing technological innovations. In addition to the data emphasis, risk prediction is analytical and automated via algorithms. Predictive policing is progressive in nature in terms of presenting as a reform that allows police to target the riskiest while reducing unnecessary contacts with innocent citizens. No longer is the vision of policing entirely reliant upon the traditional portrayal of the cop-on-the-beat responding to discrete calls for service and using gut instinct to locate potential suspects. The variety of predictive policing models is exemplified in the examples of currently used tools described herein. Some police forces are more inclined to identify violent offenders or gang members, but others are focused on the bigger picture of offending in general. The willingness of these agencies to experiment with modelling and with expanding potential data sources also attests to the promising future for risk assessment to pre-empt crime and protect their communities.

Nonetheless, the suggestion here is not that policing will be entirely, or even substantially, replaced by computer or by algorithms. Humans still must play a role in any endeavour such as this which attempts to forecast human behaviour. Humans are innately difficult to predict. Free will means that humans are active, reactive, interactive and adaptive creatures. No model, no matter how sophisticated or science-driven, can definitively determine whether an individual person will or will not in fact commit a crime in the future. In some cases, human intuition and gut instinct on the part of police officers may be better suited to the job. Recall as well, that no predictive policing tool will be able to incorporate every relevant factor in a complex world of criminal motivation and opportunity. Further, policing decisions such as whether to make an arrest or engage in a pre-emptive action should not be entirely automated. Discretion still has a place in policing. Automation cannot either entirely account for ethics. There remains some value in the human element where the consequences may be extreme to individuals, which is inevitable in a criminal justice context such as policing.

It is also the case that algorithms require human oversight. Clear policies and managerial supervision may help mitigate biases that may become embedded in algorithms. Humans must also weigh the trade-offs between the inclusion of biases against the potential of predictive abilities to protect the public. Then, to the extent that predictive policing practices will further mine private databases and open source social communications, attention to privacy issues is appropriate. While the public may be willing to accept some increasing surveillance activities in order to feel safer, this openness is not limitless. Any such qualms over privacy may vary by community values and social norms. This is one reason that experimentation in predictive policing may appropriately occur at the local policing level to allow for administrators to respond to concerns of community members.

In sum, predictive policing tools have an important role to play in the future of policing. Despite the controversies, public safety is itself a significant concern. Advancements in big data and technological innovation offer areas of significant improvements in predictive policing to efficiently and effectively assign policing resources and pre-empt threats to citizens.

References

Almond, L., McManus, M., Brian, D. and Merrington, D.P. (2017). Exploration of the risk factors contained within the UK's existing Domestic Abuse Risk Assessment Tool (DASH): do these risk factors have individual predictive validity regarding recidivism? *Journal of Aggression, Conflict and Peace Research*, 9(1), pp. 58–68.

Amnesty International. (2018). *Trapped in the matrix: secrecy, stigma, and bias in the Met's Gangs Database.* [Online]. London: Royal United Services Institute. Available at: www.amnesty.org.uk/files/2018-05/Trapped%20in%20the%20Matrix%20Amnesty%20report.pdf?lJSxllcKfkZgr4gHZsz0vW8JZ0W3V_PD= [accessed 8 August 2019].

Babuta, A., Oswald, M. and Rinik, C. (2018). *Machine learning algorithms and police decision-making: legal, ethical and regulatory challenges* [Online]. Available at· https://rusi.org/sites/default/files/201809_whr_3-18_machine_learning_algorithms.pdf.pdf [accessed 8 August 2019].

Bannon, M.M. (2017). Datafied and divided: techno-dimensions of inequality in American cities. *City & Community*, 16(1), pp. 20–24.

Bennett Moses, L. and Chan, J. (2018). Algorithmic prediction in policing: assumptions, evaluation, and accountability. *Policing and Society*, 28(7), pp. 806–822.

Brantingham, P.J. (2018). The logic of data bias and its impact on place-based predictive policing. *Ohio State Journal of Criminal Law*, 15, pp. 473–486.

Brennan-Marquez, K. (2018). Big data policing and the redistribution of anxiety. *Ohio State Journal of Criminal Law*, 15, pp. 487–493.

British Broadcasting Company (2019). *West Midlands police "fails to record 16,600 violent crimes"* [Online]. Available at: www.bbc.co.uk/news/uk-england-46867657 [accessed 11 August 2019].

Burrington, I. (2015). What Amazon taught the cops: predictive policing is just another form of supply-chain efficiency. *The Nation*. [Online]. Available at: www.thenation.com/article/what-amazon-taught-cops/ [accessed 21 August 2019].

Campbell, M.A., Gill, C. and Ballucci, D. (2018). Informing police response to intimate partner violence: predictors of perceived usefulness of risk assessment screening.' *Journal of Police and Criminal Psychology*, 33(2), pp. 175–187.

Chicago Police Department. (2019). *Subject Assessment and Information Dashboard (SAID), special order S09-11* [Online]. Available at: http://directives.chicagopolice.org/directives/data/a7a57b85-155e9f4b-50c15-5e9f-7742e3ac8b0ab2d3.html [accessed 8 August 2019].

Corbett-Davies, S. and Goel, S. (2018). *The measure and mismeasure of fairness: a critical review of fair machine learning* [Online]. Available at: https://arxiv.org/pdf/1808.00023 [accessed 10 June 2019].

Degeling, M. and Berendt, B. (2018). What is wrong with Robocops as consultants? A technology-centric critique of predictive policing. *AI & Society*, 33, pp. 347–356.

Dencik, L., Hintz, A., Redden, J. and Warne, H. (2018). *Data scores as governance: investigating uses of citizen scoring in public services* [Online]. Available at: https://datajusticelab.org/publications/ [accessed 8 August 2019].

Eaglin, J. (2017). Constructing recidivism risk. *Emory Law Journal*, 67, pp. 59–122.

Faust, K. and Tita, G.E. (2019). Social networks and crime: pitfalls and promises for advancing the field. *Annual Review of Criminology*, 2, pp. 99–132.

Favaretto, M., De Clercq, E. and Elger, B.S. (2019). 'Big data and discrimination: perils, promises and solutions: a systemic review', *Journal of Big Data*, 6, pp. 1–27.

Feeley, M.M. (2018). How to think about criminal court reform. *Boston University Law Review*, 98, pp. 673–730.

Ferguson, A.G. (2018). Illuminating black data policing, *Ohio State Journal of Criminal Law*, 15, pp. 503–525.

Ferguson, A.G. (2017a). The police are using computer algorithms to tell if you're a threat. *Time*. [Online] Available at: https://time.com/4966125/police-departments-algorithms-chicago/ [accessed 7 August 2019].

Ferguson, A.G. (2017b). Policing predictive policing. *Washington University Law Review*, 94, pp. 1109–1189.

Hamilton, M. (2019a). Debating algorithmic fairness. *UC Davis Law Review Online*, 52, pp. 261–296.

Hamilton, M. (2019b). The biased algorithm: disparate impact for Hispanics. *American Criminal Law Review*, 56, pp. 1553–1577.

Hamilton, M. (2019c). The sexist algorithm. *Behavioral Sciences and the Law*, 37, pp. 145–157.

Hamilton, M. (2015). Risk and needs assessment: constitutional and ethical challenges. *American Criminal Law Review*, 52, 231–291.

Joh, E.E. (2018). Automated policing. *Ohio State Journal of Criminal Law*, 15, pp. 559–563.

Jung, S. and Buro, K. (2017). Appraising risk for intimate partner violence in a police context. *Criminal Justice and Behavior*, 44(2), pp. 240–260.

Kaufmann, M., Egbert, S. and Leese, M. (2019). Predictive policing and the politics of patterns. *British Journal of Criminology*, 59(3), pp. 674–692.

Kearns, I. and Muir, R. (2019). *Data-driven policing and public value.* [Online] London: The Police Foundation. Available at: www.police-foundation.org.uk/2017/wp-content/uploads/2010/10/data_driven_policing_final.pdf [accessed 11 August 2019].

Klingele, C. (2019). Measuring change: from rates of recidivism to markers of desistance. *Journal of Criminal Law & Criminology*, 109(4). [Online]. Available at: http://sentencing.typepad.com/sentencing_law_and_policy/2018/03/%22Measuring%20Change:%20From%20Rates%20of%20Recidivism%20to%20Markers%20of%20Desistance%22 [accessed 15 July 2019].

Liberty. (2019). *Policing by machine: predictive policing and the threat to our rights* [Online]. Available at: www.libertyhumanrights.org.uk/sites/default/files/LIB%2011%20Predictive%20Policing%20Report%20WEB.pdf [accessed 19 March 2019].

Manning, P.K. (2018). Technology, law and policing. In: den Boer, M. (ed.) *Comparative policing from a legal perspective.* Cheltenham, UK: Edward Elgar.

Meijer, A. and Wessels, M. (2019). Predictive policing: review of benefits and drawbacks. *International Journal of Public Administration*, 42(12), pp. 1031–1039.

Metropolitan Police. (2019). *Gangs violence matrix* [Online]. Available at: www.met.police.uk/police-forces/metropolitan-police/areas/about-us/about-the-met/gangs-violence-matrix/ [accessed 8 August 2019].

New, J. and Castro, D. (2018). *How policymakers can foster algorithmic accountability.* Washington, D.C.: Center for Data Innovation. [Online]. Available at: www2.datainnovation.org/2018-algorithmic-accountability.pdf [accessed 21 August 2019].

Nilsson, P. (2019). UK police test if computer can predict criminal behaviour. *Financial Times.*

Oracle. (2015). Social-enabled policing: leverage the power of social media to enhance outcomes. [Online] Available at: www.oracle.com/us/industries/public-sector/social-enabled-policing-wp-2541916.pdf [accessed 11 August 2019].

Oswald, M., Grace, J., Urwin, S. and Barnes, G.C. (2018). Algorithmic risk assessment policing models: lessons from the Durham HART and 'experimental' proportionality. *Information & Communications Technology Law*, 27(2), pp. 223–250.

Papachristos, A.V. and Sierra-Arévalo, M. (2018). *Policing the connected world: using social network analysis in police-community partnerships* [Online]. Available at: https://ric-zai-inc.com/Publications/cops-w0859-pub.pdf [accessed 11 August 2019].

Perry, W.L., et al. (2013). *Predictive policing: the role of crime forecasting in law enforcement operations* [Online]. Rand Corp. Available at: www.rand.org/content/dam/rand/pubs/research_reports/RR200/RR233/RAND_RR233.pdf [accessed 31 March 2019].

Police Transformation Fund. (2019). *National Analytics Solution: final business case (v6.0)* [Online]. Available at: foi.west-midlands.police.uk/wp-content/uploads/2019/01/report1 .pdf [accessed 11 August 2019].

Ratcliffe, J. (2019). Predictive policing. In: Weisburd, D. and Braga, A.A. (eds.) *Police innovation: contrasting perspectives.* Cambridge: Cambridge University Press.

Ratcliff, J.H. and Kikuchi, G. (2019). Harm-focused offender triage and prioritization: a Philadelphia case study. *Policing: An International Journal*, 42(1), pp. 59–73.

Richardson, R., Schultz, J.M. and Crawford, K. (2019). Dirty data, bad predictions: how civil rights violations impact police data, predictive policing systems, and justice. *New York University Law Review* (94), pp. 192–233.

Selbst, A.D. (2017). Disparate impact in big data policing. *Georgia Law Review*, 52, pp. 109–195.

Shapiro, A. (2017). Reform predictive policing. *Nature*. [Online] Available at: www. nature.com/news/reform-predictive-policing-1.21338 [accessed 7 August 2019].

Sheehey, B. (2019). Algorithmic paranoia: the temporal governmentality of predictive policing. *Ethics and Information Technology*, 21(1), pp. 49–58.

Veale, M. (2019). *Algorithms in the criminal justice system*. London: The Law Society of England and Wales. [Online]. Available at: www.lawsociety.org.uk/support-services/research-trends/algorithm-use-in-the-criminal-justice-system-report/ [accessed 30 April 2019].

Vestby, A. and Vestby. J. (2019). Machine learning and the police: asking the right questions. Policing: A Journal of Policy and Practice, 14 June 2019. Available at: https://doi.org/10.1093/police/paz035.

Weisburd, D. et al. (2019). Proactive policing: a summary of the Report of the National Academies of Sciences, Engineering, and Medicine. *Asian Journal of Criminology*, 14(2), pp. 145–177.

West Midlands Police. (2017). *Data driven insight & data science capability for UK law enforcement* [Online]. Available at: www.excellenceinpolicing.org.uk/wp-content/uploads/2017/10/EIP17_2-5_Utilising_Data_Science.pdf [accessed 11 August 2019].

Wheeler, A.P., Worden, R.E. and Silver, J.R. (2019). The accuracy of the Violent Offender Identification Directive tool to predict future gun violence. *Criminal Justice and Behavior*, 46(5), pp. 770–788.

Williams, M.L., Burnap, P. and Sloan, L. (2017). Crime sensing with big data: the affordances and limitations of using open-source communications to estimate crime patterns. *British Journal of Criminology*, 57, pp. 320–340.

Chapter 3

Policing, AI and choice architecture

John L.M. McDaniel and Ken G. Pease

Introduction

The chapter draws upon Thaler and Sunstein's (2008) concept of 'choice architecture' to frame developments at the nexus of public policing and AI. We focus first on the concept of choice architecture as it applies to policing and, more particularly, on how the development and use of AI can play a significant role in organising contexts with a view to influencing the way police officers make decisions. Distinct sections of the chapter address choice architecture during the development of AI technologies, the ability of AI to act as a choice architect, and the choice architecture surrounding police interventions in practice. Our aim is to help police officers, policy makers and AI developers appreciate how their decision-making fits into a broader choice environment, and how their decisions and actions can affect the conduct of policing in practice.

The ubiquity of choice architecture

Those who organise contexts with a view to influencing the way other people make decisions have been described as 'choice architects', and what they do as 'choice architecture' (Thaler and Sunstein, 2008). While the designation is new, the role of the 'choice architect' has been occupied (though less often recognised) for as long as people (or deities) made consequences conditional on human choices. Interesting as a history of social and psychological influence would be, we will confine our discussion to more contemporary kinds of influence associated with the term. The supermarket is an obvious example. When shoppers enter a supermarket in the UK, their purchasing is shaped. Fresh fruit, vegetables and flowers can be found close to the entrance since consumer research has shown that the vibrant colours and smells can put people in a good mood and induce purchases of goods with a short shelf life. Music with a slow rhythm is routinely used to slow customer pace, keeping them in the shop for longer so they might spend more. Well-known products that sell well, and usually the more expensive items, are typically placed at eye-level so that they are easily spotted. Displays next to checkouts frequently contain sweets and chocolates to tempt children, likely bored with queuing. By applying these techniques, supermarkets can increase the rate at which people 'choose' particular items. They can also deter particular behaviours. Placing items most likely to be stolen in sight of checkouts limits shop theft.

The presence of choice architecture is everywhere. Physicians are choice architects when they describe a particular range of treatments to their patients and the various benefits of each (the order in which they describe them is important). Newspaper editors are choice architects when they decide which stories to publish and where they should be placed (i.e. what should go on the front page and attract most attention). As Thaler and Sunstein (2008) explain: 'just as no building lacks architecture, no choice lacks a context'. In their best-selling book *Nudge*, they reason that the choice architects who design these choice environments could, in many cases, act more responsibly to 'nudge' people towards decisions that are good for them, as opposed to exploiting their cognitive weaknesses in ways that are profitable for the company but more detrimental to the consumer's long-term health, wealth and happiness. It is unreasonable, they argued, to expect people to always be able to equip them-selves with complete information about all of the choices available, to pay full attention to the decisions that they make and to have complete self-control. Instead, it is more plausible to expect people to make bad decisions, primarily because of their inability to meet these expectations much of the time, and especially since choice architects have systematically organised various contexts in ways that make bad decisions seem like good ones.

A 'bad decision', in this context, is described as one that does not leave the person better off as judged by themselves and, most importantly, that they would not have made the decision if they had paid full attention and possessed complete information, unlimited cognitive abilities and absolute self-control. Psychologists and behavioural economists know that human judgement exhibits a whole host of heuristics and biases which render our cognitive processes markedly sub-optimal for important decisions, especially ones that are made quickly or passively (Kahneman and Tversky, 1979). Commercial entities know it too. Heuristics, biases and other cognitive weaknesses are routinely exploited by real estate agents, insurance companies, credit card providers and bookmakers, among others, to induce behaviours that they desire. Thaler and Sunstein suggest that bad decisions are so prevalent in society that the uncon-strained exercise of human judgement in important decision-making, left only to the mercy of profit-oriented companies, is almost indefensible.

The authors of *Nudge* set about laying some of the responsibility for the public's decision-making at the feet of choice architects. They recommend that, since choice architects are going to organise various contexts in any case, they should act responsibly to reorganise them in ways that enable better decisions to be made. Espousing the exercise of benign influence, Thaler and Sunstein badged their particular recommendations as 'libertarian paternalism'. Its characteristics are that the relevant interventions are designed to alter a person's behaviour in a predictable way, while modest in scale, transparent, leaving the person influenced the clear option of rejecting the influence, and deployed where people typically make choices which redound to their disadvantage. Providing better 'default options' for healthcare plans, pension policies, credit cards, phone contracts and organ donations were some of the soft forms of design-based control methods they recommended. These are examples of an eponymous 'nudge'. The flavour of libertarian paternalism was well captured in Thaler's acceptance speech for the 2017 Nobel Memorial Prize in Economic Sciences.

In *Nudge*, Thaler and Sunstein were concerned with applying libertarian paternalism and nudges to areas of 'health, wealth and happiness'. Their aim was to inspire people to become more aware of the existence and work of choice architects, and to suggest more responsible forms of behaviour. One takeaway for the reader was that we cannot choose *not* to be subjected to choice architecture. Neither will attempts to eradicate choice architecture work since any form of status quo is itself a product of choice architects. We can only choose to become aware of the choices that we face, accept that the easiest choices that we face are probably pre-prepared for us by choice architects, and decide whether we are content with them. If not, we should probably do something about it. It was not Thaler and Sunstein's intention to address all kinds of choice architects across every field. They left that to others.

Our concern in this chapter is not with libertarian paternalism nor do we advocate particular default options or any other kind of nudge. We focus on choice architecture. First, only a minority of choice architecture can be thought of as informed by libertarian paternalism. Choice architects do not need to value concepts of individual liberty and freedom of choice. Many of the choices open to prisoners on a daily basis (of which there are many) would not be described as libertarian, nor would they be characterised as entirely free of choice architecture. Similarly, attempts to organise contexts with a view to influencing the way people make decisions do not need to be as discrete as a nudge (in fact, Thaler and Sunstein encourage transparency). Choice architects can be open and entirely deliberate in their design of the choice environment to ensure that decisions and behaviours move in the directions they prefer. They may induce or coerce. An individual could be presented with no more than two options, both of which are perhaps unpleasant, or even incentivised by the promise of a benefit or threatened with unpleasant consequences so that they are more likely to choose one (Yeung, 2016).

Nudges are a particular variety of design-based regulatory techniques available to some choice architects (Yeung, 2016). Although the kind espoused by Thaler and Sunstein are designed to influence behaviours in ways that reduce harm and leave people better off as judged by themselves, at least in the long-term, they are not the only class of behavioural influence techniques. Even their well-meaning variety can be controversial because they are closely associated with ideas of covert social engineering, manipulation and deception (Yeung,

2017). Intentionally and stealthily arranging the choice environment to make it systematically more likely that a desirable action is taken can also be problematic from a human rights perspective, raising issues of liberty, freedom, transparency and democratic legitimacy among other values (Yeung, 2016; Law Society, 2019). People may feel angry and betrayed to find out that they were systematically manipulated, even to their own advantage, and especially if they were nudged by state actors. If an attempt at behavioural modification is perceived to be excessive or offensive (etching a target close to the urinal drains in police station bathrooms to enhance cleanliness should not qualify as excessive or offensive), they should be able to demand an explanation that justifies such interventions. If they cannot be justified (with reference to policy motives such as the prevention of harm), people living in a liberal democracy should be able to seek reparation and reform with minimal effort.

Nudges appear to be commonplace, and such techniques are 'dual purpose' (capable of being used for benevolence or greed, or by private or state actors), but this chapter is not about critiquing the presence of nudges in modern policing or advocating particular kinds (although we would caution against the harmful sort). We aim only to make the people working at the nexus of policing and AI, from computer scientists to police officers and politicians, more aware that, in various contexts, they *are* choice architects. We outline some general outcomes that we would consider to be better or worse than alternatives, but what these choice architects will decide to do with their considerable ability to organise contexts is largely unknown. The way that they go about organising contexts with a view to influencing the way people make decisions may be coloured by benevolence or malice or the process may end up that way. Choice architecture is rarely unbiased. Moreover, expert commentary about the future of AI in policing, the rate of advances, what forms such advances might take, and the range of plausible outcomes varies wildly. This is without even considering the outcomes that are less likely, but still possible. Within the chapter, we do a lot of hypothesising. We use a lot of 'ifs'.

There are perhaps two reasons for addressing the issue of choice architecture in relation to crime and justice. The first is simply that choice architects and those whom the decisions affect should be clear about what is happening. Thaler and Sunstein invoke John Rawls in the assertion that no choice architect should have any reservation about what they are doing becoming public. The second concerns the application of AI to policing. This remains in an embryonic state, but experience already suggests that AI systems will become choice architects. At the very least, the advent of AI marks the partial outsourcing of choice architecture in policing to AI practitioners and vendors. The focus in what follows will be on decision-making context reorganisation caused by AI developments both directly and indirectly. This is because the application of these techniques is burgeoning and their implications must be addressed.

Policing and choice architecture

The concept of choice architecture has not been readily associated with contemporary policing, yet it underlies much of what police officers do (throughout the chapter we focus on police officers, but many of the same issues can be applied to civilian staff too). Rank and file police officers are choice architects since they use a range of subtle and overt techniques to establish contexts in order to influence the way members of the public make decisions. The tone of their voice, the words that they use, their movements, the space that they afford to aggressive people and people in crisis, and their ability to convey compassion and understanding are key techniques for de-escalation, negotiation and conflict resolution (van Maanen, 1974; Muir, 1979). A civilian may not immediately recognise these techniques, but they are frequently employed by police officers to influence the individual's mood, or the mood of a larger crowd, and to shape the next decisions that they make. The issuance of fines or the use of powers of arrest are also designed to influence an individual's future decision-making, albeit in a much more overt way.

The decisions that police officers make are not determined in a vacuum either. A civilian may see a police officer who is authoritative, powerful and capable of making life-changing decisions, relying only on their independent and internal judgement, but they would be mistaken. The contexts within which police officers make decisions are intentionally influenced and explicitly organised by others. The police officer who chooses to arrest for a minor offence may have been encouraged by their line manager to take a less tolerant approach to particular types of offences. This strategy may be in response to community feedback, a critical inspectorate report or the expressed desire of politicians or newspaper editors for a more hard-line approach. The police sergeant, in particular, is an important choice architect, for they can establish for their subordinates a 'sense of permission' or 'perception of reality and purpose' of what is possible and what is not (Van Maanen, 1983). This usually centres on the expectations and standards that they apply, backed up by the threat of punishment should an officer deviate. Police officers, like most other human beings, typically care about what other people think, like to conform, and search for environmental cues about how to act (Acquisti et al., 2015). Behavioural tendencies will inevitably be reinforced, or changed, if police managers indicate, for example, that a greater reliance on AI systems and outputs represents the normal or recommended course of action in future.

Outside of the moral obligation of police officers to respond to a call for immediate police assistance (their response may be to leave it to a closer colleague), the hierarchical organisation of police inspectors, superintendents and other senior ranks will also choose where to strategically deploy their police officers and for what particular purposes. Disparate crime rates, data analysis, community feedback, newspaper reporting, external reports, consultation with elected officials and budgetary constraints, among other factors, give rise to numerous opportunities and demands for proactive policing. At any one time, police managers face an array of competing goals to pursue and configurations they can choose from. These demands cannot all be met at once. Time, personnel, logistics, money and the expectations of external stakeholders are key considerations. It is ultimately the decisions of line managers, influenced by choice architecture, that ordinarily place police officers at particular scenes, and shape the informational choice context in which the police officers' decision-making occurs. The aim, generally, is to channel attention and decision-making in the direction that aligns with the vested interests of the choice architects. Public policing is very much about the science of choice.

AI and choice architecture

We outlined the nature and role of AI in various policing contexts within the introduction to the book, so we will not cover old ground here. In short, modern policing organisations could potentially benefit from using AI systems to process information, particularly those AI systems that focus on pattern recognition and classification. Machine learning systems, for instance, are capable of processing huge volumes of data of diverse kinds and sorting locations, events or people (or whatever) into groups carrying different implications for action. The bad news is of three kinds. First, the input data available on the basis of which to classify may be a consequence of earlier policing activities. Earlier forms of choice architecture will have influenced citizen-police encounters and policing activities, and it is this data that provides the feedstock for many data-based algorithms. This means that the measures used for prediction are likely to carry some baggage that one would prefer not to carry into the mathematical enterprise, such as a host of police decisions to stop and search individuals in particular places based in part on race. The second, and related, type of bad news is the degree of uncertainty of most algorithmic outputs and predictions. There is usually a chance that they will be wrong, at least some of the time, since they must rely on partial datasets. Not all of the things that police officers do can be quantified and analysed by an algorithm. Yet, their outputs may still form part of the policing choice architecture. In brief, all AI procedures should be labelled 'handle with care' from the outset. Third, police officers are arguably as capable as other human beings of making bad decisions but, unlike civilians, they are surrounded by choice architects within and without the police organisation who are supposed to be benevolently, explicitly and purposefully designing contexts that reduce the possibility of bad decision-making (it is partially why police organisations have hierarchies in the first place). The broader choice architecture includes numerous structures and processes designed by regulators, inspectorates, complaints bodies and legislatures. Yet, bad decisions continue to be made. AI technologies have joined the fray, but not ordinarily as omniscient mediators or fixers. They too are the product of choice architecture, can function as choice architects, and can both exacerbate bad decisions and be crippled by them.

AI as a product of choice architects

Extant AI technologies in policing are the product of choice architects. Those technologies currently labelled as AI all involve machine learning and, more particularly, usually use either random forests or neural network techniques to carry out the learning task. Although both techniques are celebrated for their unpredictability and their ability to reach conclusions without direct instruction, they are designed at the outset by people and affected by the choices that their designers and users make. One of the first ways that designers and users organise contexts with a view to influencing the way AI systems make decisions is by selecting the data to feed it. The external sources (usually people) who choose what data a machine learning system can access generally have a particular objective in mind. For the designer or programmer who wants to see whether a technology can identify interesting patterns of violence, then they will acquire and use data related to violence, and not data on something like horticulture (although gardening could play a role in calming aggression). The rub here is that good data on violence is also difficult to find, and is generally of questionable quality.

Police-held data is often limited in calibre and completeness. As we outlined in the introduction to the text, police-recorded data does not measure crime but relates to the places and people that frequently request police assistance, how police officers choose to act in those spaces, what they choose to record, and the extent to which police officers direct their activities to other places and people on a more proactive footing. The choices and assumptions that they make about what is important, significant or useful will colour the entire process of collecting and organising police data. Modern history is replete with examples of individuals being stopped and searched within particular areas because their ethnicity was broadly, and wrongly, associated with various forms of criminality within those areas. Some ethnicities were regularly associated with drug dealing in particular areas or associated with muggings in others (Hall et al., 1982; Bowling and Phillips, 2003). One of the overriding problems was that many police officers could not, or chose not to, differentiate between crime and non-crime variables. Factors such as race, clothing, time, place and association were frequently linked to crime when in fact there wasn't even the smallest association to crime, only the prejudice of police officers to connect them (MacPherson, 1999; Holdaway and O'Neill, 2006). The police actions and the resultant data was nevertheless fed into policing systems over many decades. The net result is a piecemeal and often prejudiced picture.

A machine learning system that is capable only of pattern recognition and calculating probabilities generally relies on this data in a policing context. Its calculations will reflect, to various extents, how facts were chosen and weighted in the past. A cluster analysis technique known as latent class analysis, which involves grouping together items that share similar characteristics and estimating probabilities of class membership is a popular technique (Francis et al., 2004). If an individual shares some characteristics and behaviours with an identifiable group, such as offenders with a particular modus operandi or background, it can help to generate a prediction that they are likely to act in similar ways. For example, growing up in a particular area, leaving school early, and having an absent parent may be particularly strong indicators for inclusion into a class. The result is their inclusion in categories, data 'buckets' or 'behavioural tribes' on the basis of the variables they have in common (O'Neil and Schutt, 2013).

This is a characteristic that various AI systems share with traditional police approaches: the propensity to stereotype. Inferences are drawn about a person because of one or more shared interests or attributes, irrespective of their more complex life experiences, personalities and hopes for the future. AI systems that rely on this data may therefore be no more advanced than the prejudicial police officer who develops a suspicion on the basis of ethnicity, association and place alone. Drawing insights, assumptions or suspicions simply from what a person wears or who they associate with or where they choose to spend their time has long been discredited in policing (Chan, 1997; Jones, 2017), but an AI may not be able to deduce this.

One popular argument is that more data should be made available to AI systems so that they can become more objective. Data from accident and emergency departments, social care services, local authorities, education providers and private sector organisations, among other sources, could potentially assist in a more objective search for patterns and correlations. Setting AI pattern recognition systems loose on the internet is one prominent proposal, so that they can draw insights from friendship networks, the words and phrases people post online, and the people they interact with, among other factors (see Chapter 5). Some machine learning systems used by police forces in the UK and the US already examines individuals' social media feeds (Law Society, 2019). However, such activities do not necessarily shed the cloak of prejudice. Much online activity is non-crime related. Tasked with identifying patterns and correlations, and without further instruction, AI systems will inevitably make links between criminals and their language, clothing, interests and places of residence, among other factors. Another reality that undermines the case for setting machine learning systems loose on more and more databases is that their results can become more unstable (Berk and Bleich, 2014). The more data, and new types of data, an AI system is introduced to, the less relevant its original specifications and accuracy rates become.

A second way that designers and users can organise contexts with a view to influencing the way AI systems make decisions is by selecting how they receive feedback and from where. To prevent an AI system from exhausting its computational resources and running forever in order to solve intractable problems, human designers or other external sources generally 'reward' an AI system for correct inferences that they make so that new and valid conclusions can be internalised as an updated variable or rule (Lemm et al., 2011). This technique is closely associated with neural networks. By providing feedback to an AI system, the external source is acting as a choice architect. If, for example, an algorithm is taught by an external source that it is worse to overlook potential criminal activity than to have an innocent person treated as a potential criminal (i.e. false negatives are worse than false positives), the system may treat low risk people as riskier than they are. Similarly, if biased data is inputted and a programmer rewards a machine learning programme for using a mechanical thought process to produce a conclusion which is thought to be correct but which is in fact unnecessarily biased, it may serve to simply reproduce the designer's prejudice.

Whether and to what extent feedback is gathered through a statistical analysis of police data and performance measures, or through more ancillary and qualitative fieldwork-based studies involving victims, community groups, police officers and other stakeholders, among other techniques, are also important questions. Otherwise, AI programmes that receive their feedback primarily from police officers could end up giving priority to those variables and results that are popular only within police organisations (and may be detested by the wider community). A decision by the designer or user not to provide feedback might not be helpful either. Without it, an AI system might not be able to infer that it is offensive or even illegal to identify correlations between people and crime based on variables such as religion. It is partly for these reasons that, although machine learning programmes are typically designed to be as unpredictable as possible in their search for patterns and correlations, many machine learning programmes available today are given some guidance about which reasoning steps to try and which variables to use (Russell and Norvig, 2014; Law Society, 2019). The work of choice architects, thus, is central to the design and operation of AI systems in a policing context.

Choice architects may go further still. They can even pre-set the weightings that are attached to specific variables and incorporate formulae that are already known to be important determinants and predictors in order to guide machine learning systems. This process is often referred to as feature engineering. In practice, specific weightings are attached to various machine learning systems in use within some police organisations. Facial recognition technologies and risk assessment tools used in some areas tend to be high on sensitivity (spotting correlations, both strong and weak) but low on specificity (rejecting the weak, normal and innocent). Ideally, they should be sensitive enough to identify particular people's faces, voices and movements (depending upon what patterns they are designed to look for), yet specific enough to rule out those people, behaviours and things that have a passing resemblance to features they are looking for but are entirely normal. Unfortunately, this is not the case with many extant AI technologies, and intentionally so. Several tools have been designed under the working assumption that people will be prepared to live with an increase in the number of false positives if the number of false negatives can be meaningfully reduced (Berk and Bleich, 2014). In other words, it may be acceptable to misidentify lots of innocent people as long as all of the guilty people are successfully identified.

The Harm Assessment Risk Tool (HART), which uses machine learning and was developed by Durham Constabulary and researchers at Cambridge University, is perhaps a useful example of feature engineering. The tool uses the random forests technique to analyse dozens of variables, including an individual's criminal history, their age and gender, to predict whether they are low, medium or high risk of reoffending within the next two years. The output helps custody officers to determine whether individuals are suitable to be diverted away from the criminal justice system and towards an associated rehabilitation programme called 'Checkpoint' (see Chapter 8). It is tuned to favour false positives over false negatives, as the designers considered it to be more harmful to underestimate the risk posed by a high-risk offender than to overestimate the risk posed by a low-risk one (Babuta et al., 2018). Choice architects, thus, played a significant role in influencing the way that the AI system makes decisions. Although AI products are often packaged as unpredictable and objective, the reality can be rather different.

The issues of feedback and feature selection are not small or insignificant. Decisions about whether innocent people should be treated as risker than they are, or whether theft from a vehicle is worse than damage to a vehicle, or whether one conviction for serious violence is worse than two convictions for theft, may seem relatively simple. Such choices are routinely made in the design and operation of algorithmic risk assessment tools and predictive 'hotspot' mapping programmes among other technologies. However, deciding that a crime mapping technology should be developed and deployed to focus on some crimes and not others is laden with meaning. Determining which variables or outputs are most appropriate or more important within police-related AI systems involves important ethical considerations and political choices that should not be easy to make in reality (Valentine, 2019). In a liberal democracy, decisions about how crime is treated should reflect the values of a broad array of stakeholders and preferably shaped by a process of continuous debate. Some of the values under consideration may represent goals and ideals that people endorse thoughtfully, defend and use to organise their communal lives (Royal Society, 2017; Whittlestone et al., 2019). They may be rooted in cultural norms, religious views, party politics, populist ideologies or philosophical theories that do not share majority support. Values and desires that conflict with one another but are considered to be of similar importance need to be reconciled to some degree. The costs and benefits of particular technologies may not be equitably distributed across ethnic or economic groups, among other demarcations. Somebody or some group could be left worse off than others by distributive choices.

Depending on the type of feedback a machine learning system receives, it could make trade-offs that favour one particular stakeholder over another or the values and needs of the majority at the expense of minorities. Whether or not an AI system even works is often a matter of opinion. Police officers may take the view that an algorithm works because it identifies criminals most of the time, whereas a human rights lawyer may argue that the algorithm does not really work at all since it incorrectly identifies an unacceptable number of innocent people. Whether one view or both are fed back to an AI may have a significant bearing on the outputs and recommendations it generates. These costs and inequities must be properly understood before new technologies are introduced so that attempts can be made at reconciliation and mitigation. If values are unclear then efforts should be taken to clarify their meaning. Such considerations should ideally be undertaken for each new class of algorithm and AI system employed in a policing context, reconciling their individual features and practical impacts.

In addition, the choices that are made within this enterprise do not remain constant. Attitudes to offences can change over time (towards drugs, hate crime or domestic abuse, among others) so it could be regressive to embed variables too firmly within algorithms. The same is arguably true of the 'internal algorithms' of police officers, which can be influenced by heuristics and stereotypes concerning people and places that no longer carry any determinative value (and perhaps never did), so it would be sensible to avoid this happening to AI systems. Police officers' historical and 'encoded' knowledge can be particularly embedded, so an AI programme, even if it evinces considerable bias, may be a desirable improvement (see Chapter 4). That is, if it has broad public support and efforts have been made to mitigate all foreseeable harms. Thus, the process of determining which variables should be used, the ethical reasons for doing so, how much weight should be attached to them, and for what purpose, should be a hefty undertaking and necessarily so.

Giving AI systems free rein to determine values might not be palatable in comparison. A rational AI system may, for instance, reason and act logically and consistently to achieve an outcome by one measure but it need not necessarily adhere to social norms, minimise harm, weigh risk or avoid decisions that are irreversible (Bostrom, 2017). Nor have extant AI systems proven capable of solving our most complex social problems or plotting courses through them sequentially to achieve distant goals. Machine learning programmes have, for example, proven to be quite effective in detecting anomalies in medical images (like examining x-rays for cancer diagnoses) largely because they are presented with the same set of deterministic circumstances (an x-ray, that if healthy, should look a particular way). They cannot yet produce such consistency and rationality in more random, complex and partially observable environments. Equally, AIs may be capable of identifying relatively simple patterns in criminal activity but they cannot yet produce a good understanding of causation or generate a clear picture of all of the relevant structures, processes, multi-agency networks, funding requirements and psychological and behavioural skills needed to address the root causes of crime. There is little to suggest that we are on the cusp of a big breakthrough in artificial intelligence that might allow this to happen any time soon (Bostrom, 2017; Law Society, 2019). At present, as Bostrom (2017: 11) explains, behind the 'razzle-dazzle of machine learning' lies a set of mathematically well-specified trade-offs. These deserve careful consideration.

These are some of the most important features of the choice architecture surrounding the development and use of AI in policing, and so should never be outsourced to computer programmers to determine passively (Law Society, 2019). Computer scientists are singularly ill equipped to code for fairness and determine trade-offs concerning the kinds of high-stakes decisions routinely taken in the criminal justice system. Valentine (2019: 374) observes that the people making programming choices 'often work from a perspective that lacks the cultural awareness of those the technology most directly affects'. Computer scientists, particularly those who work in the commercial AI sphere, are typically more concerned with whether their algorithm proves to be correct at least some of the time, or whether it is 'good enough' despite its deductive biases, rather than with issues of the broader public good (Bostrom, 2017). For those working for 'Big Tech' companies, the money that rolls in from customers (including police forces and other public bodies), and not ideas of fairness, can be the primary barometer of success (O'Neil, 2016). Thaler and Sunstein (2008) note that private companies are usually incentivised by the market to nudge consumers in the direction that helps to maximise their profits and maintain their competitive advantages, even if it involves consumer exploitation and manipulation. Market forces alone are unlikely to protect and reconcile values in a way that we would find acceptable. The endeavour requires 'care and societal steer' (Law Society 2019: 9)

The limited understanding that some computer scientists have about the social, historical and legal milieu of the policing environment within which they operate is perhaps well illustrated in the following example. Palantir is a Silicon Valley start-up worth over $20 billion and well known for its data analysis and search algorithms, which it sells to police forces among others. It calls two of its best-selling information management and analytics systems 'Gotham' and 'Metropolis' (Waldman et al., 2018). While the terms have other colloquial uses, both Gotham and Metropolis are neighbouring fictional cities in American comic books; the homes of Batman and Superman respectively. It might seem playful for computer scientists to label their systems as such but these associations are uncomfortably reminiscent of out-dated classical criminological theories which characterise and frame crimes as an evil to be eradicated rather than as social, economic and public health problems. Similarly, within one of its network analysis programs, Palantir even inserted a playful caricature beside the names of criminals and suspects. Wearing a grey trench coat, black fedora and a black eye mask (see Brayne, 2017: 993), the caricature is clearly borrowed from the villains of 1950s Film Noir movies and comic books of the era. Using icons such as the villain in a trench coat to depict criminals, an SUV with tinted windows to mark the location of car theft, or a cockroach to mark a gang territory may be a nod to Hollywood and comic book symbolism, but these systems are used by real people, and portray people and places that computer scientists will rarely, if ever, intimately understand. An icon or symbol can be a powerful influencer and interpreted by police officers and civilians as a representation of something real (Manning, 2004).

Handing off important decisions and trade-offs to computer scientists and AI companies to determine would be reckless and the antithesis of justice as fairness (Rawls, 1985), but doing so would be in line with more traditional policing approaches. One of the major weaknesses of modern police organisations is that, without appropriate checks and balances, police leaders have a tendency to assume that they know what the public wants and societies need without actually asking, preferring to rely on their own expertise (McDaniel, 2018). This has led to accusations of depersonalisation and technocratic policing styles, culminating most noticeably in the (re)emergence of theories of community-oriented and democratic policing (Manning, 1984; Bayley, 1994). The theories cautioned that assumptions should not be made about what different people expect of the police, what they might be willing to sacrifice (for example, liberty or privacy) in return for more efficient and effective policing, or that their consent should be automatically implied. Nor should police leaders be left to individually determine how much bias is 'too much'. The public should be consulted and their societal needs and views on the impacts of policing and AI should be addressed with seriousness (Whittlestone et al., 2019). Packer's (1964) famous theoretical models of criminal justice, for example, convey the importance of sacrificing some perceived levels of efficiency (i.e. crime control) for the promise of fairness (due process). However, facilitating community-oriented policing in substance is not easy, and the enterprise is arguably made harder in light of recent research by Ipsos Mori and the Royal Society (2017: 21) which indicates that only 9 per cent of people are aware of the term 'machine learning' in any context. This lack of awareness may make it all the more tempting for AI developers and police organisations to take an easier, centralised, technocratic and dehumanised route without consultation. Many citizens may not wish to see this happen.

AI technologies as choice architects

AI technologies are not only the *product* of choice architects, from those who decide what data to use to the external sources that reward their learning, they can also *function* as choice architects. We have outlined how trade-offs, opinions, perspectives and passive decisions can shape the choice architecture that surrounds the design and operation of AI systems; similar features, in turn, allow them to function as choice architects. The reasons for this lie primarily with human police officers. Few people would claim with any seriousness that police officers would not benefit greatly from receiving more help in making decisions on a day-to-day basis. It is a truism of modern policing that police officers rarely, if ever, know anything for certain. Their ability to absorb new information is relatively limited. Like other human beings, they are generally unable to process, make sense of and fully exploit all of the information and data sets at their disposal, especially under significant time constraints. Gathering and assessing all of the relevant experiences, emotions, desires and complex histories of the people they deal with, and their competing claims, is an impossible task in the time usually allocated to them. Instead, when police officers are responding to incidents, they are expected to make relatively quick and authoritative decisions within partially observable environments while in possession of imperfect information (Skolnick, 1966; Wilson, 1968; Bittner, 1970). The information they bring with them into an encounter is far from perfect either since it will be both piecemeal and experiential in nature. Thus, their aim is to arrive at solutions that are satisfactory rather than exact or optimal in most cases.

Where serious difficulties can arise is in the subjective interpretation of what 'satisfactory' means in practice. A police officer may be satisfied because a clear decision was reached expediently, but the outcome may not be satisfactory to the civilian(s) affected. An officer may have incorrectly identified one person as an aggressor or guilty party (a 'false positive'), failed to identify who was really responsible (a 'false negative') or relied on rules of thumb that completely missed the nuances of the situation. The subjective, error-prone, and ad-hoc decisions of police officers may be nowhere near appropriate. Furthermore, decisions that appear to be quite similar on paper may be entirely inconsistent across time and place. Research suggests that policing outcomes in cases which are described and justified in similar terms, such as cases of routine traffic violations, can vary wildly (Schulenberg, 2010). Inconsistent reasoning strategies have been attributed to stereotypes, prejudices and even changes in mood over the course of a day (caused by stress, the weather, hunger or anger) among other variables (Forgas and East, 2008; Babuta et al., 2018). Police officers and staff working within police stations and back offices usually enjoy a little more time to make and review decisions, but they too are limited by time pressures, capabilities and finite information. Police officer decision-making, as with most other human decision-making processes, is an inexact and error-prone endeavour. Enter the promise of AI.

In theory, AI systems can draw upon vast data sets to identify patterns and people and generate risk scores which could better inform police decision-making and reduce levels of uncertainty and inconsistency. Police decisions, and the exercise of discretion, could be far more effective if officers knew more about the people they dealt with and the types of problems they confronted. Augmented with cameras, sensors and other types of hardware, AI systems even hold the promise of downloading and analysing real-time environmental data, potentially enhancing an officer's situational awareness (Blount, 2017). Systems can potentially provide police officers with probabilities of risk and the likely success of particular actions within dynamic and highly-charged environments. They could prompt police officers to consider something that they might not otherwise have considered or to explore an issue that appeared to be superficial at first. Virtual personal assistants or 'partners' could even ask police officers to double-check whether all relevant factors have been taken into account where it detects a departure from the 'norm'. A machine could potentially say: 'That looks weird. Would you like to reconsider that?' (HLAI, 2018). A prompt that a decision varies wildly from the median could be a helpful device for reflective practice and reduce opportunities for unnecessary or silly mistakes, or prejudicial or inconsistent decision-making. Feedback can be an important way of telling people when they are making mistakes and a strong way of motivating them (Thaler and Sunstein, 2008). Information is king within uncertain environments.

For these reasons, AI systems are particularly well placed to organise contexts in ways that influence police officer decision-making. The computing power and sheer volume of information available to them occasions acknowledgement. As Cohen and Graver observe in the next chapter, trusting computers can also be a 'very natural professional impulse' since police officers will invariably know very little about the people concerned, or the data crunched by an AI programme. AI outputs can be a very convenient source of authority, avoiding the need to give some hard thought to the complex situations that confront police officers on the ground. It is well established within policing literature that police officers tend to prize expediency over exactitude, which AI technologies can excel at. Moreover, following an AI output may feel like the easiest option to defend in conditions of uncertainty (see Chapter 8). The decision that requires the least effort or the path of least resistance is often an attractive one (Thaler and Sunstein, 2008). However, these propensities, that can cause humans to favour and defer to the outputs of automated decision-making and support systems, is a well-known cognitive weakness known as 'automation bias' (Skitka, 1999).

Automation bias becomes a problem particularly where people who are inflicted begin to make new classes of error because of their over-reliance on the capabilities and 'default options' of the algorithmic systems (Skitka, 1999). They may miss events when not explicitly prompted by an AI system (errors of omission) or do what they think the system is recommending, even when it contradicts with their training and other information (errors of commission). The experience and confidence of police officers might ultimately reduce as they become little more than passive bystanders or novices in the decision-making process. Spending less time practicing and developing their deductive reasoning skills within critical and complex environments on a regular basis may inspire more uncertainty rather than less. Tacit knowledge, nuance and intuition may be lost as police officers and analysts overestimate the abilities of AI technologies, treat them as authoritative and become intimidated by their complexity. Chan outlined in Chapter 1 how AI can cause a cultural shift as much as a technical one. The net result is that the outputs of AI systems can play a role in organising contexts in ways that influence police officers to make decisions, without even attempting to do so. AI systems, in this scenario, do not get to choose whether or not to act as choice architects, automation bias thrusts it upon them.

Automation bias can be caused by simple inertia or laziness but other cognitive weaknesses are also active at the nexus of AI and policing. These include 'confirmation bias', 'framing' and 'priming' (Valentine, 2019). Confirmation bias, which is closely associated with automation bias in this context, is a process in which police officers interpret new information in a way that confirms their initial beliefs (or an AI output) despite the presence of credible contradictory information. Framing, which can lead to confirmation bias, can cause an individual to attach particular salience to a particular factor which influences a subsequent judgement depending on how key information was presented. For example, if an algorithm calculates that there is a 60 per cent likelihood that a particular individual will be involved in a shooting in the future and this key statistic is conveyed to a police officer, they may consider the person to be high risk. However, if the statistic conveyed to the police officer is that there is a 40 per cent chance that the particular individual is entirely innocent and will not be involved in any kind of violence, they may consider the individual to be at lower risk. The calculation did not change but the information was simply presented in a different way. People tend to react differently to the same information if it is framed in different ways (Thaler and Sunstein, 2008). Priming, in turn, involves drawing people's attention to some issues and not others so that their criteria for making decisions is more limited. The ability of AI algorithms to present or prioritise one type of information over another has already led to the well documented creation of 'filter bubbles' online which can determine how people are presented with information and news stories, shaping broader norms and values among other reality distorting implications (HLAI, 2018). The way that outputs are presented by AI systems, thus, have the potential to be a powerful tool for behavioural modification.

The normative pull that can lead to a decision to delegate evidence-based reasoning to an AI, whether through automation bias, confirmation bias, framing or some other cognitive weakness, may ultimately lead to a harmful 'Asimovian' paradox where the quality of what we would refer to as good policing is reducing (Kerr and Szilagyi, 2018). Rather than improving human performance, the use of AI could quickly lead to a reduction in human ability; a feature that Bainbridge (1983) describes as one of the 'ironies of automation'. It may be akin to blindly following a Satnav over a cliff because more faith is attributed to the intelligence of an AI than the information in front of a police officer. The instincts, which humans have developed over millennia, that allow people to assess situations which they have never encountered before, even just to empathise with an individual who shoplifts because the alternative is to go home to an abusive partner, are not yet shared with AI systems. Nor can extant

AI systems fully understand the power of conveying respect to an individual in a way that defuses a situation, triggers feelings of self-worth and signals their place in society. There are major limits to what can be quantified in the form of mathematical formulae. Affording them unearned esteem not only raises the possibility of miscarriages of justice but it could ultimately threaten fundamental principles of police discretion, legitimacy and operational independence in common law jurisdictions (see Chapter 8). The latter, for example, holds that constables should never be the servant in a perverse or political master-servant relationship of any kind (Walsh, 1998). To justify police action by saying that 'the computer told me to do it' or 'I am only the messenger' is not acceptable in most policing contexts.

These cognitive weaknesses and devices for behavioural modification would not present as serious problems if AI systems were omniscient and infallible, but they are not. Many of the most influential formulas in machine learning are based on a central tenet that machines (like people) can rarely be certain about the information and evidence under consideration. They will usually lack the complete data that they need and the time needed to process it in order to be precise. Instead, inferences or 'best guesses' based on mathematical probabilities are drawn from the available information because it is the best that can be done (Russell and Norvig, 2014). Bostrom (2017: 11) describes the enterprise as an exercise in finding "shortcuts ... by sacrificing some optimality or generality while preserving enough to get high performance in the actual domains of interest". Machine learning programmes can set themselves apart from human beings by their ability to analyse vast amounts of new information and consider a huge number of different probabilities and hypothetical outcomes, rapidly and simultaneously, in order to generate 'best guesses', but they still lack certainty. This is perhaps well reflected in the on-going development of driverless cars. Even an advanced understanding of the rules of the road, tort law, criminal law, and the topography of the environment, would be not sufficient for a driverless car if it approached a ball rolling across the road in front of it, with children rapidly exiting the footpath in hot pursuit. The AI systems integral to the car would need to be able to weigh up options and make quick deductions and decisions. Relying on stochastic 'best guesses' may be an issue of life or death. It is largely due to these challenges of dealing with uncertainty that self-driving cars are presently limited to particular zones and 'test sites' in the UK and the US where risks, such as children playing in the street, are artificially restricted. Self-driving AI programmes, and all of their associated hardware, have not yet been able to use best guesses to navigate partially observable and unpredictable real-life environments in a way that humans find acceptable.

Simply using AI tools as decision support or decision guidance systems to improve levels of uncertainty and inconsistency in police decision-making, then, is not as straightforward as the casual observer might think. Mechanical processes may have the allure of consistency, integrity and transparency, but the opposite can be true. The presence of uncertainty means that they have a propensity to be wrong at least some of the time. Some AI systems and algorithms that have been developed for the criminal justice system have reported accuracy rates of between 50 and 70 per cent (Berk and Bleich, 2014; Valentine, 2019). One facial recognition technology used in the UK was reported to have been wrong almost 90 per cent of the time (BBC, 2018). In the US, Berk et al. (2009) developed a recidivist model that generated about twelve false positives for every successful forecast over a two year period. This means that several products can be wrong a significant proportion of the time, and in some cases more often than not. It is due to some of these reasons that various predictive algorithms that are available today are considered to be little more than immature systems, pseudoscientific and 'junk' (O'Neil, 2016; Fry, 2018).

Studies in the UK, the US and Australia have shown that police officers and other criminal justice practitioners are capable of exercising their substantial discretion to disregard algorithmic outputs that are clearly wrong or conflict with their better judgement (Dencik et al., 2018; Stevenson, 2018). For instance, where an algorithm generates a relatively high-risk score for violence for an infant, as happened in California (Ferguson, 2017a), it may be reasonably easy for a police officer to assume that an algorithm has made a mistake or overestimated likelihood. However, it is clearly much harder to assess the accuracy and probity of a risk score of 320 out of 500 for a particular individual. Police officers may be expected to make big decisions on the basis of little more than this incomplete piece of information. They would be expected (we assume) to factor in the variation or unexplained portion and how much weight should be attached to the possibility of error. On the basis of what researchers have reported during the piloting of algorithmic systems, and what academics think they already know about police decision-making and cognitive weaknesses in general, we have some concerns.

Police offices may be told in training that AI systems are likely to misinterpret data, classify information incorrectly and generate poor outcomes in some conditions. They may even be told that they should discount an algorithmic decision where they have any doubt about its accuracy, but the aforementioned research by various psychologists and behavioural scientists suggests that this may not count for much in practice. In the absence of a clear and obvious reason to seriously doubt the veracity of an AI output, its best guess and problem-solving capabilities are likely to be considered superior to human intuition or analysis in practice. One concern is that by trusting an AI output, the process may lead to a self-fulfilling prophecy. A hypothetical example could unfold as follows. First, if an algorithm has classified a person or place according to their likelihood of violence, which is a common feature of current models, officers may adopt a negative demeanour (body language and tone of voice etc.) from the outset. A case could, for example, involve a domestic violence call which can be particularly hazardous for police officers and suggest a 'hard' policing approach, but unbeknown to the algorithm the aggressor could be suffering from mental health problems, who would benefit from a 'soft' policing approach and the creation of a safe space for dialogue and communication (McDaniel, 2018). However, by following the algorithmic score and adopting a harder posture, the officers' demeanours may have the knock-on effect of causing an individual to react negatively to the initial interaction out of fear, or a perception of stigmatisation. The process may escalate quickly, involving the use of force (perhaps even the use of a taser or firearm), thus validating the high risk score in the first instance.

If arrested, the high risk score may subsequently increase the likelihood that the individual is denied bail or sentenced to imprisonment rather than being diverted to a rehabilitation programme, once again justifying the initial risk score. This could condemn a person's life chances further because it may affect their ability to secure employment, housing and child support, which are increasingly being influenced by AI classification technologies in a myriad of ways (Eubanks, 2018). If similar sequences occurred across places that are also designated by algorithms as high-risk zones or hotspots, the link between crime and place could be reinforced. At each stage, an algorithmic output may be proven correct partly because police officers proceeded from the outset as though it already was. This insidious process has been described as a 'pernicious' feedback loop and a 'perpetual line up' of people and places that are condemned by flawed AI or, more particularly, by how algorithm outputs are interpreted by officials and police officers on the ground (Garvie, 2016; Bennett Moses and Chan, 2018). Rather than contributing to a more objective policing style, the AI outputs may lead instead to increased alienation and disproportionality in policing, greater social control of particular parts of the population, and rising inequality, poverty and other forms of structural violence. Yet, it may continue to appear to the outside observer that an algorithm or machine learning system is accurate since its high risk designations keep coming true. The risk of AI technologies being used in ways that exacerbate injustice, inequality and poverty is considered to be so great that commentators have likened the users of some AI to small children playing with bombs (Bostrom, 2017). O'Neil (2016) goes as far as describing some of them as 'Weapons of Math Destruction (WMDs)'. The thought of bomb-like AI systems acting as choice architects in policing is far from comforting.

Unfortunately, policing has been down a similar road before. A DNA match is a probability score based on the number of markers present in a sample, yet forensic processes and the expert testimonies that went with them contributed to several serious miscarriages of justice in the recent past before their limitations and flaws were properly understood (Walker and Starmer, 1993). Confirmation bias and framing played a part. Case law is replete with examples of the admission of evidence and expert testimony that was believed to be scientific and valid at the time but was discredited years later. Various sorts of 'junk science' gained a foothold in the justice system for significant periods of time largely because of cognitive weaknesses and lack of independent scrutiny and validation (Valentine, 2019). Although one of the primary aims of the developers of these technologies is to disrupt existing practices and replace them with more efficient and convenient solutions, stakeholders must remain cognisant of cognitive weaknesses and how they can potentially be exploited by new technologies like AI, intentionally or otherwise. Consideration should be given to each new class of algorithm and AI system that is introduced so that the unique ways that each tool may influence the decision-making of police officers are properly understood and addressed. Police organisations should be able to point to rigorous empirical experiments and independent assessments to prove it. If they cannot, lives and livelihoods could be put at undue risk, repeating the errors of the past.

Choice architects within police organisations

Thus far we have outlined how choice architecture can influence the development of AI technologies and the potential of AI to function as a choice architect. Our final section concerns the choice architecture surrounding police interventions in practice. What police organisations decide to do with the AI systems they procure or develop is important, and their policies can play a significant role in organising contexts with a view to influencing how police officers use these technologies in practice. It is not the machine learning elements of algorithmic tools that decide what to do with the risk scores they generate, it is for the police organisation to make this determination by way of policy and practitioner decision-making. AI outputs can serve as a good prompt to address crime problems and other social and economic issues, but the policing organisation remains a key choice architect in influencing what happens next.

As we outlined in the introduction to the text, police officers and their wider organisations are renowned for focusing predominantly on short time-scales, and immediate solutions to pressing issues (Francis et al., 2004). As Skogan (2019: 34) observes, "street officers typically define problems very narrowly ... two thirds of the time their proposed solution [does] ... not go past arresting someone". Part of this is attributable to the uncertainty associated with longer-term strategies. The causes of crime often have socio-economic or psychological roots which police services cannot address in isolation. Partner agencies, in turn, tend to have a host of other priorities and a shared attraction to short-term measures that achieve partial results. Humans have a tendency to crave short-term gains even if they are likely to be detrimental in the longer-term (Thaler and Sunstein, 2008).

Various police services in the UK, US and Australia are currently developing and piloting AI algorithms that generate risk scores about people who are deemed to be at high risk of engaging in future offending or of being harmed (Turing Institute, 2017; see Chapter 9). They can also rank order people accordingly. These lists have become colloquially known as 'heat lists', and the high risk offenders and victims on them are often referred to as 'hot people' (Ferguson, 2017b). One of the main rationales for rank-ordering high risk individuals is the well-known fact that a large proportion of violent crime is committed by a relatively small group of high rate offenders, and committed against a relatively small number of repeat victims (Pease and Farrell, 2017). Since police services are constrained by limited resources, identifying those offenders, victims and places of highest risk means that they can concentrate their scarce resources on interventions for the small percentage of people and places that are connected to the greatest amount of harm (Sherman, 2007)

In theory, an intervention can simply involve notifying an individual of their 'at risk' status in an attempt to reduce the risk of offending or harm. An officer might visit them at home or could arrange for them to speak with a widely respected community representative, rehabilitated criminals or gang members or past victims of such offences so that they might better appreciate the nature of their current trajectory. The aim is usually to deter or protect them through persuasion (Kennedy, 2019). Alternatively, an officer might attempt to refer them to a social worker, a debt management agency, a drink or drugs rehabilitation service, a mental health well-being organisation, an employment agency or an appropriate educational provider, if it was determined that issues across one or more of these areas could be contributing to their risk score. Although the police often 'pretend that they are society's best defence against crime', it is these processes that are arguably more effective in the long-term (Bayley, 1994). Intervening for the purposes of substantially influencing the context for the offender in these ways is now commonly referred to as 'pulling levers policing' or 'focussed-deterrence' strategies (Braga et al., 2001; 2008). Such interventions have also been labelled as 'person-based predictive targeting', 'pre-crime policing' and 'hot people policing' (Perry et al., 2013; Weisburd and Braga, 2019).

There are broader arguments about whether police officers, even in partnership with other officials, are the most appropriate public officials to engage in such interventions but it is unnecessary to engage in this debate here. The key point, at least at present, is that police officers can, regardless of how unreasonable or burdensome it may be (legislators could establish clearer boundaries for police work in many areas). Although 'good police work' is closely, and somewhat unfortunately, associated with pursuing 'bad' people and cracking difficult investigations, it is the solving of broader problems that should occupy a significant proportion of police time, even if those solutions have mental health, psychological, educational or social dimensions (Goldstein, 1979; Eck, 2019). This is not to say that all police officers must spend their days thinking about the solutions to wider problems. People will call the police for help and the solution surely is not to answer the call by responding:

> Yes ma'am, your ex-husband is trying get into your house and the children are terrified. Don't worry. When the relevant social issues have been resolved, he won't want to any more!

Quick and imperfect decision-making within unpredictable and partially observable environments has an important role to play. We have already outlined how AI technologies can support and shape such processes.

Where the police organisation's role as a choice architect comes into clear focus is the setting of more strategic policies. A good example of this variety of choice architecture is the aforementioned HART tool, which is used by one police service in the UK to help custody officers determine whether individuals are suitable to be diverted away from the criminal justice system and into a rehabilitation programme. The rehabilitation part involves referrals to drug and alcohol abuse services, homeless charities or mental health practitioners where appropriate. Using the random forests technique, the system analyses dozens of variables, including the individual's criminal history, their age and gender, to predict whether they are low, medium or high risk of reoffending within the next two years (Babuta et al., 2018). The tool does not ultimately decide what to do at each of these levels, this is for the police service to decide at a policy level. In the case of HART, the policy is that if they are deemed to be at high risk then they will most likely be detained in custody, whereas if they are determined to be low risk then they are not in sufficient need of referral (but are still at risk). Only the 'medium' category are recommended for the Checkpoint programme (Oswald et al., 2018). This was ultimately a policy decision taken by Durham Constabulary, in collaboration with partner institutions such as the University of Cambridge, to set the thresholds for intervention. The police service has the final say on deciding what to do at each level, including whether to establish interventions for low risk people, and made a conscious decision to limit it in this way.

Police service have finite resources and usually far fewer resources than are needed to fully address the crime and social problems within their areas, so these types of strategic decisions are routine. Police leaders must decide what policies to apply to designated classes, whether those classes were pre-determined as part of an AI tool's design or developed by the police service in order to differentiate and categorise statistical outputs. Where classes are determined by an AI or a hand-crafted algorithm, such as hotspots which may be marked on a digital map by colour-coded squares and circles, or individuals who are designated as low risk on a heat list, policy decisions must be made about what to do, in general, and what to do about the other areas and people that did not meet the particular thresholds for inclusion (Manning, 2004; Rosenbaum, 2019). The prioritisation of one place over another, one class of offender or victim over another, or one crime type over another is a choice. Allocating resources according to perceived risk (known as risk-led policing or risk-based deployment) can leave places untended and people ignored, creating an uneven distribution of justice across place and crime type (Cook, 2006).

These context-setting decisions can subsequently influence the way that AI systems are used in practice and the way that police officers are taught to perceive particular criminals and crime types. AI developers may think it humorous to use comic book iconography and may not know the precise future uses of the technologies they develop, but police services should know exactly how the technologies they use are being applied in practice. They may not know how the tools operate internally but they should know how each technology is being systematically applied on a day-to-day basis. For example, if individuals who live in or visit places that are frequently designated as hotspots are being (lazily) classified as individuals who are interested in the same things, and if their association with property and place is defining them as targets for police action, then police administrators should be able to spot this. It could indicate that AI outputs are wrong or that police officers are misinterpreting the tools. Similarly, if people who are living in areas that are attractive to burglars because of low quality housing or drug-dealers because of population density, among other factors, are being unfairly tarred with the same brushes and subjected to disproportionate rates of police stops and property searches, these trends should show up if police administrators scrutinise police work in practice. The history of policing has shown that police organisations are susceptible to these types of stereotyping (Newburn and Jones, 2007). In some neighbourhoods, correlations between poverty, race and place meant that some groups systematically experienced less favourable treatment and more oppressive social control at the hands of police officers than their neighbours (Ferguson, 2017a). Police services should be highly sensitive to it. The strategic policies that they set and the types of police practices that they permit (silence can imply consent) play a significant role in organising contexts with a view to influencing the way police officers make decisions in practice.

Unfortunately, rather than devising effective policing strategies that speak to the real social, economic, psychological and physical reality within and without hotspots, it is not unusual for police leaders to persist with a reliance on police patrols as their primary intervention strategy. Although algorithms can now help with the optimisation of patrol time in crime hotspots (Pease and Tseloni, 2014), police patrol has long proven to be one of the most rudimentary forms of intervention available to police officers (Kelling et al., 1974; Gottfredson and Hirschi, 1990; Mazerolle and Ransley, 2006). Studying the use of one new crime mapping model, Mohler et al. (2015) found that officers were frequently sent to crime hotspot without any information, just told to go there and see what happens. If police history has taught officers anything, it is that they will rarely, if ever, stumble upon a crime in progress (Bayley, 1994). What is more likely to happen is that officers will engage more aggressively in citizen interactions, use force more often (including tasers and firearms), utilise their powers of arrest (of homeless people, for example) and stop and search (potentially guided by their prejudices) on the basis of weak justifications, simply because they have been told that an area is high risk and they need to do something about it (Eck, 2019). Instances of stop and search, vehicle stops and overt surveillance may even increase where the hotspot is identified by an algorithm because police officers may infer that it is statistically more likely that the people found there are involved in criminality. Ferguson (2017a) suggests that high-risk individuals found within hotspots may be particularly affected; their liberty may be routinely curtailed because of a quasi-permanent generalised suspicion. Where police officers are routinely armed or practice unorthodox physical restraints, the risk is not just to their liberty but also to their lives (McDaniel, 2019). Alternatively, police officers can be overly lenient in high crime areas, failing to take reports or make arrests for minor and 'normal' offences that would otherwise prompt a formal response in another (low crime) geographical location (Goldstein, 1979; Klinger, 1997). Due to the high volume of crime and the limited capability of police services to respond to all calls for service or solve the structural causes underpinning them, they may choose to focus predominantly on the more serious deviant acts reported. Rosenbaum (2019) observes that police officers can view themselves as the thin blue line around the hotspot, separating good from evil, whether that involves relying on oppressive tactics or the negotiation of conduct norms.

Unchecked use of algorithmic and AI systems can quite easily serve to reinforce forms of prioritisation, stereotyping and over-policing that have long been associated with modern police work. The use of classification algorithms may, in practice, generate the same quantity of 'dirty data' (if not in greater volumes) and the same types of pernicious feedback loops because of the way they are used by the police (Joh, 2018; Richardson et al., 2019). Crime types that were not a traditional priority, such as environmental crimes, sophisticated online scams, modern slavery or drug use in wealthy neighbourhoods and on university campuses, may remain as secondary or tertiary priorities (see Chapter 2). Inequities in the deployment of police resources and use of police powers may remain commonplace. The choice architecture surrounding police policy decisions around AI may simply continue to send police officers back to those same people and places that they regularly policed in the first instance. Rather than realising a fairer and more objective policing model, the ways that AI technologies are used by police services may contribute to the perception that policing is still something that one part of society predominantly inflicts upon another. Employing AI technologies to legitimise or add the veneer of 'science' or objectivity to unfair, biased or illegal policing practices can be thought of as a form of 'tech-washing' (Ferguson, 2017a).

None of the 'pre-crime' interventions that we have come across have gained the sort of academic approval as those created by crime scientists in recent years in an attempt to 'design out crime' (which we discussed in the introduction to the text). There is anecdotal evidence to suggest that focused-deterrence strategies, such as the sending of an intervention letter, the signing of an 'acceptable behaviour contract' or a home visit to notify an offender that they are on a heat list may even be considered to be a badge of honour for some recidivist offenders because they can convey to their peers just how dangerous they are (Rosenbaum, 2019). Violence increased after the introduction of heat lists in Chicago in the long run; and long-term crime rates rose after PredPol's crime mapping software was piloted in Kent (Chowdhury, 2018).

More consideration must be given to the arrangements in place at the policy level. Otherwise, the use of AI in policing may increasingly (and unfairly) be associated with interventions that simply do not work. While a tool itself may not be great (due to biases and best guesses), how the tool is used in the hands of a police officer may be worse, causing both police practitioners and the public to lose faith. Despondence may be particularly acute where well documented mistakes are made. As Perry et al. (2013) observe, humans tend to instinctively make judgements based on the first few successful or failed outcomes that they experience rather than over a longer time frame. Part of the responsibility for this lies with police leaders for the choices that they make with a view to influencing police officer decision-making and activity on the ground.

It is frequently argued that if machine learning algorithms can successfully identify high risk people and predict offences, then we, as a society, have a moral obligation to utilise them. However, we also have a moral obligation to strike a balance between such possibilities and key principles that define modern and progressive human societies, not least liberty, fairness and equality. The conduct of police services thus far suggests that this balance is not being struck, and that the introduction of AI technologies may only make matters worse. A variety of human biases may undermine the potential benefits that some AI technologies have, even though they carry inherent weaknesses and biases themselves. Choice architects have a major role to play in this enterprise. They can organise an AI's environment by selecting the data sets that are inputted, the weighting attached to some variables, the outputs deemed to be worthy of reward, and the feedback used. They can also organise the environment within which police officers operate and influence how they use AI outputs and perceive the policing job. Even AI systems can function as choice architects, particularly where humans subconsciously allow them to organise contexts and expect them to make sense of complex situations on their behalf.

The reality on the ground is that the choice architecture at the nexus of policing and AI appears to be ill-considered and pernicious in nature. Rather than contributing to a choice architecture that is benevolent and inclusive, the activities of police organisations appear to speak to ideas of technocracy and more centralised and dehumanised decision-making systems. Similar trends can be seen in other fields, such as healthcare (see Chapter 4). One underlying reason for this trend, which we have not yet addressed, may be the unequal relationship that exists between police services and the commercial developers of AI products. Some police services are trying to develop AI technologies in-house but this is a rarity due to the costs, resources and expertise involved. In meetings and negotiations with AI companies, senior police leaders who are responsible for commissioning new technologies are likely to lack confidence and be deferential because of their comparable lack of expertise about computer and data sciences. In conditions of uncertainty and complexity, there is a strong and natural impulse for decision-makers to defer to experts, who can then exploit their confusion (Thaler and Sunstein, 2008). Far from being a partnership of equals, the relationship between police organisations and the AI companies they deal with is similar to that of a subject (the police) and a choice architect (the AI provider), much like our shopper in the supermarket.

Pressure to commission AI technologies can also come from external consultants. Police forces pay hundreds of thousands of pounds to professional services firms to audit them for efficiencies and savings for the purposes of recommending reforms and change agendas. The solution proffered by many of these firms is to incorporate AI technologies and harness data analytics, machine learning algorithms and automation across police organisations as soon as possible to benefit from cost savings and organisational efficiencies (Deloitte, 2018). In some cases, these firms have even been directly involved in the development of AI products for the police (Law Society, 2019). Such firms must recognise that they too are choice architects, for police decision-makers will consider them to be experts in organisational efficiencies and AI in an environment where the police officer is a relative novice. They should, for instance, be careful about making gross over-simplifications about the ability of AI technologies, such as 'bots', to free up police officer and staff time in areas that are 'not particularly fun or glamorous' so that police officers and staff can 'focus where their skills are most valuable' (Deloitte, 2018: 38). This is a common cliché. Much of what police officers do is not particularly fun nor glamorous, yet it is precisely their ability to make human decisions and important trade-offs in a variety of contexts that contributes to their importance.

Police services must finally determine how to forge relationships between the AI technologies that they use and the general public who are supposed to benefit from them. As choice architects, they can organise contexts with a view to influencing the way civilians make decisions during and after interactions with police officers. Like the customer in a supermarket, how an AI is presented (or not) and how the broader environment is shaped by a choice architect can affect people's moods and feelings towards it. Unfortunately, police services in the UK, US and Australia are not routinely and pre-emptively notifying the public about the AI systems that they are developing or using, the data used to inform those systems, and the impact that they are having in practice (Ferguson, 2017a; Turing Institute, 2017; Joh, 2018; Valentine, 2019). Some police forces state that algorithms are being used only for insights and are not directly influencing police practices on the street, whereas others explain that algorithm outputs are only one factor among many, so their influence is difficult if not impossible to discern. In many cases, it is not even clear whether and to what extent AI technologies have played a large, small or no role at all in the functioning of various algorithms or calculations. Police organisations may not even know how they are being used in practice and the impact they are having simply because appropriate equality impact assessments and independent evaluations were never carried out. This is not unique to policing either. In the UK, the Law Society (2019: 4) found 'a lack of explicit standards, best practice, and openness or transparency about the use of algorithmic systems in criminal justice across England and Wales'.

It is important that if citizens want to know exactly what police officers think algorithm outputs are saying and how police officers (and staff) are applying them in practice, they should be able to find out with relative ease. Mechanisms of accountability should enable them to seek answers, raise concerns, challenge police practices and secure remedies with minimal effort (Walsh, 1998; McDaniel and Lavorgna, 2020). Extant AI technologies are not so technically novel that people should suddenly find themselves unable to ask questions of the police. 'Black box' machine learning algorithms may be constantly changing as their calculations, source code and modelling evolve rapidly, with and without human interference, but as Joh (2018) argues, if the police are able to make disclosures about their use of AI systems with reference to considerations of cost and ease of use, they should be just as prepared to explain their decision with reference to issues of legal necessity, public trust, police legitimacy and individual privacy. Conventional mechanisms of police accountability, which continue to be far from perfect, were not designed to address the sort of complex mathematical processes that exist within AI systems but they were designed to address how police officers should communicate with and justify their actions to members of the public. The use of AI in policing should be done explicitly. However, since several police services have been less than forthcoming about their uses and intentions for AI, various academic commentators have recommended a taxonomy of concepts and measures to facilitate greater accountability. These include the publication of risk and equality impact assessments before new tools are deployed, whole system evaluations as they are being piloted, and accessible remedies, among other measures (see Chapter 7). Each new mechanism of accountability may play a role in (re)organising choice environments.

Conclusion

Police services have long been concerned with command and control functions which rely on the threat of legal sanction (whether through misconduct, performance or legal processes) to explicitly influence the behaviour of police officers. External police oversight bodies evolved in recent decades to monitor and influence these processes. Community-based and political mechanisms were also established in many places to let police services know how well they were doing, and to guide their activities. However, what has been relatively neglected until now is the examination of the broader network of choice architects who play a considerable role in designing and organising contexts with a view to influencing the way police officers make decisions. The introduction of AI technologies has helped to bring some of these issues to the fore, at least in our minds. Many choice architects are probably unaware of the effects their activities are having at the police–civilian interface (the lack of evaluation suggests that this is likely the case). This chapter has outlined numerous reasons why police services, AI developers and their choice architects should proceed with caution. Human opinions and values will likely be embedded within the mathematics of AI systems and the policies of police services in some configuration, whether or not care is taken. It is not simply a question of whether models are flawed but in which ways are they flawed, and what to do about each one. Dwelling on the risks of harm and inequality more than on the potential upsides of AI technologies might be worth the effort (Law Society, 2019). Viewing developments through the lens of choice architecture may help stakeholders to determine whether they are content with the choice environments and, if not, how to effect change.

It appears less likely that policing will be transformed beyond all recognition by an uncritical reliance on AI technologies, rather they will be used to reinforce, justify and perhaps amplify the types of policing practices that police officers have long been accustomed to. Many extant AI technologies already seem to do things that the police want them to do, i.e. focus on offenders at high risk of violence and recognise wanted criminals, rather than encouraging them to engage in more resource-intensive problem-oriented policing strategies. They may even lead to police organisations using AI outputs and recommendations to purposely tighten employee surveillance and supervisory control in order to limit the discretion of police officers for narrow-minded and short-term ends. AI outputs are a convenient source of justification for a 'target culture' and can encourage technocratic decisions to be made at a greater psychological distance from the people they impact (Brundage et al., 2018). Although police officers might try to rail against such pernicious efforts, manipulate the statistics they record, continue to exercise their discretion, and hide their actions from their supervisors (Law Society, 2019), choice architecture can act as a powerful influencer of human behaviour. Without a clear understanding of the choice architecture in place, we will not be able to tell whether police officers are being influenced, or nudged, and by whom. Neither will they.

References

Acquisti, A., Brandimarte, L. and Loewenstein, G. (2015). Privacy and human behaviour in the age of information. *Science*, 347(6221), pp. 509–514.

Babuta, A., Oswald, M. and Rinik, C. (2018). Machine learning algorithms and police decision-making: legal. *Ethical and Regulatory Challenges*. London: Royal United Services Institute (RUSI).

Bainbridge, L. (1983). Ironies of automation. *Automatica*, 19(6), pp. 775–779.

Bayley, D.H. (1994). *Police for the future*. Oxford: Oxford University Press.

BBC. (2018). 2,000 wrongly matched with possible criminals at Champions League. BBC News. Accessed at: www.bbc.co.uk/news/uk-wales-south-west-wales-44007872 on 1 December 2018.

Bennett Moses, L. and Chan, J. (2018). Algorithmic prediction in policing: assumptions, evaluation, and accountability. *Policing and Society*, 28(7), pp. 806–822.

Berk, R. and Bleich, J. (2014). Forecasts of violence to inform sentencing decisions. *J Quant Criminal*, 30, pp. 79–96.

Berk, R., Sherman, L., Barnes, G., Kurtz, E. and Ahlman, L. (2009). Forecasting murder within a population of probationers and parolees: a high stakes application of statistical learning. *Journal of the Royal Statistical Society*, 172(1), pp. 1–21.

Bittner, E. (1970). *The functions of the police in modern society*. Oelgeschlager, Gunn and Hain.

Blount, K. (2017). Body worn cameras with facial recognition technology. *Crim. L. Prac.*, 3, p. 61.

Bostrom, N. (2017). *Superintelligence: paths, dangers, strategies*. Oxford: Oxford University Press.

Bowling, B. and Phillips, C. (2003). Policing ethnic minority communities. In: Newburn, Tim, (ed.) *Handbook of policing*. Devon: Willan Publishing, pp. 528–555.

Braga A.A, Kennedy D.M, Waring E.J and Piehl A.M (2001). Problem-oriented policing, deterrence, and youth violence: an evaluation of Boston's operation ceasefire. *J Res Crime Delinq*, 38, pp. 195–225.

Braga, A.A (2008). Pulling levers focused deterrence strategies and the prevention of gun homicide. *Journal of Criminal Justice*, 36(4), pp. 332–343.

Brayne, S. (2017). Big data surveillance: the case of policing, *American Sociological Review*, 82(5), pp. 977–1008.

Brundage, M. et al. (2018). *The Malicious Use of Artificial Intelligence: Forecasting, Prevention and Mitigation*. Future of Humanity Institute, University of Oxford (and others). February 2018.

Chan, J.B.L. (1997). *Changing police culture: policing in a multicultural society*. Cambridge: Cambridge University Press.

Chowdhury, H. (2018). Kent police stop using crime predicting software. *The Telegraph*, 28 November 2018.

Coles, N. (2001). It's not *what* you know—it's *who* you know that counts. Analysing serious crime groups as social networks. *The British Journal of Criminology*, 41(4/1), pp. 580–594.

Cook. D. (2006). *Criminal and Social Justice*. London: Sage.

Deloitte. (2018). Policing 4.0: deciding the future of policing in the UK.

Dencik, L., Hintz, A. and Carey, Z. (2018). Prediction, pre-emption and limits to dissent: social media and big data uses for policing protests in the United Kingdom. *New Media and Society*, 20(4), pp. 1433–1450.

Eck, J.E. (2019). Why problem-oriented policing. In: Weisburd, D. and Braga, A.A (eds), *Police Innovation: Contrasting Perspectives*. Cambridge: Cambridge University Press, pp. 165–178.

Eubanks, V. (2018) *Automating Inequality*. St Martin's Press.

Ferguson, A.G. (2017a) The rise of big data Policing: surveillance. *Race and the Future of Law Enforcement*. New York: NYU Press.

Ferguson, A.G. (2017b). Policing predictive policing. *Washington University Law Review*, 94:5, p. 1109.

Forgas, J.P. and East, R. (2008). On being happy and gullible: mood effects on skepticism and the detection of deception. Journal of Experimental Social Pscyhology, 44(5), pp. 1362–1367.

Francis, B., Soothill, K. and Fligelstone, R. (2004). Identifying patterns and pathways of offending behaviour. *European Journal of Criminology*, 1(1), pp. 47–87.

Fry, H. (2018). Hello world: how to be human in the age of the machine. London: Random House.

Garvie, C. (2016). *The perpetual line-up*. Georgetown Law Centre.

Goldstein, H. (1979). Improving policing: a problem-oriented approach. *Crime and Delinquency*, 25(2) pp. 236–258.

Gottfredson, M. R., and Hirschi, T. (1990). *A general theory of crime*. Stanford University Press.

Hall, S., Critcher, C., Jefferson, T., Clarke, J. and Roberts, B. (1982). *Policing the crisis: Mugging and law and order*. London: Macmillan.

Holdaway, S. and O'Neill, M. (2006). *Institutional racism after Macpherson: an analysis of police views*, Policing and Society, 10.1080/10439460600967885, 16, 4 (349–369).

House of Lords Select Committee on Artificial Intelligence (HLAI). (2018). AI in the UK: ready, willing and able?, Report of Session 2017–19, HL Paper 100

Joh, E.E. (2018). *Artificial intelligence and policing: first questions. Seattle University Law Review*, 41, pp. 1139–1144.

Jones, J.M. (2017). Killing fields: explaining police violence against persons of colour. *Journal of Social Issues*, 73(4).

Kahneman, D. and Tversky, A. (1979). Prospect Theory: An Analysis of Decision under Risk, Econometrica, 47(2), pp. 263–292.

Kelling, G.L., Pate, A.M., Dieckman, D., and Brown, C. (1974). *The Kansas City preventive patrol experiment: technical report*. Washington, DC: Police Foundation.

Kennedy, D.M. (2019). Policing and the lessons of focused deterrence. In: Weisburd, D. and Braga, A.A (eds), *Police innovation: contrasting perspectives*. Cambridge: Cambridge University Press, pp. 205–221.

Kerr, I. and Szilagyi, K. (2018). Evitable conflicts. *Inevitable Technologies? Law Culture and Humanities*, 14(1), pp. 45–82.

Klinger, D.A. (1997). Negotiating order in patrol work: an ecological theory of police response to deviance. *Criminology*, 35(2), pp. 277–306.

Law Society. (2019). Algorithms in the Criminal Justice System. *The Law Society Commission on the Use of Algorithms in the Justice System*, June 2019.

Lemm, S., Blankertz, B., Dickhaus, T. and Muller, K.R. (2011). Introduction to machine learning for brain imaging. *NeuroImage*, 56(2/15), pp. 387–399.

MacPherson, Lord (1999). The Stephen Lawrence Enquiry. Cm. 4262-1.

Manning, P.K. (1984). Community policing. *American Journal of Police*, 3(2), pp. 205–227.

Manning, P.K. (2004). Police technology: crime analysis. *Criminal Justice Matters*, 58, pp. 26–27.

Mazerolle, L. and Ransley, J. (2006). *Third Party Policing*. Cambridge: Cambridge University Press.

McDaniel, J.L.M and Lavorgna, A. (2020). Enhancing the transparency and account-ability of transnational police cooperation within the European Union. In: John McDaniel, Karlie Stonard and David Cox (eds), *The development of transnational policing: past, present and future*. Abingdon: Routledge.

McDaniel, J.L.M. (2018). Rethinking the law and politics of democratic police account-ability. *The Police Journal*, 91(1), 22–43.

McDaniel, J.L.M. (2019). Reconciling mental health, public policing and police accountability. *The Police Journal*, 92(1), pp. 72–94.

Mohler, G.O. et al. (2015). Randomized controlled field trials of predictive policing. *Journal of American Statistical Association*, 110(512), pp. 1399–1411.

Muir, W.K (1979). *Police: Streetcorner Politicians*. University of Chicago Press.

Newburn, T. and Jones, T. (2007) Symbolizing crime control: reflections on zero toler-ance. *Theoretical Criminology*, 11(2), pp. 221–243.

O'Neil, C. (2016). *Weapons of Math Destruction: How Big Data Increases Inequality and Threatens Democracy*. Random House.

O'Neil, C. and Schutt, R. (2013). *Doing Data Science: Straight Talk from the Frontline*. Boston: O'Reilly Media, Inc.

Oswald, M., Grace, J., Urwin, S. and Barnes, G.C. (2018). Algorithmic risk assessment policing models: lessons from the Durham HART model and 'Experimental' propor-tionality. *Information & Communications Technology Law*, 27(2), pp. 223–250.

Packer, H. (1964). Two models of the criminal process. *University of Pennsylvania Law Review*, 113(1), pp. 1–68.

Pease, K. and Farrell, G. (2017). Repeat victimisation. In: Wortley, Richard and Townsley, Michael (eds), *Environmental Criminology and Crime Analysis, 2nd Edition*. Abingdon, Oxon: Routledge, pp. 180–198.

Pease, K. and Tseloni, A. (2014). *Using Modeling to Predict and Prevent Victimization*. Springer International Publishing.

Perry, W.L. et al. (2013). *Predictive policing: the role of crime forecasting in law enforcement operations*. Rand Corporation.

Rawls, J. (1985). Justice as fairness: political not metaphysical. *Philosophy and Public Affairs*, 14(3), pp. 223–251.

Richardson, R., Schultz, J. and Crawford, K. (2019). Dirty data, bad predictions: how civil rights violations impact police data, predictive policing systems, and justice. *NYU Law Review*, 94, pp. 192–233.

Rosenbaum, D.P. (2019). The limits of hot spots policing. In: Weisburd, D. and Braga, A.A (eds), *Police Innovation: Contrasting Perspectives*. Cambridge: Cambridge University Press, pp. 314–336.

Royal Society. (2017). Machine learning: the power and promise of computers that learn by example. *The Royal Society*, April 2017 DES4702.

Russell, S. and Norvig, P. (2014). *Artificial Intelligence: A Modern Approach, 3rd Edition.* Harlow: Pearson Education Limited.

Schulenberg, J.L. (2010). Patterns in police decision-making with youth. *Crime Law and Social Change,* 53, pp. 109–129.

Sherman, L.W. (2007). The power few: experimental criminology and the reduction of harm. *Journal of Experimental Criminology,* 3, pp. 299–321.

Skitka, L. (1999). Does automation bias decision-making? *Int. J. Human-Computer Studies,* 51, pp. 991–1006.

Skogan, W. (2019). Community policing. In: Weisburd, D. and Braga, A.A (eds), *Police innovation: contrasting perspectives.* Cambridge: Cambridge University Press, pp. 27–42.

Skolnick, J.H. (1966). *Justice Without Trial: Law Enforcement in Democratic Society.* New York: John Wiley & Sons.

Stevenson, M. (2018). Assessing risk assessment in action. *Minnesota Law Review,* pp. 303–378.

Thaler, R.H. and Sunstein, C.R. (2008). *Nudge: Improving Decisions About Health, Wealth and Happiness.* New Haven, Connecticut: Yale University Press.

Turing Institute. (2017). Ethics Advisory Report for West Midlands Police.

Valentine, S. (2019). Impoverished algorithms: misguided governments, flawed technologies and social control. *Forham Urb L.J.,* pp. 364–427.

van Maanen, J. (1974). Working the streets: a developmental view of police behavior. In: H. Jacob (ed.) *The potential for reform of criminal justice.* Beverly Hills, California: Sage, pp. 53–130.

van Maanen, J. (1983). *The Boss' in Maurice Punch (ed.): Control in the Police Organisation.* MIT Press, pp. 276–308.

Waldman, P., Chapman, L. and Robertson, J. (2018). *Palantir knows everything about you.* Bloomberg.

Walker, C. and Starmer, K. (1993). *Justice in error.* London: Blackstone Press.

Walsh, D.P.J (1998). *The Irish Police: a legal and constitutional perspective.* Round Hall Sweet and Maxwell.

Weisburd, D. and Braga, A.A. (2019). *Police innovation: contrasting perspectives.* Cambridge: Cambridge University Press.

Whittlestone, J., Nyrup, R., Alexandrova, A., Dihal, K. and Cave, S. (2019). *Ethical and Societal implications of algorithms, data, and artificial intelligence: a roadmap for research.* London: Nuffield Foundation.

Wilson, J.Q. (1968). *Varieties of police behaviour.* Harvard University Press

Yeung, K. (2016). The forms and limits of choice architecture as a tool of government. *Law and Policy,* 38(3), pp. 186–210.

Yeung, K. (2017). 'Hypernudge': Big Data as a mode of regulation by design, Information. *Communication & Society,* 20(1), pp. 118–136.

Chapter 4

What big data in health care can teach us about predictive policing

I. Glenn Cohen and Harry Graver

Introduction

"Big data" already permeates our lives (Cohen and Graver, 2017; Cohen et al., 2018).[1] It can shape what music we listen to, what roads we drive on, what things we buy—even who we date. Consider a recent article in *The Guardian* titled: "I asked Tinder for my data. It sent me 800 pages of my deepest, darkest secrets" (Duportail, 2017). That being said, it's important for generalists not to take the buzzwords that often attach to "big data" and assume it involves some sort of inaccessible alchemy performed by modern Freemasons. At its core, predictive analytics—that is, what we *do* with big data—involves rather ordinary concepts. It takes past experiences, recognises patterns and makes predictions. We do this all the time in our everyday life. Recall the last time you repeated a joke to a different group of friends. In so doing, you (hopefully) thought back to how it did the first time, who laughed (and who didn't) and the setting you told it in—with those data points in mind, telling it again to new people either seems like a good idea or not. The same intuitions hold here.

But big data transforms these sorts of garden-variety predictions on two main fronts. First, on a scalar dimension, big data offers a much greater trove of information from which to make a decision from. So instead of testing your joke on one group of friends, imagine knowing how it landed across 10,000 other groups of people, sorted by demographics, with cross-sections for cadence, timing and modifications. Second, on a categorical dimension, big data involves a different mode of thinking. Predictive analytics often uses some form of machine learning—that is, an algorithm designed to analyse patterns also has the ability to independently improve upon itself based on past experience. To that end, in some instances, the way a program teaches itself to be better might not be understandable from a human perspective, creating what some have called "black box" decision-making (Kroll et al., 2017; Price II, 2016; Zarsky, 2013). In other words, people won't always be able to understand *how* an algorithm reaches a result because its original thought process might have materially changed as the product of machine learning.

As the preceding chapters make clear, the right question is not whether big data and predictive analytics are here to stay, but rather how much are they going to impact life as we know it. On this score, our chapter comes at this topic from a slightly different angle. We take two professions—police officers and doctors—and place their experiences with big data in dialogue. Policing and medicine, while naturally different in some obvious respects, actually both need to grapple with a lot of the same moral, social and legal questions that come with adopting big data programs. This is because, as we discuss below, both professions generally possess a monopoly over an acute societal vulnerability, be it safety or health, and have accordingly developed a set of settled internal norms to shape individual discretion in service of each respective function. We go about this over two Parts. Part I sets the table: we look at each profession separately and describe the big ways that predictive analytics have shaped the fields already. Part II is the meat and potatoes: we place the professions side-by-side and try to distil certain insights from the perspective of three key stakeholders—practitioners, policymakers and the polity.

PART I

Predictive analytics in policing and health care

Predictive policing

Predictions are the bread and butter of our criminal justice system. Think back to an image of a police station with red pushpins on a board mapping a crime spree. From police officers to prosecutors to judges, educated guesses have always rested at the heart of law enforcement. In light of this, the point to understand at the outset is that big data and predictive analytics—together, predictive policing—have not saddled police departments with anything *new*; rather, they have (and will continue to) transform *how* cops go about their core jobs.

Predictive policing, roughly defined, is "the application of analytical techniques—particularly quantitative techniques—to identify likely targets for police intervention and prevent crime or solve past crimes by making statistical predictions" (Perry et al., 2013). To concretise this, take the landmark case of *Terry v. Ohio*. There, the United States Supreme Court set the standard for when a police officer can stop or search someone consistent with the Constitution. The Court held that a police officer must have "reasonable suspicion." Or, in their framing: "[T]he facts available to the officer at the moment of the seizure or the search [must] warrant a man of reasonable caution in belief that the action taken was appropriate" (*Terry v. Ohio*, 1968, 392 U.S. 1, 21–22). In practical terms, this boils down to the facts on the ground combined with the personal judgment of the police officer as informed by her accumulated experience on the job (Ferguson, 2015: 336–349).

Big data totally revolutionises the *Terry* stop decision point. Understanding why this is so covers a lot of the most important and disruptive features of predictive policing today. To begin, big data has dramatically expanded the amount of information that police departments have at their fingertips. This has happened over a number of innovations in policing. For one, many departments now deploy far-reaching surveillance programs. The New York Police Department, for instance, uses the "Domain Awareness System"—a program developed with Microsoft that collects and analyses data from 3,000 cameras, 200 license-plate readers, and 2,000 radiation sensors placed around the City (Joh, 2014: 48–50). What's more, local, state and national law enforcement agencies cooperate a lot more (and a lot more efficiently) than they once did. For example, "fusion centers," developed in the aftermath of 9/11, aggregating massive troves of information, from criminal records to credit reports to insurance claims (Citron and Pasquale, 2011: 1443). Lastly, social media is a big driver behind this surge. Chicago Police, for instance, use "network analysis" to track the public social media behaviour of suspected gang members (Joh, 2014: 46–48).

Of course, the very fact that the government possesses all of this data raises a host of legal and policy questions—some of which we get into below. But the sheer mass of this new information is of little inherent value to an officer on the beat. Enter predictive policing. In particular, returning to the *Terry* stop example, predictive policing takes all of this information and provides officers with tangible outputs that can inform their decision-making. For instance, imagine you are a police officer on patrol and you see an individual pacing around a closed jewellery store. This isn't ordinarily enough to stop her under *Terry*. But suppose your department uses one of the many predictive policing tools available now that helps analyse where crimes are most likely to happen. As such, you might find yourself in one of the 500x500 foot "hot spots" where, due to a host of variables, burglaries are especially likely (Joh, 2014: 42–46). How would that impact your decision whether to stop the pacing individual (*Illinois v. Wardlow* 2000, 528 U.S. 119)? Likewise, a number of departments use programs that try to predict what individuals are most susceptible to commit a future crime. For example, Chicago, Kansas City, and New Orleans have all used programs that produce variations of a "heat list"—a list of specific persons who, because of a range of factors, are especially likely to commit a given crime (Ferguson 2017a: 1139–1143). Now suppose, due to facial recognition technology, you can tell that the person outside the jewellery store is somebody on one of those lists. Is that enough for you to stop and search the person?

The *Terry* stop example shows that while the essence of the decision points posed to officers has remained the same—here, to stop or not to stop—big data has totally changed the nature of the decision-making process because of the range of new inputs and information now available. This phenomenon can be seen from individual cops on the beat to more macro policing policies like where to locate officers or what crimes to principally focus on combatting (Ferguson, 2017b). The takeaway, as we pivot to health care, is that officers still perform similar roles today—but the *way* they do them is meaningfully changing because of big data.

Health care

The use of predictive analytics in health care is relatively recent but it has rapidly taken on many forms in short order. Consider but a few of the more interesting examples: the analysis of electronic health care records to help predict which patients have higher risks of hospital readmission (Rajkomar et al., 2018); IBM Watson's use of AI to help guide the search for genes most likely to be associated with ALS in order to guide drug development (Bakkar et al., 2018); implanted pacemakers that allow the remote monitoring of cardiac patients (Kramer and Fu, 2017); and ingestible electronic sensors, so-called "smart pills," that record when they have been ingested and send that information to the patient and his or her physician as well as the maker of the pill (Klugman et al., 2018). Again, this is just a fraction of what's out there (Cohen et al., 2018).

Big data in health care can be thought of at the macro-level as facilitating four separate goals. Consider how this comes to bear in the context of dermatology. First, democratising expertise; for instance, an artificial intelligence (AI) program that helps determine whether a skin marker is likely cancerous, which enables the average non-specialist physician or perhaps even a patient herself to make a diagnosis. Second, automating drudgery; that is, freeing up a dermatologist's time to see additional patients by automating some of her billing activities. Third, optimising resources; for example, helping a hospital system or possibly a payer determine which patients to prioritise for a visit to a dermatologist. And fourth, pushing frontiers; more specifically, augmenting the diagnostic capabilities of a dermatologist through programs like an AI that can detect cancerous lesions much earlier in their development (Price II, 2019; Cohen et al., 2014).

Naturally, these innovations come with a range of legal questions. We can't get into all of them here, but the following list offers an illustrative taste: who owns patient records, such as electronic health records, in what circumstances can they be data mined and does that require explicit consent (Cohen, 2018: 209; Kulynych and Greely, 2017)? What does "privacy" mean when it comes to medical big data, and are downstream protections (such as those of anti-discrimination law) enough to protect patient, or are upstream collection limits needed (Price II and Cohen 2019)? How does the Health Insurance Portability and Accountability Act (HIPAA) in the US and the General Data Protection Regulation (GDPR) in Europe apply to health care big data, and how might it be altered to deal with the unique privacy issues raised by big data (Price II and Cohen, 2019; Cohen and Mello, 2018; Riley: 251; Terry, 2017)? What liability do physicians, hospitals and insurers face if they rely on algorithms (especially more "black box" ones) to direct patient care, and how will courts frame the relevant duties (Froomkin, Kerr and Pineau, 2019;

Cohen et al., 2014: 1142; Price II, 2015: 443–453)? Which (if any) uses of AI in health care should require regulatory pre-approval and are traditional medical regulators (e.g. the Food and Drug Administration (FDA), European Medicines Agency (EMA)) well suited for the task (Cohen et al., 2014; Price II, 2017: 439–442)? What mechanisms exist to deal with the under-inclusion of minority health care data in typical AI training data sets potentially leading to biased results? (Malanga et al., 2018: 98). These questions do not lend themselves to easy answers. But as we turn to the next Part and begin to put policing and medicine in dialogue, we can begin to glean certain insights that can help shape solutions to these difficult problems.

PART II

The professions in dialogue

This Part contains seven themes that we find are especially salient when evaluating the impact of big data on medicine and policing. We've organised them across three perspectives. First, the practitioners; the doctors and cops themselves. Second, the policymakers; the political actors tasked with the big decisions concerning whether or how to integrate a predictive analytics program. And third, the polity; the political community actually impacted by these decisions.

Practitioners

Role disruption

From the Hippocratic Oath to "Protect and Serve," there are certain notions about what it *means* to be a doctor or police officer. These "professions," as we see it, are somewhat different than ordinary jobs (Pepper, 1986; Wasserstrom, 1975). Both doctors and cops are given a monopoly over a particular social problem: health and safety, respectively. And to gain the privilege of being a part of this restricted domain, individuals need to undergo extensive, specialised training. Against this backdrop, each profession has developed a set of distinctive norms that guide decision-making and discretion. In short, the combination of power and judgment rests at the definitional core of each role.

Critically, big data directly implicates this fundamental nexus point. In particular, the way that predictive analytics programs interact with human judgment will have lasting, transformative impacts on how practitioners conceive of their professional purpose. The medical context offers a clear picture of this dynamic. Suppose you are a doctor and you have a patient with a certain liver problem that could be addressed either with prescription drugs or a more invasive surgery. The former option is less risky, but also less effective. And suppose your hospital employs a predictive analytics program that recommends the surgery. What do you tell the patient? Perhaps something like: "Well, the algorithm we used examined your electronic health records and based on its predictive model, the surgery is more likely to produce good health outcomes for you in your case."

The nature of this interaction, and the role of the doctor, is fundamentally different from what most of us are used to in a medical encounter. In many respects, the doctor becomes less of the *decider* and more of the *messenger*. To be sure, this experience likely fluctuates depending on a handful of factors. For instance, how "black box" the algorithm is; how much the physician is allowed to deviate from its recommendation either as a matter of hospital policy, malpractice pressure or insurance reimbursement; and how it is integrated into workflow process (for example, whether the physician even reviews the recommendation and in what depth) (London, 2019).

The same sort of phenomenon exists today in policing. Consider the Manhattan District Attorney's Criminal Strategies Unit (CSU). The CSU uses predictive analytics to determine what individuals are particularly likely to continually commit serious crimes. As such, police officers and prosecutors work in conjunction to figure out both where to police most effectively and also how to prosecute such individuals once arrested. The upshot is that an individual's threat profile, as determined by this program, can be dispositive in how they are treated by the justice system—from the chance of arrest on the front end to the sentence recommendation on the back end. As with the medical context, big data alters the choice architecture here for cops because a number of threshold decisions are either automated or substantially shifted to big data programs (see Chapter 3).

One important item to flag here is that the above point has almost nothing to do with the efficacy of a given predictive analytics program. Put differently, the role-disruptive impact of integrating big data into policing or health care is inevitable irrespective of the results it produces. In both instances, what used to be quintessential opportunities for an individual's personal judgment are now endeavours partially shared with machines. Accordingly, for practitioners, the initial considerations with big data are likely going to be more concerned with *means* than *ends*. For instance, predictive analytics programs can create pressure on practitioners to focus more on compiling inputs and overseeing the propriety of algorithmic outputs, instead of fashioning individual judgments. Of a part with this, training and education might begin to take on different priorities, placing a greater premium on understanding the operation of predictive programs. We build out these more ideas in the next section. The big point we want to emphasise here, though, is that both policing and health care are professions that have developed around a core of human judgment—and because big data necessarily reshapes that core, it will unavoidably impact how these practitioners conceive of themselves.

Automation bias and discretion

In tandem with the role disruption noted above, predictive analytics can lead to a very natural professional impulse, especially as these programs get more sophisticated: just trust the computers. We do this already in many contexts. For instance, it's increasingly rare to drive anywhere these days without the assistance of Google Maps or Waze. While these applications have a tremendous upside, there are accompanying dangers to pushing human judgment too much out of the equation. For this reason, we strongly believe that the experiences of predictive analytics in both health care and policing underscore that such technologies must *complement* rather than *supplant* human judgment. Put differently, we think these programs should be treated like Popeye treated spinach; something that could empower us to conquer our most pressing problems, but a pretty ineffective freestanding solution to any of those very issues.

In our view, three intertwined dangers are particularly apparent. First, and most importantly, a skewed balance between deference and discretion leads to worse results. Ziad Obermeyer and Zeke Emanuel (2016: 1217) have observed in the medical setting that "letting the data speak for themselves can be problematic. Algorithms might 'overfit' predictions to spurious correlations in the data, or multiple collinear, correlated predictors could produce unstable estimates." Second, bad results for cutting-edge technologies often lead to disproportionate public blowback. Recall the backlash Uber received when one of its self-driving car models killed a woman in Arizona. This was certainly cause for concern, but when it comes to new technologies we tend to forget the "as against what" question. Put differently, the right question shouldn't be whether these cars might hurt people, but rather whether will they do a better job than the status quo where tens of thousands of Americans are killed every year in car accidents. Third, and relatedly, this blowback ultimately chills further innovation, compounding the aforementioned problems. Big changes in health care and policing require meaningful public buy-in—as well as government-backed capital—which is immediately and perhaps incommensurately impaired when these technologies fail.

These risks make clear that practitioners need to have a stable ex ante framework for how to balance human discretion and machine judgment as part of their reshaped roles. Pulling from the extant literature on policing and health care, we've identified three guideposts. First, it's perhaps most important for practitioners to be aware of what predictive analytics *don't do*, rather than intimately understand *how* they do what they do. By design, big data programs were never designed for users to "set it and forget it." The dangers of such a mindset are well illustrated by an example from Rich Caruana and colleagues: A "neural net" form of AI was developed and shown to be generally more accurate at predicting the probability of death from pneumonia than the leading alternatives (Caruana et al., 2015). The neural net ranked asthmatics as being at a lower risk for death by pneumonia than the general population. This is contrary to the received view and practice that a patient with asthma is in fact at *higher* risk. Had the neural net discovered a surprising "ground truth" that bucked conventional wisdom? No. The reason the program reached its conclusion is that asthmatics are admitted directly into an intensive care unit (ICU) for more aggressive medical care, thereby reducing the probability of death as against the general population. But blindly following the model without stopping to consider this would have led to asthmatics receiving less care notwithstanding their higher risk.

Second, in light of the limitations inherent to predictive analytics programs, it's crucial for practitioners to establish clear decision architectures that maintain the integrity of a holistic review. Professor Michael Rich has drawn an instructive analogy as part of a broader Fourth Amendment analysis between predictive policing initiatives and drug sniffing dogs: their outputs—be it names, locations or barks—are factors in the analysis but not the whole inquiry (Rich, 2016: 902). Third, practitioners also need to establish a mechanism for consistent reform and adaptation to account for innovation and technological change. Any such process must be incremental and, for it to succeed, take regular stock of shifting internal norms and external societal input. To be sure, this sort of recurring calibration is hard. If practitioners are too resistant to predictive analytics, and accordingly rely excessively on human judgment, we'll lose out on a promising area of innovation. By defaulting too heavily or too quickly to the same programs, however, we possibly welcome arbitrary decision-making, sub-par results and stunted public confidence. But the difficulty of this task on the front end doesn't negate its necessity.

Policymakers

The duty of explanation

As this book makes clear, there are innumerable policy considerations bound up in the decision to adopt a given predictive analytics program. One constant across initiatives, though, is the duty of policymakers to provide an explanation of their decision. In particular, when it comes to shaping policy for law enforcement or health care—fields, as discussed above, that deal exclusively with particular social vulnerabilities—recipients of those services are owed some sort of rational account for why things are the way they are. Of course, accessible "reason-giving" is difficult for almost any political program, from tax policy to where to place a post office. And this already hard task is made immensely more difficult by the nature of big data, where its innate complexity and "black box" qualities make its content largely impenetrable. For that reason, we want to place the cart before the horse a bit and focus on *how* policymakers should explain a decision to adopt a predictive analytics program rather than the decision to do so in the first place.

The health care context offers valuable insight here. In particular, the medical experience with big data underscores the importance of focusing on what *kind* of explanation adequately counts for the sort of reason-giving we have in mind. Today, in traditional non-AI forms of medicine, there is a surprising amount of information that is not only unknown to the physician, but is also not currently knowable by anyone. But this knowledge gap has not led to a widespread disavowal of modern medicine or an attack on the legitimacy of the practice. Alex London describes the current landscape quite nicely:

> [C]linicians prescribed aspirin as an analgesic for nearly a century without understanding the mechanism through which it works. Lithium has been used as a mood stabilizer for half a century, yet why it works remains uncertain. Large parts of medical practice frequently reflect a mixture of empirical findings and inherited clinical culture. In these cases, even efficacious recommendations of experts can be atheoretic in this sense: they reflect experience of benefit without enough knowledge of the underlying causal system to explain how the benefits are brought about.
>
> (London, 2019: 49)

As the above examples show, what matters most for health care is that the relevant stakeholders have confidence *that* a given policy works (London, 2019.). That confidence, moreover, is not necessarily tied to understanding *why* that policy works in practice. If this all seems strange, consider the prevalence of randomised clinical trials—a bedrock method of testing that deals with figuring out the results of a given program without necessarily understanding *how* those results came to be.

We wonder whether this sort of "clinical trial approach" could carry over to law enforcement. Put otherwise, for policing, is simply explaining the before-and-after enough? There are reasons to think this wouldn't be the case. In particular, in part because of an occasionally fraught history between the police and certain policed communities, coupled with the lack of a fiduciary one-to-one relationship between police officers and the policed (as compared to doctors), a different type of "explainability" might be necessary. Even if, for instance, a policymaker could demonstrate with the same confidence of a medical clinical trial that a surveillance algorithm led to a clear reduction in property crimes, that sort of efficiency-oriented explanation might not be enough. As built out more below, there are dignitarian and equitable considerations that come to bear in policing that might force policymakers to have to explain how a given program works. What's more, latent trust gaps might cause communities to be sceptical of policy results provided by the police, and in turn might insist that policymakers show their homework.

When it comes to the duty of explanation, therefore, the touchstone is stakeholder acceptance. So what happens when the regulated community does not accept the "explanation" such that it is? When they say we want to know *why* or *how* not just *that* it works? Or when the "ways of knowing" within a community differ from, say, that of the randomised clinical trial? Or perhaps the most difficult situation, when many within the minority aggrieved by the decision have an epistemology that differs from the majority who approves it (Kahan, Hoffman and Braman, 2009)? Contrasting health care with law enforcement helps us see that efficiency-oriented explanations are not necessarily always sufficient. And when they are not, policymakers will be forced to figure out how to articulate the *how* in order to achieve sufficient public buy-in for a given program.

Transparency and trade secrets

The main claim of the previous section is that there are clearly foreseeable circumstances where a policymaker is well advised to go beyond adequately demonstrating that a given program works and into showing *why* that program works. To our mind, one of the biggest hurdles to overcome on this front is, as Professors Neil Richards and Jonathan King (2013) have labelled it, the "transparency paradox." In their words, despite "promises to use [big data] to make the world more transparent," actually "its collection is invisible, and its tools and techniques are opaque, shrouded by layers of physical, legal, and technical privacy by design." We have seen some features of this paradox already. For one, in some instance big data's inherent complexity and "black box" qualities may make fully understanding a predictive analytics program difficult or impossible. This is especially true when such programs improve upon themselves through a process of machine learning that humans ex post cannot adequately decipher.

In this section, we focus on another aspect of the problem: the role of trade secrets as a strategy to protect investment. Law enforcement and health care professionals largely come at transparency from opposite angles, with the former more sceptical than the latter. But the two face a common issue that flows from their reliance on private sector intellectual property. To begin, broader pushes for transparency mesh differently with law enforcement and health care. In the policing context, transparency initiatives can raise problematic circumvention concerns. The Internal Revenue Service (IRS), for instance, has developed an algorithm that combs through tens of millions of pages of tax filings to help determine which taxpayers should be audited. If the IRS was forced to disclose the ins-and-outs of its proprietary program, any self-respecting tax schemer would simply adjust accordingly. The same intuition holds for the predictive policing examples we've seen so far. Recall the social media or "hot spot" analysis referenced above. If the cities using those programs were forced to disclose the accounts they followed or the areas they planned on targeting, the initiatives would be practically worthless. In short, the fact that criminals may "game the system" inform the police's relationship to transparency.

By contrast, these kinds of gamesmanship or circumvention concerns are much less present when it comes to health care. Indeed, from a doctor or hospital's perspective, there are few structural obstacles pushing for greater transparency. This is in large part due to the fact that there is much more of an alignment in interests between doctors and patients than there is with, say, police officers and criminals. Patients, physicians and hospital systems share the goal of reducing hospital readmission or determining whether a patient is suffering from a subdural hematoma. And in the great run of cases patients will have little incentive nor ability to use knowledge of the analytics to circumvent it.

However, even though the incentives regarding transparency are at a high-level inverted between policing and health care—with the former perhaps inclined against and the latter more in favour—the two professions face a common hurdle in trade secrets and intellectual property (Mattioli, 2014). Put plainly, the private companies that develop many of these predictive analytics programs have no interest in their investment-laden secret sauce being made public and can impede the public's effort to learn about the details of the algorithms impacting their lives. For a useful example in the policing context, consider a recent case from the state of Wisconsin's Supreme Court which held that a company did not have to disclose the source code of its algorithm even though the state had used it in determining the length of a convicted person's criminal sentence (State v. Loomis, 2016, 881 N.W.2d 749, 752, 760–761, 766–768). In the health care context, there is a similar problem. "Complex medical algorithms are generally hard for others to evaluate: their inner workings are (by definition) either complex or actually opaque, and in many circumstances, information about how they are developed and validated is kept secret" to protect the investment and profits of the developer (Price II, 2017: 433).

We would suspect that health care professionals face an easier road in dealing with the problem posed by trade secrets. First, with health care, there exists a centralised regulatory gatekeeper in the FDA that can set the terms for entry for big data programs, as opposed to the decentralisation of local police departments each of whom will make their own decisions. Second, the interests of the relevant stakeholders are all aligned in favour of transparency. By contrast, in policing both the makers and users, police departments are more likely to have shared interests in maintaining secrecy and are more likely to be aligned against the calls for transparency of the populations on whom the analytics are used (the public).

Notwithstanding the difficulties in achieving more transparency in the policing sphere, we think movements in this direction are essential. More transparency is necessary for two legitimacy-related interests. First, the efficacy of major police initiatives often turns on a baseline of acceptance from the community being policed. Professor David Weisburd captures this point well: "Consensus and transparency ... can enhance the legitimacy of police intrusions that are necessary to intercept criminals for violating 'risk laws,' such as those against carrying guns or driving while intoxicated" (Weisburd, 2016: 678). Second, transparency is necessary for the legitimacy that comes from political accountability. As Professors Barry Friedman and Maria Ponomarenko have explained:

> Numerous studies have shown that individuals are far more likely to comply with the law and to cooperate with law enforcement authorities when they perceive their actions as legitimate—and that one critical component

of legitimacy is the perception that police officials are responsive to community demands.

(Friedman and Ponomarenko, 2015: 1881)

So what are policymakers to do? In light of the above, we think that the health care context can provide some clues for policymakers involved in policing. One approach would be to alter underlying intellectual property law. For example, current trade secrecy protections could be replaced with forms of exclusivity that require disclosure as the price of intellectual property protection. Alternatively, policymakers could rely more on third-party auditing either by accreditation organisations or public regulators in the event private companies affirmatively resist public disclosure (Cohen et al., 2018; Price II, 2017: 471). Of course, concerns about "capture" would have to be addressed here. In any event, what is clear is that the need to crack the transparency paradox is a likely prerequisite for any policymaker looking to fulfil their duty of explanation as well as garner sufficient political acceptance necessary for predictive analytics programs to work as intended.

Scarcity and the inevitability of distributional choices

The last topic we want to focus on for policymakers—on top of the duty of explanation and the inherent difficulty in discharging that duty posed by the transparency paradox—is a point we believe will have to be addressed in virtually any defence of a predictive analytics program: the distribution of winners and losers. One of the best "jingle" selling points for predictive analytics is that they "allow you to do more with less." For police departments and hospitals, often faced with tight budgets in light of the problems they need to solve, this advantage is particularly appealing. But while predictive analytics can help maximise certain efficiencies or lower specific costs, distributional choices will remain inevitable.

The inevitability of distributional choices is perhaps clearest in the health care context. Consider a hypothetical situation that one of us has posited regarding a hospital's intensive care unit (ICU) (Cohen et al., 2014: 1139). Of course, an ICU has a limited number of beds and attendant doctors. Suppose you are a physician and one of your patients has moderate organ dysfunction. Do you send her to the ICU? On the one hand, after your preliminary examination of her you are convinced she likely would benefit from the stay. On the other hand, she is not in absolutely critical condition and it's quite possible a range of other people would benefit more from an ICU bed. Now imagine that there is a predictive analytics program that could compile and analyse the health profiles of every patient and can offer a view on who should ultimately get a bed. What to do?

There are a couple of things to keep in mind when thinking about this decision prudently. For one, as noted above, we can't forget the "as against what" question. We should imagine a possible world where the predictive analytic is in place and one where it is not, generating at least hypothetically a patient who would have received an ICU bed then and will not receive one now. To determine which world to strive towards we will need to develop some sort of normative metric for why the latter is *better* than the former, and vice versa. In the health care context, this metric intuitively could be something like "what improves the overall health of the patient population." But even this approach involves inherent sub-questions. Should older and younger patients be weighted equally? What about healthier versus sicker patients? Those sick due to personal decisions or vices versus those who have genetic illnesses?

In so many words, the merits of a distributional choice—that is, figuring out whether a community is better off from a given policy decision—is often a rabbit-duck. Two (or more) groups can stare at the same result and see something entirely different. New York City's experience with NYPD's "stop, question and frisk" program is illustrative of this. There, if a police officer had "reasonable suspicion" (recall *Terry* above), she could stop and question an individual on the street. If the officer determined that further action was needed, she retained the power to "frisk" the individual for possible weapons and the like. Former Mayor Mike Bloomberg, former Chief of Police Raymond Kelly, and scores of other political leaders championed the program as a driving reason behind New York City's massive fall in violent crime. Community groups, academics and activists, however, vociferously criticised the program as racially discriminatory, destructive to police–civilian relations and ineffective. Indeed, justifying a distributional choice is a heavy lift. And as the above suggests, it's likely harder with policing. A big reason why is that it's not wholly clear who are the winners and losers. With health care, we have patients who are "sick" and those who are "healthy." But with law enforcement, we're largely dealing with hypotheticals. One can be quite sure that the rate of burglaries in a given neighbourhood can fall from X to Y. However, it is difficult to determine how to weigh the interests of those given homeowners versus the externalities of the policing practice, the fact other social forces might have caused the fall in crime, and the interests of the homeowners who houses *were* burglarised (and perhaps wouldn't have been in the previous system).

When it comes to explaining and justifying a distributional choice, we feel the health care context again offers a helpful starting point. Two lessons in particular stand out. First, as a general rule, it's likely a mistake to use a Pareto-oriented normative criterion (one where a program is only permissible if it leaves nobody worse off) for evaluating distributive choices. Pareto models only make sense if we think the system that existed before the program-readjusted distribution (call it "T1") has some inherent normative weight. But this seems wrong. Suppose you are the patient who would have received the ICU bed in the example above at T1. Now would you have an entitlement to that bed *even if* you receiving it would not improve the overall health of the population (as compared to where the predictive analytics program is in place; call it "T2")?

To argue yes would have to imbue T1 with a particular, unearned moral significance that T2 somehow lacks. Indeed, had we started with the T2 world, you'd be hard pressed to argue that we should chuck the predictive analytics program in order to benefit you, despite its broader effects. To be sure, things are often more complicated. There are a range of possible theories of distributional justice—from utilitarian to prioritarian to sufficientarian—and the answer as to which is suitable might vary by the nature of the good or service and the community. But the bigger point is that requiring Pareto superiority as a criterion does not seem like a good way to handle the sort of inevitable distributional choices posed by predictive analytics.

Second, there will be increasing pressure on decision-makers to justify that they should be the people who decide these important questions. At the current moment, the implementation of predictive analytics in health care settings largely seems to be the result of centralised decision-making, often by the hospital itself. And while there may be some attempt to canvass community views, it is fair to say this has not been the driver in most instances. But involving other stakeholders and, in turn, spreading the decision-making power across other stakeholders, is not impossible. Norman Daniels (2007: 274–296), for example, has championed the "Accountability for Reasonableness" framework in the context of meeting heath care needs fairly—and, potentially, this or other frameworks might be adapted for other settings, including policing.[2] Lastly, it's important to remember that "systems play out differently in the real world than in the simulation [and] affected communities may react to the analytics in question and alter the distribution of benefits and losses" (Cohen and Graver, 2017: 463). As such, distributional analysis is seldom one and done. To the extent policymakers and communities discern and understand whatever distributional choice they made, in light of the opacity inherent to big data programs, those choices will need to be continually reassessed as they play out in practice.

The polity

Bias and equality

It's a common refrain that algorithms are only as good as their data. As then-Judge Neil Gorsuch noted when on the Tenth Circuit Court of Appeals: "Garbage in, garbage out. Everyone knows that much about computers: you give them bad data, they give you bad results" (*United States v. Esquivel-Rios*, 2013, 725 F.3d 1231, 1234). Turning to the vantage point of the impacted political community, one variant of this concern is particularly prominent: that the respective programs fail to treat minority groups as well as majority ones. Indeed, one of the biggest pitfalls in evaluating a predictive analytics program is to assume it's automatically objective because its "thinking" is done by a machine. The simple reason is that each component part of an algorithm is the product of human decision-making; from the factors considered, to how they are weighed, to the data itself. What's more, any underlying biases that are produced by a program can be subtly compounded by machine learning.

When looking at the policing and health care literature, we see this common concern stem from opposite forces. For policing, discrimination largely takes the form of *over*-inclusion; that is, either the data is skewed too heavily to one group or a program disproportionately targets the same. For health care, however, the issue is with *under*-inclusion; minority groups are at risk of being disproportionately *under*-represented in relevant data, which accordingly causes algorithms to be less responsive to their needs. It's helpful to start by taking each in turn.

The bias-based criticism of predictive policing can be roughly boiled down to disquiet about discrimination squared. On this view, discriminatory practices by law enforcement already cause disparate treatment in policed communities (Simmons 2016). As such, the underlying data available for predictive programs—from who is stopped to who is arrested, and the like—is tainted with racial bias. To boot, the argument goes, this already present discrimination can be made worse by biases within algorithms employed by police departments. On the other hand, others have stressed the potential for predictive policing to bring about more effective and neutral policing. For example, Professor David Weisburd (2016: 686) has held that "hot spots policing properly implemented is likely to lead to less biased policing than traditional strategies" and there's currently "little evidence that hot spots policing per se leads to abusive policing practices." And departments across the United States have continued to increasingly adopt predictive policing tactics as ways to improve services and curb systematic biases. Cities are often divided, as the recent debate over Detroit's "Project Green Light" surveillance and facial recognition program has demonstrated (Harmon, 2019).

We see a similar but inverted dynamic in health care. Here, problems with bias derive from too *little* attention from relevant institutions. In particular, certain demographics simply don't engage with the health care system as much as others. And when programs know more about some and less about others, they work better for the former at the possible expense of the latter. For example, Ziad Obermeyer and Sendhil Mullainathan recently examined racial bias in a commercial algorithm that is deployed nationwide today by many prominent Accountable Care Organizations. Using data from large hospitals, they show that black and white patients with the same algorithmic risk scores have very different actual health, with black patients having significantly more chronic illness than white enrolees at the same risk score. In short, this means that white patients are favoured for enrolment in beneficial care management programs over black patients with the same health state (Obermeyer and Mullainathan, 2019: 89).

When thinking about the issue of potential bias with predictive analytics in policing or health care, we see at least two major threshold considerations that an impacted polity should keep in mind. First, these programs need to be evaluated against the baseline of the status quo rather than in a vacuum—the "as against what" question noted above. It is critical to remember that a flawed program may nonetheless be a desirable improvement on present circumstances if those present circumstances evince even more bias. Second, because big data is so difficult to decipher and explain, as discussed above, communities need to negotiate on the front end for an evaluative mechanism that can allow the public to remain informed on how a program is operating. For instance, Professor Andrew Ferguson (2017a: 1119) has offered a nine-factor framework for assessing bias in predictive policing programs. To what extent these or a myriad of other approaches will work, and under what circumstances, remains to be seen. What is clear is that for a predictive analytics program to be sustainable, system designers must design and implement a framework for evaluating bias that is both visible and understandable.

Privacy

The last theme we turn to is the intersection between predictive analytics and privacy. "Privacy," of course, is a bit of a wiggle word. Here, we generally understand it as Samuel Warren and Louis Brandeis (1890: 193) put it—in short, the "right to be let alone." Privacy concerns feature prominently in both law enforcement and health care, but interestingly for somewhat opposite reasons. In particular, privacy interests are implicated by predictive policing when something goes *right*. Consider, for example, the increased use of facial recognition software in American airports. When the program works as designed, a person is identified from the crowd and linked to whatever other information the government has on her. Put simply, the program works because she is no longer a stranger. By contrast, privacy interests typically come to the fore in the health care context when something goes *wrong*. When predictive analytics work they can tell us something useful about the patient and her health *without* revealing her identity. It is when a program is susceptible to de-identification techniques, data breaches or something similar that privacy is impaired. But even though privacy features within policing or health care somewhat differently, the same societal bargain cuts across both professions. In other words, for predictive analytics programs to be accepted in either setting, the polity needs to agree to a deal: a tradeoff between the risk of losing privacy (either directly, by design, in the policing context or indirectly, by risk of error, with health care) and the benefits of big data.

In cutting this bargain, however, it's hard to really measure each side of the ledger. On that score, the health care literature again offers a useful framing. In particular, predictive analytics in medicine often implicate both *consequentialist* and *dignitarian* concerns:

> Consequentialist concerns result from negative consequences that affect the person whose privacy has been violated. These can be tangible negative

consequences—for example, one's long-term-care insurance premium goes up as a result of additional information now available as a result of a breach of privacy, one experiences employment discrimination, or one's HIV status becomes known to those in one's social circle—or these can be the emotional distress associated with knowing that private medical information is "out there" and potentially exploited by others: consider the potential for increased anxiety if one believed one was now susceptible to identity theft, even before any misuses of identity have occurred.... Deontological concerns do not depend on experiencing negative consequences. In this category, the concern from a privacy violation manifests even if no one uses a person's information against this person or if the person never even becomes aware that a breach has occurred.

(Price II and Cohen, 2019: 38)

Both kinds of harms can arise in both of our contexts. In policing, consequentialist concerns might involve mistaken identification and harassment. In health care, this might involve a higher-than-otherwise cost for life insurance. The deontological concerns in health care might centre around the loss of control over who accesses one's data, even if one is well-protected against adverse actions against oneself. In policing this might include the general chilling effect of knowing that big brother has perhaps crafted a "mosaic" of your identity from the collection of small data points (Kerr, 2012). Communities need to have a robust discussion about both the nature and degree of interests implicated by predictive analytics programs. To that end, to the extent practicable, communities may insist on learning the types of information that a given program would require. As such, even if it is difficult to understand exactly *how* the program works, the polity can have a sense of the trade-off; a rough idea of what they're giving up and a decent sense of what they'll get in return. As above, too, the privacy issue is best understood as the sort of bargain that isn't a one-off deal. Due to the rapidly changing nature of this technology as well as the proliferation of data available about individual persons, the privacy trade-off must be taken as an on going, regularly re-upped societal agreement. This is because the technical fact of data triangulation; the multiple separate privacy harms might aggregate to be more or less than the sum of their parts; and the social expectations of privacy and its importance vary over time and by community (Price II and Cohen, 2019: 38).

Conclusion

The preceding themes all involve different sorts of trade-offs and bargains posed by the integration of big data into our daily lives. For instance, political communities are going to have to figure out where to strike the balance between privacy and efficacy. Likewise, policymakers will need to settle on a rough normative criterion to evaluate the inevitable distributional choices posed by predictive analytics. And practitioners will have to reconceive of their roles enough so that they can ensure big data will complement rather than supplant their expert judgment.

A final point we want to note is that in order for these important and recurring decisions to be made, we need to become more comfortable with making big calls on incomplete information. When it comes to big data, we'll never have a full picture. Indeed, some of that is up to us, as the foregoing discussion of trade secrets lays out. But a lot of it isn't—the "black box" nature of some forms of machine learning is here to stay. For those reasons, stakeholders should endeavour to be thoughtful while also aware of the limits of their ability to be thorough. Yogi Berra, as was his wont, offered a useful reminder: "It's tough to make predictions, especially about the future."

Acknowledgement

We thank Daniel Sieradzki for excellent research assistance.

Notes

1 This chapter builds on ideas the two of us first discussed in an article, see Cohen, I.G. and Graver, H.S. (2017), "Cops, docs, and code: a dialogue between big data in health care and predictive policing," *UC Davis Law Review*, 51(2), pp. 437–474, and in a book that one of us has recently edited, see Cohen, I.G. et al. (eds) (2018), *Big data, health law, and bioethics*. Cambridge: Cambridge University Press.

2 See Daniels, N. (2007), *Just health: meeting health needs fairly*, Cambridge: Cambridge University Press, pp. 274–296. Daniels' model requires that rationales for making decisions must be publicly accessible, that the rationales must be relevant and evidence based, that a mechanism exists for appealing decisions and their rationales, and that there is a compliance system to make sure the preceding conditions are met (Ibid).

References

Bakkar, N. et al. (2018). Artificial intelligence in neurodegenerative disease research: use of IBM Watson to identify additional RNA-binding proteins altered in amyotrophic lateral sclerosis. *Acta Neuropathologica,* 135(2), pp. 227–247.

Caruana, R. et al. (2015). Intelligible models for healthcare: predicting pneumonia risk and hospital 30-day readmission. In: *Proceedings of the 21th ACM SIGKDD International Conference on Knowledge Discovery and Data Mining*, Sydney, Australia, 10–13 August. New York: Association for Computing Machinery, pp. 1721–1730.

Citron, D.K. and Pasquale, A. (2011). Network accountability for the domestic intelligence apparatus. *Hastings Law Journal*, 62(6), p. 1443.

Cohen, I.G. et al. (2014). The legal and ethical concerns that arise from using complex predictive analytics in health care. *Health Affairs*, 33(7), pp. 1139–1147.

Cohen, I.G. and Graver, H.S. (2017). Cops, docs, and code: a dialogue between big data in health care and predictive policing. *UC Davis Law Review*, 51(2), pp. 437–474.

Cohen, I.G. et al. (eds) (2018). *Big data, health law, and bioethics*. Cambridge: Cambridge University Press.

Cohen, I.G. (2018). Is there a duty to share health care data? In: Cohen, I.G. et al. (eds), *Big data, health law, and bioethics*. Cambridge: Cambridge University Press, p. 209.

Cohen, I.G. and Mello, M.M. (2018). HIPPA and protecting health information in the 21st century. *Journal of the American Medical Association*, 320(3), pp. 231–232.

Daniels, N. (2007). *Just health: meeting health needs fairly*. Cambridge: Cambridge University Press, pp. 274–296.

Duportail, J. (2017). I asked Tinder for my data. It sent me 800 pages of my deepest, darkest secrets. *The Guardian*. Available at: www.theguardian.com/technology/ 2017/sep/26/tinder-personal-data-dating-app-messages-hacked-sold [accessed 18 September 2019].

Ferguson, A.G. (2015). Big data and predictive reasonable suspicion. *University of Pennsylvania Law Review*, 163(2), pp. 336–349.

Ferguson, A.G. (2017a). Policing predictive policing. *Washington University Law Review*, 94(5), pp. 1139–1143.

Ferguson, A.G. (2017b). *The rise of big data policing: surveillance, race, and the future of law enforcement*. New York: NYU Press.

Friedman, B. and Ponomarenko, M. (2015). Democratic policing. *New York University Law Review*, 90(6), p. 1881.

Froomkin, A.M., Kerr I.R., and Pineau, J. (2019). When AIs outperform doctors: the dangers of a tort-induced over-reliance on machine learning, *Arizona Law Review*, 61(1), pp. 33–99.

Harmon, A. (2019). As cameras track Detroit's residents, a debate ensues over racial bias. *New York Times*. Available at: www.nytimes.com/2019/07/08/us/detroit-facial-recognition-cameras.html [accessed 18 September 2019].

Illinois v. Wardlow. (2000). 528 U.S. 119.

Joh, E.E. (2014). Policing by numbers: big data and the Fourth Amendment. *Washington Law Review*, 89(1), pp. 42–46, 48–50.

Kahan, D.M., Hoffman, D.A., and Braman, D. (2009). Whose eyes are you going to believe? Scott v. Harris and the perils of cognitive illiberalism. *Harvard Law Review*, 122(3), pp. 837–906.

Kerr, O.S. (2012) The mosaic theory of the Fourth Amendment. *Michigan Law Review*, 111(3), p. 311–354.

Klugman C.M. et al. (2018). The ethics of smart pills and self-acting devices: autonomy, truth-telling, and trust at the dawn of digital medicine. *American Journal of Bioethics*, 18(9), pp. 38–47.

Kramer, DB and Fu, K. (2017). Cybersecurity concerns and medical devices: lessons from a pacemaker advisory. *Journal of the American Medical Association*, 318(21), pp. 913–917.

Kroll, J.A. et al. (2017). Accountable algorithms. *University of Pennsylvania Law Review*, 165(3), pp. 633–705.

Kulynych, J. and Greely, H.T. (2017). Clinical genomics, big data, and electronic medical records: reconciling patient rights with research when privacy and science collide. *Journal of Law and Biosciences*, 8(1), pp. 94–132.

London, A.J. (2019). Artificial intelligence and black-box medical decisions: accuracy versus explainability. *Hastings Center Report*, 49(1), pp. 15–21.

Malanga, S.E. et al. (2018). Who's left out of big data? How big data collection, analysis, and use neglects populations most in need of medical and public health research and interventions. In: Cohen, I.G. et al. (eds) *Big data, health law, and bioethics*. Cambridge: Cambridge University Press, p. 98.

Mattioli, M. (2014). Disclosing big data. *Minnesota Law Review*, 99(2), pp. 535–583.

Nickeas, P. et al. (2017). Chicago police express frustration after more than 100 shot in violent Fourth of July weekend. *Chicago Tribune*. Available at: www.chicagotribune. com/news/breaking/ct-chicago-july-4-weekend-shootings-violence-20170705-story.html [accessed 18 September 2019].

Obenmeyer, Z. and Emanuel, E.J. (2016). Predicting the future—big data, machine learning, and clinical medicine. *N Engl J Med*, 375(13), p. 1217.

Obenmeyer. Z. and Mullainathan, S. (2019). Dissecting racial bias in an algorithm that guides health decisions for 70 million people, *FAT* '19 Proceedings of the Conference on Fairness, Accountability, and Transparency*, Atlanta, Georgia, 29–31 January. New York: ACM Publications, p. 89.

Pepper, S.L. (1986). The lawyer's amoral ethical role: a defense, a problem, and some possibilities. *American Bar Foundation Research Journal*, 11(4), pp. 613–635.

Price II, W.N. (2015). Black-box medicine. *Harvard Journal of Law and Technology*, 28(2), pp. 443–453.

Price II, W.N. (2016). Big data, patents, and the future of medicine. *Cardozo Law Review*, 37(4), pp. 1401–1453.

Price II, W.N. (2017). Regulating black-box medicine. *Michigan Law Review*, 116(3), pp. 439–442.

Price II, W.N. (2019). Medical AI and contextual bias. *Harvard Journal of Law and Technology*, 33.

Price II, W.N. and Cohen, I.G. (2019). Privacy in the age of medical big data. *Nature Medicine*, 25(1), pp. 37–43.

Perry, W.L. et al. (2013). *Predictive policing: the role of crime forecasting in law enforcement operations*, Rand Corporation, doi.org/10.7249/RR233.

Rajkomar, A. et al. (2018). Scalable and accurate deep learning with electronic health records. *Nature Project Journals Digital Medicine*, 1(18).

Rich, M.L. (2016). Machine learning, automated suspicion algorithms, and the Fourth Amendment. *University of Pennsylvania Law Review*, 164(4), p. 902.

Richards, N.M. and King, J.H. (2013). Three paradoxes of big data. *Stanford Law Review Online*, 66, pp. 41–46.

Riley, M.F. (2018). Big Data, HIPPA, and the common rule: time for big change? In: Cohen, I.G. et al. (eds), *Big data, health law, and bioethics*. Cambridge: Cambridge University Press, p. 251.

Simmons, R. (2016). Quantifying criminal procedure: how to unlock the potential of big data in our criminal justice system. *Michigan State Law Review*, 2016, pp. 947–1017.

State v. Loomis. (2016). 881 N.W.2d 749, 752, 760–761, 766–768.

Terry v. Ohio. (1968). 392 U.S. 1, 21–22.

Terry, N.P. (2017). Regulatory disruption and arbitrage in health-care data protection. *Yale Journal of Health Policy, Law, and Ethics*, 17(1), pp. 143–208.

United States v. Esquivel-Rios. (2013). 725 F.3d 1231, 1234.

Warren, S.D. and Brandeis, L.D. (1890). The right to privacy. *Harvard Law Review*, 4(5), p. 193.

Wasserstrom, R. (1975). Lawyers as professionals: some moral issues. *Human Rights*, 5(1), pp. 1–24.

Weisburd, D. (2016). Does hot spots policing inevitably lead to unfair and abusive police practices, or can we maximize both fairness and effectiveness in the new proactive policing? *University of Chicago Legal Forum*, 2016, p. 678.

Zarsky, T.Z. (2013). Transparent predictions. *University of Illinois Law Review*, 2013(4), pp. 1503–1570.

Chapter 5

Artificial intelligence and online extremism

Challenges and opportunities

Miriam Fernandez and Harith Alani

Introduction

Radicalisation is a process that historically used to be triggered mainly through social interactions in places of worship, religious schools, prisons, meeting venues, etc. Today, this process is often initiated on the Internet, where radicalisation content is easily shared, and potential candidates are reached more easily, rapidly, and at an unprecedented scale (Edwards and Gribbon, 2013; Von Behr et al., 2013). In recent years, some terrorist organisations succeeded in leveraging the power of social media to recruit individuals to their cause and ideology (Farwell, 2014). It is often the case that such recruitment attempts are initiated on open social media platforms (e.g. Twitter, Facebook, Tumblr, YouTube) but then move onto private messages and/or encrypted platforms (e.g. WhatsApp, Telegram). Such encrypted communication channels have also been used by terrorist cells and networks to plan their operations (Gartenstein-Ross and Barr, 2016).

To counteract the activities of such organisations, and to halt the spread of radicalisation content, some governments, social media platforms and counter-extremism agencies are investing in the creation of advanced information technologies to identify and counter extremism through the development of Artificial Intelligent (AI) solutions (Correa and Sureka, 2013; Agarwal and Sureka 2015a; Scrivens and Davies, 2018). These solutions have three main objectives: (i) **understanding** the phenomena behind online extremism (the communication flow, the use of propaganda, the different stages of the radicalisation process, the variety of radicalisation channels, etc.), (ii) automatically **detecting** radical *users* and *content*, and (iii) **predicting** the adoption and spreading of extremist ideas.

Despite current advancements in the area, multiple challenges still exist, including: (i) the lack of a common definition of prohibited radical and extremist internet activity, (ii) the lack of solid verification of the datasets collected to develop detection and prediction models, (iii) the lack of cooperation across research fields, since most of the developed technological solutions are neither based on, nor do they take advantage of, existing social theories and studies of radicalisation, (iv) the constant evolution of behaviours associated with online extremism in order to avoid being detected by the developed algorithms (changes in terminology, creation of new accounts, etc.), and (v) the development of ethical guidelines and legislation to regulate the design and development of AI technology to counter radicalisation. In this book chapter we provide an overview of the current technological advancements towards addressing the problem of online extremism (with a particular focus on Jihadism). We identify some of the limitations of current technologies and highlight some of the potential opportunities. Our aim is to reflect on the current state of the art and to stimulate discussions on the future design and development of AI technology to target the problem of online extremism.

An overview of existing approaches

A wide range of work has emerged in the last few years that applied and developed AI technologies with the aim of examining the radicalisation phenomenon, and understanding the social media presence and actions of extremist organisations (Correa and Sureka, 2013; Agarwal and Sureka, 2015a; Scrivens and Davies, 2018).

Broadly, these works can be categorised as (see Figure 5.1): (i) those that focus on the intelligent, large-scale analysis of online radicalisation to better understand this phenomenon, (ii) those that focus on the automatic detection

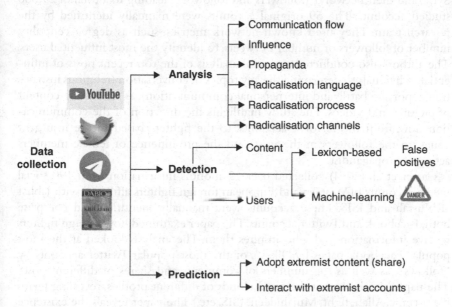

Figure 5.1 Overview of AI approaches to counter online radicalisation.

of radicalisation, including the detection of radical *content* online, as well as the detection of radical *user* accounts, and (iii) those that focus on the automatic prediction of radicalisation (adoption of extremist content, interaction with extremist accounts, etc.). Note that, while we do not present an exhaustive list of works in this chapter, the following sections aim at providing an overview of some representative approaches, including their main objective, the data they used to support their research, the key algorithms used, and the main output of their work.

Analysis

Works that have focused on the application of AI technologies for the intelligent, large-scale analysis of radicalisation (see Table 5.1) have different objectives. Among these objectives we can highlight: (i) studying the communication flow within the online medium (Klausen, 2015), (ii) analysing influence (Carter et al., 2014), (iii) investigating how propaganda is presented and spread online (Chatfield et al., 2015; Badawy and Ferrara, 2018), (iv) observe the evolution of radicalisation language (Vergani and Bliuc, 2015), (v) study the radicalisation process (Bermingham et al., 2009; Rowe and Saif, 2016), and (vi) the analysis of the different online radicalisation channels.

Klausen (2015) studied the role of social media, and particularly Twitter, in the jihadists' operational strategy in Syria and Iraq. During 2014, they collected information on 59 Twitter accounts of Western-origin fighters known to be in Syria, and their networks (followers and followees), leading to a total of 29,000 studied accounts. The 59 original accounts were manually identified by the research team. They used known network metrics, such as degree-centrality, number of followers or number of tweets, to identify the most influential users. The authors also conducted a manual analysis of the top recent posts of influential individuals to determine the key topics of conversation (religious instruction, reporting battle and interpersonal communication), as well as the content of pictures and videos. The study highlights the direction of the communication flow, from the terrorist accounts, to the fighters based in the insurgent zones, to the followers in the west, and the prominence of female members acting as propagandist.

Carter et al. (2014) collected over 12-months information from 190 social media accounts of Western and European foreign fighters affiliated with Jabhat al-Nusrah and ISIS. These accounts were manually identified and comprise both, Facebook and Twitter accounts. The paper examined how foreign fighters receive information and who inspires them. The analysis looked at the most popular Facebook pages by "likes", or the most popular Twitter accounts by "follows", as well as the numbers of comments and shares of different posts. The paper also looked at the word clouds of different profiles, revealing terms like islamic, Allah, fight, Mujahideen, ISIS, etc.) The paper reveals the existence of spiritual authorities who foreign fighters go to for inspiration and guidance.

Table 5.1 Approaches that focus on the analysis of online radicalisation.

Work	Goal	Data	AI algorithm / technique	Conclusions
Klausen (2015)	Study the communication flow in the jihadists' operational strategy in Syria and Iraq	59 pro-ISIS Twitter accounts (manually assessed) and their networks (29,000 accounts)	Social network analysis in combination with manual analysis of accounts, tweets and images	Communication flow, from the terrorist accounts, to the fighters based in the insurgent zones, to the followers in the west. Prominence of female members acting as propagandist
Carter et al. (2014)	Examine how foreign fighters receive information and who inspires them (influence)	190 pro-ISIS Twitter and Facebook accounts (manually assessed)	Manual annotation and assessment of accounts in combination with social network analysis	Existence of spiritual authorities who foreign fighters look to for inspiration and guidance
Chatfield et al. (2015)	Investigate how ISIS members/supporters used Twitter to radicalise and recruit other users	3,039 tweets from one account of a known ISIS "information disseminator" (Twitter)	Social network analysis combined with manual analysis of content	Posts about propaganda, radicalisation and terrorist recruitment mentioning international media, regional Arabic media, IS sympathisers and IS fighters.
Vergani and Bliuc (2015)	Investigated the evolution of the ISIS's language	first 11 issues of Dabiq, the official ISIS's internet magazine	Natural Language Processing based on LIWC (Linguistic Inquiry and Word Count)	Use expressions related to achievement, affiliation and power. Emotional language. Mentions of death female and religion and use of internet jargon
Rowe and Saif (2016)	Study Europe-based Twitter users before, during, and after they exhibited pro-ISIS behaviour to better understand the radicalisation process	727 pro-ISIS Twitter accounts. Categorised as pro-ISIS base on the use of radicalised terminology and sharing from radicalised accounts	Modelling and analysis of diffusion over time-series data	Prior to being activated/radicalised users go through a period of significant increase in adopting innovations (i.e. communicating with new users and adopting new terms). Social homophily has a strong bearing on the diffusion process of pro-ISIS terminology.

(continued)

Table 5.1 Cont.

Work	Goal	Data	AI algorithm / technique	Conclusions
Bermingham et al. (2009)	Explore the use of sentiment and network analysis to determine whether a YouTube group was used as radicalisation channel	135,000 comments and 13,700 user profiles. YouTube group manually assessed	Social network analysis and content analysis (including the automatic extraction of topics and sentiment)	The group was mostly devoted to religious discussion (not radicalisation). Female users show more extreme and less tolerant views
Badawy and Ferrara (2018)	Explored the use of social media by ISIS to spread its propaganda and recruit militants	1.9 million Twitter posts by 25K ISIS and ISIS sympathisers' accounts	Lexicon-based approach to classify each tweet into violence, theological, sectarian and others, and an over-time analysis of tweets and correlation with real-events	Violence-driven, theological and sectarian content play a crucial role in ISIS messaging. There is a connection between online rhetoric and events happening in the real world
Lara-Cabrera et al. (2017)	Translate a set of indicators found in social science models into a set of computational features to identify the characteristics of users at risk of radicalisation	17K Twitter posts from pro-ISIS users provided by Kaggle (Kaggle, 2019). 76K tweets from pro-ISIS users provided by Anonymous. 173K tweets randomly selected	Five indicators are modelled based on lexicons (frustration, negative content, perception of discrimination, negative ideas of Western society and positive ideas about Jihadisim) and their density distribution is observed within the data	The proposed indicators do indeed characterise radicalised users. Authors define as the next step the use of these indicators as features to create Machine Learning classifiers for the automatic classification of users at risk of radicalisation

Chatfield et al. (2015) investigated how ISIS members/supporters used Twitter to radicalise and recruit other users. For this purpose, they study 3,039 tweets from one account of a known ISIS "information disseminator". Two annotators categorised those posts manually as: propaganda (information), radicalisation (believes in support of intergroup conflict and violence), terrorist recruitment (enticing others to join in fighting the jihad war) and other. Examples of these tweets and their content is provided as a result of this exercise. The analysis also studied the frequency and times of posting, indicating highly active users, as well as the network of users mentioned in the tweets, which were manually categorised as: international media, regional Arabic media, IS sympathisers and IS fighters.

Vergani and Bliuc (2015) investigated the evolution of the ISIS's language by analysing the text contained in the first 11 issues of Dabiq; the official ISIS internet magazine in English. To conduct their analysis they made use of the Linguistic Inquiry and Word Count (LIWC) text analysis program. Their analysis highlighted: (i) the use of expressions related to achievement, affiliation and power, (ii) a focus on emotional language, which is considered to be effective in mobilising individuals, (ii) frequent mentions of death, female and religion, which are related to the ISIS ideology and the recruitment of women to the cause, and (iv) the use of internet jargon ("btw", "lol", etc.), which may be more effective in establishing a communication with the youngest generations of potential recruits.

While Klausen (2015), Carter et al. (2014) and Chatfield et al. (2015) studied the social media behaviour of users once radicalised, Rowe and Saif (2016) studied the social media actions and interactions of Europe-based Twitter users before, during and after they exhibited pro-ISIS behaviour. Starting from 512 radicalised Twitter accounts, manually identified in the work of O'Callaghan (2014), they collected their followers, filtered those based in Europe and determined whether those followers were radicalised based on two hypotheses: (i) use of pro-ISIS terminology, a lexicon was generated to test this hypothesis, and (ii) content shared from pro-ISIS accounts. Their filtering process led to the study of 727 pro-ISIS Twitter accounts and their complete timelines. The study concluded that prior to being activated/radicalised users go through a period of significant increase in adopting innovations (i.e. communicating with new users and adopting new terms). They also highlight that social homophily has a strong bearing on the diffusion process of pro-ISIS terminology through Twitter.

Bermingham et al. (2009) looked at the user profiles and comments of a YouTube video group whose purpose was "the conversion of infidels" with the aim of assessing whether users were being radicalised by the group and how this was reflected in comments and interactions. They collected a total of 135,000 comments posted by 700 members and 13,000 group contributors. They performed term frequency to observe the top-terms used in the group as well as sentiment analysis over a subset of comments filtered by a list of keywords of interest (Islam, Israel, Palestine, etc.). They also used centrality measures to identify influencers. They observed that the group was mostly devoted to religious discussion (not radicalisation) and that female users show more extreme and less tolerant views.

Badawy and Ferrara (2018) explored the use of social media by ISIS to spread its propaganda and to recruit militants. To do so, they analysed a dataset of 1.9 million tweets posted by 25K ISIS and ISIS sympathisers' accounts. They distinguish three different types of messages (violence-driven, theological and sectarian content) and they traced a connection between online rhetoric and events happening in the real world. In 2017, Lara-Cabrera et al. (2017) translated a set of indicators found in social science theories of radicalisation (feelings of frustration, introversion, perception of discrimination, etc.) into a set of computational features (mostly sets of keywords) that they could automatically extract from the data. They assessed the appearance of these indicators in a set of 17K tweets from pro-ISIS users provided by Kaggle (2019), a set of 76K tweets from pro-ISIS users provided by Anonymous and a set of 173K tweets randomly selected by opening the Twitter stream. The authors concluded that, while the proposed metrics showed promising results, these metrics were mainly based on keywords. More refined metrics can therefore be proposed to map social science indicators.

Detection

While in the previous section we discuss examples of works which have attempted to analyse the phenomenon of online extremism, with the aim of understanding the different actors involved, and how the process kick-starts and evolves, in this section we focused on those works who have attempted to provide technological solutions to automatically detect the presence of radical *content* and *users* online (see Table 5.2). Works focused on content have attempted to identify radical material (either text, images or videos), while works focused on users have attempted to automatically identify those social media accounts exhibiting radicalisation signs (using radical rhetoric, sharing radical material, etc.). It is important to highlight here that the automatic detection and categorisation of *users* as radical or extremist is a particularly difficult and sensitive problem, since the wrong categorisation of a user as radical (false positive error) may result in an innocent person being subjected to surveillance or policing investigation. In this section we give an overview of some of these works, focusing on their key objectives, the AI methods applied or proposed, the datasets used to conduct the research, and the key obtained outputs.

In 2013, Berger and Strathearn (2013) developed an approach to detect individuals more prone to extremism (white supremacy in this case) among those with an interest in violent ideologies. Their approach started by collecting the social networks of 12 known extremists on Twitter (3,542 accounts were collected using this process and a maximum of 200 tweets per account was

Table 5.2 Approaches that focus on the detection of online radicalisation.

Work	Goal	Data	AI Algorithm / Technique	Conclusions
Berger and Strathearn (2013)	Identify individuals prone to extremism from the followers of extremist accounts (user detection)	3,542 Twitter accounts (followers of 12 known pro-ISIS accounts)	Designed a scoring system to measure "influence" and "Exposure" based on interactions such as replies, retweets, or direct messages	High scores of influence an exposure showed a strong correlation to engagement with the extremist ideology (manual evaluation)
Berger and Morgan (2015)	Create a demographic snapshot of ISIS supporters on Twitter and outline a methodology for detecting pro-ISIS accounts (user detection)	20,000 pro-ISIS Twitter accounts (7,574 manually annotated to test classification)	A Machine Learning (ML) classifier was trained based on 6,000 accounts and tested with 1574. No details are provided on the ML method used.	The authors concluded that pro-ISIS supporters could be identified from their profiles descriptions: with terms such as succession, linger, Islamic State, Caliphate State or In Iraq all being prominent
Saif (2017)	Create classifiers able to automatically identify pro-ISIS users in social media (user detection)	1,132 Twitter users (566 pro-ISIS, 556 anti-ISIS). Annotation based on the terminology used and the sharing from known radicalised accounts	SVM classifiers are created based on n-grams, sentiment, topic and network features. The authors also proposed classifier based on semantic features (frequent patterns extracted from a knowledge-graph).	Classifiers trained on semantic features outperform those trained from lexical, sentiment, topic and network features
Fernandez and Alani (2018)	Explore the use of semantic context to create more accurate radicalisation detection methods (user detection)	17K tweets from pro-ISIS users and 122K tweets from 'general' Twitter users available via the Kaggle data science community (Kaggle, 2019)	Semantic extraction of entities, entity types, topics and categories from a knowledge graph (to model context) and incorporation of such context as features into SVM, Naive Bayes and Decision Tree classifiers.	Semantic information can help to better understand the contextual variances in which radicalisation terms are used when conveying 'radicalised meaning' vs. when not. Understanding such variances can help to create more accurate radicalisation detection methods.

(continued)

Table 5.2 Cont.

Work	Goal	Data	AI Algorithm / Technique	Conclusions
Fernandez et al. (2018)	Measure the influence of online radicalisation that a user is exposed to. Design a computational method based on the social science theory of roots of radicalisation (Schmid, 2013; Borum, 2016) (user detection)	17K tweets from pro-ISIS users and 122K tweets from 'general' Twitter users available via the Kaggle data science community (Kaggle, 2019)	Use word vectors to model the micro (individual), meso (social) and macro (global) radicalisation influence. Cosine similarity is used to compare such vectors against a Lexicon of radical terms	There is an important need to leverage closer the knowledge of theoretical models of radicalisation to design more effective technological solutions to track online radicalisation.
Agarwal and Sureka (2015b)	Automatic identification of hate and extremism promoting tweets (content detection)	10,486 hate and terrorism-related Twitter posts (extracted based on hashtags) + 1M random tweets annotated by students for validation	They tested KNN and LibSVM classifiers based on religious, offensive, slang, negative emotions, punctuations and war related terms	Presence of religious, war related terms, offensive words and negative emotions are strong indicators of a tweet to be hate promoting
Ashcroft et al. (2015)	Automatically detect messages released by jihadist groups on Twitter (content detection)	2,000 pro-ISIS Twitter posts (containing pro-ISIS terminology and extracted from the accounts 6,729 ISIS sympathisers), 2,000 anti-ISIS tweets (extracted from manually assessed anti-ISIS accounts), 2000 random tweets.	Trained classifiers (SVM, Naive Bayes and Adaboost) based on stylometric (n-grams, hashtags, word frequency, etc.), time-based and sentiment features	Fridays are a key date to spread radical tweets. Automatic detection is viable but can never replace human analysts. It should be seen as a complementary way to detect radical content

analysed). Using the 3,542 accounts collected using this method, the work measured three dimensions for each user: (i) their influence (number of times their content was retweeted), (ii) exposure (number of times they retweeted other's content), and (iii) interactivity (by looking for keywords in tweets like DM -Direct Message- or email). They concluded that high scores of influence and exposure showed a strong correlation to engagement with the extremist ideology. Manual analysis of the top 200 accounts was used for evaluating the proposed scoring.

In 2015, Berger and Morgan (2015) aimed at creating a demographic snapshot of ISIS supporters on Twitter and outline a methodology for detecting pro–ISIS accounts. Starting from a set of 454 seed accounts (identified in Berger and Strathearn, 2013) and recursively obtaining followers of those accounts and filtering them based on availability of the account, robot identification, etc., they obtained a final list of 20,000 pro–ISIS accounts to analyse. They estimated that at least 46,000 pro–ISIS accounts were active (as of December 2014). They created classifiers from a subset of 6,000 accounts that were manually annotated as ISIS supporters or non-supporters. The authors concluded that pro–ISIS supporters could be identified from their profile descriptions: with terms such as succession, linger, Islamic State, Caliphate State or In Iraq all being prominent. When testing this classifier with 1,574 manually annotated accounts they obtained 94% of classification accuracy. However, profile information was only available for around 70% of accounts.

Saif (2017) proposed a semantic graph-based approach to identify pro vs. anti–ISIS social media accounts. By using this graph, the authors aimed at capturing the relations between terms (e.g. countries *attacking* ISIS vs. countries *attacked* by ISIS) as well as contextual information based on the co-occurrence of terms. Their work hypothesised that, by exploiting the latent semantics of words expressed in social media content, they could identify additional pro–ISIS and anti–ISIS signals that could complement the ones extracted from previous approaches. The authors developed multiple classifiers and showed that their proposed classifier, trained for semantic features, outperformed those trained from lexical, sentiment, topic and network features. Evaluation was done on a dataset of 1,132 Twitter users (with their timelines): 566 pro–ISIS accounts, obtained from Rowe and Saif (2016), and 566 anti–ISIS users, whose stance was determined by the use of anti–ISIS rhetoric.

Fernandez and Alani (2018) hypothesise that a key reason behind the inaccuracy of radicalisation detection approaches is their reliance on the appearance of terminologies and expressions regardless of their context. The authors therefore explore: (i) how pro–ISIS users and non pro–ISIS users (journalists, researchers, religious users, etc.) use the same words and expressions, (ii) if there exist any divergence in how the same words are used, and (iii) if this context divergence can be helpful to create more accurate radicalisation detection methods. The work uses 17K tweets from pro–ISIS users and 122K tweets from 'general' Twitter users available via the Kaggle (2019) datasets. This work concludes that the identification of language divergence between these groups can lead to more accurate user and content detection mechanisms.

Stepping aside from the categorisation of users as 'radical' or 'non-radical', Fernandez et al. (2018) proposed an approach to measure the influence of online radicalisation that a user is exposed to. The proposed approach renders the social science theory of 'roots of radicalisation' (Schmid, 2013; Borum, 2016) into a computational model that computes the micro (individual, i.e. originating from the user himself), meso (social, i.e. originating from the user's social network) and macro (global, i.e. originating from events happening in the world) radicalisation influence a user is exposed to based on her social media contributions. The work used 17K tweets from pro-ISIS users and 122K tweets from 'general' Twitter users available via the Kaggle (2019) data science community, and concluded that there is an important need to leverage more strongly the knowledge of theoretical models of radicalisation to design more effective technological solutions for the tracking of online radicalisation.

Agarwal and Sureka (2015b) investigated techniques to automatically identify hate and extremism promoting tweets. Starting from 2 crawls of Twitter data they used a semi-supervised learning approach based on a list of hashtags (#Terrorism, #Islamophobia, #Extremist) to filter those tweets related to hate and extremism. The training dataset contained 10,486 tweets. They used random sampling to generate the validation dataset (1M tweets). Tweets were in English and manually annotated by four students. They created and validated two different classifiers (KNN and SVM) based on the generated datasets to classify a tweet as hate promoting or unknown. By creating and validating these classifiers, they concluded that the presence of religious, war related terms, offensive words and negative emotions are strong indicators of a tweet to be hate promoting.

Ashcroft et al. (2015) investigated the automatic detection of messages released by jihadist groups on Twitter. They collected tweets from 6729 Jihadist sympathisers. Two additional datasets, one of 2,000 randomly selected tweets, and one of tweets from accounts manually annotated as anti-ISIS, were collected for validation. Numbers of tweets for the pro and anti-ISIS datasets were not reported, but based on the provided experiments we estimated they should be around 2,000 each. SVM, Naive Bayes and Adaboost classifiers were trained with this data using stylometric, time and sentiment features. Authors concluded that Fridays are a key date to spread radical tweets and that automatic detection is viable but can never replace human analysts. It should be seen as a complementary way to detect radical content.

Prediction

Regarding prediction of radicalisation (see Table 5.3), we can highlight the works of Magdy et al. (2016) and Ferrara et al. (2016). Magdy et al. (2016) proposed an approach to identify Arab Twitter accounts explicitly expressing

Table 5.3 Approaches that focus on the prediction of online radicalisation.

Work	Goal	Data	AI Algorithm / Technique	Conclusions
Magdy et al. (2016)	Proposed an approach to predict future support or opposition to ISIS	57,000 Twitter users who authored or shared tweets mentioning ISIS. Categorised as pro or anti-ISIS based on the use of the full name of the group vs. an abbreviated form	SVM classifier based on bag-of-words features, including individual terms, hashtags, and user mentions	Pro- and anti-ISIS users can be identified before they voice explicit support or opposition.
Ferrara et al. (2016)	Propose a computational framework for detection and prediction of: adoption of radical content and interaction with pro-ISIS accounts	Over 3M Twitter posts generated by over 25 thousand extremist accounts (manually identified, reported, and suspended by Twitter). 29M posts from the followers of these accounts	Random forest and logistic regression classifiers are used for classification and prediction based on user metadata and activity features, time features, and features based on network statistics	The ratio of retweets to tweets, the average number of hashtags adopted, the sheer number of tweets and the average number of retweets generated by each user, systematically rank very high in terms of predictive power

positions supporting or opposing ISIS. They collected 57,000 Twitter users who authored or shared tweets mentioning ISIS and determined their stance based on the use of the full name of the group vs. an abbreviated form. They then created classifiers to predict future support of opposition to ISIS based on the users' timelines before naming ISIS. The authors conclude that Pro- and anti-ISIS users can be identified before they voice explicit support or opposition. Ferrara et al. (2016), in turn, proposed a computational framework for detection and prediction of extremism in social media. For this purpose, they used a dataset of over 3M tweets generated by over 25 thousand extremist accounts, who have been manually identified, reported, and suspended by Twitter (Ferrara, 2017), and a dataset of 29M posts from the followers of these users. Random forest and logistic regression were used for classification and prediction based on user metadata and activity features, time features, and features based on network statistics. Two types of predictions were made: (i)

Figure 5.2 Main challenges of the development of AI applications to counter radicalisation.

whether the follower will adopt extremist content (retweet from a known pro-ISIS account), and (ii) whether the follower will interact (reply) with a known pro-ISIS account. The authors concluded that the ratio of retweets to tweets, the average number of hashtags adopted, the sheer number of tweets and the average number of retweets generated by each user, systematically rank very high in terms of predictive power.

Challenges

Despite the previous advancements in the area, multiple challenges still exist when targeting online radicalisation. These challenges include: (i) the ones that are derived from conducting research with Big Data such as (Volume – large amounts of content, Velocity – new content quickly produced, Variety – heterogeneity of the data and the information sources where data is produced, and Veracity – quality of the information), (ii) the ones that are derived from the application of technology into a new field (such as technology adoption by users), and (iii) the ones that are specific to online radicalisation research and the development of AI applications to counter radicalisation. Although we acknowledge the challenges derived from the use of big data, and the challenges for relevant stakeholders to adopt novel counter radicalisation technology, in this book chapter we aim to focus on the specific challenges of the design and development of AI solutions to counter radicalisation. We have identified six main challenges in this work (see Figure 5.2). These challenges are described in the following subsections.

Defining radicalisation

One of the key challenges of the design and development of AI technology to target radicalisation is the lack of a common definition of prohibited radical and extremist internet activity, which can impede optimal enforcement

(Housen-Couriel et al., 2019). Online radicalisation is a global phenomenon, but it is perceived differently in different regions of the world, and hence it is complicated to have a single unique and globally accepted definition (Meserole and Byman, 2019).

Currently, many governments around the world are pressurising globally operating Tech companies, such as Google, Facebook and Twitter, to remove and block radical content and accounts. However, no clear definitions of what constitutes a radical piece of content, or a radical account are provided with these government regulations, which means that Tech companies have to set up their own definitions and to decide which content they block or which content they keep online, with the corresponding ethical implications that this entails (Saltman, 2019). Initiatives such as the *Global Internet Forum*, or *Tech Against Terrorism* have emerged in recent years with the idea of formalising definitions and fostering collaborations among Tech companies, civil society, academics, governments and supra-national bodies such as the European Union (EU) and United Nations (UN). However, more dialog and collaboration across these organisations is needed to reach a consistent definition.

Data collection, verification and publication

Another very important challenge when researching online radicalisation is the availability and quality of data used to study this phenomenon. As we have seen in the previous works, multiple datasets have been collected for studying

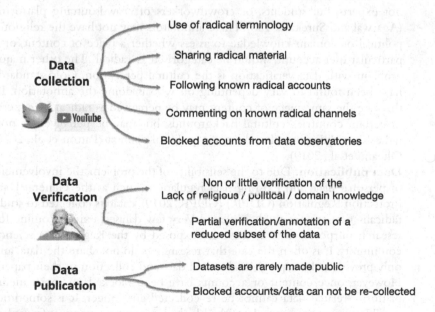

Figure 5.3 Mechanisms used for data collection, verification and publication.

radicalisation. However, many of these datasets are collected based on certain assumptions (e.g. accounts that use radical terminology or share radical material (Rowe and Saif, 2016; Magdy et al., 2016), accounts that follow known radical accounts (Chatfield et al., 2015), accounts that participate/comment in particular YouTube channels known to disseminate radical content (Bermingham et al., 2009)) but in many occasions, neither those assumptions, nor the data collected based on those assumptions, are properly verified. It is therefore unclear how the amount of noise (content that is not reliable or credible) that exists in those datasets is affecting the quality and validity of the insights gained from that data (Parekh et al., 2018). In this section we report on the problems derived from the current mechanisms used for data collection, verification and publication (see Figure 5.3).

- **Data collection:** As reported in the previous section, common methods used for data collection include: (i) data collected based on the appearance of certain terms ('ISIS', 'daesh', etc.), (ii) data collected based on users sharing a particular URL / image or piece of radical material, (iii) data collected from followers' of known radical accounts, (iv) data collected from users that comment in radical channels (such as YouTube channels), and (v) data collected for accounts that have been blocked or suspended (using data archives gathered by data observatories).
- **Data verification:** Once data is collected based on these assumptions, these data is either not verified, or partially verified, i.e. only a subset of the data is labelled by human annotators. These annotators are generally not experts, but students, or crowdworkers of crowdsourcing platforms (Agarwal and Sureka 2015b). These annotators may not have the religious, political or domain knowledge to assess whether a piece of content, or a particular user account, should be categorised as 'radical'. The other major problem with data verification is the cultural perception. Gold standards have been found to vary depending on who is doing the annotation. In this case the same piece of content may be perceived as radical by experts of certain countries/cultural backgrounds, but may be perceived as non radical in a different cultural / socio-political context (Patton et al., 2019, Olteanu et al., 2019).
- **Data publication:** Due to the sensibility of the problem, the involvement of personal data, and existing data regulations, such as the General Data Protection Regulation (GDPR) (GDPR, 2019), datasets collected to study radicalisation are not publicly shared. Very few datasets existing online for research purposes, such as the ones exposed by the Kaggle data science community. It is often the case that researchers do not share the data, and only provide a description of the used data and collection in their papers. However, once content or accounts have been blocked on social media platform, related data cannot be re-collected any longer. It is sometimes possible to retrieve a sample of the blocked content or accounts from data

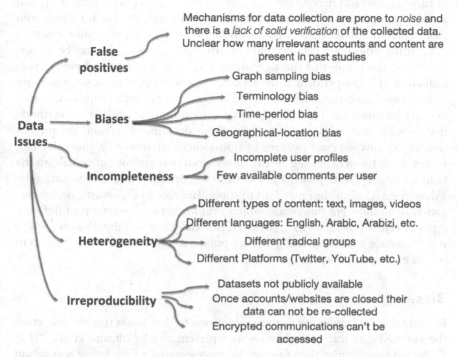

Mechanisms for data collection are prone to *noise* and there is a *lack of solid verification* of the collected data. Unclear how many irrelevant accounts and content are present in past studies

False positives

Biases
Graph sampling bias
Terminology bias
Time-period bias
Geographical-location bias

Data Issues

Incompleteness
Incomplete user profiles
Few available comments per user

Heterogeneity
Different types of content: text, images, videos
Different languages: English, Arabic, Arabizi, etc.
Different radical groups
Different Platforms (Twitter, YouTube, etc.)

Irreproducibility
Datasets not publicly available
Once accounts/websites are closed their data can not be re-collected
Encrypted communications can't be accessed

Figure 5.4 Problems with existing datasets to study radicalisation.

observatories (Ferrara, 2017), but it is unknown what percentage of such information is lost.

In the following subsections we describe some of the challenges derived from the existing data collection, verification and publication mechanisms (see Figure 5.4).

Noisy data (false positives)

Since existing data collection mechanisms to study online radicalisation are prone to noise, and the collected data is not verified, or only partially verified, the generated datasets could include an unknown amount of false positives (i.e. content and user accounts that, while categorised as radical, are indeed not radical). Examples include content and accounts reporting current events, e.g. "Islamic State hacks Swedish radio station", sharing harmless religious rhetoric, e.g. "If you want to talk to Allah, pray. If you want Allah to talk to you, read the Qur'an", or sharing counter extremism narratives and material, e.g. "armed Jihad is for defence of Muslim nation, not for establishment of the Khilafah". Parekh and colleagues (Parekh et al., 2018) highlighted this problem in their analysis and stressed the fact that "nobody knows how many irrelevant accounts are present in past studies and therefore much of what is known from past studies of online jihadist behavior is highly skewed by irrelevant accounts".

Learning from noisy data not only means that analysis results may be imperfect, but it also means that the algorithms developed to detect and predict radicalisation may not perform at the reported levels of correctness, since they are trained based on erroneously labelled data. Since irrelevant accounts may erroneously be categorised as 'radical', based on existing data collection methods, it is possible that, while training from these data, the detection and prediction algorithms associate patterns of non-radical accounts (e.g. journalist that report about terrorist-related events, or religious non violent individuals) to the radical category. Note that the erroneous categorisation of a user as radical by a developed AI algorithm may lead to surveillance, or in the worst case, investigation of an innocent individual, which calls for better assessments of different types of errors (Olteanu et al., 2017). Additionally, because the datasets used to train these algorithms are not generally public, it is not possible to verify up to which extent they contain noisy data.

Biases

Existing data collection mechanisms are prone to data biases (i.e. the distortion the sampled data that compromises its representatives) (Olteanu et al., 2019). Collected samples may therefore not be representative of the larger population of interest. Common biases across online radicalisation research include: the terminology bias, the time-period bias, the graph-sampling bias and the geographical location bias. However, it is relevant to note that demographic (age/gender, etc.), as well as behavioural biases (e.g. the various ways in which users connect and interact with one another), may also exist within the collected datasets.

- **Terminology:** When data is collected based on restricted lexicons (i.e. selected terms and expressions), these lexicons may cover only a fraction of the topics or entities (persons, organisations, etc.) discussed by radical groups. They may also cover only the terminology of a particular subgroup, or even only one language (e.g. Arabic). Collected content and accounts are therefore biased to the original lexicons used for collection. It is therefore important to acknowledge that the obtained findings (or developed radicalisation detection classifiers) may not be general but restricted to particular topics of discussion.
- **Time-period:** Data collections are generally restricted to particular time periods (generally a few months). Data is therefore biased to the world events happening during those particular months (i.e. particular terror attacks, regions of the world, political and religious figures, etc.). Classifiers may therefore learn that naming certain political or religious figures, or

locations, are reliable indicators to determine whether a piece of content, or a user account, is radical. However, as time evolves, those locations, those popular figures, those events, may not be relevant or even discussed any longer. In certain cases, they may even become discriminative of the opposite class (e.g. locations under control by a radical group that become liberated) Hence, classifiers trained on data collected in the past to detect and predict radicalisation in the present, or the future, may not perform with the expected level of correctness.

- **Graph-sampling:** The discovery of related accounts is generally based on graph sampling methods, where related accounts are discovered from the social graph of known radical (i.e. seed) accounts. The expanded dataset therefore depends on the choice of the initial seed accounts. The other key problem is the type or relations selected to do graph sampling, since in the case of *'followers'*, irrelevant or noisy accounts, such as reporters and researchers, who are just 'listening' to jihadist accounts, are likely to be included (Klausen, 2015; Parekh et al., 2018).
- **Geographical:** Some data collections are restricted to particular regions of the world (e.g. western countries (Rowe and Saif, 2016)). Variations in user-generated content, particularly text, are well documented across and within demographic groups. Findings about 'radicalisation' based on such samples may hence not be generalisable to other regions in the world.

Incompleteness

When datasets are collected based on keywords, or when data is gathered based on comments on particular YouTube channels, or social media groups, the collected datasets contain very few posts (if more than one) associated to a particular user account (incomplete user profiles). This means that, for most user accounts, only a partial view of the history (or timeline) of such account is available. This limits the type of research that can be conducted, since it is very difficult (if not impossible) to study the behavioural evolution of users towards more radical views if their historic posts are not available. Since social media platforms sometimes close radical accounts fairly quickly, recollecting data from such accounts is no longer possible. Similarly, although accounts that get blocked tend to resurface under different names (Conway et al., 2017), those accounts do not have historical data, and therefore AI solutions need to deal with a 'cold start' problem (i.e. accurate inferences cannot be drawn from accounts for which we have not yet gathered sufficient information).

Additional elements of incompleteness within existing datasets are the collected social graphs. In most occasions only a partial sample of the social graph of the collected accounts is being gathered (incomplete social graphs). Some researchers tried to reproduce social graphs based on implicit connections (e.g. users mentioning other users within the content (Fernandez et al., 2019)), when the explicit (friend/follower) relations among accounts are not available.

Heterogeneity (variety of content)

Another relevant consideration is the heterogeneity of the data. Online data comes in multiple languages, from multiple platforms, in multiple formats (audio, video, text) and from multiple radical groups and subgroups. The development of 'generic' online radicalisation detection methods in an ever changing and heterogeneous world is a complex and challenging task.

- **Language:** Online data comes in multiple languages, sometimes underrepresented languages or forms of text, such as Arabizi (Arabic language written in Latin Script (Tobaili et al., 2019)). Multiple challenges arise when dealing with the multilingual sea of data available online: (i) the lack of resources and local expertise to analyse underrepresented languages, (ii) the automatic identification of the written language, since not only languages coexist across different pieces of content, but the same piece of content may contain terms and expressions in more than one language, and (iii) the informality of social media language, which is an added challenge to the multilinguality of the text. Note that terms and expressions in social media are sometimes written without following standard morphological, or syntactic rules (e.g. 'Heeeeeello' vs. Hello). It is also the case that communities and social groups often invent and adopt terms to define new realities. For example, the acronym KTHHFV, adopted within extreme misogynist communities refers to a kissless, touchless, hugless, handholdless, friendless, virgin person (Farrell et al., 2019). Not only are those new terms and expressions not available within standard dictionaries, but also the meanings of those terms and expressions are not known outside the communities that invented and adopted them, hence expert or inside knowledge is needed to capture these complex semantics.
- **Platforms:** radical content is shared in multiple social networking platforms, including Twitter, Reddit, YouTube, Whatsapp, Telegram, etc. Each platform differs on how content is posted (e.g. Twitter limits the amount of characters of a posts while other platforms don't have length restrictions) or how user relations are established (e.g. Twitter distinguishes between 'followers – people who follow a user account' and 'followees – people to whom the user account follows') whether others, like Whatsapp, do not consider bidirectional relationships. There are also distinctions on how content is shared, how accounts are referred to, or named, whether videos can be streamed, etc.
- **Radical groups:** Not only different accounts may express different extremist ideologies (Jihadist, Far-right, extreme misogyny, etc.), but also within the same extremist ideology we may find different groups. These groups, while having some common ground, differ in their interpretation of concepts, and in their attitudes and actions. Not only these groups

coexist within the online world, they also merge and shift depending on real-world events, interests and conflicts.

- **Content types:** In the online world different types of content emerge including videos, images, text, etc. The automatic processing of multi-media content is very different than the processing of textual content. Combinations of AI techniques are therefore needed to understand the complete picture of the radical material being disseminated.

Irreproducibility

A key problem of existing radicalisation research is the lack of reproducibility, since datasets used to study radicalisation are not shared, and once user accounts or content are blocked, data can no longer be recollected.

- **Datasets are not publicly available:** As mentioned when describing existing data publishing methods, while multiple datasets have been collected for research, due to the sensitivity of the data, and to comply with existing social networking sites regulations (Twitter, 2019), and data regulations, such as GDPR (2019), researchers are not sharing the collected datasets. This implies that: (i) further assessments over the data are very difficult to perform, and (ii) researchers struggle to build on previous studies and developed systems to further advance research.
- **Once accounts/websites are closed data cannot be recollected:** Researchers working in online radicalisation sometimes share the IDs of forums/groups, accounts or posts (Farrell et al., 2019), so that other researchers can recollect the data. The problem in this case is that, if the collected accounts were indeed radical, or the collected content exhibited radical terminology or material, they will be blocked at the time of recollection. Moreover, according to the data regulations of some social media platforms, like Twitter (2019), researchers and practitioners that collect data are responsible of making all reasonable efforts to delete the collected content, if such content is deleted, gains protected status or is suspended (unless otherwise prohibited by applicable law or regulation, and with the express written permission of Twitter). This regulation makes it even more difficult to maintain datasets to study radicalisation.
- **Encrypted and private communications cannot be accessed:** Extremist organisations sometimes move from the public sphere to a more private medium. This is for example the case of the Islamic State (IS), which moved many of its communications to Telegram due to the disruption they suffered on more visible platforms such as Twitter (Conway et al., 2017). Platforms such as Telegram or Whatsapp offer end-to-end encrypted communications. Therefore, messages sent via private channels, groups and chats cannot be collected. Journalist and researchers have nonetheless gathered and studied information from these platforms via public

Telegram channels, and by infiltrating private groups (Clifford and Powell, 2019). IS has also started to experiment with the Decentralised Web. Platforms such as RocketChat and ZeroNet proved attractive for IS media operatives since the developers of those platforms are unable to act against content that is stored on user-operated servers or dispersed across the user community (King, 2019).

Research methodologies

Various problems and challenges are also derived from the research methodologies used to investigate online radicalisation. We will discuss in this section two common issues: (i) the lack of a control group to contrast research findings, and (ii) the lack of comparison across existing technological solutions.

Lack of comparison against a control group

One of the key problems with existing radicalisation research is the lack of comparison against a control group. Most data analysis approaches are based on the study of datasets containing radical content, or radical accounts (Bermingham et al., 2009; Chatfield et al., 2015; Rowe and Saif, 2016; Badawy and Ferrara, 2018). Based on the analysis of these datasets, these works make conclusions on the most discriminative features or characteristics of radical content and users. However, they do not investigate how these features differ from those of a control group (e.g. religious not violent accounts, accounts from journalist reporting about related events, counter-extremist accounts, and accounts from users with no particular relation with radicalisation). Unless such comparisons are made, it is not possible to claim that certain terms, behaviours, networks, etc., are specific of extremist content or accounts.

In the case of the creation of detection and prediction approaches, most works use a control group, so that the AI algorithms can learn the key discriminative features and divergences between the radical and the non-radical control group. The key problem with some of these works is that, in the majority of the cases, the used control group is composed by randomly collected posts and user accounts (Agarwal and Sureka 2015b; Lara-Cabrera et al., 2017). These are the accounts of average social platform users (who may talk about their work, their pets, or other topics not even partially related with extremism or radicalisation). The key challenge however, lies on differentiating radical accounts from those that, despite using the same terminology, reporting the same events, or talking about the same topics, are indeed not radical (e.g. accounts or religious not violent individuals, journalist accounts, counter-terrorism accounts, etc.). While some works have attempted to generate control-group datasets by considering similar lexicons to collect radical and non-radical accounts (Fernandez and Alani, 2018), those accounts are not-verified, and it is therefore not possible to determine whether the control group contains representative examples of the above mentioned categories, or simply standard Twitter users that at some point in time share the same terminology than the radical group under study. Another issue emerges when the control group is collected in a different time period (Lara-Cabrera et al., 2017). Classifiers may then select as discriminative features of the non-radical class terms, like political figures, simply because these terms did not exist in the previous time period when the radical group was collected.

Lack of comparison across approaches

The other main issue that we observe within the literature is the lack of comparison across existing approaches. Different works have analysed and are trained over different datasets, making results and approaches not easily comparable. In Correa and Sureka (2013) and Agarwal and Sureka (2015a), the authors conducted an extensive survey of the techniques used to identify and predict radicalisation in social media. From these systematic literature reviews, and the overview provided in this paper, we can observe the use of multiple techniques within different subfields of AI including:

- *Natural Language Processing* (NLP) and the use and development of lexicons to interpret text (Vergani and Bliuc, 2015; Fernandez et al., 2018; Badawy and Ferrara, 2018).
- *Machine Learning* (ML) mostly supervised approaches (SVM, Linear Regressions, Naive Bayes, Decision Trees, and lately deep-learning models) for the automatic detection and prediction of radicalisation (Berger and Morgan, 2015; Agarwal and Sureka 2015b).
- *Semantic Web technologies* (entity and relation extraction and analysis) (Saif et al., 2017; Fernandez and Alani, 2018) to better identify the semantic *context* in which words and expressions are used, or the context in which certain entities (persons, organisations, locations) are mentioned, as a way to improve the accuracy of existing algorithms for radicalisation detection.
- *Information Retrieval techniques* (IR), particularly the use of *ranking* methods and *recommender systems* (Fernandez et al., 2018; Fernandez et al., 2019), as a way to filter and rank content and accounts rather than providing a binary categorisation (radical vs. non-radical).

However, while literature surveys have attempted to identify the wide range of AI techniques used to counter online radicalisation, to the best of our knowledge, there are no replication studies in the literature attempting to compare existing approaches and techniques. Comparative studies could help to determine which features, or which classification methods do actually perform more reliably, accurately and efficiently, and under which contexts, when countering online radicalisation. It's also important to note that the algorithms designed and developed by Tech companies (such as Twitter, Google or Facebook) are not public, and therefore not available for comparison.

Lack of cooperation across research fields

Understanding the mechanisms that govern the process of radicalisation, and online radicalisation in particular, has been the topic of investigation in multiple research fields including: social sciences (Schmid, 2013; Hafez and Mullins, 2015), psychology (Moghaddam, 2005; Van der Veen, 2016), computing (Agarwal and Sureka, 2015a), policing (Silber et al., 2007), and governance (European Parliament, 2019). These efforts however, have mostly evolved in silos, and most of the existing works towards the design and development of AI technology to counter online radicalisation are neither based on, nor do they take advantage of, the existing theories and studies of radicalisation coming from social sciences, psychology or policing.

Models from social science, psychology and policing have investigated the factors that drive people to get radicalised (Moghaddam, 2005) (e.g. failed integration, poverty, discrimination), their different roots (Schmid, 2013; Borum, 2016) (micro-level, or individual level, mesolevel, or group/community level, and macro-level, or global level, the influence of government and society at home and abroad), and how the radicalisation process happens and evolves, i.e. what are its different stages (Silber et al., 2007) (e.g. pre-radicalisation, self-identification, indoctrination, Jihadisation). However, very few works in the literature (Lara-Cabrera et al., 2017; Fernandez et al., 2018) have used the learning from these models to create more effective radicalisation analysis and detection methods. AI technology development needs to leverage closer the knowledge of theoretical models of radicalisation to design more effective technological solutions to target online radicalisation.

Adaptation of extremist groups

While multiple efforts are being made to design and develop effective AI solutions that automatically identify and block radical accounts, or that stop the viral spreading or radical content, extremist groups are adapting their behaviour to avoid being detected, or to resurface once they have been blocked (Conway et al., 2017). We list here some of the adaptation techniques used by these groups to maintain their online presence (Bodo, 2018).

- **Content adaptation**: In order to avoid being flagged by AI technology, extremist organisations adapt their content, either by replacing/modifying terms, or by distorting the audio and pixilation of images and videos (Stalman, 2019).
- **User-account adaptation:** Some extremist groups use proxies, such as media organisations or local charities, to post content on the platforms for them to avoid being detected (Frenkel and Hubbard, 2019). In the cases where the accounts are blocked, extremist groups manage to keep re-emerging within the same platform under different names, using a variety of strategies to be found by their followers (Conway et al., 2017).

- **Platform adaptation:** In some cases, extremist groups also change platforms. An example is the Islamic State (IS), which in recent years moved many of its communication to Telegram (al-Lami, 2018; Clifford and Powell, 2019) due to the disruption they faced on more visible platforms such as Twitter (Conway et al., 2017), and more recently they are exploring the use of the decentralised Web via platforms like RocketChat and ZeroNet (King, 2019).
- **Technology adaptation:** Extremist organisations make use of the latest technological developments in order to increase the spread of their message. A key example of this is the use of life-stream videos. For example, during the recent attack at Christchurch, New Zealand, the video of the shooting was spread all around the Internet. Despite the efforts of tech companies to contain the virality, many hours after the shooting, various clips of the video were still searchable (Lapowsky, 2019).

Ethics and conflicts in legislation

Another key challenge of the design, development and use of AI to counter radicalisation is that technology needs to comply with legislation that can sometimes be ambiguous or contradictory, particularly when it comes to the tension between security, privacy and freedom of expression. The European Commission, for example, is proposing legislation to ensure all member states bring in sanctions against those who repeatedly fail to respond to removal orders of radical content, facing penalties up to 4% of their global revenue. The draft regulation was approved by Members of the European Parliament (MEPs) in April 2019 (European Parliament, 2019). Critics, including internet freedom think tanks and big tech firms, claim the legislation threatens the principles of a free and open internet (Porter, 2019). Another example is the regulation that will force WhatsApp, Facebook and other social media platforms to disclose encrypted messages from suspected terrorists under a new treaty between the UK and US (Swinford, 2019), with a similar law is already approved in Australia. Privacy advocates are highly critical and have highlighted the potential negative implications that these regulations will have for future cases on privacy and government surveillance.

The other key issue that emerges from the use of AI to counter online radicalisation is the need for a constant review of ethical guidelines in order to assess the risk of the proposed technology and address them through reflexivity and anticipation (Troullinou and d'Aquin, 2018). Processes and decisions, once undertaken by humans, are now computer-driven, increasingly derived through AI powered by big data. And, while reports from the European Union (EU) (European Commission, 2018) state the need of AI to be based on values of respect for human dignity, freedom, democracy, equality, the rule of law, and respect for human rights; the reality is that the rapid and ethically careless development of AI has led to serious adverse effects that go against these values

(Harford, 2014). In the case of the development of AI systems to counter online extremism, the wrong categorisation of a user as 'radical' or 'extremist' may result in an innocent person being subjected to surveillance. It is therefore extremely important to consider potential sources of inaccuracy of automatic AI-powered radicalisation detection approaches, and to have a constant reflection and continuous change in ethical guidelines to reduce the potential negative impact of AI developments.

Opportunities

The challenges and issues reported above open a wide range of opportunities for the improvement of AI solutions to counter online radicalisation. We highlight here six main lines of research that we hope to inspire the design and development of future AI technology: (i) stronger collaboration across research disciplines and organisations, (ii) creation of reliable datasets to study online radicalisation, (iii) development of comparative studies, (iv) contextual adaptation of technological solutions (v) better integration of humans and technology, and (vi) ethical vigilance.

Collaboration across research disciplines and organisations

Since 2017 several initiatives, such as the Global Internet Forum, or Tech Against Terrorism have emerged, putting Tech Companies in contact with Governments, Civil Societies, researchers and NGOS in order to have a better understanding of what radicalisation is, and how to stop the online phenomenon. These initiatives are helping to create consensus, and to define more clearly what constitutes radical and extremist internet activity, since tech companies should not be the 'deciders' of content moderation (Saltman, 2019). It is also necessary to include different points of view on the discussion table, to ensure the right balance between security, privacy, freedom of expression and content moderation.

While initiatives have emerged to ensure a wide range of organisations are collaborating towards the development of AI solutions to counter radicalisation, synergies across different research fields (psychology, social science, policing, computer science) are yet to become a reality (Scrivens and Davies, 2018). AI design and development can strongly benefit from leveraging closer the knowledge of theoretical models of radicalisation, and the empirical evidence gathered through policing research, to design more effective technological solutions to target online radicalisation.

Creation of reliable datasets to study radicalisation

As we observed in the previous section, the majority of ground truth datasets used to study online radicalisation lack of solid verification. We continue to observe false positives, incompleteness and biases in those datasets. Many datasets used in radicalisation studies are no longer available and recollecting that data is no longer possible. Obtaining and annotating data to create reliable gold standard datasets (as well as sharing them for reproducibility purposes) are key future steps for research on online radicalisation.

Comparative studies

As previously reported, different AI approaches have been developed to counter online radicalisation. However, while some of these approaches target the same objective (e.g. identify radical content / identify radical accounts), they have not been compared against one another. Replication studies are therefore needed to assess existing approaches and techniques, to understand their strengths and limitations and to determine which ones should be applied and under which conditions.

Contextual adaptation of technological solutions

As mentioned in our first reported challenge, radicalisation needs to be understood in context (time, geographic location, culture, etc.). The same piece of content may be deemed as radical within a particular region of the world, and as non-radical in a different region. Similarly, as shown by Fernandez and Alani (2018), contextual divergences also emerge within the use of radicalisation terms, and understanding such nuances can help to enhance existing radicalisation detection approaches. It is therefore important to develop robust technological solutions, able to adapt to the different contexts in which they may need to operate.

Better integration of humans and technology

Radicalisation is a human-driven problem, and to develop effective AI solutions to counter this problem it is important to introduce humans in the loop. Human feedback and expertise can be applied at various levels including:

- Co-creation with users: technology development could benefit from the use of co-creation to ensure that different points of view and perspectives are gathered and that this complex problem is targeted simultaneously from different angles.
- Technology and humans deciding together: Expertise may be needed to review complex software decisions. Developing technology that facilitates that human expertise is integrated in the decision-making process could help mitigating the impact of erroneous or controversial outputs.
- Human feedback for technology adaptation: The development of technology that gathers and integrates human feedback can help ensuring that algorithms are retrained, capturing evolving behaviours, themes, and novel radicalisation strategies.

Ethical vigilance

As we previously discussed, there is a strong tension between ensuring security, privacy, and freedom of expression, when targeting online radicalisation. Ethical methodologies are therefore needed to track the human and societal effects of AI technologies during the design, development, and post-production processes. Particularly, the development of post-market ethical monitoring methods will be needed to further refine, confirm or deny, the safety of a particular technology after it is used to counter online extremism, helping to identify potential unforeseen negative effects.

Conclusions

In this chapter we have provided an overview of the current AI technological advancements towards addressing the problem of online extremism, identified some of the limitations of existing solutions, and highlighted some opportunities for future research. We hope the provided critical reflections will stimulate discussions on the future design and development of AI technology to target the problem of online extremism.

References

Agarwal, S. and Sureka, A. (2015a). Applying social media intelligence for predicting and identifying on-line radicalization and civil unrest oriented threats. arXiv preprint arXiv:1511.06858.

Agarwal, S. and Sureka, A (2015b). Using knn and svm based one-class classifier for detecting online radicalization on twitter. In: *International Conference on Distributed Computing and Internet Technology*. Springer, 431–442.

al-Lami, M (2018). Jihadist media's cat and mouse game. *BBC Monitoring*. https://monitoring.bbc.co.uk/inside-bbcm/7.

Ashcroft, M., Fisher, A., Kaati, L., Omer, E. and Prucha, N. (2015). Detecting jihadist messages on twitter. In Intelligence and Security Informatics Conference (EISIC), 2015 European. IEEE, 161–164.

Badawy, A. and Ferrara, E. (2018). The rise of jihadist propaganda on social networks. *Journal of Computational Social Science*, 1(2), pp. 453–470.

Berger, J.M. and Morgan, J. (2015). The ISIS Twitter Census: Defining and describing the population of ISIS supporters on Twitter. *The Brookings Project on US Relations with the Islamic World*, 3, 20 (2015), 4–1.

Berger, J.M. and Strathearn, B. (2013). Who Matters Online: Measuring influence, evaluating content and countering violent extremism in online social networks. International Centre for the Study of Radicalisation and Political Violence (2013).

Bermingham, A., Conway, M., McInerney, L., O'Hare, N. and Smeaton, A.F (2009). Combining social network analysis and sentiment analysis to explore the potential for online radicalisation. In Int. Conf. Advances in Social Network Analysis and Mining (ASONAM'09).

Bodo, L. (2018). Now you see it, now you don't? Moving beyond account and content removal in digital counter-extremism operations. www.voxpol.eu/now-you-see-it-now-you-dont-moving-beyond-account-content-removal-in-digital-counter-extremism-operations/ [accessed 1 February 2019].

Borum, R. (2016). The etiology of radicalization. In: G. LaFree and J. Freilich (eds), *The Handbook of the Criminology of Terroris*. Oxford: Wiley.

Carter, J.A, Maher, S. and Neumann, P.R. (2014). Greenbirds: Measuring importance and influence in Syrian foreign fighter networks.

Chatfield, A.T, Reddick, C.G, and Brajawidagda, U. (2015). Tweeting propaganda, radicalization and recruitment: Islamic state supporters multi-sided twitter networks. In Proceedings of the 16th Annual International Conference on Digital Government Research. ACM, 239–249.

Clifford, B. and Powell, H. (2019). Encrypted extremism. Inside the English-speaking Islamic State ecosystem on telegram. Program on extremism https://extremism.gwu.edu/sites/g/files/zaxdzs2191/f/EncryptedExtremism.pdf.

Conway, M. et al. (2017). Disrupting Daesh: Measuring takedown of online terrorist material and its impacts. *Studies in Conflict and Terrorism*, 42(1–2), 141–160, DOI: 10.1080/1057610X.2018.1513984.

Correa, D. and Sureka, A. (2013). Solutions to detect and analyze online radicalization: a survey. arXiv preprint arXiv:1301.4916.

Edwards, C. and Gribbon, L. (2013). Pathways to violent extremism in the digital era. *The RUSI Journal*, 158, 5 (2013), 40–47.

European Commission. (2018). Communication Artificial Intelligence for Europe (2018). https://ec.europa.eu/digital-single-market/en/news/communication-artificial-intelligence-europe.

EU Expert Group. (2008). Radicalisation Processes Leading to Acts of Terrorism. A Concise Report prepared by the European Commission's Expert Group on Violent Radicalisation. Submitted to the European Commission on 15 May.

European Parliament. (2019). Legislative resolution of 17 April 2019 on the proposal for a regulation of the European Parliament and of the Council on preventing the dissemination of terrorist content online (COM(2018)0640 – C8-0405/2018 – 2018/0331(COD)), www.europarl.europa.eu/doceo/document/TA-8-2019-0421_EN.html.

Farrell, T., Fernandez, M., Novotny, J. and Alani, H. (2019). Exploring Misogyny across the Manosphere in Reddit. In: WebSci '19 Proceedings of the 10th ACM Conference on Web Science, pp. 87–96.

Farwell, J.P. (2014). The media strategy of ISIS. *Survival*, 56(6), 49–55.

Fernandez, M. and Alani, H. (2018). Contextual semantics for radicalisation detection on Twitter. In: Semantic Web for Social Good Workshop (SW4SG) at International Semantic Web Conference 2018, 9 Oct 2018, CEUR.

Fernandez, M, Asif, M. and Alani, H. (2018). Understanding the roots of radicalisation on twitter. Proceedings of the 10th ACM Conference on Web Science. ACM.

Fernandez, M.; Gonzalez-Pardo, A. and Alani, H. (2019). Radicalisation Influence in Social Media. *Journal of Web Science*, Vol.6.

Ferrara, E. (2017). Contagion dynamics of extremist propaganda in social networks. *Information Sciences*, 418 (2017), 1–12.

Ferrara, E., Wang, W.Q, Varol, O., Flammini, A. and Galstyan, A. (2016). Predicting online extremism, content adopters, and interaction reciprocity. In *International Conference on Social Informatics*. Springer, 22–39.

Frenkel, S. and Hubbard, B. (2019). After Social Media Bans, Militant Groups Found Ways to Remain. *The New York Times*. www.nytimes.com/2019/04/19/technology/terrorist-groups-social-media.html [accessed 1 September 2019].

Gartenstein-Ross, D. and Barr, N. (2016) The Myth of Lone-Wolf Terrorism. The Attacks in Europe and Digital Extremism. Foreign Affairs. www.foreignaffairs.com/articles/western-europe/2016-07-26/myth-lone-wolf-terrorism [accessed 2 February 2019].

Hafez, M. and Mullins, C. (2015). The radicalization puzzle: A theoretical synthesis of empirical approaches to homegrown extremism. *Studies in Conflict and Terrorism*.

Harford, T. (2014). Big data: A big mistake? *Significance*, 11(5), 14–19.

Housen-Couriel, D., Ganor, B., Yaakov, U.B, Weinberg, S. and Beri, D. (2019). The International Cyber Terrorism Regulation Project. https://rusi.org/publication/other-publications/international-cyber-terrorism-regulation-project [accessed 2 October 2019].

Kaggle. (2019). Datasets to study radicalisation. www.kaggle.com/fifthtribe/how-isis-uses-twitter, www.kaggle.com/activegalaxy/isis-related-tweets [accessed 30 October 2019].

King, P. (2019). Analysis: Islamic State's experiments with the decentralised web. BBC Monitoring. https://monitoring.bbc.co.uk/product/c200paga [accessed 1 November 2019].

Klausen, J. (2015). Tweeting the Jihad: Social media networks of Western foreign fighters in Syria and Iraq. *Studies in Conflict and Terrorism*, 38, 1.

Lapowsky, I. (2019). Why Tech Didn't Stop the New Zealand Attack From Going Viral. *WIRED*. www.wired.com/story/new-zealand-shooting-video-social-media/ [accessed 2 November 2019].

Lara-Cabrera, R., Gonzalez-Pardo, A. and Camacho, D. (2017). Statistical analysis of risk assessment factors and metrics to evaluate radicalisation in Twitter. Future Generation Computer Systems.

Magdy, W., Darwish, K. and Weber, I. (2016). #FailedRevolutions: Using Twitter to study the antecedents of ISIS support. First Monday, (S.l.), Jan. ISSN 13960466.

Meserole, C. and Byman, D. (2019). Terrorist definitions and designations lists. What technology companies need to know. *Global research network on terrorism and technology*. Paper No. 7.

Moghaddam, F.M. (2005). The staircase to terrorism: A psychological exploration. *American Psychologist*, 60(2), 161.

Moskalenko, S. and McCauley, C. (2009). Measuring Political Mobilization: The Distinction Between Activism and Radicalism, *Terrorism and Political Violence*, 21:2, 239–260, DOI: 10.1080/09546550902765508

O'Callaghan, D., Prucha, N., Greene, D., Conway, M., Carthy, J. and Cunningham, P. (2014). Online social media in the Syria conflict: Encompassing the extremes and the in-betweens. In: Int. Conf. Advances in Social Networks Analysis and Mining (ASONAM). Beijing, China.

Olteanu, A. et al. (2019). Social data: Biases, methodological pitfalls, and ethical boundaries. *Frontiers in Big Data*, 2, 13.

Olteanu, A., Talamadupula, K. and Varshney, K.R. (2017). "The limits of abstract evaluation metrics: The case of hate speech detection". Proceedings of the 2017 ACM on Web Science Conference. ACM.

Parekh, D. et al. (2018). "Studying Jihadists on Social Media: A Critique of Data Collection Methodologies". Perspectives on Terrorism, 12(3), 5–23.

Patton, D.U. et al. (2019). "Annotating Twitter Data from Vulnerable Populations: Evaluating Disagreement Between Domain Experts and Graduate Student Annotators".

Porter, J. (2019). Upload filters and one-hour takedowns: the EU's latest fight against terrorism online, explained. The Verge. www.theverge.com/2019/3/21/18274201/european-terrorist-content-regulation-extremist-terreg-upload-filter-one-hour-takedown-eu [accessed 1 September 2019].

Rowe, M. and Saif, H. (2016). Mining Pro-ISIS Radicalisation Signals from Social Media Users. In Int. Conf. Weblogs and Social Media (ICWSM). Cologne, Germany.

Saif, H., Dickinson, T., Kastler, L., Fernandez, M. and Alani, H. (2017). A semantic graph-based approach for radicalisation detection on social media. In: European Semantic Web Conference. Springer, 571–587.

Saltman, E. (2019). Global Research Network on Terrorism and Technology. www.youtube.com/watch?v=82L3ziU4LkM.

Schmid, A.P (2013). Radicalisation, de-radicalisation, counter-radicalisation: A conceptual discussion and literature review. ICCT Research Paper 97, 22.

Scrivens, R. and Davies, G. (2018). Identifying radical content online. https://policyoptions.irpp.org/magazines/january-2018/identifying-radical-content-online/ [accessed 4 September 2019].

Silber, M.D, Bhatt, A. and Senior Intelligence Analysts. (2007). Radicalization in the West: The homegrown threat. Police Department New York.

Swinford, S. (2019). Police can access suspects' Facebook and WhatsApp messages in deal with US. The Times. www.thetimes.co.uk/edition/news/police-can-access-suspects-facebook-and-whatsapp-messages-in-deal-with-us-q7lrfmchz [accessed 2 November 2019].

Tobaili, T., Fernandez, M., Alani, H., Sharafeddine, S., Hajj, H. and Glavas, G. (2019). SenZi: A Sentiment Analysis Lexicon for the Latinised Arabic (Arabizi). In: International Conference Recent Advances In Natural Language Processing (RANLP 2019). pp. 1204–1212.

Troullinou, P. and d'Aquin, M. (2018). Using Futuristic Scenarios for an Interdisciplinary Discussion on the Feasibility and Implications of Technology. In: A.M. Cirucci and B. Vacker (eds), Black Mirror and Critical Media Theory. Rowman and Littlefield.

Twitter. (2019). Twitter Data policies and privacy regulations 2019. https://cdn.cms-twdigitalassets.com/content/dam/legal-twitter/site-assets/privacy-policy-new/Privacy-Policy-Terms-of-Service_EN.pdf, https://twitter.com/en/privacy, https://developer.twitter.com/en/developer-terms/policy [accessed 4 November 2019].

van der Veen, J. (2016). Predicting susceptibility to radicalization: An empirical exploration of psychological needs and perceptions of deprivation, injustice, and group threat.

Vergani, M. and Bliuc, A. (2015). The evolution of the ISIS' language: a quantitative analysis of the language of the first year of Dabiq magazine. *Sicurezza, Terrorismo e Società = Security, Terrorism and Society*, 2(2), 7–20.

von Behr, I., Reding, A., Edwards, C. and Gribbon, L. (2013). Radicalisation in the digital era: The use of the Internet in 15 cases of terrorism and extremism. www. rand.org/content/dam/rand/pubs/research_reports/RR400/RR453/RAND_ RR453.pdf [accessed 1 September 2019].

Chapter 6

Predictive policing and criminal law

Manuel A. Utset

Introduction

Crime prediction technologies are routinely used by police to make law enforcement decisions (Perry et al., 2013). Predictive policing, as this practice is known, makes use of machine predictions about the place and time when crimes are likely to occur and about the identity of potential offenders and victims. Proponents of the practice argue that these predictive technologies help increase the overall level of deterrence (Mohler et al., 2015), but the evidence on deterrence is still, at best, inconclusive (Bennett Moses and Chan, 2018). At the same time, there is growing evidence that predictive policing comes at a cost, including the potential for errors and biases that are difficult to detect and prevent (Ferguson, 2017). This chapter considers whether, in light of these issues, predictive policing can be justified as a viable deterrence tool, and if so, under what circumstances, and at what costs. It will focus in particular on the use of predictive policing tools as a deterrence in real-time (what I will refer to as 'real time policing').

Real-time policing, as I will use the term, takes place within a small temporal window, starting when an offender decides to commit a crime and ending when the crime is completed and the offender has fled the crime scene. During this crime window, an offender undertakes a set of actions that can trigger criminal liability not just for the underlying crime, but also for inchoate offenses and a set of other corollary crimes. The chapter argues that real-time policing helps increase the overall level of deterrence by increasing the aggregate expected sanctions from following through with a planned crime. The chapter also identifies an important commitment problem that can lead to systematic underdeterrence of crimes that create relatively small losses. A statement by the state that it will fully enforce crimes after the fact will not be credible whenever the costs of investigating these crimes are much higher than the losses they produce. The chapter argues that real-time policing is a way for the state to precommit to enforce these low-loss crimes.

Real-time policing provides two other deterrence and crime-prevention benefits. Confronting offenders during the small crime window allows police to send salient signals about the expected costs of violating the law. The chapter argues that these salient signals can help better deter offenders who are highly impatient or have weak self-control. They also help deter two other types of offenders: those who commit crimes 'erroneously' because they are mistaken about the true magnitude of expected sanctions; and offenders embarking on a series of crimes in which they will learn-by-doing. This chapter describes a number of contexts in which offenders would be underdeterred if society relies on standard deterrence levers, but in which real-time policing can help close the deterrence gap.

Real-time policing, as the concept is used in this chapter, refers specifically to the real-time interaction between police and offenders during the crime window described above. Predictive policing algorithms can play an important role in real-time policing, as can other technologies that provide police with timely, actionable intelligence and other information that enhances their situational awareness (Wilson, 2019). But police services must also examine whether the utilization of real-time crime forecasts and intelligence sufficient to drive real-time policing can be justified given the social costs involved. Each of the important questions outlined above will be examined within this chapter, which is divided into four parts. Part I provides an overview of standard deterrence approaches, including punishment-focused and police-focused deterrence regimes. Part II describes the most common uses of predictive technologies in law enforcement. Part III identifies a number of contexts in which real-time policing can help to better deter offenders and to prevent undeterred offenders from committing crimes; and Part IV describes a number of limitations of relying on machine predictions to make policing decisions.

Part I: Crime prevention and law enforcement

This part provides a brief overview of crime deterrence theories. It begins by describing the rational offender assumption commonly made in deterrence models. It then compares the punishment-focused deterrence approach of conventional law and economics models with the policing-focused deterrence approach that is influential among criminologists and police departments. The last section unpacks the concepts of crime prevention, law enforcement and real-time policing.

A. Rational offenders and the expected benefits and costs of crime

Under the conventional law and economics approach, rational offenders will choose to commit crimes whenever the expected benefits are greater than the expected costs (Posner, 1985). To fully deter potential offenders, society must set the expected punishment sufficiently high so that it exceeds the offenders' expected benefits. Offenders considering committing a crime will take into account the punishment they will face if they are arrested and convicted. These include the actual sanctions and any other disutility from being arrested, such as shaming (Nagin and Paternoster, 1993). The probability of punishment will depend on how much society invests in law enforcement. As a result, society has two main levers for increasing expected sanctions: it can increase the amount of the gross punishment or it can increase the probability of punishment.

B. Punishment-focused deterrence

The conventional law and economics approach to criminal law and deterrence assumes that the primary goal of the criminal justice system is to maximize aggregate social welfare (Polinsky and Shavell, 2000). The conventional approach concludes that a punishment-focused deterrence policy will, as a general matter, maximize aggregate social welfare. Under the punishment-focused approach, society will first increase the gross punishment as much as possible—until increasing it further will not yield further deterrence. Only then should society turn to investing in policing to increase the probability of punishment (Becker, 1968).

The general argument is based on two assumptions. First, risk-averse offenders are deemed to react more to increases in the delayed punishment than to increases in the probability of punishment (Chalfin and McCrary, 2017). Secondly, it is assumed that society will punish offenders using fines and resort to incarceration—a much costlier form of punishment—only if offenders are unable to pay monetary fines (Polinsky and Shavell, 2000).

There are two reasons why it is difficult to justify the conventional punishment-focused deterrence approach. First, the costs to society of imprisonment can be significant. They include the losses experienced by the offender's family and the costs of running a prison system (Posner, 1985). As the number of wealth-constrained offenders increases, so do the costs of running a punishment-focused deterrence regime. Secondly, there is evidence suggesting that offenders react more to an increase in the probability of punishment than to an increase in the severity of punishment, although the evidence is mixed (Nagin, 2013; Loughran, Paternoster and Weiss, 2015).

C. Police-focused deterrence

Criminologists have tended to give greater weight to the role played by police in deterring crime (Nagin, 2013). They have drawn a distinction between two forms of policing. In reactive policing, police get deployed after the fact, when victims or third parties report crimes (Willis, 2014). Reactive policing has come under sustained criticism and given way to proactive policing, a set of strategies that focus on using police proactively to prevent crime (Harmon and Manns, 2017). One proactive strategy, hot spot policing, is based on the premise that crime tends to cluster in particular geographical areas. This leads to the conclusion that, given limited law enforcement resources, society should focus on policing those areas (Sherman and Weisburd, 1995). Problem-oriented policing is a longer-term proactive strategy. It focuses on identifying and addressing core problems that give rise to criminal misconduct within particular communities. Problem-oriented policing pays special attention to the relationship between potential victims and offenders and the environments in which they interact (Braga, 2014).

Whether proactive policing is a better deterrence strategy than punishment-focused deterrence or reactive policing is still an open question. For one thing, it is difficult to disentangle and fully identify how offenders react to the various deterrence levers, or the extent to which changes in deterrence policies achieve their desired effect—for example, whether an observed reduction in crime is due to higher sanctions, greater police presence, or the mere fact that a greater number of potential offenders are behind bars (Chalfin and McCrary, 2017).

D. Long-term and short-term deterrence

We can distinguish between long-term and short-term deterrence. In long-term deterrence contexts, offenders deliberate over future crime opportunities and decide either to obey the law or to commit a crime at some point in the future. In short-term deterrence contexts, offenders face immediate crime opportunities and must decide what to do. Rational offenders who from a long-term perspective have concluded that a crime is not worthwhile will not change their minds when faced with an immediate opportunity to commit that crime, unless, of course, they have new information. Whether or not offenders have considered the pros and cons of violating the law ahead of time, they will need to do so when faced with an immediate crime opportunity. Or more precisely, a rational offender would want to undertake such a short-term cost-benefit analysis. In short, what ultimately matters is what offenders do when faced with an immediate opportunity to commit a crime. An offender who is undeterred at that point will form an intention to commit the crime and will start to execute it. At that point, the undeterred offender will either be able to conclude the crime or will be prevented from completing it either by the police or a third party. We are only concerned here with real-time police interventions to prevent an undeterred offender from committing the crime.

E. Real-time policing and enforcing the criminal law

This chapter focuses on a relatively narrow definition of law enforcement and crime prevention. Law enforcement, as we will use the term, requires the existence of criminal laws, a means for enforcing those laws, and stated consequences for those who violate the law. Both reactive and proactive policing involve law enforcement tasks. But the move from reactive to proactive policing was motivated, at least in part, by a concern that reactive policing focused too much on enforcing the criminal law instead of proactively preventing crime (Goldstein, 1979).

We can divide the enforcement of criminal law into two parts. The first is an ex-ante threat that if an offender violates the law, the police will undertake to investigate the crime and bring the offender to justice. The second part is an ex-post execution of that threat. Real-time policing brings both the ex-ante law enforcement threat and ex-post execution of that threat to bear within a relatively small crime window. The window begins when an offender has an immediate opportunity to commit a crime and ends when an offender finishes the crime and escapes the crime scene. During this crime window, the police engage in ex-ante law enforcement by attempting to change the minds of undeterred offenders who have formed an intention to commit a crime. An offender confronted by the police in real-time will take into account that new information and recalculate the costs and benefits of continuing with the crime.

An offender who either does not observe the police presence or decides to commit the crime regardless will either finish the crime and escape or will be arrested in mid-stream. In this second type of scenario, real-time policing moves to ex post law enforcement: identifying in real-time that a crime is occurring, identifying the offender and making an arrest. If this fails, then the police will resort to reactive policing. The effectiveness of real-time policing strategies will depend in large part on how well the police are able to predict potential criminal activity.

Part II: Machine predictions and policing

This part begins with a brief overview of machine predictions. It then describes the use of machine learning algorithms for making place-based and person-based crime predictions, as well as a series of AI technologies used to enhance situational awareness.

A. Machine learning: a brief overview

Some machines can learn the same way that humans do—through experience. A child can learn to tell the difference between cats and dogs by receiving instructions from an adult about features relevant to distinguishing cats and dogs, looking at photographs with cats and dogs, and receiving feedback: 'yes that's right' or 'no, try again'. After a while, the child is shown a photo that she has never seen before of a dog, and exclaims: 'dog'. This sort of supervised learning also works with machines. But machines are able to sift more quickly through larger amounts of data. They can thus learn some things quicker than humans can.

Machines are fed training data, appropriately tagged with the associations to be learned, and with each pass, the machine will output a rule—for example, 'picture that has features, 1, 2 and 3 = picture of dog'. The machine will receive feedback through a loss function that captures how close it was to the mark, adjust the rule incrementally and make new predictions. This will continue until the machine's predictions are sufficiently accurate on that training data. After that, the machine is tested using test data it has never seen before. If the rule yields sufficiently accurate predictions on the test data, it will be used to make future predictions; if it does not, then the machine will continue learning on the training data, until the rule it outputs meets the requisite level of accuracy on new data (Chollet, 2017).

B. Place-based predictions

Place-based prediction systems issue predictions of when and where a crime may occur. Police departments rely on these predictions to decide where and when to deploy officers. Place-based prediction systems are trained using historical crime data and a set of crime features that have been identified as relevant by criminologists and other domain experts. For example, some place-based systems rely on findings that certain crimes, such as burglaries, often have a short-term effect on criminal activity. They tend to trigger the same or similar crimes, much in the way that earthquakes trigger aftershocks (Mohler et al., 2015). Other place-based systems, such as risk terrain models, focus on a wider set of crime features—for example, place-specific features, routine activities of offenders and victims, temporal cycles and weather patterns (Piza and Gilchrist, 2018).

C. Person-based predictive policing

Predictive algorithms are also used to try to identify "potential offenders". For example, Chicago's Strategic Subject Algorithm produces risk assessment scores that attempt to capture the likelihood that an individual will be involved in a shooting incident, either as an offender or victim. These risk scores are produced using criminal records and features such as prior involvement in gunshot incidents, age, arrest record and gang affiliation.

D. Real-time situational awareness technologies

Real-time policing also relies on other AI and machine learning technologies that can provide police real-time intelligence and thus increase situational awareness. These technologies include automatic license plate readers (Lum et al., 2019), facial recognition systems (Bowling and Iyer, 2019), voice identification systems (Morrison et al., 2016), audio gunshot sensor technology (Carr and Doleac, 2018), natural language processing of social media feeds (Bennett Moses and Chan, 2018) and object recognition and object tracking technologies (Saikia et al., 2017; Xu et al., 2016).

Part III: Real-time policing and crime prevention

It is important to identify those contexts in which real-time policing aided by predictive technologies can have the greatest impact on crime prevention. Real-time interactions will send offenders salient signals of the expected costs of following through with a crime. They can thus help change the minds of otherwise undeterred offenders who have formed an intention to violate the law. Real-time policing can also target a subset of offenders who are undeterrable and have to be intercepted in real-time. This part begins by describing the important role of inchoate offenses and corollary crimes within a real-time policing system. The second section argues that real-time policing helps society precommit to enforce certain low-loss crimes that would be under-enforced if society relies solely on ex-post reactive policing. The third section identifies four contexts in which the salient enforcement signals sent by real-time policing helps deter offenders who would be otherwise underdeterred. The fourth section describes two contexts in which offenders would be underdeterred under any deterrence scheme and must thus be intercepted in real-time to prevent them from committing crimes.

A. Inchoate and corollary crimes

This section argues that inchoate offenses and corollary crimes play an important role in real-time policing. Inchoate offenses punish individuals who have exhibited an intention to commit a particular crime, but have not harmed anyone. Attempt liability is triggered whenever an individual has taken substantial steps toward the commission of the underlying offense. Conspiracy liability is triggered whenever two or more individuals agree to engage in criminal conduct or aid in the commission of a crime. Solicitation to commit a crime is triggered when one individual asks another individual to commit a crime. A common justification for inchoate offenses is that they allow the police to lawfully intercede to prevent serious crimes, something that can have a material impact in increasing overall social welfare (Chalfin and McCrary, 2018). For example, an individual who has taken substantial steps towards committing a murder or robbery can be arrested for attempted murder or attempted robbery.

In addition to inchoate offenses, there are a set of corollary crimes that are often triggered during the preparation or commission of more serious crimes. These corollary crimes include offenses such as: possession of burglary tools with the intent to commit a burglary; possession, without a permit, of materials to make destructive devices or explosives; and possession of machine guns, sawed-off shotguns, other illegal firearms, or bulletproof vests while committing other offenses. Arresting an offender for corollary crimes can also help prevent serious crimes in real-time. Inchoate offenses and corollary crimes also help increase the overall level of deterrence. Offenders considering committing a crime will take into account not just the expected sanctions for that crime, but also the expected sanctions from inchoate offenses and corollary crimes that they may trigger while committing the underlying crime.

B. Precommitment and credible law enforcement policies

Real-time policing allows the state to precommit to enforce property crimes and other low-loss crimes that it may not have an incentive to enforce after the fact. I will refer to a 'low-loss crime' as one that creates a social loss that is materially lower than the costs of investigating it after the fact. Suppose that the state issues a threat to investigate and prosecute low-loss crimes. Some offenders will conclude that if they call the state's bluff and offend the state will not follow through with its enforcement threat. Such non-credible law enforcement threats will lead to underdeterrence. To close this deterrence gap the state can invest in a proactive policing strategy. This sort of commitment problem is common in a number of other contexts in which ex-ante and ex-post incentives diverge (Schelling, 1960). For example, an established firm may threaten to retaliate against new entrants by cutting prices drastically to assure that new entrants cannot survive. In order for this threat to be credible, it has to be the case that if a new entrant disregards the threat, the established firm will have an ex-post incentive to follow through and cut prices.

Burglaries are low-loss crimes. The average loss per burglary is relatively small and thus the ex-post incentive to expend law enforcement resources to identify and arrest offenders after the fact is relatively small. For example, according to FBI Uniform Crime Data, in 2017 the aggregate property loss from burglaries was $3.4 billion. The average loss per burglary was only $2,416. And only 13.5% of the reported burglaries in 2017 were solved (United States Department of Justice, 2018). There are of course various explanations for the low clearance rates for burglaries, but one plausible explanation is that society has an ex-post incentive to underinvest in solving burglaries.

C. Real-time policing, salient signals and deterrence

This section identifies four contexts in which offenders would be underdeterred if society relies on punishment-focused deterrence or on ex post reactive policing, and in which real-time policing can help close the deterrence gap.

Myopic offenders

When offenders commit crimes they receive an immediate benefit and trigger a potential, but delayed punishment. This temporal gap between an offense and its punishment can lead to the systematic underdeterrence of impatient offenders. Offenders, like other individuals, give greater weight to immediate costs and benefits, and discount future ones. Offenders who are more impatient or myopic will discount delayed sanctions by a greater amount than their more patient counterparts. This discounting will be even greater when prison sentences are involved since the disutility from a prison sentence is experienced incrementally over time (Polinsky and Shavell, 1999).

Real-time policing makes more salient to myopic offenders that the police may intervene to make an arrest before they can complete the crime or flee the crime scene. It also sends these offenders a more salient signal of the consequences of crime—the punishment that they will experience if arrested and convicted. This includes both formal sanctions imposed by the state and more immediate informal sanctions, such as shaming. Both of these side effects of real-time policing will increase the overall level of deterrence. Importantly, the more impatient an offender the greater the increase in the level of deterrence.

Self-control problems and time-inconsistent misconduct

In the previous section, we assumed that an offender's level of impatience remains constant over time. However, people routinely make long-term plans to act patiently, but reverse those long-term preferences when faced with the prospect of immediate gratification. Individuals who are overoptimistic about their future willpower will exhibit self-control problems. Suppose that an offender has determined that the delayed expected sanctions of a crime are greater than its immediate benefits—for example, the crime would yield an immediate benefit of $1,000 but trigger delayed expected sanctions of $1,500 (after discounting for the type of impatience discussed above). The offender therefore concludes to obey the law. However, now suppose that the next day the offender has an opportunity to commit that crime. If the offender has a preference for immediate gratification, he will now give added weight to the immediate $1,000 that the crime would yield. If the offender's preference for immediate gratification is sufficiently great, he will reverse his long-term pref-erence and commit the crime. After doing so, the offender will again conclude to obey the law in the future. But the next time that the offender has an oppor-tunity to commit the crime, he again yields to the temptation of immediate gratification. For example, dieters may decide each day that tomorrow they will definitely abstain from eating cake, and yet yield repeatedly to the immediate gratification provided by each slice of cake. Offenders with a preference for immediate gratification can exhibit similar self-control problems and engage in 'nibbling opportunism', repeatedly overriding their long-term preference to obey the law (Utset, 2007). Whether offenders engage in repeated nibbling opportunism depends on how accurately they can predict their future will-power and on the availability of commitment devices to prevent their future selves from yielding to the pull of immediate gratification.

Real-time policing can be seen as a state-provided commitment device for offenders with this sort of self-control problem. It increases the immediate costs of planning and executing crimes, and makes more salient the delayed punishment. The greater an offender's preference for immediate gratification, the greater weight he will give to the immediate costs he must incur to counteract the added risks brought about by real-time policing.

Real-time policing can also lead offenders with self-control problems to repeatedly delay committing crimes that they planned to commit. Suppose that a crime will provide an immediate benefit of $1,500 and trigger expected sanctions of $1,000. An offender facing such a prospect is underdeterred and will make a plan to commit the crime. However, on the day of the crime, he will again give greater weight to the immediate costs imposed by real-time policing. If those magnified immediate costs are sufficiently great, the offender will put off committing a crime, even though from a detached long-term perspective, he had concluded that the crime was worthwhile. Again, to the extent that the offender is sufficiently overoptimistic about his future willpower, he may repeatedly put off committing the crime. One can refer to this sort of repeated procrastination in committing a planned crime, as time-inconsistent obedience (Utset, 2007). The salient presence of police can thus deter offenders in real-time, even though those same offenders are not deterred by the actual delayed sanctions.

Perceptual deterrence and 'erroneous crimes'

Real-time policing can help to better deter offenders who are underdeterred because they have formed incorrect beliefs about the true magnitude of the expected sanctions (Apel, 2013). If these offenders remain underdeterred they will end up committing crimes that, on average, yield negative returns. From an economic perspective, these 'erroneous crimes' harm both the crime victims and the misinformed offenders.

Offenders may form incorrect crime-related beliefs due to the fact that information about expected sanctions is highly complex. An offender trying to ascertain the probability of being arrested and convicted of a crime will need to make sufficiently accurate predictions about police deployments, prosecutorial practices, and the sentences that judges may impose. Offenders may also form incorrect beliefs in instances in which crime-related information is not sufficiently salient to impact their day-to-day decisions about whether to commit crimes. For example, in other contexts, a number of studies have found that consumers are less likely to pay attention to non-salient information. This includes hidden taxes, hidden shipping costs, financial information disclosed to markets on Fridays, and financial information that require market participants to draw inferences based on the interconnection between companies (Chetty, Looney and Kroft, 2009).

Real-time policing provides offenders with current and salient information about the probability that they will be arrested if they commit a crime. As such, it helps reduce the social losses from erroneous criminal activity. The informational signal sent by ex post reactive policing is less salient and less likely to affect an offender's short-term decision to commit a crime.

Learning from crime and serial offenders

When planning crimes, offenders will have to make predictions about the expected benefits and expected sanctions from crime. Since the latter depends on the likelihood that offenders will escape detection, offenders will also try to make predictions about their criminal skills—their ability to plan, execute and cover-up crimes. As with many types of skills, offenders will learn from experience. In planning a particular crime, offenders will take into account both the actual returns from that crime and the future returns from crimes that they will be able to plan and execute more efficiently, due to learning-by-doing. An offender who expects to undertake a series of crimes may want to invest in acquiring this sort of crime-related information. Additionally, if *offender A* commits a crime, *offender B* may be able to learn some of this crime-related information by observing offender A, or hearing about the crime after the fact.

These learning effect make deterrence more complicated. With each crime, an offender's expected benefits may increase and the expected costs decrease (although with diminishing returns). Forward-looking serial offenders are underdeterred by delayed sanctions because they are in essence making up-front investments that will yield positive returns only after they commit a sufficient number of successful crimes.

One way to close this deterrence gap is to punish serial offenders more harshly the more crimes that they commit. Such a strategy is often used to deter repeat offenders. However, repeat offenders are, by definition, unsuccessful offenders—after all, they have been convicted previously, have reoffended, and have been arrested once again. But the serial offenders that I have in mind are successful offenders who commit crime after crime and get away with it. The heightened sanctions issued to repeat offenders tend to underdeter serial offenders. One way to effectively deter them is to increase expected sanctions by an amount that will cancel out the increased criminal efficiency from learning-by-doing. But a second deterrence strategy is to rely more heavily on real-time policing. By increasing the likelihood that serial offenders will be intercepted in mid-crime, real-time policing helps increase the offenders' costs of relying on learning-by-doing to sharpen their criminal skills.

D. Real-time intervention

In the crime contexts described in the previous section, real-time policing helps deter crime either by making law enforcement signals more salient or by intercepting undeterred offenders in mid-crime. This section identifies two contexts in which offenders would not be deterred, even with salient law-enforcement signals. These offenders have to be confronted by the police in real time and prevented from completing their crimes.

The projection bias and hot-state crimes

At the time of committing crimes, offenders have to predict the disutility that they will feel if they are arrested and punished. This sort of prediction about future preferences is subject to a number of potential distortions. One type of distortion is the projection bias (Loewenstein, O'Donoghue and Rabin, 2003). Suppose that two individuals are deciding what to order for tomorrow's lunch. One of them has just finished lunch and is sated; the other has not eaten anything since breakfast and is very hungry. Their current state—being sated or hungry—should not affect their predictions of how hungry they will be tomorrow. But anecdotal evidence and numerous empirical studies suggest otherwise (Read and Van Leeuwen, 1998). In fact, when making predictions about future preferences, people routinely let their current preferences influence those predictions.

Even when people know that they are likely to experience such a projection bias, they still tend to underappreciate how much it will affect their predictions. For example, hungry supermarket shoppers who are aware that their hunger combined with the projection bias will tempt them to purchase more food than they had planned (per their grocery lists) still routinely yield to that temptation (Gilbert, Gill and Wilson, 2002).

The projection bias can lead offenders to underappreciate the full weight of the disutility they will experience if they are arrested and punished. This will lead to underdeterrence: offenders will commit more crimes than they would if they could accurately predict their future preferences. This underdeterrence problem is further magnified if offenders commit crimes while in hot psychological states (Loewenstein, 1996). Hot states—which include anger, sexual arousal and addictive cravings for drugs and alcohol—can hijack an offender's deliberations, prodding them to act without giving much thought to the consequences.

Reactive policing regimes will do relatively little to deter offenders who commit crimes while in hot psychological states, or who merely mispredict the disutility they would feel if arrested and punished. Real-time policing regimes, on the other hand, allow for real-time interventions to prevent hot-state crimes.

Risky crimes

Some offenders, such as gang members, engage in highly risky criminal misconduct: crimes with very high-expected benefits (both tangible and intangible) but also very high-expected costs (Papachristos et al., 2015). These expected costs can be divided into crime-related and punishment related costs. Crime-related costs include the potential of being injured or killed while committing a crime. How does one effectively deter serial offenders who commits crimes in which the expected crime-related costs are greater than the highest possible expected punishment? For example, assume that the expected crime-related costs to a gang member include a 20% of dying violently within five years, and that the gang member is committing a set of crimes that cannot be punished with the death sentence. When crime-related costs greatly exceed the expected punishment if an offender is arrested and convicted, standard deterrence strategies do not work. In this sort of situation, real-time policing strategies becomes critical, since they allow the police to intercept these undeterred offenders in real-time. Incapacitation then becomes the second-best approach for crime prevention.

Part IV: The social costs of relying on machine predictions in policing

So far we have focused on the potential benefits of real-time policing. However, as mentioned above, real-time policing relies on place-based and person-based predictions produce by machine learning algorithms. As we will see in this part, there are important social costs associated with the use of machine-based predictions in policing. As policymakers consider implementing real-time policing strategies they will have to weigh these social costs against the benefits described in Part III. The goal of the chapter is not to provide a full evaluation of the pros and cons of real-time policing but to provide an overview of the principal benefits and costs involved and to provide a general framework that can be used to examine in more detail the full implications of real-time policing.

A. Fairness and accuracy

The increased use of predictive policing and predictive adjudication technologies has led to myriad criminal procedure, privacy and bias concerns. As to the latter, there is a valid concern that algorithms trained on historical crime data will learn explicit and implicit biases captured by that data (Ferguson, 2012; Mayson, 2018; O'Donnell, 2019). Biased prediction rules can lead to real-time policing strategies that unfairly profile certain individuals and communities. Additionally, these prediction rules can exhibit feedback loops that can further exacerbate the biased predictions (Lum and Isaac, 2016). These bias, privacy and criminal procedure problems create social costs that need to be taken into account when evaluating real-time policing strategies that depend on predictive policing algorithms.

Even if machine predictions are free of bias, they may still produce inaccurate results. In this context, accuracy refers to the fraction of crime predictions that yield correct results: actual crimes, in the case of place-based predictions, and actual offenders or victims, in the case of person-based predictions. Even if the police make a sufficiently accurate decision about the location of a crime, once officers arrive, they still need to identify potential offenders (Mohler, 2014). Errors at this point can create high social costs. Singling out, stopping, questioning, and possibly frisking law-abiding individuals not only harm those individuals, but also produce longer-term, residual social costs, including the undermining of trust and the loss of confidence in the police's ability to do their job. This erosion of trust and confidence can in turn lead to a decrease in overall deterrence. For example, the police's ability to identify potential and actual offenders depends in part on the willingness of law-abiding citizens to trust the police with information (Manski and Nagin, 2017).

B. Machine predictions and indirect, non-transparent deterrence

As we saw above, real-time policing relies heavily on the ability of police to arrest offenders for inchoate offenses and corollary crimes. This reliance comes at a cost. One would expect that as police departments resort more to real-time policing, the number of offenders arrested for inchoate offenses and corollary crimes will increase. This in turn will lead policymakers concerned with increasing deterrence and real-time crime prevention to create new inchoate offenses and corollary crimes. But this sort of derivative crimes are not benign. Instead, they allow society to deter certain types of behaviour in an indirect, non-transparent manner, and as such they create a number of social costs.

Additionally, as the accuracy of predictive technologies increases, it will be easier for policymakers to identify behaviours or events that are highly correlated with the behaviour prohibited by a particular underlying crime. In other words, predictive algorithms can be used to identify and extract crime features that are useful for deterring certain types of behaviour, either directly or indirectly. If the predictions are sufficiently accurate, policymakers can deter that underlying crime indirectly by creating additional corollary crimes or by adding additional prohibitions to existing ones. For example, Section 466 of the California Penal Code, which criminalizes possession of burglary tools with intent to feloniously use them, lists: picklock, crowbar, screwdriver, vise grip pliers, slidehammer, slim jim, tension bar, tubular lock pick, bump key and porcelain spark plug chips, amongst many other instruments and tools.

C. Switching to more serious crimes under a proactive predictive policing regime

The predictive technologies used in policing rely on machine learning algorithms that work best when they can be trained with a large number of examples. It follows that these algorithms will be most useful for very common crimes and much less useful for uncommon crimes. All other things being equal, predictive policing will lead to more arrests for common crimes, such as drug crimes and property crimes. Suppose that the gross punishment for these crimes stays the same. Rational offenders will then have an incentive to switch to less common crimes that are underenforced by policing regimes that rely on machine predictions, and thus have lower expected sanctions. This shift in crimes can lead to a reduction of social welfare.

More generally, when policymakers are setting up a regime to deter crime, they need to take into account the problem of marginal deterrence—more serious crimes should have higher expected sanctions than less serious crimes, if not offenders will switch to more serious crimes. So to the extent that predictive policing leads to higher expected punishment for a set of less-serious crimes, it will be necessary to increase the expected punishment for more serious crimes in order to achieve marginal deterrence. However, there is a limit to how high policymakers can set gross punishments, particularly when there is a positive probability that individuals may be wrongfully convicted.

D. Machine predictions and police judgements

When individuals and machines make predictions, they use information in their possession, including what they have learned from past experience, to determine the likelihood that a course of action will produce a specific result. Whether current predictive policing technologies in fact yield better predictions than those made by experienced police officers is an open question. In fact, some experienced officers believe that the place-based and person-based predictions produced by machines do not add new information but merely restate obvious facts that experienced officers already know (Brayne, 2017). At the same time, increasing reliance on predictive technologies can erode the overall prediction expertise of police officers. On the other hand, it is likely that, in the long run, data mining and machine learning models will be able to make better and faster predictions regarding off-site strategies that require quick analysis of large amounts of data.

While machine predictions help reduce some of the uncertainty surrounding decisions, there will still be some residual decisional uncertainty that has to be resolved by making judgments. More specifically, predictions help identify the consequences and payoffs associated with various courses of action and the potential trade-offs involved. But even if machine learning models produce highly accurate predictions, people will still need to use judgment to negotiate these trade-offs (Agrawal, Gans and Goldfarb, 2019). It follows that predictions are just one part of predictive policing. Once predictions are made, officers must be able to act on the predictions by making effective judgments (Koper, Lum and Willis, 2014). Some of this judgment-craft is learned over time, through experience, and is difficult to teach to others—particularly machines. This sort of tacit knowledge is an important part of police craft, and a type of skill that machines are unlikely to usurp (Willis and Mastrofski, 2018). But in order to acquire and keep this type of craft knowledge, police officers need to have sufficient discretion to make decisions in different types of contexts (Willis, Koper and Lum, 2018). This discretion can be circumscribed if police departments begin to rely inflexibly on machine predictions. This is more likely to happen as predictive policing models increase in accuracy.

Machines can also get in the way of community policing. Community policing not only helps develop trust between communities and police officers, it also helps officers acquire situational skills that they can later use when making quick judgments in mid-crisis. There is a danger that police departments will continue to replace more traditional community policing with crime-focused-policing, in which police interactions with communities focuses on short-term crime-prevention instead of longer-term crime-prevention built on trust and repeated interactions in non-confrontational scenarios.

E. The costs of proactive deterrence policies

Each time that a police department deploys officers, it makes an investment in either proactively preventing crime or reactively solving them. The return on these law enforcement investments depends on whether or not the police make sufficiently accurate predictions about future and past crimes, respectively. If the police deploys and comes up empty, that investment will be lost. If the deployment creates other social losses—such as stopping, questioning and frisking law-abiding citizens—undoing those losses will take time and further investments.

Real-time policing and other proactive policing strategies require an earlier investment in law enforcement under conditions of greater uncertainty. The greater this uncertainty, the greater the value of waiting to deploy police officers until after some of that uncertainty is resolved. It follows that, all other things being equal, reactive policing provides police departments with more options—including, the option to deploy fewer officers or none at all. However, waiting until crimes occur comes at a cost: the losses incurred by crime victims. As these losses increase, so does the value of trying to prevent crime through real-time policing and other proactive approaches. It follows, that reactive policing is more costly when the undeterred crimes are more serious, such as murder, rape and armed robbery.

Conclusion

In this chapter, I argued that given the social costs created by the use of predictive technologies in law enforcement—predictive policing—scholars and policymakers advocating the use of these technologies need to identify how, if at all, predictive policing creates value. I focused on one potential source of value: the use of predictive algorithms to help police engage in short-term deterrence and real-time intervention to arrest undeterred offenders in mid-crime. I refer to this practice as real-time policing. In particular, real-time policing focuses on a relatively small crime-window. The window begins at the time that a potential offender is faced with an immediate crime opportunity. At that point, the offender must decide whether or not to violate the law. The crime window comes to an end either when the offender decides to forego the crime opportunity or when an undeterred offender has completed the crime and fled the crime scene.

Offenders may forego an immediate crime opportunity because they had already concluded ahead of time that obeying the law was the best possible strategy and they have not received any new information to make them change their minds—long-term deterrence. Using real-time policing to confront such offenders is wasteful. However, some offenders faced with a crime opportunity are undeterred: they will violate the law unless they receive new information to make them change their minds. An important goal of real-time policing is to send salient law enforcement signals to these undeterred offenders about the consequences of going through with those crimes. This chapter identified various types of crime contexts and offenders that fall under this short-term undeterred category.

For example, delayed sanctions and reactive policing strategies will, as a general matter, underdeter myopic offenders and offenders with self-control problems. One way to better deter myopic and akratic offenders is to provide them with salient signals of future sanctions or to require them to incur additional immediate costs at the time of executing a crime. Some offenders are undeterred because they have formed incorrect beliefs about the true magnitude of the expected sanctions they would face if they partake of a crime opportunity. The salient law-enforcement information provided by real-time policing can help correct these erroneous beliefs of offenders. Real-time policing can also help increase the level of deterrence for serial offenders.

In this chapter, I also argued that even salient law enforcement signals provided by real-time policing will systematically underdeter certain types of offenders. Offenders are deterred when they deliberate about the pros and cons of committing a crime and conclude to obey the law. However, some offenders commit crimes when in hot-psychological states—that is, in states in which they have temporarily lost their ability to objectively deliberate about whether a crime is in fact worthwhile. Such undeterred offenders must be intercepted in a timely fashion and prevented from going through with the crime. There is a second type of undeterred crime that is best addressed through real-time police interventions: crimes that are so dangerous to execute that the threat of punishment is unlikely to change an offender's mind.

In this chapter, I also showed that inchoate offenses and corollary crimes help increase the aggregate amount of deterrence faced by potential offenders. These derivative crimes can act as important law enforcement tools for intercepting offenders during the crime window targeted by real-time policing.

Some low-loss crimes, such as property crimes, can be much costlier to investigate, solve and prosecute, after the fact than the losses that they produce to society. Rational offenders knowing this will assume that society's threat to enforce these low-loss crimes is not credible. They may thus call society's bluff and violate the law. I argue that real-time policing strategies are a commitment device through which society can precommit to enforce these low-loss crimes.

The chapter also makes a more general argument: in order to effectively execute a real-time policing scheme, police must be able to make accurate predictions of potential crimes and future offenders and victims, as well as be able to make quick, real-time crime scene decisions. Machine predictions and real-time AI tools such as facial recognition technologies and license-plate readers can all play critical roles in real-time policing. But as the article shows, the use of these technologies comes at a cost. A principal goal of this chapter was to provide a conceptual framework within which to identify and measure the potential benefits of continuing to develop and deploy predictive and AI technologies in policing. It has done so by showing a number of contexts in which real-time policing is particularly well suited to deter and prevent certain types of crimes and offenders.

References

Agrawal, A., Gans, J. S. and Goldfarb, A. (2019). Artificial intelligence: The ambiguous labor market impact of automating prediction. *Journal of Economic Perspectives*, 33(2), pp. 31–50.

Apel, R. (2013). Sanctions, perceptions, and crime: Implications for criminal deterrence. *Journal of Quantitative Criminology*, 29(1), pp. 67–101.

Becker, G. S. (1968). Crime and punishment: An economic approach. *Journal of Political Economy*, 76(2), pp. 169–217.

Bennett Moses, L. and Chan, J. (2018). Algorithmic prediction in policing: assumptions, evaluation, and accountability. *Policing and Society*, 28(7), pp. 806–822.

Bowling, B. and Iyer, S. (2019). Automated policing: The case of body-worn video. *International Journal of Law in Context*, 15(2), pp. 140–161.

Braga A.A. (2014). Problem-Oriented Policing. In: Bruinsma G., Weisburd D. (eds) *Encyclopedia of Criminology and Criminal Justice*. Springer, New York, NY.

Brayne, S. (2017). Big data surveillance: The case of policing. *American Sociological Review*, 82(5), pp. 977–1008.

Carr, J.B. and Doleac, J. L. (2018). Keep the kids inside? Juvenile curfews and urban gun violence. *Review of Economics and Statistics*, 100(4), pp. 608–618.

Chalfin, A. and McCrary, J. (2017). Criminal deterrence: A review of the literature. *Journal of Economic Literature*, 55(1), pp. 5–48.

Chalfin, A. and McCrary, J. (2018). Are U.S. cities underpoliced? Theory and evidence. *Review of Economics and Statistics*, 100(1), pp. 167–186.

Chetty, R., Looney, A. and Kroft, K. (2009). Salience and taxation: Theory and evidence. *American Economic Review*, 99(4), pp. 1145–1477.

Chollet, F. (2017). *Deep Learning with Python*. Greenwich, CT: Manning Publication Co.

Ferguson, A.G (2012). Predictive policing and reasonable suspicion. *Emory Law Journal*, 62(2), pp. 259–325.

Ferguson, A.G. (2017). Policing predictive policing. *Washington Law Review*, 94(5), pp. 1109–1189.

Gilbert, D.T., Gill, M.J. and Wilson, T.D. (2002). The future is now: Temporal correction in affective forecasting. *Organizational Behavior and Human Decision Processes*, 88(1), pp. 430–444.

Goldstein, H. (1979). Improving policing: A problem-oriented approach. *Crime & Delinquency*, 25(2), pp. 236–258.

Harmon, R. and Manns, A. (2017). Proactive policing and the legacy of Terry. *Ohio Journal of Criminal Law*, 15(1), pp. 1–19.

Koper, C.S., Lum, C. and Willis, J.J. (2014). Optimizing the use of technology in policing: Results and implications from a multi-site study of the social, organizational, and behavioural aspects of implementing police technologies. *Policing (Oxford)*, 8(2), pp. 212–221.

Loewenstein, G. (1996). Out of control: Visceral influences on behaviour. *Organizational Behavior and Human Decision Processes*, 65(3), pp. 272–292.

Loewenstein, G., O'Donoghue, T. and Rabin, M. (2003). Projection bias in predicting future utility. *Quarterly Journal of Economics*, 118(4), pp. 1209–1248.

Loughran, T.A., Paternoster, R. and Weiss, D.B. (2015). Deterrence. In: A. Piquero (ed), *The Handbook of Criminological Theory*, pp. 50–74.

Lum, C. et al. (2019). The rapid diffusion of license plate readers in US law enforcement agencies. *Policing*, 42(3), pp. 376–393.

Lum, K. and Isaac, W. (2016). To predict and serve? *Significance*, 13(5), pp. 14–19.

Manski, C.F. and Nagin, D.S. (2017). Assessing benefits, costs, and disparate racial impacts of confrontational proactive policing. *Proceedings of the National Academy of Sciences of the United States of America*, 114(35), pp. 9308–9313.

Mayson, S.G. (2018). Bias in, bias out. *Yale Law Journal*, pp. 1–59.

Mohler, G. (2014). Marked point process hotspot maps for homicide and gun crime prediction in Chicago. *International Journal of Forecasting*, 30(3), pp. 491–497.

Mohler, G. et al. (2015). Randomized controlled field trials of predictive policing. *Journal of the American Statistical Association*, 110(512), pp. 1399–1411.

Morrison, G.S. et al. (2016). INTERPOL survey of the use of speaker identification by law enforcement agencies. *Forensic Science International*, 263, pp. 92–100.

Nagin, D.S. (2013). Deterrence: A review of the evidence by a criminologist for economists. *Annual Review of Economics*, 5(1), pp. 83–105.

Nagin, D.S. and Paternoster, R. (1993). Enduring individual differences and rational choice theories of crime. *Law & Society Review*, 27(3), pp. 467–496.

O'Donnell, R.M. (2019). Challenging racist predictive policing algorithms under the equal protection clause. *New York University Law Review*, 94(3), pp. 544–580.

Papachristos, A.V. et al. (2015). The company you keep? The spillover effects of gang membership on individual gunshot victimization in a co-offending network. *Criminology*, 53(4), pp. 624–649.

Perry, W. et al. (2013). *Predictive Policing: The Role of Crime Forecasting in Law Enforcement Operations, Predictive Policing: The Role of Crime Forecasting in Law Enforcement Operations*. RAND Corporation.

Piza, E.L. and Gilchrist, A.M. (2018). Measuring the effect heterogeneity of police enforcement actions across spatial contexts. *Journal of Criminal Justice*, 54 (January–February 2018), pp. 76–87.

Polinsky, A.M. and Shavell, S. (1999). On the disutility and discounting of imprisonment and the theory of deterrence. *Journal of Legal Studies*, 28(1), pp. 1–16.

Polinsky, A.M. and Shavell, S. (2000). The economic theory of public enforcement of law. *Journal of Economic Literature*, 38(1), pp. 45–76.

Posner, R.A. (1985). An economic theory of the criminal law. *Columbia Law Review*, 85(6), pp. 1193–1231.

Read, D. and Van Leeuwen, B. (1998). Predicting hunger. The effects of appetite and delay on choice. *Organizational Behavior and Human Decision Processes*, 76(2), pp. 189–205.

Saikia, S. et al. (2017). Object detection for crime scene evidence analysis using deep learning. *ICIAP*, pp. 14–24.

Schelling, T.C. (1960). *The Strategy of Conflict*. Cambridge, MA: Harvard University Press.

Sherman, L.W. and Weisburd, D. (1995). General deterrent effects of police patrol in crime 'HOT SPOTS': A randomized, controlled trial. *Justice Quarterly*, 12(4), pp. 625–648.

United States Department of Justice, Federal Bureau of Investigation. (September 2018). Crime in the United States, 2017.

Utset, M.A. (2007). Hyperbolic criminals and repeated time-inconsistent misconduct. *Houston Law Review*, 44(3), pp. 609–677.

Willis, J.J. (2014). *A Recent History of the Police, Oxford Handbook of Police and Policing.* Oxford: Oxford University Press.

Willis, J.J., Koper, C.S. and Lum, C. (2018). Technology use and constituting structures: Accounting for the consequences of information technology on police organisational change. *Policing and Society*, 30(5), pp. 483–501.

Willis, J.J. and Mastrofski, S.D. (2018). Improving policing by integrating craft and science: what can patrol officers teach us about good police work? *Policing and Society*, 28(1), pp. 27–44.

Wilson, D. (2019). Platform policing and the real-time cop. *Surveillance and Society*, 17(1/2), pp. 69–75.

Xu, Z. et al. (2016). Semantic enhanced cloud environment for surveillance data management using video structural description. *Computing*, 98, pp. 35–54.

Part II

Police accountability and human rights

Part II

Police accountability and
human rights

Chapter 7

Accountability and indeterminacy in predictive policing

Aaron Shapiro

Introduction

From the warehouse to the courthouse, artificial intelligence (AI) and machine learning have become the 'new normal' (Raman, 2019). Private and public institutions now outsource many of their decision-making functions to automated systems, and the speed at which this 'AI revolution' (Harari, 2017) has progressed has left little time for reflection on how the systems work 'in the wild' (Green, 2019), how they transform the institutional contexts into which they are thrust or whether they might disparately impact the communities they are meant to benefit. Algorithmic assessments and risk predictions now determine if we're creditworthy (Citron and Pasquale, 2014; Hurley and Adebayo, 2017) or whether we'll make good employees (Ajunwa, 2020; Bogan, 2019), tenants (Kayyali, 2016; Selbst, 2019; Shaw, 2018) and customers (Gandy, 1993; Turow, 2013; Zwick and Denegri Knott, 2009). They govern who among the poor deserve public benefits or access to public housing (Eubanks, 2011; 2018), and calculate which defendants should be released on bail and which offenders can get out on parole (Angwin et al., 2016; Dressel and Farid, 2018; Green, 2018). Each of these applications proceeds under the technophilic banners of objectivity, neutrality and efficiency (cf. Miller, 2018), and each has the potential to disparately impact society's most vulnerable (Barocas and Selbst, 2016) – all despite minimal public input or external checks and balances.

It should come as no surprise then that AI has become cause for public concern. Activists are no longer alone in calling out online platforms' monopolistic behaviour (Marshall, 2017), nor is algorithmic bias the sole purview of disciplinarily siloed academics. The anxiety is now mainstream (Ip, 2017), and the producers of automated decision-making systems – computer scientists, engineers and technologists – are taking note. Students and faculty at elite institutions now demand that ethics courses be incorporated into undergraduate and graduate computer science curricula (Karoff, 2019). Meanwhile, the Association for Computing Machinery (ACM) – the flagship society for computer scientists and professionals – has responded to mounting calls for fairer, more transparent and more accountable algorithms (Diakopoulos et al., n.d.) by hosting an annual interdisciplinary conference on those very themes (ACM, 2019). And while these developments are certainly remarkable, they also leave unresolved how ideals like fairness, accountability and transparency might translate into meaningful safeguards in the institutional settings where automated decision-making systems are being taken up (cf. Ananny and Crawford, 2018).

Nowhere is this question more pressing than in the context of law enforcement, where police leaders and intellectuals harbour lofty ambitions for 'big data policing' (Brayne, 2017; Ferguson, 2017a), automated surveillance (Andrejevic, 2019; Gates, 2011) and 'real-time' algorithmic investigatory tools (Wilson, 2019). As in other institutional settings, the hype around new technology prompted a rush to embrace machine learning and AI as solutions to broader institutional woes, including shrinking departmental budgets and waning legitimacy (cf. Beck and McCue, 2009) – again without sufficient public engagement or reflection, and again raising red flags. Like other contexts, too, everyday decisions in law enforcement have significant consequences for the policed – the difference between a felony and a misdemeanour, an unnecessary arrest and a clean record. While many researchers (myself included; Shapiro, 2017) have called for increased fairness, transparency and accountability as bulwarks against these consequences, I fear that such calls may also be somewhat naïve about the institutional cultures of policing (cf. Benbouzid, 2019). What could 'fairness' mean for an institution that in the US has its origins in repressing worker organising or criminalising African Americans before and after the abolition of slavery (Hartman, 1997; Vitale, 2017; Wood, 2011)? What might 'transparency' mean for a force whose culture of solidarity and institutional virtue still promotes a 'blue wall of silence' (Chin and Wells, 1997; Kleinig, 2001)?

The most widely used, and broadly critiqued, of the new police technologies is 'predictive policing', a phrase that has at various points described nearly any imaginable application of machine learning and AI to crime analysis and prediction – from crowd management to terrorism deterrence (National Institute of Justice, n.d.). Today, predictive policing is most closely associated with two types of modelling: offender-based models predict individual recidivism risk or the likelihood of becoming involved in gang activity (Angwin et al., 2016; Dressel and Farid, 2018; Green, 2018; Jefferson, 2017b), while the more common and generally less controversial geospatial modelling predicts crime-risk by location and time (Shapiro, 2017).

Dozens if not hundreds of US police departments now use some form of geospatial modelling (Green, 2019; Robinson and Koepke, 2016), and many started doing so in the midst of crisis. Predictive policing was heralded as a tool of reform and was often the technological vanguard in police efforts to salvage legitimacy after civil rights violations. Civilian footage of officers using excessive and sometimes deadly force against unarmed African Americans led to investigations that, in turn, exposed extensive malpractice at the institutional level (e.g. US Department of Justice, 2015). Many agencies faced the embarrassing possibility of oversight from the Obama Administration's Department of Justice (DOJ) (Ferguson, 2017a; Richardson, Schultz and Crawford, 2019). Alongside other technological fixes such as body-worn cameras (see Mateescu, Rosenblat and Boyd, 2016), predictive policing was framed as the solution to bad decision-making on the ground. A discourse that I have elsewhere described as 'predictive policing for reform' (Shapiro, 2019) emphasised the algorithm's rationalisation benefits, with data-driven predictions promising to optimise law enforcement practices and improve public safety and criminal justice outcomes (Corbett-Davies, Goel, and González-Bailon, 2017; Siegel, 2018; see also Miller, 2018).

But claims to the value of predictive policing for reform were met with accusations that it would merely exacerbate already-biased and discriminatory police practices. Critics charged that because crime-prediction algorithms are trained on data managed by police, the systems simply 'learn' to see crime in the same way that police do – and thereby perpetuate the same problematic practices that prompted the institutional crisis in the first place (cf. American Civil Liberties Union, 2016; Ensign et al., 2017; Lum and Isaac, 2016; Richardson, Schultz and Crawford, 2019; Selbst, 2017). According to some, even systems designed to enhance fairness or transparency – for instance, by excluding race from the analysis or by making code available for public review – nonetheless "lack ... rigorous methodology and accountability" when put into practice (Richardson, Schultz and Crawford, 2019: 199; Barocas and Selbst, 2016; Selbst, 2017).

Clearly, accountability has intuitive appeal here, both as a metric for evaluating policies around police use of technology and to gauge the ethical merit of the predictive algorithms themselves (cf. Brauneis and Goodman, 2018). But are these the same accountabilities? While some have discussed the relationship between algorithmic accountability and police accountability more broadly (e.g. Brayne, Rosenblat and Boyd, 2015; Richardson, Schultz and Crawford, 2019; Zarsky, 2013), it is also true that many of predictive policing's most vocal advocates, such as former Los Angeles and New York City Police Commissioner William Bratton, routinely invoke the moral connotations of accountability as a rationale *for* predictive policing, not as a charge against it (Black, 2016; Bratton, 2018; Bratton and Anderson, 2018). Such ambiguity is troublesome. For if given enough ideological wiggle room, technology vendors and police leaders can justify nearly any conceivable technocratic intervention in policing, regardless of its potential impact.

What exactly do we mean, then, when we talk about accountability in policing and AI? Being as precise as possible on this point is critical if we are to develop policies to more effectively govern how law enforcement uses AI and machine learning. In the next section, I briefly discuss the role that accountability has played historically in shaping modern policing. Building on this, I distinguish three sets of accountability concerns as they pertain to predictive policing – *public accountability, supervisory accountability* and *algorithmic accountability*. Public accountability describes the extent to which police are answerable to external governance bodies, while supervisory accountability refers to structures internal to police institutions. These two concerns recur due to the police's ambiguous role within liberal–democratic governance, and their relationship evolves in tandem with shifting understandings of the police's mandate. Algorithmic accountability, by contrast, describes concerns specific to the use of automated decision-making systems, and in particular issues of data-quality, opacity and explainability.

The chapter then moves to a case study of the geospatial predictive policing platform HunchLab, and is based on ethnographic research that I conducted with the product team. HunchLab provides a unique lens for examining how questions of accountability motivate and interact with the design of predictive policing systems because the product team was sympathetic to both sides of the predictive policing debate – that is, they believed that algorithms have the potential to expand the police's public safety benefits and mitigate police harms through its rationalisation benefits, but they also recognised that without appropriate measures, algorithms will simply reproduce policing's deep-seated biases and discriminatory practices. As the team worked to translate their ethical commitments into technical mechanisms, however, their solutions generated a new set of concerns around measurement, validation and falsifiability. These epistemic concerns complicate core assumptions for police accountability in the era of AI, and the chapter concludes with suggestions towards a normative framework that can take these into account without losing sight of the police's problematic relationship to democratic governance.

Police, accountability, transparency and reform

Since the earliest modern forces were commissioned in the 18th and 19th centuries, police authority and autonomy have been met with allegations of unaccountability (de Lint, 2000; Edwards, 2001). Indeed, the history of modern policing and its reforms could be told through the constantly evolving prism of what an 'accountable' police force might look like – or, in other words, how we should govern the relationship between actually existing police forces and liberal–democratic institutions (Dubber and Valverde, 2008; Sklansky, 2008a).

In the US, early police forces were generally answerable only to the political-party machines that ran City Hall, meaning that there were few, if any, mechanisms for establishment outsiders to challenge police actions. With the growth of organised crime in the 1920s and 1930s, calls for reform echoed from the popular outcry of progressive reformers to newspaper editorials and eventually to politicians' own mouths. In 1929, President Herbert Hoover appointed the Wickersham Commission to investigate law enforcement's ineffectual response to organised crime under Prohibition (cf. Wright, 2012). Meanwhile, leading police intellectuals, such as Berkeley, California Chief of Police August Vollmer and Theodore Roosevelt as police commissioner of New York City, launched comprehensive professionalisation campaigns, urging police departments to rationalise their procedures through new investigatory standards and patrol technologies (Berman, 1987; Carte and Carte, 1975; Sklansky, 2014). This involved, for instance, the pioneering development of radio-patrol cars, fingerprinting and records management databases, along with several other crime-fighting and forensic techniques (Battles, 2010; Reeves and Packer, 2013) – all lending a veneer of expertise and authority to the police while distancing law enforcement from the gang-like authority of political patronage.

Accountability efforts in the 'reform' era (Kelling and Moore, 1988) were refracted through the lens of the police's socially and politically dictated mandate: fighting rising crime rates as effectively as possible. To be more accountable to the public, early-to-mid-20th century commissioners such as Los Angeles Police Chief William Parker initiated significant technological and institutional reforms. As criminologist George Kelling explains,

> In the name of eliminating corrupt political influences from policing, [police reformers] attempted to change the nature of the business from crime prevention to reactive law enforcement. They restructured police organizations, revised administrative processes, developed new tactics, and redefined the relationship between police and citizens – each, more or less successfully – all with an eye toward gaining administrative control of police, whether field commanders, supervisors, or patrol officers.
>
> (Kelling, 1999: 6)

In other words, the more the police advanced both technologically and organisationally toward optimising their reactive crime-fighting apparatus, the more professional, and thus accountable, they were perceived to be. That is, at least to some members of society. To poor and racial-minority communities, the professionalised police were no less caustic a force than before. For black Americans, forced by white terrorism in the south to migrate and re-build their lives in inner city enclaves in the north, a more 'professional' police force meant a more-organised repressive regime, neither more nor less accountable than anything before (Williams and Murphy, 1990).

Additionally, because line officers were subject to stricter standards (such as dress and behaviour codes and new training and educational requirements), professionalisation efforts were met with significant institutional resistance. And while the rank-and-file eventually adapted to the new requirements (largely through mass unionisation and collective bargaining negotiations; cf. Juris, 1971), suburbanising white America was being exposed for the first time throughout the 1960s to televised images of police violence. Police departments across the US used aggressive and sometimes deadly tactics to quell civil rights and anti-war protests (Kelling and Moore, 1988). Unwarranted and often deadly use of force against African Americans went unpunished, prompting widespread urban unrest (Levy, 2018; Sugrue, 2014). With a lack of checks on police, internal corruption ran rampant (Sherman, 1978). Even Kelling – whose research and advocacy helped advance the police's 'culture of control' (Garland, 2001) through programs like 'broken windows' and 'order-maintenance' enforcement (Harcourt, 2001) – would concede that the mid-century reforms had adverse effects on the police's relationship to society. As policing became more internally rigid and controlled, its inner workings became less transparent and its actions less accountable to outside institutions. Agency leaders appealed to the complexity of investigatory techniques, data management systems, crime-targeting strategies and so on, justifying their authority and autonomy under the pretence that would-be criminals could 'game' the system if police operations were more transparent; at the same time, the rank-and-file's increasingly militant unionism bolstered the police's infamous 'blue-wall' – an professional culture of 'silence' as a virtue (Chin and Wells, 1997; Kleinig, 2001).

After the social and political turmoil of the 1960s, then, new reform efforts gained momentum, but the demands were different. As the police entered into what Kelling and criminologist Mark Moore (1988) called the 'community problem-solving era', the emphasis shifted from professionalisation to community relations and institutional transparency (see also Kelling, Wasserman, and Williams, 1988). The new reforms were driven by an evolving sense of democratic governance, now refracted through the lens of 'community' as the preferred locus of action and agency (Rose, 1996; Sklansky, 2008a). The police were no longer expected to be efficient in reacting to crimes already committed, but to be proactive in establishing and building community relationships and trust. Institutional transparency thus became tied to accountability to the extent that it could improve community-police relations. As public policy scholar James F. Gilsinan (2012: 93) writes of policing, "[I]n the lexicon of dyadic American folk sayings, 'motherhood and apple pie' is being joined by 'transparency and accountability'". The twinning of these ideals is now common: a failure in transparency implies a failure of accountability (Levine, 2019; Luna, 2000). Legal theorist David Harris (2013: 878) explains the rationale: "by making the workings of government open to public scrutiny, the public will better understand what those in charge are doing, and can hold officials accountable in appropriate ways". And in the era of community policing, this logic was grafted onto law enforcement bodies. If we can't know what the police are up to, then we can't challenge their decisions or hold agencies and officials accountable for their actions or failures (Luna, 2000; Zarsky, 2013). In this "new world of police accountability", as criminologists Sam Walker and Carol Archbold (2019: 8) call it, the "core meaning of police accountability" is that "police are answerable to the public" as a "basic principle of a democratic society".

The extent to which these community-oriented reform efforts actually enhanced transparency – and by extension, the new police accountability – remains an open question (Friedman, 2016; McDaniel, 2018). Although the International Association of Chiefs of Police (IACP) claims 'transparency' as a core value (IACP, 2018), scholars of policing continue to discover that police agencies are themselves undemocratic, and that their relationship to public institutions and democratic norms is shaky at best (Fagan, 2016; Sklansky, 2008a; 2008b; 2014; Schwartz, 2016; Walker, 2016; Woods, 2015). Police insist on discretionary authority and continue to abhor transparency's 'sunlight' to the extent that it threatens institutional autonomy. Historically and globally, law enforcement agencies have tended to operate as authoritarian exceptions to liberal governance, with strict chain-of-command structures and sovereign interpretations of the law that leave little flexibility for public input or participation (Dubber and Valverde 2006; 2008). And while there have been experiments in running police departments more democratically, criminologist David Alan Sklansky (2008a; 2008b) observes that these routinely fail. "The agenda of police reform", Sklansky writes (2008b: 110), has "been shaped and limited by authoritarian assumptions about the nature of the police workplace: democracy in the broader society has been thought to require placing police officers under rigid, comprehensive rules, imposed from outside, or at least from the top". These same 'authoritarian assumptions' continue to thwart efforts toward increased police transparency – despite the fact that the 'rigid, comprehensive rules' of policing continue to promote illegitimate practices disproportionately impacting poor and minority communities, such as citation and arrest quotas and racial profiling (Bronstein, 2014).

By invoking Sklansky's critique of police professionalisation, my point is not to advance an alternative proposal for how police institutions should be organised or governed. Rather, it is simply to highlight the persistence of ambiguities and tensions in police institutions' relationships to democratic governance. We saw the interplay between institutional transparency and accountability continue to play out in the rise of CompStat, a data-driven, crime-reduction strategy pioneered in the 1990s by the then-NYPD Commissioner William Bratton as an 'accountability system' (Bratton and Anderson, 2018; Bratton and Malinowski, 2008; Gilsinan, 2012). CompStat is essentially a programmatic managerial reform, designed to make district commanders more accountable to department executives. It involves intense tribunal-like meetings (fictionalised, famously, in *The Wire*), where crime data is sacrosanct as evidence of police performance. Many departments today open at least some of their CompStat meetings up to public observation and publish crime statistics, and often point to these measures as evidence of institutional transparency. But insofar as CompStat represents progress in police 'accountability', it does so only to the extent that it reinvigorates earlier reformers' emphasis on the mandate to fight crime as effectively as possible, and little else. CompStat may have augmented mid-20th century professionalisation campaigns with an aura of technological sophistication through computerised crime mapping, but the rationale was nearly identical; rather than quelling organised crime, in the CompStat era, it was street crimes. And while CompStat has been thoroughly critiqued – for relying too heavily questionable crime numbers and arrest rates, imposing an authoritarian rigidity in the name of 'accountability' and promoting the over-policing of low-income, racial-minority communities (Eterno and Silverman, 2012;

Garrett, 2001; Hanink, 2013; Harcourt, 2001; Kaufman, 2016) – it has none-theless been credited with lowering crime rates across the US, and continues to be held up as the gold standard for 'accountability' in police departments across the world (e.g. de Maillard, 2018; Mazerolle, Rombouts, and McBroom, 2007).

Three accountabilities

Keen readers may protest that in giving this account, I have deliberately conflated two distinct senses of police 'accountability' (cf. Chan, 1999). On the one hand are calls for police forces to become more accountable to the publics they serve – that is, rather than answering to corrupt political machines or, later, to complex investigatory procedures, crime-fighting strategies and insti-tutional bureaucracies. This sense is often referred to as 'external' accountability (e.g. Moore and Braga, 2003). On the other hand is a notion of accountability that is entirely internal – where being more accountable means making the hierarchical structures of policing institutions more tractable, such that respon-sibility for a failure or wrongdoing runs up the chain of command. On this view, superiors are accountable for the actions of subordinates, and everyone accountable to the department brass – which, in turn, must answer to elected officials. For simplicity's sake, we can call these the *public* and *supervisory* notions of police accountability, respectively. And in response to the keen reader, I'd only emphasise that for a large portion of US policing's history, these two account-ability functions overlapped, such that the more rigid and tightly controlled the internal hierarchy, the more accountable the police were perceived to be externally – and vice versa. For example, as criminologists Moore and Anthony Braga (2003: 441) argue for CompStat, the "only way for police managers to acquire a strong current of accountability through their organizations is to build behind them a powerful, persistent constituency that demands from their organization the same things that they are demanding, and to attach a measure-ment system to these particular values". It was only relatively recently that the merits of supervisory accountability systems like CompStat were challenged on their face, with calls mounting for greater transparency into institutional decision-making processes as a way to enhance public accountability in the form of relationships with community stakeholders.

What drives the changing relationship between public and supervisory accountabilities? On the one hand are shifting demands placed on police departments. With calls for the police to be more effective in their ability to react to crime, supervisory accountability reigns; when police are tasked with building trust in their jurisdiction's communities, public accountability is the name of the game. But this is only part of the story. On the other hand, and without defaulting to a techno-determinist narrative, we can say with some confidence that technology also plays a role. As police historian Willem de Lint (2000) observed, there is an implicit connection between police account-ability and new police technologies: "With each new technology", de Lint wrote (2000: 70, emphasis added), "a fuller and more penetrating gaze has been envisioned, *both of the police into the polity and of police supervision on police officer mobilization*". In other words, as advances in mobility (as in the squad car) and communications (as in the two-way radio) expand the police power, they do so ambivalently because they also "structure the decision-making of individual officers on patrol to organizationally vetted formats" (2000). A technology like body-worn cameras, for example, was framed as a solution to mounting accountability concerns because it expanded supervision of officers' activities in the field; at the same time, however, its penetration 'into the polity' through a mobilisation of surveillance cameras also provoked new anxieties (Mateescu, Rosenblat and Boyd, 2016). Technology's dual gaze was certainly how Bratton and his team imagined CompStat in the 1990s (better crime data = greater supervisory accountability = greater public accountability), and it is how predictive policing systems are designed today. Where CompStat tightens the managerial coupling of police executives and district commanders, predictive policing tightens supervisory control over officers in the field, such that their decisions – about where to patrol, when and for how long – are likewise structured to 'organizationally vetted formats' (see also Benbouzid, 2019).

But as a new police technology, predictive policing raises a distinct set of anxieties that exceed the traditional frames of public and supervisory accountability. First and foremost are straightforward transparency issues. Department contracts with predictive policing vendors have been shrouded in secrecy and thus aroused suspicion prima facie. The Brennan Center for Justice at New York University, for example, had to sue the City of New York to access information about the NYPD's predictive policing trials (Levinson-Waldman and Posey, 2018). In other cases, politicians and city government officials were left in the dark about police use of predictive algorithms. Silicon Valley data analytics giant Palantir worked with the New Orleans Police Department for years without City Councilmembers' knowledge (Winston, 2018), while the San Francisco Police Department went behind the backs of the city's civilian police-oversight body to discuss a contract with geospatial crime-analytics firm PredPol (Bond-Graham, 2013). This unwarranted secrecy transformed predictive policing overnight into a symbol of unaccountable policing – an aura that never attached to CompStat's supervisory interventions in quite the same way. So while police leaders and intellectuals continue to view predictive policing as a positive refinement upon CompStat's supervisory interventions – or as Bratton (2018: 7) puts it, "the CompStat of the '90s on steroids in the 21st century" (see also Bratton and Anderson, 2018) – to critics, the blatant disregard for public input suggested an outright affront to accountability concerns.

The bipolar responses to predictive policing is unsurprising, especially if we consider that most systems were introduced in a period when police killings of unarmed African Americans seemed to be recurring at an unprecedented rate. As critical legal scholar Andrew Guthrie Ferguson (2017a: 29) observes, predictive policing and other 'big data' technologies "grew out of crisis and a need to turn the page on scandals that revealed systemic problems with policing tactics". The six-million-dollar predictive policing experiment underway in Chicago, for example, is part of broader reform efforts at the Chicago PD. These were triggered by a DOJ investigation at the department after dash-cam video showed Officer Jason Van Dyke shooting and killing unarmed teenager Laquan McDonald. "In response to demonstrated human bias", Ferguson (2017a: 26) writes, "it is not surprising that the lure of objective-seeming, data-driven policing might be tempting".

It is also not surprising that critics were wary of 'objectivity' claims. Beyond the initial transparency concerns, then, are anxieties around algorithmic decision-making itself – whether it is appropriate in the first place for a machine to be making high-impact decisions in patrol resource-allocation. Much of the critique has been levelled at the data. Because predictive policing algorithms are trained on crime data managed by police, the systems will learn only from the police's already-biased choices about what to count as a crime (Gilsinan, 2012), where to patrol (Ensign et al., 2017; Lum and Isaac, 2016) and who to target (Jefferson, 2017a; 2017b).

While all of these concerns are legitimate and certainly warrant further investigation, I want to focus the remainder of the chapter on what I think are more fundamental questions. For behind any data-quality issue are epistemic anxieties provoked by the algorithm itself. I say that this anxiety is fundamental because, as a number of scholars have shown, even when technology producers design a system with fairness, transparency or accountability in mind, discrimination and unfairness can emerge as an artefact of the machine learning process itself (Barocas and Selbst, 2016; Roth, 2019). It is therefore crucial that institutions be capable of giving adequate accounts of the machine learning process – of the AI's 'reasoning'. Often, this notion of 'accountability' is discussed in terms of explainability (cf. Bennett Moses and Chan, 2018). In predictive policing, this could mean something as simple as why an officer was sent to this intersection and not another. For example, legal scholars Lyria Bennett Moses and Janet Chan (2018) argue that if an officer can't explain why the algorithm sent her to a particular location, then her accountability is limited in the literal sense of being unable to give an account of her actions – at least, without defaulting to the technology itself in the explanation. The temptation here is to 'tech-wash' the decision – to invoke the supposed objectivity and neutrality of the algorithm rather than explaining how the decision was made – producing an account that is neither normatively acceptable (given the stakes of policing) nor legally sufficient in a courtroom context (Ferguson 2011; 2017a; 2017b).

Critical data scholars Andrew Selbst and Solon Barocas (2018) argue that machine learning models defy explanation for two distinct but related reasons: models can be both *inscrutable* – the rules that the model follows are hard to identify – and *nonintuitive* – because it is unclear why the rules are what they are. And because many predictive policing applications use machine learning to model crime, they too can be inscrutable and nonintuitive. Consider the geo-spatial predictive policing platform HunchLab. We will focus on this product in the next section. For now, it is only necessary to know that HunchLab uses thousands of variables in its modelling. Machine learning algorithms mine the data to sort through all of those variables and produce a crime model that is tailored to each crime-type in each jurisdiction. Because of this tailoring, the model's 'rules' – or more precisely, the series of variables that the machine identifies as statistically significant predictors of a crime's occurrence – will differ across crime-types within the same jurisdiction; but they will also differ across jurisdictions for the same crime-type. If you were to apply the model for, say, burglaries in Philadelphia to burglaries in San Francisco, the results wouldn't be very accurate at all; likewise, if you applied the model for burglaries in Philadelphia to larceny in Philadelphia, the performance would be just as poor. This tailoring makes the modelling inscrutable because the 'rules' are highly specified, making explanation more difficult. But the models can also be nonintuitive. This is the case when the 'rules' for predicting burglaries are set by machine-detected correlations that make little sense to human interpreters. HunchLab uses moon phase as a temporal input, and if the system were to create a rule based on a correlation between 'waning gibbous' and assaults, then human interpreters would likely have a difficult time explaining the rationale behind this nonintuitive setting.

Given these issues with the decision-making systems themselves, we can count *algorithmic accountability* as encompassing concerns distinct from the public and supervisory accountabilities. For one, a police department could take any number of steps to improve the sense of accountability and trans-parency around predictive policing – for instance, by opening the acquisition process to public comment, publicising the technology's adoption and even pro-viding explanations for how the modelling works (cf. Brauneis and Goodman, 2018) – but nonetheless fail to identify the exact 'rules' of a jurisdictionally and crime-specific model or give a meaningful account of why the rules are what they are. In this case, the algorithmic decisions would remain inscrut-able and nonintuitive despite transparency efforts (cf. Ananny and Crawford, 2018). Likewise, predictive policing could satisfy calls for supervisory account-ability – for instance, with automated vehicle location (AVL) signals notifying supervisors that officers are patrolling where they are supposed to (cf. Sherman, 2013) – without the officers ever needing to explain or even understand why they were assigned to that particular block or intersection.

In short, algorithmic accountability captures anxieties stemming from the algorithm's potential to short-circuit institutional efforts to enhance account-ability on other fronts. As critical information scholar Jenna Burrell (2016: 1) argues, machine learning algorithms present threats to transparency on mul-tiple fronts, including intentional corporate or state secrecy, technical illiter-acies as well as the "characteristics of machine learning algorithms and the scale required to apply them usefully" – each a distinct threat to our ability to account for automated decision-making and each requiring a distinct response (see also Zarsky, 2016).

To date, however, most critiques of predictive policing have emphasised the first and second of Burrell's opacities, leaving aside the characteristics of machine learning algorithms as they're actually applied. In other words, explainability is not the only epistemic anxiety that algorithmic accountability must address. If we're to make sense of AI's impact on policing, then we also need to address lingering epistemological assumptions about how algorithms work in and on the world – that is, not only what the 'rules' are and why, but how the models operate 'in the wild'; how they affect the objects and dynamics they are meant to merely represent (Hacking, 1983; Mackenzie, 2015). As I illustrate in the following section, at the centre of predictive policing is a profound *indeterminacy* with the potential to undermine even the most well-intentioned justifications for automated decision-making. Unlike explainability, indeterminacy is not an artefact of the algorithm *per se*; rather, it results from how the algorithm becomes entangled with the world it purports to merely operate on (Introna, 2016). As sociologist Adrian Mackenzie (2015: 442) argues, "the problem of using machine learning … is that the effectiveness of any given predictive model is hard to measure because so many other things are changing at the same time". The same is true for the dynamics that predictive policing attempts to model and anticipate: how do we measure the model's 'effectiveness' when it intervenes unto that which it represents (Hacking, 1983)?

Algorithmic indeterminacy

On October 3, 2018, the publicly traded police technology firm ShotSpotter, Inc. announced its purchase of HunchLab, a geospatial predictive policing platform previously produced by Philadelphia-based analytics firm Azavea. ShotSpotter specialised in gunshot detection systems, and the company planned to integrate the gunshot data with HunchLab's crime-forecasting to generate 'predictive models and patrol missions in real time' (ShotSpotter, 2018). Business observers predicted that the acquisition would give ShotSpotter a significant advantage over competitors (GovTech Biz, 2018) – not only because of the data fusion, but because HunchLab enjoyed a reputation as one of – if not *the* – most sophisticated and advanced crime-modelling systems available (cf. Egbert, 2019). William Bratton, who enjoys a seat on ShotSpotter's corporate board, remarked that the 'combination of HunchLab with ShotSpotter will accelerate the maturation of the [predictive policing] category and result in even greater value to police departments' (ShotSpotter, 2018). On the whole, it was a good day for ShotSpotter's investors.

I conducted ethnographic research with the product team at Azavea before they sold Hunchlab to ShotSpotter, and the following case study is based on my observations from 2015–2016. While I can't validate that ShotSpotter continues to manage HunchLab in exactly the same way that Azavea did, the rhetoric around the acquisition suggests that this is likely the case (cf. GovTech Biz, 2018). A good deal of HunchLab's reputation owed to its sophisticated crime modelling. After landing a grant from the National Science Foundation, Robert Cheetham, Azavea's founder and president, hired mathematician and statistician Jeremy Heffner to manage the project. Heffner introduced cutting-edge techniques from AI and machine learning to the new HunchLab proto-type. With these techniques, the team was able to avoid commitments to any particular crime-forecasting or modelling approach. With enough pro-cessing power, Heffner reasoned, several crime-modelling approaches could be incorporated into a single, theory-agnostic meta-model. These included an early warning system that Cheetham developed for the Philadelphia PD in the early 2000s; 'near repeat' analysis, a forecasting technique based on the spa-tial and temporal distribution of crimes (e.g. Townsley, Homel and Chaseling 2000; 2003); and 'risk terrain modeling' (RTM), an approach that examines the proximity of crimes to key urban features such as bars, churches, transporta-tion hubs, and so on to create spatial risk profiles (Caplan, Kennedy and Miller 2011). HunchLab's machine learning algorithm would simply parse through combinations of these forecasting methods – represented as series of variables – to determine the model of best fit based on signals in the local data. In other words, 'HunchLab 2.0' (Azavea, 2015) adopted a key tenet of the 'big data' revo-lution: throw as many theories as possible at the data and let the machine sort out the most precise 'recipe' for predicting an outcome (Mayer-Schönberger and Cukier, 2013).

HunchLab subscribers received access to several algorithmic features, but the core risk-prediction algorithm was called 'Predictive Missions'. This is what modelled the various criminological methods together to generate geospatial risk scores. Every 'instance' of the Predictive Missions algorithm – that is, each jurisdiction-specific set of crime models – was trained on five years' worth of local crime-data as well as several non-crime-related data-sets, such as census data, weather patterns, moon cycles, school schedules, holidays, concerts and events calendars, and so on. All of these were then mapped onto a grid of 500 square-foot cells laid over the client's jurisdiction and a series of thousands of decision trees recursively partitioned the data based on crime outcomes in each grid cell; if a crime occurred, then the regressions determined which variables influenced the occasion of that crime and to what extent, weighting the model accordingly and tailoring it to the local data. The result was a hyper-localised and hyper-sensitive crime forecasting algorithm, with accuracy measurements sometimes coming in as high as ninety-two per cent (for comparison, PredPol, HunchLab's primary competitor, reports measurements of a 'predictive accuracy index' at around fifty percent at highest; see Mohler et al., 2015). As I noted earlier, because Predictive Missions adjusted weights according to local crime data, models for the same crime differed across jurisdictions. And because sub-scribing departments' data was updated daily, the weighting for each crime-type would change over time.

HunchLab boasted of this sophistication to potential clients, and if crime data was publicly available for a jurisdiction – which is common thanks to increasingly popular 'open data' initiatives – a HunchLab product specialist could create a mock-up model and present it during a sales pitch. To do so, he or she simply needed to withhold recent crime events from the data used to train a mock-up and then juxtapose them with the crime predictions. But HunchLab's reputation was about more than just the modelling. Based on what I observed, it is fair to say that HunchLab enjoyed a unique status in the police technology sector as the ethical alternative in an increasingly crowded field – a repute that owed in large part to Azavea's unwillingness to take on investors or go public. Where most competitors were brought to market by large corporations (IBM, Microsoft and Motorola to name a few) or backed by venture capital (as with PredPol) or covert government seed funding (as with Palantir; cf. Robinson and Koepke 2016; Winston 2018), Azavea was unbeholden to shareholders, investors or state intelligence. Instead, it adhered to a strict set of criteria for corporate social responsibility, environmental sustainability and transparency, all of which earned the firm a certification as a 'social benefit' company, or B-Corp. (In fact, when Azavea sold HunchLab to ShotSpotter, Cheetham penned a blog post explaining that HunchLab ultimately failed to align with the company's core values; see Cheetham, 2019.) Perhaps, then, it was for the sake of transparency that Cheetham and Heffner were willing to recognise a fundamental but rarely acknowledged contradiction: the algorithm's accuracy can only be measured *before* a department starts using the predictions to allocate patrols. Once officers start patrolling based on the algorithm, the system's performance can no longer be validated. The police's visible presence in the predicted grid cell affects what happens there, meaning that the 'ground truth' data ceases to be a controlled sample. This dynamic confounds performance metrics because there is no basis for comparison.

Heffner conceptualised the problem as a paradox animated by competing probabilities: *detection* – the increased likelihood that an officer observes a crime taking place in a predicted grid cell – and *deterrence* – the increased likelihood that his or her visible presence will prevent the predicted crime from taking place. Detection and deterrence pull in opposite directions, and neither can be attributed to the predictions with any certainty. With crime and policing configured as 'metastable states coexisting in one and the same modulation' (Deleuze, 1992: 5), the ability to isolate effects becomes impossible. Like the Heisenberg uncertainty principle or post-humanist theories of performativity (e.g. Barad, 2003), HunchLab conceived the double optics of police patrols – the officers in the field both observable and observing – as introducing uncertainty at the same time that it generates new data. The result is an uncertainty inherent to prediction in general (Mackenzie, 2015) but which has largely been ignored in debates over predictive policing's merit.

What are the implications of indeterminacy for accountability concerns? The most obvious issue is accuracy. Even if a crime analyst or district commander could explain the 'rules' of a model and how they were set, the fact that the algorithm's accuracy can't be tested or evaluated after it has been put to use should discredit the validity of those rules in the first place – it is simply impossible to give a sufficient account of the relationship between the model and the real-world conditions that it is supposed to represent. But the HunchLab team took the opposite view. Acknowledging indeterminacy didn't stop them from selling software. If indeterminacy is an unavoidable by-product of any predictive system, they reasoned, then one might as well capitalise on the rationalisation benefits to rein in arbitrary decision-making in policing. The task, as Cheetham, Heffner and others on the team saw it, was to exploit indeterminacy to improve police outcomes – to make the distribution of police resources and public safety benefits more equitable and more efficient. And to do so would require greater efforts to capture, measure and analyse the predictions' effects in and on the dynamics of crime and patrol. Just as Google experiments with changes to its algorithm or interface design monitoring usage, the goal would be to "fold the performativity of models back into the modelling process", as Mackenzie (2015: 443) puts it – to statistically represent prediction's performative effects within the predictive apparatus.

In the context of predictive policing, this 'folding' can work if the desired outcomes are observable behaviours or actions. If clients want predictions to lead to higher arrest rates, this can be modelled because it is observable in the data. But to HunchLab, as well as to proponents like Bratton – who routinely invokes Robert Peel's (1829) principles of policing that "[t]he test of police efficiency is the absence of crime and disorder, not the visible evidence of police action in dealing with it" (cf. Bratton, 2014) – deterrence and prevention are paramount as safeguards against the 'the potential harm caused by over-policing' (HunchLab, n.d.). However, the emphasis on deterrence introduces yet another paradox: an event deterred is by definition unobservable (as in the truism that you can't prove a negative). Of course, prevention rates can be inferred by comparison between a treatment group and a control (e.g. Hunt, Saunders, and Hollywood 2014; Mohler et al., 2015; Ratcliffe, Taylor, and Askey 2017), but this will always be an imperfect estimation as no two jurisdictions, beats or patrol shifts are identical. Further, maintaining a control group necessarily means only partially implementing predictions, a prospect that may not be terribly enticing to clients given that they are paying handsomely for the technology.

The HunchLab team was not interested in using crime predictions to increase arrest rates. As Cheetham (2018) would later write on the Azavea blog,

> we believe that too many people are arrested in the United States' and that the criminal justice system has been both biased and destructive to many groups in our society, particularly to minorities and immigrants. Arresting more people is not our goal and should not be the objective of law enforcement agencies.

They therefore sought ways to measure and optimise the immeasurable – deterrence. The problem thus became a question of proxies and counterfactuals (Morgan and Winship, 2007), and this required looping in more data: if deterrence is the desired outcome, and deterrence is immeasurable, then adding data points that co-occur with the absence of crime can serve as a proxy.

We see this, for instance, in a discussion that Heffner and former product specialist Chip Koziara led in an online webinar about 'prescriptive analysis in policing' (Azavea, 2014). In business analytics, prescription occupies a more complex register than prediction. Rather than merely predicting an outcome based on past events, prescription is about determining the best course of action from among a set of options in order to optimise outcomes (Ransbotham, Kiron and Prentice, 2015). A 'prescriptive policing' approach, then, would need to reverse-engineer from the desired outcome – deterrence – to identify the best course of action to get there. As Heffner and Koziara saw it, to achieve this, the analysis and software would need to be constructed "not only [to] make accurate forecasts of where and when crimes are likely to occur, but also to help inform the decisions [that police] make in terms of what to do in those locations" (Azavea, 2014). By creating new variables for police activity (such as how long an officer patrols a predicted grid cell or what he or she does while in that zone), the prescriptive design would link deterrence with other information, thereby rendering it legible to the machine through the proxy. "You build a predictive model and within the course of that predictive model it explicitly represents different possible decisions that you could make, models them, and then gives an explicit recommendation about the decision that you should make to effect the change that you want in the outcome" (Azavea, 2014).

A similar logic motivated an index called 'predictive efficacy'. In a partnership with Temple University criminologist Jerry Ratcliffe, Heffner and others on the team had been working on a modelling system called HarmStat during my observations. HarmStat was based on the progressive notion that low-income and minority communities are as likely to view police as a hostile force as they are to see law enforcement as a necessary measure for survival and social control (cf. Bell, 2016). HarmStat's objective was therefore to quantify 'police harm' and place it on the same analytic plane as 'crime harm', such that the two could be optimised through a cost-benefit analysis. Predictive efficacy served as a weighting metric. Where the quantification of crime–harms could be estimated using sentencing guidelines, police harms were calculated based on an estimate of each crime's predictability – the idea being that highly unpredictable crimes like homicide will require more police resources and an amplified presence in an area, and thereby increased the likelihood of adverse interactions between police and the community, but that these high-impact crimes are more important to prevent from community members' perspective. So while a violent crime such as assault may be more difficult to predict than a property crime like burglary or larceny (e.g. Ratcliffe, Taylor and Askey 2017), community members are more likely to prioritise police intervention unto violent crimes; if efforts to thwart more easily predictable crimes have greater success rates, the payoff for preventing the less predictable and more harmful violations would be higher, justifying greater expenditure of patrol resources – and more potential police harm to the community.

While the logic makes sense intuitively, HarmStat glosses over the indeterminacy baked into its own modelling. 'Predictive efficacy' was an estimation of predictability and deterrence, which remained unobservable. And even if a prescriptive design could produce a sufficient proxy, HarmStat would still assume an immeasurable and unvalidated precision to the crime predictions. Say, for example, that the algorithm gave a false positive by predicting a crime that would *not* have occurred regardless of police intervention. Because accuracy can no longer be evaluated, there's no mechanism to detect and correct the error, and as such the machine receives positive feedback – a 'reward' – for its recommendation because no crime occurred. The risk here is an inflation of 'predictive efficacy' – or, in other words, a ratcheting of Type I errors – where deterrence is incorrectly and systematically attributed to police activity. If the algorithm were at all inaccurate, it could learn to favour police intervention – an outcome that meets textbook definitions of bias and, by HarmStat's own reasoning, negatively impacts poor, racial-minority communities.

A similar risk carried over into another HunchLab feature called 'Advisor'. Like the vision for 'prescriptive policing', Advisor would help clients experiment with police tactics to gather evidence for effective deterrence techniques. On the surface, Advisor appeared to simply automate the randomised control trial (RCT) methodology: clients could use the feature to test out different tactical responses to 'crime problems' and evaluate the outcomes relative to a control group. As one programmer on the HunchLab team put it, with Advisor,

> we could start to see how different tactics perform in actually deterring crime… If we know that police officers went into an area and they were there but the crime still occurred, but the same type of crime is predicted in another area and they did different tactics, then we could start evaluating the types of tactics to use in each situation, and stuff like that.
>
> (Author's notes, 19 November 2015)

Given the indeterminacies detailed above, however, it is also the case that Advisor abandons some fundamental tenets of the experiment design, leading to a kind of rough-and-dirty approach to evidence gathering that extends indeterminacy into new areas. In one of Advisor's formats, clients evaluated a specific tactic for its deterrence effects. For example, after a wave of home burglaries, clients might use Advisor to test 'high visibility patrols' or 'canvassing residents and local businesses' to see whether these have an effect on the burglary rate. While the program came pre-loaded with suggestions (e.g. 'writ[ing] reports while parked in patrol cars at high risk locations'), these were also customizable fields that users could update at their discretion to match preferred nomenclature or tactical approaches. After the tactics are delineated, Advisor would then monitor the rate of home burglaries and compare outcomes in the test area to "what likely would have happened had you not been doing the field test" (Azavea, 2015).

Advisor's emphasis on pragmatic experimentalism echoed calls from criminologists and law enforcement intellectuals for police to adopt a more iterative and evidence-based approach to patrol. Between 2014 and 2016, the National Institute of Justice ran the Randomized Control Trial Challenge, promising grants of $100,000 to five police departments interested in conducting research on innovative police managerial strategies. Jim Bueermann, president of the Police Foundation, predicted that by 2022, every police department would have a resident criminologist to test strategic efficacy (Cohen McCullough and Spence, 2012). Similarly, criminologist Lawrence Sherman (2013) forecast that by 2025, command staffs will be deploying technologies to test patrol efficiencies on a regular basis. As Heffner rightly argued both in our discussions and publicly, such experimentation can be burdensome and expensive for local departments, especially if a substantial grant is absent. Institutional pressures can also be prohibitive. With CompStat's lingering impact on departmental expectations, the pressure to demonstrate strategic effectiveness through crime reductions or increased arrest rates "can lead to a sort of risk aversion", as Heffner put it, with commanders becoming "less likely to experiment with things ... Because if we can just keep things generally as they are, they will likely turn out the same way at the next CompStat meeting – and so that's a safe move" (Azavea, 2015).

Heffner is not wrong here. Institutional procedures have a way of gaining a momentum that makes change difficult, and Advisor was marketed as a way to overcome these barriers – through automation, easy-to-use interface design and lower thresholds for statistical significance – and always with the goal of making policing more accountable to evidence. The trouble was that like prescriptive policing and like HarmStat, Advisor was built upon indeterminacies. When the system evaluated the effectiveness of any crime-fighting tactic, it compared the outcome in the assigned cell not against an actual control group but an algorithmically generated simulation of crime outcomes – an unvalidated prediction of 'what likely would have happened'. The default is, again, to the crime predictions, which again risks inflating results to favour police action. The result is therefore something like a fraction without a denominator, an RCT without a control, an unfalsifiable finding. And because the tactics field was customisable, there was nothing to prevent users – district commanders, for instance – from inputting a tactic like 'stop and frisk' that's already known to disparately impact low-income and minority communities. Sacrificing scientific rigor for good-enough estimations *could* lead to less-discriminatory tactics; but it could also mean an optimised version of the same old discriminatory practices. Faith, perhaps the ultimate antidote to accountability, is simply placed in police departments' willingness to test out less harmful strategies – canvassing rather than stopping and frisking, for example. Algorithmic 'rewards' are set to inform the system how to sort outcomes as positive or negative, but if the only data legible to the system are arrests or proxies of the immeasurable, then programs like Advisor will only ever learn to reproduce the patrol tactics most in need of change (Jefferson, 2017a; 2017b; Robinson and Koepke, 2016).

Towards a police accountability frame for the age of AI

Each of these initiatives – prescriptive policing, HarmStat and Advisor – reflected Azavea's efforts to leverage the algorithm to improve policing – to "reduc[e] [the] harm associated with over-policing, and … [help] officers find the best tactical solutions to improve their communities" (HunchLab, n.d.). In the end, though, each of these efforts was scaffolded upon an epistemological fallacy – a faith in the algorithm, not only to send officers to the best locations or to use the best tactics, but to provide evidence for its own effectiveness. Perhaps these shaky foundations shouldn't be surprising, given that predictive policing attempts to model and anticipate something as dynamic, complex, mutable and socially contingent as 'crime'. What counts as measurable, modellable and statistically scrutable in the first place is a fraught question (Bowker and Star, 1999; Gitelman, 2013), and what counts as crime depends not only on the whims of policy, regulation, legislation and criminological theory (Garland, 2001) but on the discretion of individual officers in the field. Predictive policing's promise was always to be more precise and certain – "to reduce uncertainty so that police can approach the allocation of resources in an optimal manner" (Brantingham, 2018: 473) – to rein in human error and discretion, and structure decision-making to "organizationally vetted formats" (de Lint, 2000: 70). But as we've seen, the danger of using technology to make these decisions, as Ben Green (2019) argues, "is that we will misinterpret them as technical problems that do not require political deliberation … blind[ing] us to the full possibilities to reform the policies and practices that technology purports to improve". In the case of HunchLab, the epistemic and ethical anxieties around crime and its prevention are simply imported onto the plane of machine-detectable patterns.

If predictive policing fails on its promises, then where do we stand on accountability? If structuring patrol decisions to algorithmically vetted formats increases supervisory accountability and, by some proponents' accounts, public accountability, then it does so by making sacrifices in algorithmic accountability. This is an old pattern. For decades it was thought that police autonomy and authority – and by extension, limited transparency and accountability – were justified to the extent that they made police more accountable as crime-fighters and stewards of the public's trust; today it is algorithmic autonomy and authority that get justified for the same goals.

Perhaps the problem is the entire set of assumptions that we've built up around police accountability and new technologies. After all, 19th and 20th century policing didn't exactly produce institutions known for their transparency and accountability. Why then should we map the expectations of police accountability onto the algorithm? A far more helpful starting point is to imagine the algorithm as an institution-extending mechanism in the first instance – not an alien technology imported onto a stable set of patrol practices, but rather a *remediation* of the patrol – not unlike the uniform, the beat, the patrol route or radio-car. And if the algorithm extends the institution by remediating it, then we might learn from HunchLab's efforts to wrangle with algorithmic indeterminacy that *the institution of policing itself is built upon shaky ground*. The algorithm – indeed, technology – won't save you.

To grapple with police accountability in the age of AI, then, we must take up the difficult task of reconciling what I have described here as public, supervisory and algorithmic conceptions of accountability – to think through these anxieties and concerns together. And so to conclude, I wish to submit a framework that I believe to be a useful starting point for doing so, even if it is not entirely suited to the complexity of the task. First, rather than conceiving of police accountability as distinct from technological concerns, we could instead think through *institutional accountability* as the ethical calculus behind any decision to expand police autonomy and discretion – regardless of whether that decision is made by a human or a machine. Any policy that constricts external transparency must be thoroughly vetted through the lens of the police's responsibility and answerability to external stakeholders. From this point of view, decisions to be secretive about the adoption of predictive policing would clearly be unwarranted, as would any undisclosed use of surveillance technologies – from cell-site simulators to facial recognition-enabled cameras. The point is not to simply foreclose upon the possibility of autonomy and discretion, but to create effective institutional checks and balances that force police to provide a more thorough and public account for the need to do so. If new police technologies expand the police power ambivalently, as de Lint (2000) suggests, then institutional accountability provides the frame for evaluating how the balance between public and supervisory accountabilities is struck.

Second, given the indeterminacy discussed throughout the chapter, we can conceive of *epistemic accountability* as the police's responsibility to provide sufficient explanations, both for their own decision-making processes and for the limitations of explainability itself. At the very least, epistemic accountability would require police to be upfront about what can and what cannot be known about a crime-fighting strategy, whether it is as broad as 'hot spot policing' or as specific as the algorithmic identification of a street-corner for patrol. Building on the notion of 'distributed epistemic responsibility' in moral philosophy (e.g. Simon, 2015), epistemic accountability describes a collective rather than individual sense of responsibility, with decision-making and knowledge-production shared across humans, automated systems and institutions. From this point of view, it would not be enough for a police department to simply claim that an 'accountability system' like CompStat ensures that crime is being addressed. The department would need to provide an account of how crime is counted, measured, represented, analysed and so on, and to justify the relationship between the metrics, the analytics and the human activity they are meant to represent. Epistemic accountability requires the institution to be answerable to what can be known, by what techniques and with what effects. In this sense, the obligation to account for causality and indeterminacy would be identical. A department using HunchLab would need to understand and be capable of explaining why and how indeterminate predictions are used to deter crime. By the same token, a department *not* using a predictive policing system would be held to the same standards: what methods does the agency use to allocate its patrol resources? The point is to develop mechanisms that can sort good-faith efforts to deter crime, minimise harm and prevent over-policing from those that might simply exploit the imprimatur of objectivity and neutrality of predictive policing as a public relations tool.

Finally, *egalitarian accountability* would provide a means for expanding citizens' power to set the police mandate by evaluating not only the distribution of crimes, but the police's distribution of both public safety benefits and harm. Based on Elizabeth Anderson's (1999: 289) theory of 'democratic equality', it holds that the 'principles of distribution' must be integrated with "the expressive demands of equal respect". In other words, evaluations of police performance (insofar as they also satisfy institutional and epistemological accountabilities) must expand their metrics and analytics to ensure that socially beneficial policing outcomes – letting-alone, letting-be, respecting – are as legible to the mathematics and statistics of machine learning as policing's social harms – arrest rates, use of force, racial profiling and so on. As it stands, policing strategies in the US start from the premise that some neighbourhoods have the misfortune of being overburdened with crime while others don't, and that policing's harms are justified to the extent that they're merely a byproduct of its benefits (cf. Harcourt, 2001). If this were the case, then we would also see a more equitable rates of arrest or excessive use of force across racial and class lines, which is decidedly not so. If the best measure of the police's success is, to quote Peel (1829: 1) again, "the absence of crime and disorder, not the visible evidence of police action in dealing with it", then our problem is that we lack mechanisms for ensuring a more democratic distribution of this absence; all we have to work with is "visible evidence of police action". Perhaps this means coming up with systems that, in practice, look a lot like HarmStat – systems where police recognise their unique capacity to inflect harms at the same time that they 'serve and protect'. But unlike HarmStat, the police must be able to do this while still satisfying the demands of institutional and epistemic accountability – that is, by recognising, accounting for, scrutinising and attempting to rectify our inability to measure socially beneficial outcomes. Without these kinds of accountability interventions, predictive policing will remain little more than an algorithmic salve on an on going institutional crisis.

References

ACM. (2019). ACM FAT* conference examines fairness, accountability and transparency of algorithmic systems. Available at: www.acm.org/media-center/2019/january/fat-2019 [accessed: 25 September 2019].

Ajunwa, I. (2020). The paradox of automation as anti-bias intervention. *Cardozo Law Review*, 41 (forthcoming). Available at: https://papers.ssrn.com/sol3/papers.cfm?abstract_id=2746078 [accessed 25 September 2019].

American Civil Liberties Union (ACLU). (2016). *Predictive policing today: A shared statement of civil rights concerns.* Available at: www.aclu.org/other/statement-concern-about-predictive-policing-aclu-and-16-civil-rights-privacy-racial-justice [accessed 25 September 2019].

Ananny, M. and Crawford, K. (2018). Seeing without knowing: Limitations of the transparency ideal and its application to algorithmic accountability. *New Media & Society*, 20(3), pp. 973–989.

Anderson, E. (1999). What is the point of equality? *Ethics*, 109(2), pp. 287–337.

Andrejevic, M. (2019). Automating surveillance. *Surveillance & Society*, 17(1/2), pp. 7–13.

Angwin, J., Larson, J., Mattu, S., and Kirchner, L. (2016). Machine bias. *ProPublica*. Available at: https://www.propublica.org/article/machine-bias-risk-assessments-in-criminal-sentencing [accessed 25 September 2019].

Azavea. (2014). Beyond the box: Towards prescriptive analysis in policing. *YouTube*. Available at: www.youtube.com/playlist?list=PL0avZRN-1JNmpWCHou4ydBvjyFg2wvfEY [accessed 27 June 2019].

Azavea. (2015). HunchLab Advisor: Know what works. *YouTube*. Available at: www.youtube.com/watch?v=hHDJfHPYTsU&list=PL0avZRN-1JNmpWCHou4ydBvjyFg2wvfEY&index=15&t=0s [accessed 27 June 2019].

Barad, K. (2003). Posthumanist performativity: Toward an understanding of how matter comes to matter. *Signs*, 28(3), pp. 801–831.

Barocas, S. and Selbst, A.D. (2016). Big data's disparate impact. *California Law Review*, 104, pp. 671–732.

Battles, K. (2010). *Calling all cars: Radio dragnets and the technology of policing.* Minneapolis, MN: University of Minnesota Press.

Beck, C. and McCue, C. (2009). Predictive policing: What can we learn from Wal-Mart and Amazon about fighting crime in a recession? *Police Chief*. Available at: http://acmcst373ethics.weebly.com/uploads/2/9/6/2/29626713/police-chief-magazine.pdf [accessed 27 September 2019].

Bell, M.C. (2016). 'Situational Trust: How Disadvantaged Mothers Reconceive Legal Cynicism. *Law & Society Review*, 50(2), pp. 314–347.

Benbouzid, B. (2019). To predict and to manage: Predictive policing in the United States. *Big Data & Society*, 6(1). doi: 10.1177/2053951719861703.

Bennett Moses, L. and Chan, J. (2018). Algorithmic prediction in policing: Assumptions, evaluation, and accountability. *Policing and Society*, 28(7), pp. 806–822.

Berman, J.S. (1987). *Police administration and progressive reform: Theodore Roosevelt as police commissioner of New York.* Westport, CT: Greenwood Press.

Black, D. (2016). Predictive policing is here now. *Manhattan Institute*. Available at: www.manhattan-institute.org/html/predictive-policing-here-now-8563.html [accessed 25 September 2019].

Bogen, M. (2019). All the ways hiring algorithms can introduce bias. *Harvard Business Review*, 6 May. Available at: https://hbr.org/2019/05/all-the-ways-hiring-algorithms-can-introduce-bias [accessed 25 September 2019].

Bond-Graham, D. (2013). All tomorrow's crimes: The future of policing looks a lot like good branding. *SF Weekly*. Available at: www.sfweekly.com/news/all-tomorrows-crimes-the-future-of-policing-looks-a-lot-like-good-branding/ [accessed 1 September 2019].

Bowker, G.C. and Star, S.L. (1999). *Sorting things out: Classification and its consequences.* Cambridge, MA: MIT Press.

Brantingham, P.J. (2018). The logic of data bias and its impact on place-based predictive policing. *Ohio State Journal of Criminal Law*, 15(2), pp. 473–486.

Bratton, W. (2014). Manhattan Institute: Bill Bratton on the future of policing. *YouTube*. Available at: www.youtube.com/watch?v=X_xjqOp7y0w [accessed 26 September 2019].

Bratton, W.J. (2018). Cops count, police matter: Preventing crime and disorder in the 21st century. *The Heritage Foundation*. Available at: www.heritage.org/sites/default/files/2018-03/HL1286.pdf [accessed 25 September 2019].

Bratton, W.J. and Anderson, B.C. (2018). William Bratton on 'precision policing'. *City Journal*. Available at: www.city-journal.org/html/william-bratton-precision-policing-16084.html [accessed 25 September 2019].

Bratton, W.J. and Malinowski, S.W. (2008). Police performance management in practice: Taking COMPSTAT to the next level. *Policing: A Journal of Policy and Practice*, 2(3), pp. 259–265.

Brauneis, R. and Goodman, E.P. (2018). Algorithmic transparency for the smart city. *Yale Journal of Law and Technology*, 20, pp. 103–176.

Brayne, S. (2017). Big data surveillance: The case of policing. *American Sociological Review*, 82(5), pp. 977–1008.

Brayne, S., Rosenblat, A. and Boyd, D. (2015). Predictive Policing. *Data & Civil Rights*, Washington, DC. Available at: https://datasociety.net/output/data-civil-rights-predictive-policing/ [accessed 26 September 2019].

Bronstein, N. (2014). Police management and wuotas: Governance in the CompStat era. *Columbia Journal of Law and Social Problems*, (4), pp. 543–582.

Burrell, J. (2016). How the machine "thinks": Understanding opacity in machine learning algorithms. *Big Data & Society*, 3(1), doi: 10.1177/2053951715622512.

Caplan, J.M., Kennedy, L.W. and Miller, J. (2011). Risk Terrain Modeling: Brokering criminological theory and GIS methods for crime forecasting. *Justice Quarterly*, 28(2), pp. 360–381.

Carte, G.E. and Carte, E.H. (1975). *Police reform in the United States: The era of August Vollmer, 1905–1932.* Berkeley, CA: University of California Press.

Chan, J. (1999). Governing police practice: Limits of the new accountability. *British Journal of Sociology*, 50(2), pp. 251–270.

Cheetham, R. (2019). Why we sold HunchLab. *Azavea*, 23 January. Available at: www.azavea.com/blog/2019/01/23/why-we-sold-hunchlab/ [accessed 27 June 2019].

Chin, G.J. and Wells, S.C. (1997). The "blue wall of silence" as evidence of bias and motive to lie: A new approach to police perjury. *University of Pittsburgh Law Review*, 2, pp. 233–300.

Citron, D.K. and Pasquale, F. (2014). The scored society: Due process for automated predictions. *Washington Law Review*, 89(1), pp. 1–34.

Cohen McCullough, D.R and Spence, D.L. (2012). American Policing in 2022: Essays on the Future of a Profession. U.S Department of Justice.

Corbett-Davies, S., Goel, S. and González-Bailon, S. (2017). Even imperfect algorithms can improve the criminal justice system. *The New York Times*. Available at: www.nytimes.com/2017/12/20/upshot/algorithms-bail-criminal-justice-system.html [accessed: 26 September 2019].

Deleuze, G. (1992). Postscript on the societies of control. *October*, 59 (Winter), pp. 3–7.

Diakopoulos, N., Friedler, S.A., Arenas, M., Barocas, S., Hay, M. et al. (n.d.) *Principles for accountable algorithms and a social impact statement for fairness, accountability and transparency in machine learning*. Available at: www.fatml.org/resources/principles-for-accountable-algorithms [accessed 25 September 2019].

Dressel, J. and Farid, H. (2018). The accuracy, fairness, and limits of predicting recidivism. *Science Advances*, 4(1), doi: 10.1126/sciadv.aao5580.

Dubber, M.D. and Valverde, M. (2006). Introduction: perspectives on the power and science of police. In: Dubber, M. D. and Valverde, M. (eds.) *The new police science: The police power in domestic and international governance*. Palo Alto, CA: Stanford University Press, pp. 1–16.

Dubber, M.D. and Valverde, M. (2008). Introduction: Policing the *Rechtsstaat*. In: Dubber, M. D. and Valverde, M. (eds.) *Police and the liberal state*. Palo Alto, CA: Stanford University Press, pp. 1–14.

Edwards, C. (2001). Democratic control of the police: How 19th century political systems determine modern policing structures. In: Enders, M. and Dupont, B. (eds.) *Policing the lucky country*. New South Wales: Hawkins Press, pp. 13–21.

Egbert, S. (2019). Predictive policing and the platformization of police work. *Surveillance & Society*, 17(1/2), pp. 83–88.

Ensign, D., Friedler, S.A., Neville, S., Scheidegger, C., and Venkatasubramanian, S. (2017). Runaway feedback loops in predictive policing. *Conference on Fairness, Accountability, and Transparency in Machine Learning*, New York University, New York, February 2018. Available at: http://arxiv.org/abs/1706.09847 [accessed 27 June 2019].

Eterno, J.A. and Silverman, E.B. (2012). *The crime numbers game: Management by manipulation*. Boca Raton, FL: CRC Press.

Eubanks, V. (2011). *Digital dead end: Fighting for social justice in the information age*. Cambridge, MA: MIT Press.

Eubanks, V. (2018). *Automating inequality: How high-tech tools profile, police, and punish the poor*. New York: St. Martin's Press.

Fagan, J. (2016). Terry's original sin. *University of Chicago Legal Forum: Policing the Police*, 2016, pp. 43–98.

Ferguson, A.G. (2011). Crime mapping and the Fourth Amendment: Redrawing "high-crime areas". *Hastings Law Journal*, 63(1), pp. 179–232.

Ferguson, A.G. (2017a). *The rise of big data policing: Surveillance, race, and the future of law enforcement*. New York City: NYU Press.

Ferguson, A.G. (2017b). The "smart" Fourth Amendment. *Cornell Law Review*, 102, pp. 547–632.

Friedman, B. (2016). Secret policing. *University of Chicago Legal Forum: Policing the Police*, 2016, pp. 99–124.

Gandy, O. (1993). *The panoptic sort: A political economy of personal information*. Boulder, CO: Westview Press.

Garland, D. (2001). *The culture of control: Crime and social order in contemporary society.* Chicago, IL: University of Chicago Press.

Garrett, B. (2001). Remedying racial profiling. *Columbia Human Rights Law Review*, (1), pp. 41–148.

Gates, K.A. (2011). *Our biometric future: Facial recognition technology and the culture of surveillance.* New York, NY: NYU Press.

Gilsinan, J. (2012). The numbers dilemma: The chimera of modern police accountability systems. *St. Louis University Public Law Review*, 32(1), pp. 93–110.

Gitelman, L. (ed.) (2013). *'Raw data' is an oxymoron.* Cambridge, MA: The MIT Press.

GovTech Biz (2018). Gunshot Detection Company ShotSpotter Acquires Predictive Policing Software. *GovTech Biz.* Available at: www.govtech.com/biz/Gunshot-Detection-Company-ShotSpotter-Acquires-Predictive-Policing-Software.html [accessed 26 September 2019].

Green, B. (2018). "Fair" risk assessments: A precarious approach for criminal justice reform. In: *5th Workshop on Fairness, Accountability, and Transparency in Machine Learning.* Stockholm. Available at: https://scholar.harvard.edu/files/bgreen/files/18-fatml.pdf.

Green, B. (2019). *The smart enough city: Putting technology in its place to reclaim our urban future.* Cambridge, MA: The MIT Press. Text available at: https://smartenoughcity.mitpress.mit.edu/.

Hacking, I. (1983). *Representing and Intervening.* New York, NY: Cambridge University Press.

Hanink, P. (2013). Don't trust the police: Stop question frisk, CompStat, and the high cost of statistical over-reliance in the NYPD. *Journal of the Institute of Justice and International Studies*, 13, pp. 99–114.

Harari, Y.N. (2017). Reboot for the AI revolution. *Nature News*, 550(7676), pp. 324–327.

Harcourt, B.E. (2001). *Illusion of order: The false promise of broken windows policing.* Cambridge, MA: Harvard University Press.

Harris, D.A. (2013). Across the Hudson: Taking the stop and frisk debate beyond New York City. *New York University Journal of Legislation and Public Policy*, 16, pp. 853–880.

Hartman, S.V. (1997). *Scenes of subjection: Terror, slavery, and self-making in nineteenth-century America.* New York, NY: Oxford University Press.

HunchLab. (n.d.). 'Resources', *HunchLab.* Available at: www.hunchlab.com/resources/ [accessed 1 October 2019].

Hunt, P., Saunders, J. and Hollywood, J.S. (2014). *Evaluation of the Shreveport Predictive Policing Experiment,* RAND Corporation. Available at: https://www.rand.org/pubs/research_reports/RR531.html [accessed 25 September 2019].

Hurley, M. and Adebayo, J. (2017). Credit scoring in the era of big data. *Yale Journal of Law and Technology*, 18(1), pp. 148–216.

IACP. (2018). *TRUST initiative report.* Alexandria, VA: International Association of Chiefs of Police. Available at: www.theiacp.org/sites/default/files/2018-10/Final%20Trust%20Initiative%20Report.pdf [accessed 25 September 2019].

Ip, C. (2017). In 2017, society started taking AI bias seriously. *Engadget.* Available at: www.engadget.com/2017/12/21/algorithmic-bias-in-2018/ [accessed 25 September 2019].

Introna, L.D. (2016). Algorithms, governance, and governmentality: On governing academic writing. *Science, Technology, & Human Values*, 41(1), pp. 17–49.

Jefferson, B.J. (2017a). Digitize and punish: Computerized crime mapping and racialized carceral power in Chicago. *Environment and Planning D: Society and Space*, 35(5), pp. 775–796.

Jefferson, B.J. (2017b). Predictable policing: Predictive crime mapping and geographies of policing and race. *Annals of the American Association of Geographers*, 108(1), pp. 1–16.

Jenkins, S. (dir.) (2017). *Burn mother*cker, burn!* SHOWTIME www.sho.com/titles/3445958/burn-motherf-cker-burn [accessed 26 September 2019].

Juris, H.A. (1971). The implications of police unionism. *Law & Society Review*, 6(2), pp. 231–245.

Karoff, P. (2019). Harvard works to embed ethics in computer science curriculum. *Harvard Gazette*. Available at: https://news.harvard.edu/gazette/story/2019/01/harvard-works-to-embed-ethics-in-computer-science-curriculum/ [accessed 25 September 2019].

Kaufman, E. (2016). Policing mobilities through bio-spatial profiling in New York City. *Political Geography*, 55, pp. 72–81.

Kayyali, D. (2016). Big data and hidden cameras are emerging as dangerous weapons in the gentrification wars. *Quartz*. Available at: https://qz.com/763900/surveillance-and-gentrification/ [accessed 25 September 2019].

Kelling, G.L. (1999). *'Broken windows' and police discretion*. NCJ 178259. Washington, DC: National Institute of Justice. Available at: www.ncjrs.gov/pdffiles1/nij/178259.pdf [accessed 25 September 2019].

Kelling, G.L. and Moore, M.H. (1988). The evolving strategy of policing. *Perspectives on Policing*, 4, pp. 1–16.

Kelling, G.L., Wasserman, R. and Williams, H. (1988). Police accountability and community policing. *Perspectives on Policing*, 7, pp. 1–8.

Kleinig, J. (2001). The blue wall of silence: An ethical analysis. *International Journal of Applied Philosophy*, 15(1), pp. 1–23.

Levine, K. (2019). Discipline and policing. *Duke Law Journal*, 68(5), pp. 839–905.

Levinson-Waldman, R. and Posey, E. (2018). Court rejects NYPD attempts to shield predictive policing from disclosure. *Brennan Center for Justice*. Available at: www.brennancenter.org/blog/court-rejects-nypd-attempts-shield-predictive-policing-disclosure [accessed 25 September 2019].

Levy, P.B. (2018). *The great uprising: Race riots in urban America during the 1960s*. Cambridge: Cambridge University Press.

de Lint, W. (2000). Autonomy, regulation and the police beat. *Social & Legal Studies*, 9(1), pp. 55–83.

Lum, K. and Isaac, W. (2016). To predict and serve? *Significance*, 13(5), pp. 14–19.

Luna, E. (2000). Transparent policing. *Iowa Law Review*, 85, pp. 1108–1194.

Mackenzie, A. (2015). The production of prediction: What does machine learning want? *European Journal of Cultural Studies*, 18(4–5), pp. 429–445.

de Maillard, J. (2018). Police performance regimes and police activity: CompStat in Paris and London compared. *European Journal of Criminology*, 15(5), pp. 589–608.

Marshall, J. (2017). Yep, platform monopolies are a thing. *Talking Points Memo*. Available at: https://talkingpointsmemo.com/edblog/1058277 [accessed 26 September 2019].

Mateescu, A., Rosenblat, A. and Boyd, D. (2016). Dreams of accountability, guaranteed surveillance: The promises and costs of body-worn cameras. *Surveillance & Society*, 14(1), pp. 122–127.

Mayer-Schönberger, V. and Cukier, K. (2012). *Big Data*. Boston, MA: Houghton Mifflin.

Mazerolle, L., Rombouts, S. and McBroom, J. (2007). The impact of COMPSTAT on reported crime in Queensland. *Policing: An International Journal of Police Strategies & Management*, 30(2), pp. 237–256. doi: 10.1108/13639510710753243.

McDaniel, J.L.M (2018). Rethinking the law and politics of democratic police accountability. *The Police Journal*, 91(1), pp. 22–43.

Miller, A.P. (2018). Want less-biased decisions? Use algorithms. *Harvard Business Review*. Available at: https://hbr.org/2018/07/want-less-biased-decisions-use-algorithms [accessed 25 September 2019].

Mohler, G.O., Short, M.B., Malinowski, S., Johnson, M., Tita, G.E., et al. (2015). Randomized controlled field trials of predictive policing. *Journal of the American Statistical Association*, 110(512), pp. 1399–1411.

Moore, M.H. and Braga, A.A. (2003). Measuring and improving police performance: The lessons of CompStat and its progeny. *Policing: An International Journal*, 26(3), pp. 439–453.

Morgan, S.L. and Winship, C. (2007). *Counterfactuals and causal inference: Methods and principles for social research*. New York, NY: Cambridge University Press.

National Institute of Justice. (n.d.). *Predictive policing symposiums: November 18, 2009 & June 2–3, 2010*. Washington, D.C.: National Institute of Justice. Available at: www.ncjrs.gov/pdffiles1/nij/242222and248891.pdf [accessed 25 September 2019].

Peel, R. (1829). 'Principles of law enforcement'. Available at: www.durham.police.uk/About-Us/Documents/Peels_Principles_Of_Law_Enforcement.pdf [accessed 25 September 2019].

Raman, A. (2019). AI is the new normal: Recap of 2018. *Microsoft Azure Blog*. Available at: https://azure.microsoft.com/en-us/blog/ai-is-the-new-normal-recap-of-2018/ [accessed 25 September 2019].

Ransbotham, S., Kron, D. and Prentice, K. (2015). Minding the analytics gap. *MIT Sloan Management Review*, pp. 62–68.

Ratcliffe, J.H., Taylor, R.B. and Askey, A.P. (2017). *The Philadelphia predictive policing experiment: Effectiveness of the prediction models*. Philadelphia, PA: Temple University. Available at: bit.ly/CSCS_3PE [accessed 25 September 2019].

Reeves, J. and Packer, J. (2013). Police media: The governance of territory, speed, and communication. *Communication and Critical/Cultural Studies*, 10(4), pp. 359–384.

Richardson, R., Schultz, J. and Crawford, K. (2019). Dirty data, bad predictions: How civil rights violations impact police data, predictive policing systems, and justice. SSRN Scholarly Paper ID 3333423. Rochester, NY: Social Science Research Network. Available at: https://papers.ssrn.com/abstract=3333423 [accessed 15 May 2019].

Robinson, D. and Koepke, L. (2016). *Stuck in a pattern: Early evidence on 'predictive policing' and civil rights*. Washington, DC: Upturn Available at: www.teamupturn.com/reports/2016/stuck-in-a-pattern [accessed 25 September 2019].

Rose, N. (1996). The death of the social? Re-figuring the territory of government. *Economy and Society*, 25(3), pp. 327–356.

Roth, A. (2019). Algorithmic unfairness without any bias baked in. *Adventures in Computation*, 26 January. Available at: http://aaronsadventures.blogspot.com/2019/01/discussion-of-unfairness-in-machine.html [accessed 27 September 2019].

Royal Thai Embassy. (2016). NYPD training Thai police in higher-tech crime fighting. Available at: https://thaiembdc.org/2016/05/23/nypd-training-thai-police-in-higher-tech-crime-fighting/ [accessed 25 September 2019].

Schwartz, J.C. (2016). Who can police the police? *University of Chicago Legal Forum: Policing the Police*, 2016, p. 437.

Selbst, A.D. (2017). Disparate impact in predictive policing. *Georgia Law Review*, 52, pp. 109–195.

Selbst, A.D. (2019). A New HUD Rule Would Basically Permit Discrimination by Algorithm. *Slate*. Available at: https://slate.com/technology/2019/08/hud-disparate-impact-discrimination-algorithm.html [accessed 25 September 2019].

Selbst, A.D. and Barocas, S. (2018). The intuitive appeal of explainable machines. *Fordham Law Review*, 87(3), pp. 1085–1139.

Shapiro, A. (2017). Reform predictive policing. *Nature News*, 541, pp. 458–460.

Shapiro, A. (2019). Predictive policing for reform? Indeterminacy and intervention in big data policing. *Surveillance & Society*, 17(3/4), pp. 456–472.

Shaw, J. (2018). Platform real estate: Theory and practice of new urban real estate markets. *Urban Geography*. doi: 10.1080/02723638.2018.1524653.

Sherman, L.W. (1978). *Scandal and reform: Controlling police corruption*. Berkeley, CA: University of California Press.

Sherman, L.W. (2013). The rise of evidence-based policing: Targeting, testing, and tracking. *Crime and Justice*, 42(1), pp. 377–451.

ShotSpotter. (2018). ShotSpotter Announces Acquisition of HunchLab to Springboard into AI-Driven Analysis and Predictive Policing. Available at: www.shotspotter.com/press-releases/shotspotter-announces-acquisition-of-hunchlab-to-springboard-into-ai-driven-analysis-and-predictive-policing/ [accessed 26 September 2019].

Siegel, E. (2018). How to fight bias with predictive policing. *Scientific American*. Available at: https://blogs.scientificamerican.com/voices/how-to-fight-bias-with-predictive-policing/ [accessed 25 September 2019].

Simon, J. (2015). Distributed epistemic responsibility in a hyperconnected era. In: Floridi, L. (ed.), *The Onlife Manifesto: Being Human in a Hyperconnected Era*. Cham: Springer International Publishing, pp. 145–159.

Sklansky, D.A. (2008a). *Democracy and the police*. Palo Alto, CA: Stanford University Press.

Sklansky, D.A. (2008b). Work and authority in policing. In: Dubber, M. D. and Valverde, M. (eds), *Police and the Liberal State*. Palo Alto, CA: Stanford University Press, pp. 110–135.

Sklansky, D.A. (2014). The promise and perils of police professionalism. In: Brown, J. M. (ed.) *The Future of Policing*. London and New York: Routledge, pp. 343–354.

Sugrue, T.J. (2014). *The origins of the urban crisis: Race and inequality in postwar Detroit*. Princeton, NJ: Princeton University Press.

Townsley, M., Homel, R. and Chaseling, J. (2000). Repeat burglary victimisation: Spatial and temporal patterns. *Australian & New Zealand Journal of Criminology*, 33(1), pp. 37–63.

Townsley, M., Homel, R. and Chaseling, J. (2003). Infectious burglaries: A test of the near repeat hypothesis. *The British Journal of Criminology*, 43(3), pp. 615–633.

Turow, J. (2013). *The daily you: How the new advertising industry is defining your identity and your worth*. New Haven, CT: Yale University Press.

US Department of Justice. (2015). *Investigation of the Ferguson Police Department*. Washington, DC: US Department of Justice Civil Rights Division. Available at: www.justice.gov/sites/default/files/opa/press-releases/attachments/2015/03/04/ferguson_police_department_report.pdf [accessed 25 September 2019].

Vitale, A.S. (2017). *The end of policing*. London; New York: Verso.

Walker, S. (2016). Governing the American police: Wrestling with the problems of democracy. *University of Chicago Legal Forum: Policing the Police*, 2016, pp. 615–660.

Walker, S.E. and Archbold, C.A. (2019). *The new world of police accountability*. Third edition. Los Angeles, CA: SAGE.

Williams, H. and Murphy, P.V. (1990). The evolving strategy of police: A minority view. *Perspectives on Policing*, 13, pp. 1–16.

Wilson, D. (2019). Platform policing and the real-time cop. *Surveillance & Society*, 17(1/2), pp. 69–75.

Winston, A. (2018). Palantir has secretly been using New Orleans to test its predictive policing technology. *The Verge*. Available at: www.theverge.com/2018/2/27/17054740/palantir-predictive-policing-tool-new-orleans-nopd [accessed 25 September 2019].

Wood, A.L. (2011). *Lynching and spectacle: Witnessing racial violence in America, 1890–1940*. Chapel Hill, NC: The University of North Carolina Press.

Woods, J.B. (2015). Decriminalization, police authority, and routine traffic stops. *UCLA Law Review*, (3), pp. 672–759.

Wright, R.F. (2012). The Wickersham Commission and local control of criminal prosecution. *Marquette Law Review*, (4), pp. 1199–1220.

Zarsky, T. (2013). Transparent predictions. *University of Illinois Law Review*, 2013(4), pp. 1503–1570.

Zarsky, T. (2016). The trouble with algorithmic decisions: An analytic road map to examine efficiency and fairness in automated and opaque decision making. *Science, Technology, & Human Values*, 41(1), pp. 118–132.

Zwick, D. and Denegri Knott, J. (2009). Manufacturing customers: The database as new means of production. *Journal of Consumer Culture*, 9(2), pp. 221–247.

Chapter 8

Machine learning predictive algorithms and the policing of future crimes

Governance and oversight

Alexander Babuta and Marion Oswald

Introduction

UK police forces collect a vast amount of digital data from many different sources, but have historically lacked the technological capabilities needed to analyse this data to improve effectiveness and efficiency (Babuta, 2017). However, as data continues to evolve in volume and complexity, there is increasing interest in the use of data analytics and machine learning tools to improve decision-making and service provision within policing in England Wales (The Law Society of England and Wales, 2019). This follows the trend already seen in the United States, where 'predictive policing' algorithms have been gaining traction for some years (Bachner, 2013; Joh, 2014; Ferguson, 2017). While the statistical methods underpinning these technologies have existed for many years, significant advances in computing power and the availability of large volumes of digital data have now enabled rich insights to be rapidly extracted from large, disparate data sets.

While often presented as novel and futuristic, predictive analytics was first implemented in UK policing more than ten years ago, but traditionally focussed on spatial analysis of past crime data, to predict locations where crime is most likely to occur in the near future (Bowers, Johnson and Pease, 2004; Johnson, 2008; Johnson et al., 2007). While various field trials have shown this technology to be more likely to predict the location of future crime than non-algorithmic methods (Mohler et al., 2015), the use of these tools has so far been limited and localised to individual forces: responses to Freedom of Information requests suggest that 12 (out of 45) UK police forces are currently using, trialling, planning to use or trial predictive mapping software, or have done so in the past few years (Liberty, 2019). Numerous bodies that have scrutinised the police's use of technology have urged forces to make more effective use of such tools to better direct operational activity at the local level (HMIC, 2017; London Assembly, Budget and Performance Committee, 2013; Europol, 2017). Police forces' apparent disinclination to deploy this technology on a wider scale could be partly due to an absence of authorised professional guidance, leading to a lack of clarity over how to address legal and ethical concerns, as well as concerns regarding public and media opposition.

More recently, research has focussed on developing algorithms to support risk assessment and resource prioritisation related to *individuals*. Perhaps the most widely publicised example of such a tool is Durham Constabulary's Harm Assessment Risk Tool (HART), a machine learning algorithm that assigns individuals 'risk scores' corresponding to their predicted likelihood to reoffend (Oswald et al., 2018). A number of other notable initiatives are underway. West Midlands Police has created its own internal Data Analytics Lab. In parallel, a data ethics committee, the first of its kind within UK policing, was established to advise the Chief Constable and Police and Crime Commissioner (PCC) on the police force's data analytics projects. Avon and Somerset Constabulary uses predictive risk models to assess a range of factors, including likelihood of re-offending, likelihood of victimisation or vulnerability, and likelihood of committing a range of specific offences (Liberty, 2019). Through an app on their mobile and tablet devices, neighbourhood officers can instantly access the 'risk profile' for each offender registered in the force area, which are re-calculated on a daily basis. Hampshire Constabulary is also currently developing a machine learning tool to predict risk of domestic violence offending (Terzis, Oswald and Rinik, 2019).

While police forces have only recently implemented statistical ('actuarial') offender assessment tools, elsewhere in the criminal justice system, similar technology has been used for many years. As Craig and Beech describe, "in North America and the United Kingdom, actuarial risk assessment has permeated the entire criminal justice system" (Craig and Beech, 2009: 197). Some of these tools are purely actuarial methods that do not incorporate any human judgement, while others encourage the assessor to use the output of the algorithmic prediction in combination with their professional judgement to arrive at an overall assessment. The most commonly used tools are the Offender Assessment System (OASys), the national risk and needs assessment tool for adult offenders, used by HM Prison and Probation Service (HMPPS) to measure individuals' likelihood of reoffending and to develop individual risk management plans (Howard, Clark and Garnham, 2006; National Offender Management Service, 2015) and the Offender Group Reconviction Scale (OGRS), an actuarial tool used by HMPPS to assess reoffending risk at pre-sentence court report stage, post-sentence, or for offenders who receive out of court disposals (Copas and Marshall, 1998; Howard et al., 2009; National Offender Management Service, 2015). Various other systems have been developed for specific purposes, such as risk assessment of young offenders (Youth Justice Board, 2000; Wilson and Hinks, 2011), violent offenders (Harry, Rice and Quinsey, 1993; Quinsey et al., 2006) and sexual offenders (Thornton et al., 2003; Craig, Beech and Browne, 2006). In many cases, these statistical scoring systems are not used for risk management purposes *per se*, but for 'screening', i.e. to identify a smaller subset of a given population of offenders who require further, more detailed risk assessment. However, the legal and ethical implications of using such statistical scoring systems in an operational policing environment are considerably different to when they are used for offender management purposes or in a clinical setting.

More generally, recent years have seen a proliferation in the use of algorithmic methods across the UK public sector. It is beyond the scope of this chapter to discuss these projects in any detail, however, the reader is directed to a recent report on the use of data scoring in public services published by Cardiff University's Data Justice Lab (Dencik et al., 2018; Jansen, 2019). It is important to note that there is a lack of reliable research demonstrating the potential benefits and 'predictive performance' of such data scoring tools. In the specific context of offender risk assessment, it has been argued that the performance of statistical methods has been significantly overstated, and that they are of little use in identifying the specific nature and causes of risk, or measures that can be taken to reduce that risk (Cooke and Michie, 2013; Hart, Michie and Cooke, 2007; Webster, Haque and Hucker, 2013; Douglas, Yeomans and Boer, 2005). The debate is ongoing.

Much commentary has highlighted potential risks and issues regarding the introduction of AI and machine learning into police decision-making, particularly relating to the impact on individual rights (Liberty, 2019; Richardson et al., 2019; Bennett Moses and Chan, 2018; Lynskey, 2019). There tends to be a divide between those focused upon strengths and opportunities of data science and those who stress the risks and issues. Within the policing context, the authors' previous research has drawn attention to the limited evidence base on the efficacy and efficiency of different systems, their cost-effectiveness, their impact on individual rights and the extent to which they serve valid policing aims (Babuta, Oswald and Rinik, 2018; Babuta and Oswald, 2019). Meijer and Wessels argue for more research into how predictive models work in practice (to see if drawbacks actually occur) (Meijer and Wessels, 2019), and a recent US report on predictive policing by the 'Partnership on AI' (an organisation bringing together for-profit and non-for-profit bodies working on AI) found that more research is required on how data-enabled risk assessment tools inform human decisions, in order to determine what forms of training will support principled and informed application of these tools, and where gaps exist in current practice (Partnership on AI, 2019). It is important to note that the concerns that have been raised regarding the risks of implementing 'predictive policing' tools are largely based on research conducted in the US, and there is a lack of sufficient evidence to demonstrate the extent to which these concerns are applicable to the UK policing context.

In addition to the common law, a number of legal frameworks within the law of England and Wales are applicable to the development and deployment of AI in UK policing. While this chapter cannot do justice to them all, it will include comment in particular upon obligations pursuant to the European Convention on Human Rights, taking effect through Section 6, Human Rights Act 1998, and administrative law principles applicable to lawful public sector decision-making (Oswald, 2018; Grace, 2019; Cobbe, 2018). These legal frameworks are primarily principles-based, meaning that often-difficult context-specific judgements are required on a case-by-case basis regarding such issues as the justification and relevance of data inputs, and the necessity and proportionality both of the data analysis and the way in which the output is then used. Furthermore, the lack of guidance frameworks regarding methods of 'testing' these technologies, particularly within operational environments (Babuta, Oswald and Rinik, 2018; Fussey and Murray, 2019), and the absence of clear scientific standards by which to judge the validity and fairness of the outputs (Hildebrandt, 2018; Oswald, 2020), add considerably to the challenge. In the absence of clear organisational guidelines and codes of practice, it may be difficult for police decision-makers to assess whether the development and deployment of a particular algorithmic tool meets the legal requirements of the various frameworks mentioned above.

In the following section, we review the extent to which predictive assessments supported by machine learning connect with the public protection functions and duties of the police under common law.

Functions of the police in England and Wales under the common law

The operational independence of the police in upholding the law (*Fisher v The Mayor of Oldham* 143 LTR 281), including as regards the deployment of resources and discretion to investigate, is said to be a fundamental principle of policing in England and Wales (The Policing Protocol Order, 2011). A chief constable holds office under the Crown, and is accountable 'to the law' for the exercise of police powers (The Policing Protocol Order, 2011). Under the Police Reform and Social Responsibility Act 2011 (Schedule 2), a chief constable "may do anything which is calculated to facilitate, or is conducive or incidental to, the exercise of the functions of chief constable." In order to decide whether particular information acquisition or data analysis can be regarded as incidental or consequential, the functions of a chief constable need to be understood. But where do we find these functions, or indeed of any constable within a police force of England and Wales? Despite the raft of legislation since the 1980s regulating various aspects of police activity, the underlying legal authority of the office of constable in England and Wales still stems from the common law, as does the constable's duty to maintain the Queen's Peace without fear or favour (The Policing Protocol Order, 2011). "Police constables owe the public a common law duty to prevent and detect crime. That duty reflects a corresponding common law power to take steps in order to prevent and detect crime" *(R (Bridges) v Chief Constable of the South Wales Police* [2019] EWHC 2341 (Admin)). This contrasts with the UK intelligence agencies and the National Crime Agency, the functions of which are now defined in statute (Security Service Act 1989; Intelligence Services Act 1994; Crime and Courts Act 2013) and the statutory duties of constables within the police services of

Northern Ireland and Scotland (Police and Fire Reform (Scotland) Act 2012; Police (Northern Ireland) Act 2000).

The 'Peace' in common law, fundamental to the functions of the English and Welsh police, has traditionally been linked with rioters and other 'barators' (Justices of the Peace Act 1361) although the concept relates more widely to "public quietness and tranquillity, and the entitlement of every citizen to go about his or her lawful business without interference from malevolent forces" (Lord Judge, 2011). Police duties and other powers related to the breach of the peace are there to fill in the gap left by statutory powers of arrest relevant only to defined crimes, powers which Fenwick has described as "immensely broad and bewilderingly imprecise" (Fenwick, 2009).

This is not to say that general police powers, responsibilities and particular areas of focus (such as public order) are not subject to a plethora of definitions, statutory requirements, codes of practice and other guidance regulating intrusive and coercive powers, use of data, out of court disposals, formulation of crime and disorder reduction strategies, positive obligations under Articles 2 and 3 ECHR, and subjecting policing activities to regulatory and political oversight.[1] While much of the policing landscape is heavily regulated by statute (thus significantly limiting the role of common law), the fundamental question of what the police in England and Wales are there to do – their *function* – still falls within the remit of the common law, and how this is achieved is left to a great extent to the discretion of the Chief constable, accountable to the common law, by way of judicial review against public law and human rights principles. Where there are gaps in statute that are not explicitly accounted for within existing legal frameworks – as could be argued in the case of new technologies such as AI and 'predictive policing' – the onus rests on the force to justify such activity as legitimate for carrying out the function of the police in accordance with the common law.

This approach has consequences. The overarching duty to uphold the law and protect the Peace within the common law permits a degree of flexibility and adaptability, both as regards prioritisation and deployment of resources, and in respect of what preserving the Peace might require at any given time. While in the past, measures to tackle rioters, rebels and outlaws on the highway were likely the priority, today the police may be more concerned with gangs, anti-social behaviour, mental health and domestic abuse, as activities that may threaten "the entitlement of every citizen to go about his or her lawful business without interference from malevolent forces" but may not justify a 'full' criminal justice response. Such duties may overlap with obligations imposed by article 2 of the European Convention on Human Rights ECHR), which can imply a positive obligation to take preventative operational measures to protect a person whose life is at risk (*Osman v United Kingdom* [1998] 29 EHRR 245), such as a victim or witness to a crime, thus emphasising the importance of police risk assessments and the policy that informs them (*LXD v The Chief constable of Merseyside Police* [2019] EWHC

1685 (Admin)). Furthermore, circumstances may arise when priorities conflict. Enforcement of the law may, for instance, be incompatible with the maintenance of order (Police Foundation and Policy Studies Institute, 1996). The common law allows the chief constable the discretion to balance prevention and detection of crime, and maintaining the Peace.

We might look to the Association of Chief Police Officers (ACPO)[2] Statement of Mission and Values (2011) as the clearest modern explanation of what the police themselves think they are there to do. This sets out that:

> The mission of the police is to make communities safer by upholding the law fairly and firmly; preventing crime and antisocial behaviour; keeping the peace; protecting and reassuring communities; investigating crime and bringing offenders to justice.

No single activity is favoured, thus allowing the adaptation of priorities as circumstances and demands dictate. Linked with the Statement of Mission and Values is the police officer's oath of attestation which includes a commitment to "cause the peace to be kept and preserved and prevent all Offences against people and property" (College of Policing), indicating the importance of the Peace, and the prominence given to the preventative aspect of policing. This is also reflected in the Peelian Principles of policing by consent: Principle 1, "The basic mission for which the police exist is to prevent crime and disorder"; Principle 9, "The test of police efficiency is the absence of crime and disorder, not the visible evidence of police action in dealing with it" (College of Policing, Code of Ethics Reading List).

The very flexibility of the police's functions can however cause uncertainty and dispute. Millie (2013: 82–93) argues that police officers "clearly do not intervene in 'every kind of emergency'; however their remit has grown to such an extent that what is regarded as legitimate police activity is perhaps too wide". Millie (2013) lists a wide range of activities in his article: "crime fighting, crime reduction, dealing with anti-social behaviour, tackling terrorism, public reassurance, traffic duties, immigration control, schools work, offender management, event security, disaster management, making people feel safer". This has implications regarding the 'necessity analysis' of deploying new technology for a specific policing purpose, if such an analysis is founded on a subjective interpretation of what constitutes 'legitimate policing activity'. In their review of the National Analytics Solution, (a project to trial predictive analytics techniques for policing involving a number of major police forces), the Alan Turing Institute Data Ethics Group and the Independent Digital Ethics Panel for Policing concluded that:

> We see the NAS as moving law enforcement away from its traditional crime-related role and into wider and deeper aspects of social and public policy. This move requires explanation, justification and legitimation,

especially where the ethical dimensions and principles of such policing roles are not well established. The NAS can be viewed as a charter for significant broadening of policy and governance. This would be a significant change with profound ethical, institutional and policy implications.

> (The Alan Turing Institute Data Ethics Group and the
> Independent Digital Ethics Panel for Policing, 2017)

The NAS project team responded that they did not believe that the above comment reflected the modern police service:

> While the core function of the Police is the prevention and detection of crime there are numerous areas where we invest resource not directly linked to this such as – inter alia – locating missing persons, dealing with people in crisis with mental health issues (often as a joint team with health services), road traffic accidents including fatalities where there is no element of criminal activity, dealing with the homeless, responding to suicide, domestic abuse where there is no recordable crime and dealing with anti-social behaviour issues that do not constitute crime but nevertheless have the ability to have a significant impact on the quality of life of the public affected by them.
>
> (National Analytics Solution project team, 2018)

The preventative and public protection mission often overlaps with other agencies, leading to questions as to the appropriateness of such police involvement (House of Commons Home Affairs Committee, 2007: 8). The preventative and 'keeping the peace' functions of the police arguably suffer from a lack of clarity and development of what could be called 'Austerity AI' in conjunction with those aims that have been subject to criticism. In parallel, the police are increasingly required to pick up the slack left by cuts to other public services, most notably local ambulance trusts and mental health services (Babuta, 2017b), raising further questions regarding the delineation of responsibilities between the police and other agencies when it comes to intervention and prevention measures.

'Austerity AI' and the problem of prioritisation

Recent decades have seen an increased focus on risk-based approaches to the prioritisation of resources and triaging of offenders (Yeung, 2018), coupled with a rise in risk management and public protection approaches to future offending (Millie, 2013; Heaton, Bryant and Tong, 2019) and an emphasis on vulnerability (Grace, 2015). Sommerer argues that this may lead to a shift away from defined criminal offences to a more 'diffuse' category of algorithmically defined risk-based behaviour and attitudes (Sommerer, 2018). Reduction in police officer numbers has also created a perceived need to work differently and prioritise effectively. In their report on citizen scoring in public services, Dencik et al. (2018) found:

A recurring theme in the rationale for implementing data systems is the context of austerity, with managers and developers often responding to significant cuts by trying to use data to better target resources. This speaks to the contextual duality of data-driven technologies as one of data-rich and resource-poor contexts.

'In accordance with law'

The difference in approach to police duties and functions between England and Wales and the rest of the UK has direct relevance to the legal justification of algorithmic tools designed to support the police's functions. According to the European Convention on Human Rights (ECHR), an interference by a police force with an individual human right by way of 'Austerity AI' and associated personal data processing must be 'in accordance with law', 'necessary' and 'proportionate' in the interests of public safety or for the prevention or detection of crime. For a measure to be 'in accordance with law', it must be 'accessible' to the person concerned and foreseeable as to its effects, including as to the scope and discretion conferred on the police (*M.M. v. the United Kingdom* (Application no.24029/07).

In Scotland and Northern Ireland, the relevant statutes both confirm that activities relating to preventing crime and preserving order are part of the police's duties (Police and Fire Reform (Scotland) Act 2012, s20; Police (Northern Ireland) Act 2000, s32), and due regard must be had to 'policing principles'. In Scotland, these principles include the statement that 'the main purpose of policing is to improve the safety and well-being of persons, localities and communities in Scotland.' (Police and Fire Reform (Scotland) Act 2012, s32). In Northern Ireland, the principles focus upon carrying out functions to secure the support, and with the cooperation, of the local community (Police (Northern Ireland) Act 2000, s31A).

Regarding England and Wales, Hale LJ in *Michael v The Chief constable of South Wales Police* said that: "There is no doubt that the police owe a positive duty in public law to protect members of the public from harm caused by third parties". (*Michael v The Chief constable of South Wales Police* [2015] UKSC 2, para. 195) This common law duty also relates to the positive obligations under Articles 2 and 3 of the European Convention on Human Rights (ECHR) to protect individuals from real and immediate risks of victimisation and violence (*Chief constable of Hertfordshire v Van Colle* [2008] UKHL 50). In *Catt*, however, although noting general police powers under English common law and declining to make a definitive ruling, the European Court of Human Rights expressed concern that 'the collection of data for the purposes of the [domestic extremism] database [in this case] did not have a clearer and more coherent legal base' (*Catt v UK* Application no. 43514/15). In reviewing South Wales Police's use of facial recognition, the High Court in *Bridges* was more bullish, finding that (in contrast to physically intrusive acts) the police's common law powers were 'amply sufficient' for photography in public places, biometric matching and compilation of watch-lists (*R (Bridges) v Chief Constable of the South Wales Police* [2019] EWHC 2341 (Admin), paras 68–78).[3]

While many uses of data analytics for policing may prove uncontentious within the common law framework discussed above, expansion into algorithmic predictions of future risk, and the further disclosure of those predictions (for interventions that may or may not be statutorily defined) based on a common law justification could be regarded as a step too far. Such activities are not intrusive in the same way as a physical search or taking of fingerprints. However use of an algorithmic prediction in policing does not seem comparable to overt facial recognition, described by the High Court in *Bridges* as "no more intrusive than the use of CCTV on the streets" (*R (Bridges) v Chief Constable of the South Wales Police* [2019] EWHC 2341 (Admin), para 75). Neither does it seem as straightforward as the obtaining and storing of personal information, as approved by the Supreme Court in *Catt*, (*R (Catt) v Association of Chief Police Officers* [2015] AC 1065) especially if the algorithmic process creates a new category of uncertain or contestable information that may then directly affect an individual's treatment or categorisation. The contrast with the statutory functions (although widely drawn) of the Scottish and Northern Irish police, the intelligence agencies and National Crime Agency (and the associated provisions around obtaining, using and disclosing information[4]) may come further into focus as scrutiny of the use of algorithmic tools and other experimental technology gains traction. This suggests an urgent need for a public debate over the role of the police and the concepts of public safety, prevention and wellbeing in an algorithm-assisted environment.

Furthermore, in considering the second limb of the ECHR test, the necessity and proportionality analysis, and despite the margin of appreciation given to national authorities, lack of clarity regarding the function to which the interference relates inevitably carries with it a risk that necessity will be challenging to make out, in terms of demonstrating how the interference answers a 'pressing social need' and that the reasons for it are relevant and sufficient (*S and Marper v United Kingdom* 30562/04 [2008] ECHR 1581). As Grace (2019) points out, "there are as yet considerable unknowns as to what should be considered to be the proportionate storage or *use* of algorithmically-generated predictions of risk as a type of police intelligence".

Discretion in police decision-making

Police work involves considerable autonomy and discretion (Lister and Rowe, 2015), not only around strategic and policy matters but also for day-to-day operational decisions often taken by lower ranks (Wilson, 1978). Such discretion recognizes the fallibility of various rules with their field of application (Hildebrandt, 2016). The first Principle of the College of Policing's Authorised Professional Practice on 'Risk' states that "the willingness to make decisions in conditions of uncertainty (i.e. risk taking) is a core professional requirement of all members of the police service" (College of Policing Authorised Professional Practice). This discretion is not unlimited however and public law expects discretion to be exercised reasonably, and the duty to enforce the law upheld (*R v Metropolitan Police Commissioner ex. P. Blackburn* [1968] 2 QB 118; *R v Chief constable of Sussex ex. P. International Trader's Ferry Ltd.* [1999] 2 AC 418). Conversely, discretion must not be fettered unlawfully, by, for instance, failing to take a relevant factor into account when making a decision, such as, by only considering factors that may indicate risk or potential for harm rather than those that might indicate the opposite.

Algorithms have the potential to package relevant factors in a way that could facilitate more efficient decision-making (Babuta, Oswald and Rinik, 2018), contributing to the identification of the factors most relevant to the decision at hand. These tools present a number of threats, however, to legitimate discretionary decision-making. Unnuanced risk scores have been demonstrated to be highly influential on human decision-makers (Cooke, 2010). Their 'binary nature' may even eliminate any discretionary power to deal with the 'hard cases' (Bayamlıoğlu and Leenes, 2018). A significant issue with categorising risk using whole numbers is that this method treats nominal variables as if they were scale, implying some form of objective assessment (Heaton, Byrant and Tong, 2019), or indeed to conclude that someone categorised as 'low risk' needs no help or intervention for their particular circumstances.

Police forces that have implemented predictive algorithms have stressed that such tools are being used in a way that 'supports' and 'enhances', rather than replaces, professional judgement (Durham Constabulary, 2017; Oswald, Grace, Urwin and Barnes, 2018). In its Authorised Professional Practice on Risk, the College of Policing likewise notes that "RI [risk identification], RA [risk assessment] and RM [risk management] tools should be regarded as an excellent but limited, means of improving the likelihood of identifying and preventing future offending or victimisation. They can enhance professional judgement but not replace it" (College of Policing Authorised Professional Practice). Nevertheless, a statistical prediction may have a significantly prejudicial effect on the human decision-making process. As Cooke and Michie point out, 'it is difficult for the decision-maker to disregard the number and alter their evaluation even if presented with detailed, credible and contradictory information' (Cooke and Michie, 2013).

The way that officers react to algorithmic outputs, and whether they will be prepared to override algorithmic recommendations with their own judgement, may depend to a large extent on the force's attitude to risk and the extent to which individual officers are held responsible for the consequences of alleged omissions and the criticisms made with the benefit of hindsight (Heaton,

Bryant and Tong, 2019). Dencik et al.'s case study of Avon and Somerset police's Qlik tool highlights police officers' frustration that the tool initially generated scores that were contrary to their own knowledge and judgement of the individuals concerned (Dencik et al., 2018). This resulted in further development of the tool in terms of data inputs and use of relevant intelligence that remained uncodified: "that breakdown in the relationship isn't going to go into Qlik Sense because it's not a crime, it's an intelligence report and Qlik Sense doesn't pick up intelligence. So we were quite frustrated by that at the beginning" (Avon and Somerset inspector quoted in Dencik et al., 2018). Concern was also expressed that too much importance was attached to the tool, resulting in nervousness about the 'defenceability' of taking action contrary to the algorithmic recommendation (Avon and Somerset inspector quoted in Dencik et al., 2018).

Beyond assessing the relevance and importance of factors which may or may not be coded into a statistical model, officer discretion is also crucial when deciding what further action will be taken on the basis of the risk assessment or forecast. The College of Policing notes that statistical prediction "is recognised as more accurate than unstructured judgement, but is inflexible and blind to specific contexts" (College of Policing Authorised Professional Practice). A numerical 'risk score' provides the decision-maker with no insight into the specific nature or causes of risk, nor guidance as to what intervention measures can be taken to address the risk (Cooke and Michie, 2013). The third principle of the APP on 'Risk' states that "[r]isk taking involves judgement and balance. Decision makers are required to consider the value and likelihood of the possible benefits of a particular decision against the seriousness and likelihood of the possible harms" (College of Policing Authorised Professional Practice). It follows that the soundness and fairness of an officer's decision-making is judged largely on whether they have considered the relative potential benefits and harms of different outcomes. Such a risk-benefit analysis may be highly context-specific and subjective, requiring careful consideration of a range of possible scenarios, including their likelihood and severity.

The ability to assess 'un-thought of' and uncodified relevant factors as part of the decision-making process must be preserved if discretion is to be applied appropriately. We have previously argued that AI and machine learning tools should not be inserted into a process that requires the exercise of discretion where the tool prevents that discretion; either because all of the factors relevant to the decision cannot be included, or required elements of the decision itself cannot be appropriately codified into, or by, the algorithm (Oswald, 2018). Use of an algorithmic tool should similarly not prevent the consideration of a range of different potential interventions or measures that can be taken to reduce any identified risk. Furthermore, as Lynskey points out in connection with the prohibition on automated decision-making in Article 11 of the Law Enforcement Directive and the question of adverse effect, much "depends on how the decision-making process occurs in practice. In this context, one would need to gauge to what extent the final decision entails the discretion and judgment of the officer making that decision" (Lynskey, 2019). Practical considerations, in particular design of the human-computer interface, the avoidance of unnuanced framing of results (such as 'traffic-lighting' of risk levels), and organisational culture and processes, will be crucial to these issues.

Impact on rights

It is not our intention here to repeat the extensive research and commentary available on the issues of data protection, privacy, discrimination and bias, and transparency and explainability as these relate to machine learning. We instead refer back to the preventative and public protection role of the police supported by machine learning risk assessment tools. From the perspective of the police, it is clearly preferable to predict and prevent crime before it happens, rather than simply responding to and investigating criminal events after they have occurred. Few would question the validity of this logic as the rationale for implementing 'predictive policing' technology. However, legal and ethical issues arise when these preventative strategies involve interventions or other 'pre-crime' policing activities which may interfere with individuals' human rights or civil liberties, because they have been statistically identified as posing some risk of future offending. Furthermore, strategies of 'smart prevention' risk weakening society's moral narrative by disrupting conventional understanding of criminal responsibility and focusing upon reducing practical options to commit crime rather than moral reasons for compliance (Brownsword, 2019).

A potential risk in this regard is that the subjects of a 'data scoring' system are implicitly assessed based on the extent to which they conform to a particular group or 'class', rather than being considered as an individual case. In the context of criminal offending, this issue has been recognised for well over a hundred years. As Holmes remarks to Watson in *The Sign of the Four* (Conan Doyle's second Sherlock Holmes mystery):

> While the individual man is an insoluble puzzle, in the aggregate he becomes a mathematical certainty. You can, for example, never foretell what any one man will do, but you can say with precision what an average number will be up to. Individuals vary, but percentages remain constant.
>
> (Doyle, 1890)

While often presented as an individual-level prediction, the output of a statistical risk assessment tool can be better understood as a group-level classification or categorisation. Rather than answering the question, 'what is the *likelihood* that this individual will behave in a certain way?', the algorithm is in fact answering a different question: 'to what extent is this individual *similar to* other individuals in the data who went on to behave in a certain way?' Predictive judgments can be meaningful when applied to groups of offenders but, at an individual level, predictions are considered by many to be imprecise (Sutherland et al., 2012).

The distinction between group-level classification and individual-level prediction is crucial, but often overlooked or misinterpreted.

When using group classification methods as a means of 'risk scoring' at the individual level, there is a risk that the police's preventative role may deviate from individual justice to group-based intervention, potentially adversely discriminating against individuals on the basis of the extent to which they conform to a certain 'profile' as identified in historic data. This may engage the Equality Act (and public sector equality duty pursuant to that Act) if such discrimination were to correspond to one or more protected characteristics, and could also result in the creation of new targeted groups not linked to protected characteristics, on the basis of systematic 'profiling' of individuals (Bennett Moses and Chan, 2018). When the risk scoring system also uses measures of association with known offenders as a predictor of risk, as in the Metropolitan Police's 'Gangs Matrix', individuals may be labelled as higher risk merely as a result of association with a particular group or network. This raises further questions around rights to non-discrimination under Article 26 of the International Covenant on Civil and Political Rights (ICCPR), as well as Articles 8 and 14 ECHR (corresponding to the right to respect for private and family life, home and correspondence, and protection from discrimination, respectively).

In practice, inclusion of measures of association as 'risk predictors' can lead to individuals being treated as 'guilty by association', even if there is no evidence to suggest they have been involved in criminal activity. Amnesty's investigation into the Gangs Matrix concluded that

> once on the matrix, they become *de facto* 'gang nominals', a label which carries the stigma and suspicion of involvement in violent crime … the person is often automatically treated as someone who poses a risk of violence – even if they should not be on the matrix, or are on the matrix only because they have been a victim of violence.
>
> (Amnesty, 2018: 19)

The ICO's investigation into the Gangs Matrix found numerous breaches of data protection laws, concluding that "[t]he Gangs Matrix does not clearly distinguish between the approach to victims of gang-related crime and the perpetrators, leading to confusion amongst those using it" (Information Commissioner's Office, 2018). This 'presumption of guilt' resulting directly from the algorithmic risk score may raise questions regarding the engagement of Article 6 ECHR (the right to a fair trial), where the assessment of guilt has in effect been pre-determined prior to any trial. Sommerer argues for a new broad reading of the presumption of innocence, "a reading not limited to the criminal trial, but instead also related to risk assessments … where the criminal justice system attaches materially negative consequences to an individual's high-risk score", thus applying the presumption not only to the past, but to future prejudgments (Sommerer, 2018: 58). Commenting on the COMPAS tool used for bail assessments in the US, Sommerer notes further that "the likelihoods turn into 'legal truth' for defendants when a judge at a bail hearing is presented with a high-risk classification (which generally neglects to mention the underlying statistics)" (Sommerer, 2018). A new broad presumption would therefore require a special uniform standard of certainty to apply to the ranking of an individual as high risk and therefore attaching to them potentially negative criminal justice consequences. This would also suggest the need for laws, codes of practice and procedures relating to the recording, retaining and disclosure of material relevant to a criminal investigation to be reviewed in the light of the use of machine learning generated recommendations or classifications.

Beyond risks of discrimination, profiling and privacy violations, risk scoring of individuals based in part on their known associates and network of contacts may also lead to a 'chilling effect' where individuals become reluctant to go about their normal social activities, thereby engaging Articles 10 and 11 ECHR (right to freedom of expression, and right to freedom of assembly and association, respectively). In their independent report on the Metropolitan Police's trial of live facial recognition technology, Fussey and Murray noted that

> the deployment of LFR technology may generate a chilling effect whereby individuals refrain from lawfully exercising their democratic rights due to a fear of the consequences that may follow. For instance, they may be reluctant to meet with particular individuals or organizations, to attend particular meetings, or to take part in particular protests, at least in part due to the fear of 'guilt by association'.
>
> (Fussey and Murray, 2019: 36)

The sharing of data between other agencies may also contribute to this chilling effect, causing individuals to become reluctant to engage with other public services for fear that their interaction with these services may be subsequently coded into a statistical model and used as an indicator of future risk. Amnesty concluded that

> [d]ata sharing between the police and other government agencies means that this stigmatising 'red flag' can follow people in their interaction with service providers, from housing to education, to job centres. It is important to examine the impact this has on their rights.
>
> (Amnesty, 2018: 3)

Therefore, while use of police data alone to train predictive systems carries risks concerning bias and discrimination, the use of a wider range of data sets from other sources can affect individuals' rights and freedoms in other, more complex ways which may be difficult to quantify or even identify.

Finally, while the risk of being subject to intervention or interference from police and other authorities is often discussed as a potential negative outcome of being subject to a risk scoring system, being judged as *ineligible* for a particular intervention or initiative could also impact on individuals' rights in a way that is far harder to detect. Risk scoring systems are trained to identify statistically significant correlations and patterns in historic data. Some variables may not be statistically significant because they do not appear very frequently in historic data, but are very strong predictors when they do occur. Variables can also interact with each other in ways that are not captured by the algorithm. As a result, there is a risk that the algorithm may not take account of factors which are relevant to an individual's risk of offending (either because these factors are too rare to be captured by a statistical model, or because they interact in a way that is not coded into the algorithm), meaning those individuals then fail to receive the support they need to prevent them engaging in problematic behaviour.

Safeguards, governance and oversight

There are various stakeholders in the 'regulatory space' relevant to police use of predictive analytics (Hancher and Moran, 1998). As mentioned previously, police use of analytics engages aspects of various legal frameworks, codes of practice and professional standards, and there is a lack of coordination and clarity regarding delineation of responsibilities as regards scrutiny, oversight and regulation. Some stakeholders play a major role in overseeing and setting professional standards for policing in England and Wales, such as Chief Constables, Police and Crime Commissioners (PCCs), the College of Policing, the NPCC, the Home Office and Her Majesty's Inspectorate of Constabulary and Fire and Rescue Services (HMICFRS). Others have a more limited remit or one confined to specific issues, such as the Investigatory Powers Commissioner's Office (IPCO), the Information Commissioner's Office (ICO) and other commissioners or regulators such as the Surveillance Camera Commissioner and Forensic Science Regulator. In addition, a number of other bodies are engaging in advisory or investigatory activities, including the Centre for Data Ethics and Innovation (an advisory body currently situated within the Department for Digital, Culture, Media and Sport), the Office for Artificial Intelligence, Parliamentary committees, other independent committees, and various non-government academic and campaigning organisations with sector expertise or policy-making functions.

But despite this crowded 'regulatory space', there is a lack of clarity regarding who should take the lead in providing national guidance and oversight of compliance in relation to police use of analytics. As a result of this lack of national leadership and guidance, forces continue to operate with a great deal of autonomy when it comes to technological development, with different forces investing in different pieces of technology for the same purposes. This lack of national coordination results in duplication of efforts, unnecessary overspending, and a lack of compatibility and interoperability between local, regional and national information systems.

The College of Policing's Authorised Professional Practice (APP) is the official source of professional practice for policing in England and Wales. It includes sections on Management of Police Information (MoPI), risk assessment, intelligence management and a Code of Ethics based on the Principles of Public Life developed by the Committee on Standards in Public Life. Police officers and staff are expected to have regard to this APP in discharging their responsibilities, but individual forces have the autonomy to operate outside of these nationally agreed guidelines if deemed appropriate. The NPCC is of particular importance given its role in the national operational implementation of standards and policy and joint approaches on information management and technology. The NPCC Coordination Committees (of which there are eleven, each led by a Chief Constable) are responsible for identifying additional guidance that may need to be incorporated into APP, and these are submitted for consideration by the College's 'Gateway Group'. APP is subject to ongoing review in consultation with the relevant National Policing Business Area.

HMICFRS has a clear oversight and inspection remit as part of its annual PEEL (police effectiveness, efficiency and legitimacy) inspections, Data Integrity inspections, and national thematic inspections. Adherence to APP and other College of Policing standards is assessed as part of these inspections. However, HMICFRS is not a regulator, rather an 'inspectorate', meaning it has no enforcement powers. The recommendations produced as part of HMICFRS inspections are not legal requirements, and chief constables and PCCs have a considerable degree of discretion in deciding how (if at all) to act upon these recommendations. PCCs are required to publicly respond to HMICFRS inspections within a period of 56 days, summarising the action to be taken in response to each recommendation. Closely related to the HMICFRS inspection framework is the generation of 'force management statements', which include the chief constable's own evaluation and projections for the coming year against a set of pre-determined criteria.

While the policing inspection programme and framework for 2019/20 includes specific thematic inspections focussed on cyber-crime, this does not extend to wider issues concerning digital investigation and intelligence, or methods of data exploitation. Since 2015, HMICFRS has inspected forces' crime-recording practices as part of an ongoing rolling programme, covering the extent to which forces are adequately recording crime data. It is a natural progression for this inspection framework to be expanded to include forces' use of analytical tools applied to this data, against a set of national standards in the form of APP. At present, the 'ALGOCARE' guidance (Oswald et al., 2018) is the only *de-facto* national guidance in this area, and has recently been adopted by the NPCC Business Change Council and recommended to chief constables alongside additional explanatory documentation (Terzis, Oswald and

Rinik, 2019). A new set of APP could build on the existing 'ALGOCARE' guidance and provide a set of national standards against which forces can be inspected as part of future HMICFRS inspection programmes. This guidance could also assist policing bodies in crafting appropriate contract specifications and standards for AI tools, and should include advice on how performance should be tested and judged.

Beyond HMICFRS, the ICO has a specific regulation and enforcement function relating to data protection, and may issue enforcement notices to police forces when it identifies a breach of data protection laws. However, as discussed in this chapter, police use of algorithms can impact on human rights and civil liberties in multiple ways beyond those captured in data protection legislation, and there is an argument that the ICO's remit may need to be expanded to account for the relevance of these other legal frameworks. However, this is an unrealistic prospect at present as the ICO is critically under-resourced. The ICO's data protection functions are funded solely by notification fees paid by organisations that process personal data ('data controllers'). The monetary penalties generated by ICO enforcement activity are paid into the Treasury's Consolidated Fund and not kept by the ICO, meaning it lacks the resources needed to take on additional investigation and enforcement responsibilities beyond data protection.

When algorithms are used in a context that would require a warrant under relevant surveillance legislation (Regulation of Investigatory Powers Act 2000; Investigatory Powers Act 2016), IPCO also has an important regulation and enforcement function. This includes ensuring that input data is not held for longer than is justified and is only used for the purposes specified in the initial warrant. In a recent investigation into the Security Service (MI5's) collection and analysis of communications data, IPCO identified serious compliance risks relating to the length of time that data collected under lawful interception warrants was stored within one or more of MI5's technology environments (Javid, 2019). However, in most cases the algorithmic tools discussed in this chapter would not be used in a way that would require a warrant and would therefore remain outside IPCO's remit. It is possible that IPCO's remit will need to be expanded in future to account for the use of potentially intrusive technologies which does not necessarily meet the threshold of 'surveillance' as defined in current legislation.

Beyond *ex post facto* oversight of the police's compliance with relevant legislative requirements, another challenge lies in ensuring that the analytical tools being used meet the necessary scientific standards to render them accurate and reliable enough to be used in an operational policing environment. Predictive algorithms produce probabilistic forecasts, not certainties, and the margin of error associated with these forecasts can vary considerably from one tool to the next. There are no minimum standards for the scientific validity and relevance of algorithmic outputs, which would enable the police to judge the level of confidence to assign to a prediction. The Forensic Science Regulator could potentially play an important role here – particularly if such tools were to be used in a criminal justice context – but currently lacks the statutory enforcement powers needed to enforce such quality standards (Tully, 2019).

Beyond ensuring compliance with 'the letter of the law', independent ethics committees can also provide oversight and scrutiny of police use of data analytics. The promotion of ethical principles and guidelines has been gaining traction, although many of these initiatives can be criticised for a high level of abstraction, limited consideration of existing legal and regulatory regimes, and lacking any enforcement or oversight mechanisms. By contrast, two public sector ethics committees established specifically to oversee innovative data analytics projects are worthy of consideration: the National Statistician's Data Ethics Advisory Committee (NSDEC) and the West Midlands Police and Crime Commissioner and West Midlands Police Ethics Committee. Both these committees operate in accordance with terms of reference, and review submissions against specified principles, which include legal compliance. Both committees have a commitment to transparency, with papers and minutes published online (subject to any necessary operational confidentiality).

The West Midlands committee's terms of reference tasks the committee with tracking a project from development to deployment, as it is anticipated that unforeseen consequences could occur when a project moves from the development stage to operational roll-out, with the PCC and chief constable required to respond to the Committee's feedback and provide reasons for any disagreement with the Committee's recommendations. Based on the proceedings of the NSDEC since 2015, the Statistics Authority has developed self-assessment and 'precedent' administrative processes, allowing researchers to assess projects in advance of full ethical review by NSDEC and compare new proposals against projects previously approved by NSDEC.

Although entitled 'ethics' committees, the remit of these bodies is not in fact narrowly defined; they could be said rather to be oversight committees, testing proposals against the 'public good', and providing the benefit of a 'fresh pair of eyes.' The structure of these bodies might usefully be further studied in order to provide a template that could be used more widely within policing for oversight of the deployment of AI. Many police forces have already established Ethics Committees (not necessarily focussed on technology). A draft terms of reference was produced by the College of Policing, noting that "[e]thics Committees offer an opportunity for the Police Service to develop a structured environment in which to discuss and debate some of the most difficult and contentious issues we face" (College of Policing). In May 2019 the London Policing Ethics Panel published its final report on live facial recognition, in which it issued a number of recommendations to the force regarding ongoing use of the technology (London Policing Ethics Panel, 2019). However, more detailed technical analysis is required to understand these complex issues in sufficient detail, and it is essential that such committees include members with specific data science expertise.

Conclusion

Bearing in mind the significant impact the police's use of predictive analytics can have on citizens' civil liberties, and the various legal frameworks that may be engaged by the use of this technology, the lack of any clear national guidance or professional standards is a cause of great concern. In the long term, primary legislation may be required to account for these advances in the police's use of technology. Specifically, the roles and responsibilities of the police of England and Wales may need to be explicitly defined in the form of statutory functions, as is the case with the police services of Scotland and Northern Ireland. This may be necessary not just for police use of algorithms, but more generally to provide reassurances regarding the legitimacy of the 'public protection' and preventative functions of various policing powers and duties. In the short to medium term, it is essential to develop a clear framework to facilitate trials of experimental technology, in order to judge its relative benefits and harms in a controlled environment, before such tools are deployed operationally in a way that could interfere with individuals' human rights and civil liberties. Failure to do so could erode public trust in the police and undermine future attempts to engage in meaningful dialogue.

Notes

1   Police and Criminal Evidence Act 1984, Criminal Justice and Public Order Act 1994, Police Act 1996, Human Rights Act 1998, Crime and Disorder Act 1998, Police Reform and Social Responsibility Act 2011, Legal Aid, Sentencing & Punishment of Offenders Act 2012, Police (Conduct) Regulations 2012, Data Protection Act 2018, Protection of Freedoms Act 2012, Criminal Procedure and Investigations Act 1996, Terrorism Act 2000, Regulation of Investigatory Powers Act 2000, Investigatory Powers Act 2016, Code of Ethics, Management of Police Information, to name but a few.
2   Now the National Police Chiefs' Council (NPCC).
3   Since writing, the Court of Appeal has partially overturned the High Court decision on the basis that there were fundamental deficiencies in the legal framework and therefore in the quality of law: [2020] EWCA Civ 1058.
4   See for instance s1(5) Crime and Courts Act 2013: "The NCA is to have the function (the 'criminal intelligence function') of gathering, storing, processing, analysing, and disseminating information that is relevant to any of the following—(a) activities to combat organised crime or serious crime; (b) activities to combat any other kind of crime; (c) exploitation proceeds investigations ..."

References

ACPO (2011). *Statement of Mission and Values.*
The Alan Turing Institute Data Ethics Group and the Independent Digital Ethics Panel for Policing (2017). 'Ethics Advisory Report for West Midlands Police'.
Amnesty (2018). *Inside the Matrix.*
Babuta, A. (2017a). Big Data and Policing: An Assessment of Law Enforcement Requirements, Expectations and Priorities. *RUSI Occasional Papers.* London: Royal United Services Institute.

Babuta, A. (2017b). A thinning blue line? The context of current debate on Britain's police levels. *RUSI Commentary*. London: Royal United Services Institute.

Babuta, A. and Oswald, M. (2019). Data analytics and algorithmic bias in policing. *RUSI Briefing Paper*. London: Royal United Services Institute.

Babuta, A., Oswald, M. and Rinik, C. (2018). Machine Learning Algorithms and Police Decision-Making: Legal, Ethical and Regulatory Challenges. *RUSI Whitehall Reports*, 3–18. London: Royal United Services Institute.

Bachner, J. (2013). *Predictive policing: preventing crime with data and analytics*. IBM Center for the Business of Government.

Bayamlıoğlu, E. and Leenes, R. (2018). The "rule of law" implications of data-driven decision-making: a techno-regulatory perspective. *Law, Innovation and Technology*, 10(2), pp. 295–313.

Bennett Moses, L. and Chan, J. (2018). Algorithmic prediction in policing: assumptions, evaluation, and accountability. *Policing and Society*, 28(7), pp. 806–822.

Bowers, K.J., Johnson, S.D. and Pease, K. (2004). Prospective hot-spotting: the future of crime mapping? *British Journal of Criminology*, 44(5), pp. 641–658.

Brownsword, R., (2019). *Law, Technology and Society: Re-imaging the Regulatory Environment* Abingdon: Routledge.

Catt v UK (Application no. 43514/15).

Chief constable of Hertfordshire v Van Colle [2008] UKHL 50.

Cobbe, J. (2018). 'Administrative Law and the Machines of Government: Judicial Review of Automated Public-Sector Decision-Making', a pre-review version of a paper in Legal Studies, Forthcoming. Available at SSRN: https://ssrn.com/abstract=3226913 or http://dx.doi.org/10.2139/ssrn.3226913 [accessed 10 October 2019].

College of Policing (2014). *The Code of Ethics Reading List*.

College of Policing (2015). *Authorised Professional Practice: Understanding risk and vulnerability in the context of domestic abuse*.

College of Policing, 'Ethics Committees'. Available at: www.college.police.uk/What-we-do/Ethics/Documents/Ethics_Committees.pdf [accessed 10 October 2019].

Cooke, D. J. (2010). More prejudicial than probative. *The Journal of the Law Society of Scotland*, 55, 20–23.

Cooke, D.J. and Michie, C. (2013). Violence risk assessment: from prediction to understanding–or from what? To why? In: Logan, C. and Johnstone, L. (eds.) *Managing Clinical Risk*. London: Routledge, pp. 22–44.

Copas, J., and Marshall, P. (1998). The Offender Group Reconviction Scale: A Statistical Reconviction Score for Use by Probation Officers. *Journal of the Royal Statistical Society. Series C (Applied Statistics)*, 47(1), 159–171.

Craig, L. and Beech, A.R. (2009). Best practice in conducting actuarial risk assessments with adult sexual offenders. *Journal of Sexual Aggression*, 15, p. 197.

Craig, L.A., Beech, A. and Browne, K.D. (2006). Cross-validation of the risk matrix 2000 sexual and violent scales. *Journal of interpersonal violence*, 21(5).

Crime and Courts Act, 2013.

Dencik, L., Hintz, A., Redden, J. and Warne, H. (2018). *Data Scores as Governance: Investigating uses of citizen scoring in public services*. Research Report, Cardiff University.

Douglas, K.S., Yeomans, M. and Boer, D.P. (2005). Comparative validity analysis of multiple measures of violence risk in a sample of criminal offenders. *Criminal Justice and Behavior*, 32(5), pp. 479–510.

Doyle, A.C. (1890). *The sign of the four*. London: Spencer Blackett.

Durham Constabulary written evidence to Commons Science and Technology Committee inquiry into algorithms in decision making, 26 April 2017.

Europol (2017). *Serious and Organised Crime Threat Assessment 2017: Crime in the Age of Technology*. The Hague: Europol

Fenwick, H. (2009). Marginalising human rights: breach of the peace, "kittling", the Human Rights Act and public protest. *Public law*, 2009(4).

Ferguson, A.G. (2017). *The rise of big data policing: Surveillance, race, and the future of law enforcement*. New York: NYU Press.

Fisher v The Mayor of Oldham 143 LTR 281.

Fussey, P. and Murray, D. (2019). *Independent Report on the London Metropolitan's Police Service's Trial of Live Facial Recognition Technology*. University of Essex.

Grace, J. (2015). Clare's Law, or the national Domestic Violence Disclosure Scheme: the contested legalities of criminality information sharing. *The Journal of Criminal Law*, 79(1), pp. 36–45.

Grace, J. (2019). "Algorithmic impropriety" in UK policing? *Journal of Information Rights, Policy and Practice*, 3(1).

Hancher, L. and Moran, M. (1998). Organizing Regulatory Space. In R. Baldwin, C. Scott and C. Hood (eds), *A Reader on Regulation*, Oxford: Oxford University Press.

Harris, G.T., Rice, M.E. and Quinsey, V.L. (1993). Violent recidivism of mentally disordered offenders: The development of a statistical prediction instrument. *Criminal Justice and Behavior*, 20(4), pp. 315–335.

Hart, S.D., Michie, C. and Cooke, D.J. (2007). Precision of actuarial risk assessment instruments: Evaluating the "margins of error" of group v. individual predictions of violence. *The British Journal of Psychiatry*, 190(S49), pp. s60–s65.

Heaton, R., Bryant, R. and Tong, S. (2019). Operational risk, omissions and liability in policing. *The Police Journal*, 92(2), pp. 150–166.

Hildebrandt, M. (2016). New animism in policing: re-animating the rule of law. *The SAGE Handbook of Global Policing*, pp. 406–28.

Hildebrandt, M. (2018). Preregistration of machine learning research design. In: E. Bayamlioglu, I. Baralouc, L. Janssens and M. Hildebrandt (eds), *Cogitas Ergo Sum: 10 Years of Profiling the European Citizen*. Amsterdam: Amsterdam University Press.

HMIC. (2017). *PEEL: Police Effectiveness 2016: A National Overview*. London: Her Majesty's Inspectorate of Constabulary.

House of Commons Home Affairs Committee. (2007–8). Policing in the 21st Century. Seventh Report of Session 2007–8 HC 364-1.

Howard, P., Clark, D. and Garnham, N. (2006). *An Evaluation and Validation of the Offender Assessment System (OASys)*. London: Home Office.

Howard, P. and Francis, B. and Soothill, K. and Humphreys, L. (2009). *OGRS 3: The revised Offender Group Reconviction Scale*. Research Summary, 7/09. London: Ministry of Justice.

Information Commissioners Office. (2018). Enforcement notice issued to Metropolitan Police Service. 16 November 2018.

Intelligence Services Act 1994.

Jansen, F. (2019). *Data Driven Policing in the Context of Europe*, working paper, 7 May 2019.

Javid, S. (2019). Investigatory Powers Act 2016: Safeguards Relating to Retention and Disclosure of Material: Written statement by Sajid Javid – HCWS1552, 9 May 2019.

Joh, E.E. (2014). Policing by numbers: big data and the Fourth Amendment. *Wash. L. Rev.*, 89.

Johnson, S.D. (2008). Repeat burglary victimisation: a tale of two theories. *Journal of Experimental Criminology*, 4(3), pp. 215–240.

Johnson, S.D., Birks, D.J., McLaughlin, L., Bowers, K.J. and Pease, K. (2007). Prospective crime mapping in operational context: Final report. *UCL, Jill Dando Institute of Crime Science: London, UK*.

Justices of the Peace Act 1361.

The Rt Hon The Lord Judge, Lord Chief Justice Of England And Wales. (2011). The Police Foundation's John Harris Memorial Lecture. *Summary Justice In And Out Of Court*, Drapers Hall, London, 7 July 2011.

Kent Police Corporate Services Analysis Department. (2014). PredPol Operational Review [Restricted and Heavily Redacted]. Available at: www.statewatch.org/docbin/uk-2014-kent-police-predpol-op-review.pdf [accessed 10 October 2019].

The Law Society of England and Wales. (2019). *Algorithms in the Criminal Justice System*. London: The Law Society.

LXD v The Chief constable of Merseyside Police [2019] EWHC 1685 (Admin).

Lister, S. and Rowe, M. (2015). 'Accountability of policing', In *Accountability of Policing*, pp. 1–17. London: Routledge.

Liberty (2019). *Policing by machine: predictive policing and the threat to our rights*. Available at: file:///C:/Users/jmcda/Downloads/LIB-11-Predictive-Policing-Report-WEB.pdf [accessed 1 April 2019].

London Assembly, Budget and Performance Committee. (2013). *Smart Policing*.

London Policing Ethics Panel. (2019). *Final report on live facial recognition*.

Lynskey, O. (2019). Criminal justice profiling and EU data protection law: precarious protection from predictive policing. *International Journal of Law in Context*, 15(2), pp. 162–176.

M.M. v. the United Kingdom (Application no. 24029/07).

Meijer, A. and Wessels, M. (2019). Predictive Policing: Review of Benefits and Drawbacks. *International Journal of Public Administration*, pp.1–9.

Michael v The Chief constable of South Wales Police [2015] UKSC 2.

Millie, A. (2013). What are the police for? Re-thinking policing post-austerity. In: Brown, J.M., *The Future of Policing* (pp. 82–93). Abingdon: Routledge.

Mohler, G.O., Short, M.B., Malinowski, S., Johnson, M., Tita, G.E., Bertozzi, A.L. and Brantingham, P.J. (2015). Randomized controlled field trials of predictive policing. *Journal of the American Statistical Association*, 110(512), pp. 1399–1411.

National Analytics Solution project team. (2018). Response to The Alan Turing Institute and IDEPP, 2018.

National Offender Management Service. (2015). A compendium of research and analysis on the Offender Assessment System (OASys), 2009–2013. London: NOMS.

Osman v United Kingdom [1998] 29 EHRR. 245.

Oswald, M. (2018). Algorithmic-assisted decision-making in the public sector: framing the issues using administrative law rules governing discretionary power. In: 'The growing ubiquity of algorithms in society: implications, impacts and innovations' issue of Philosophical Transactions of the Royal Society A.

Oswald, M. (2020). Technologies in the twilight zone: Early lie detectors, machine learning and reformist legal realism. *International Review of Law, Computers & Technology*, 34(2) 214–231.

Oswald, M., Grace, J., Urwin, S. and Barnes, G.C. (2018). Algorithmic risk assessment policing models: lessons from the Durham HART model and "experimental" proportionality. *Information & Communications Technology Law*, 27(2), pp. 223–250.

Partnership on AI (2019). *Annual Report: Building a connected community for responsible AI.* Available at: www.partnershiponai.org/wp-content/uploads/2021/01/PAI-2019-Annual-Report.pdf [accessed 1 February 2020].

Police Foundation and Policy Studies Institute. (1996). The Role and Responsibilities of the Police.

Police and Fire Reform (Scotland) Act. (2012).

Police (Northern Ireland) Act. (2000).

The Policing Protocol Order. (2011). Cm. 2850.

Police Reform and Social Responsibility Act. (2011). c.13 Schedule 2.

Quinsey, V.L., Harris, G.T., Rice, M.E. and Cormier, C.A. (2006). *Violent offenders: Appraising and managing risk.* American Psychological Association.

R (Catt) v Association of Chief Police Officers [2015] AC 1065.

R v Chief constable of Sussex ex. P. International Trader's Ferry Ltd. [1999] 2 AC 418.

R (Bridges) v Chief Constable of the South Wales Police [2019] EWHC 2341 (Admin).

R v Metropolitan Police Commissioner ex. P. Blackburn [1968] 2 QB 118.

Richardson, R., et al. (2019). Dirty Data, Bad Predictions: How Civil Rights Violations Impact Police Data, Predictive Policing Systems, and Justice. *New York University Law Review Online.*

S and Marper v United Kingdom 30562/04 [2008] ECHR 1581 (4 December 2008).

Security Service Act 1989.

Sommerer, L. M. (2018). The Presumption of Innocence's Janus Head in Data-Driven Government. In: E. Bayamlioglu, I. Baralouc, L. Janssens, M. Hildebrandt (eds.), *Cogitas Ergo Sum: 10 Years of Profiling the European Citizen.* Amsterdam: Amsterdam University Press.

Sutherland, A.A., Johnstone, L., Davidson, K.M., Hart, S.D., Cooke, D.J., Kropp, P.R., Logan, C., Michie, C. and Stocks, R. (2012). Sexual violence risk assessment: An investigation of the interrater reliability of professional judgments made using the Risk for Sexual Violence Protocol. *International Journal of Forensic Mental Health,* 11(2), pp. 119–133.

Terzis, P., Oswald, M. and Rinik C (2019). *Shaping the State of Machine Learning Algorithms within Policing,* 26 June 2019. Winchester: University of Winchester.

Thornton, D., Mann, R., Webster, S., Blud, L., Travers, R., Friendship, C. and Erikson, M. (2003). Distinguishing and combining risks for sexual and violent recidivism. *Annals of the New York academy of sciences,* 989(1), pp. 225–235.

Tully, G. (2019). Forensic Science Regulator annual report 2018.

Webster, C.D., Haque, Q. and Hucker, S.J. (2013). *Violence Risk-assessment and Management: Advances through Structured Professional Judgement and Sequential Redirections.* Oxford: John Wiley & Sons.

Wilson, E., and Hinks, S (2011). Assessing the predictive validity of the Asset youth risk assessment tool using the Juvenile Cohort Study (JCS). *Ministry of Justice Research Series,* 10(11).

Wilson, J.Q. (1978). *Varieties of Police Behaviour: The Management of Law and Order in eight Communities, with a New Preface by the Author.* London: Harvard University Press.

Yeung, K. (2018). Algorithmic regulation: A critical interrogation. *Regulation & Governance,* 12(4), pp. 505–523.

Youth Justice Board. (2000). *ASSET: Explanatory Notes.* London: Youth Justice Board.

Chapter 9

'Algorithmic impropriety' in UK policing contexts

A developing narrative?

Jamie Grace

Introduction

The inevitable greater use of algorithmic police intelligence analysis tools (APIATs) by UK police forces, as something that is to be done for the 'public good', is a conflicted and unproven stance, or at least is a matter of perspective and priority (O'Neil, 2009). Each element of AI in policing that is a 'public good' to one person (resources more accurately targeted, recidivists deterred, and potential harms prevented) can entail for some people a more obvious opportunity to see controversy (a sticking plaster for austerity cuts to criminal justice agencies, stigmatisation and the unfair labelling of some offenders, and the erosion of civil liberties). This tension over whether AI in policing is a 'public good' is the essential question in the use of the technology in policing contexts, and specifically the use of machine learning in offender risk prediction. It is sometimes immediately apparent to see the potential unfairness or risks of biases in a paper proposal from a police force as to how they would like to use data (and as is discussed below), but less obvious to see potential risks to public health, or access to justice, in uses of the same type of data technologies in practice, since these wider risks may take a longer time to emerge or to be verified.

This chapter seeks to draw out lessons for policymakers from early skirmishes in the field of 'predictive policing', where the hope is that 'algorithmic impropriety' could be better avoided. 'Algorithmic impropriety', as I have written elsewhere (Grace, 2019: 1), "is something that could be seen as [a breach of] the combination of administrative law grounds of review as part of a bundle of accountability standards that draw on wider bodies of law", in 'calling out' the mis-use or unlawfulness of particular deployments of machine learning technology in a specific policing context. This unfairness or mis-use could be as a result of one or more of 'data inequalities', 'accuracy biases' and 'decisional opacity' (Grace, 2019). The chapter focuses in particular on the proposed and developmental work of West Midlands Police, which is currently developing a risk profiling tool using machine learning approaches (a new APIAT), and which could identify more than 8,000 'High Harm Offenders' to be managed more intensively, police resources permitting, across the West Midlands, UK.

Algorithms in the UK public sector

Algorithmic risk prediction practices, while still in their infancy (particularly so in policing circles), might be representative of a greater shift toward algorithmic governance in the longer term. In the short term, these practices can often be portrayed as problematic. For example, Philip Alston, the UN Special Rapporteur on Human Rights and Extreme Poverty at the time of writing, has argued that the "British welfare state is gradually disappearing behind a webpage and an algorithm, with significant implications for those living in poverty" (Alston, 2019: 13). For governance to be fair, then data governance must be fair, because data enables governance. Hildebrandt (2009) argues that democracy depends on both individuals being able to formulate their own ideas in a private sense, and yet also depends on a public degree of accountability and transparency in relation to state institutions in the way that they use data about individuals to make decisions affecting their lives. Taking the development of the printing press as a transformative technological tool of governance comparable in its revolutionary power to the potential of 'big data' twinned with machine learning tools, Hildebrandt (2009: 300) notes that:

> While the printing press first allowed the rule by law (the sovereign using written codes as a means to rule his subjects), it later enabled the rule of law (the internal division of sovereignty that separates the enactment of legal rules by the legislator from their interpretation in a court of law).
>
> (2009: 300)

For algorithmic police intelligence analysis tools to be moved in their use, from not just simply tools to more efficiently rule *by* law, but to become tools to better secure the rule *of* law by, through and against law enforcement bodies, methods must be developed to enhance the deliberative democratic basis of these APIATs. Ten years ago, Hildebrandt wrote that (2009: 307): "Creating transparency and privacy-enhancing tools should enable a citizen to contest the application of (group) profiles, rejecting the idea that one can be judged on the mere basis of a correlation." This is because, of course, and as Holmes reminds us: "Problems arise with false correlations …" (2017: 58). In policing contexts these false correlations may be discriminatory, or be a factor in depriving a person of their liberty, or facilitating a disruption of their family life, and so on.

Worryingly, in our contemporary society we run the risk of predictive analytics supported by 'big data' being *too* influential on the humans 'in the loop' (Keats Citron and Pasquale, 2014). As noted by Holmes (2017: 3), there was a historical usage of the term 'data' to mean an article of faith:

The Oxford English Dictionary attributes the first known use of the term ['data'] to the 17th-century English cleric Henry Hammond in a controversial religious tract published in 1648. In it Hammond used the phrase 'heap of data' in a theological sense, to refer to incontrovertible religious truths.

And yet the same data science that builds an algorithm for use in a policing context can highlight for us the degree of expected (in)accuracy – what the algorithm alone cannot do is recommend that its predictions can be trusted, or should be. Some writers have set out examples of why contextual knowledge is vital in determining the ability of an algorithm to get at 'the truth'. For example, the acceptability of the balance between 'statistical sensitivity' and 'statistical specificity' of an algorithm, and thus the overall number or rate of 'false positives', will depend greatly on the prevalence of risk in the overall population whose data are processed by the tool concerned. Haigh gives the following hypothetical example of a terrorist profiling tool in an airport, where an emphasis has been placed on statistical sensitivity (and an algorithm emphasising detection over the avoidance of false positives) (Haigh, 2012: 101–102):

> suppose that the probability a real terrorist evades [profiling in airport] checks is tiny, 1/10,000, while the chance that an innocent person is led away for an intensive interrogation is a miniscule 1/100,000. How likely is it that someone picked out is guilty? ... We cannot answer the question without some idea of the would-be passengers who are terrorists. Try one in a million – frighteningly high, given that Heathrow handles ... fifty million passengers a year. But the figures assure us that, even with fifty potential terrorists, it is overwhelmingly likely that all will be detected. ... Unfortunately, five hundred innocent passengers will also be detained! Among those stopped by this system, fewer than 10% are terrorists. And if there are fewer than fifty terrorists, the chance that someone who is stopped is indeed guilty are even lower. Detection methods must have much better performance figures if they are to be useful.

As well as substantive issues of accuracy and false positive rates, there are questions of procedural justice posed by the use of AI in policing contexts. Boden (2018) acknowledges that something in meaning and nuanced can be lost in explaining or investigating issues by using a chat-bot, even a state of the art one. Is it merely enough that information is gleaned by the police from a victim of crime, using an AI-powered simulacrum of an investigating officer? Isn't something of police legitimacy lost along the way?

These questions of the type of legitimacy fostered by the use of algorithmic police intelligence analysis tools are crucial ones to be posed in this pivotal era for 'big data' in policing contexts, since much the data drawn upon is indicative of the discriminatory treatment of ethnic minorities and the working class (and members of the ethnic minority working class) as disproportionately vulnerable citizens and residents in the UK.

Nevertheless Her Majesty's Chief Inspector of Constabulary, Sir Thomas Winsor, argues that (2018: 34): "…there is real potential for technology, such as artificial intelligence (AI) and machine learning, to make the police more effective and efficient. [If] the police are going to be able to prevent and detect crime in the future – particularly technology enabled crime – they need to invest now in the technology and training to do so." Sir Thomas' call for investment and emphasis on the cost-effectiveness of policing through data analytics (not yet well-substantiated in practice, to the knowledge of this author, but often cited in theory), bears repeating in detail here (2018: 35):

> The opportunity here is not only to get machines to do faster what the police already do. It is also to use technology to achieve police objectives in ways we have not even thought of yet, and might never. Instruments and technology exist today which can process information far faster, more efficiently and more reliably and effectively than any human could. But, even more significantly, the capability exists now to devise ways of learning – of machines thinking for themselves – which no person has ever achieved, and perhaps no person ever could. Preventing, investigating and determining the causes of crime all involve numerous complex factual permutations, unpredictable human behaviour and random as well as intended events. This is the perfect field for the application of smart [analytics]. Of course, this technology costs money. But if the police invest now, working with the experts who have created and are developing these capabilities, this powerful technology has the potential to make them more efficient, and achieve huge advances in public safety and security, and timely justice.

The Gangs Matrix case study

While the Gangs Matrix used recently in London is not a machine learning-based tool, it is a scoring system which gives rise to problems that are indicative of the general trend. The system, operated by the Metropolitan Police over a period of years, is a worthy case study that shows that police investment in database technologies must be done with requisite care, and the use of predictive tools undertaken with requisite due process. In November 2018, the Information Commissioner's Office (ICO) published an Enforcement Notice which highlighted failings on the part of the Metropolitan Police Service in operating its Gangs Matrix (ICO, 2018). The Enforcement Notice found that there were breaches of the data protection principles under the Data Protection Act 1998 (which was in force for much of the life of the Gangs Matrix from inception) as well as suggestions of a breach of the public sector equality duty under the Equality Act 2010. In December 2018, the Mayor's Office for Policing and Crime (MOPAC) published a review of the use of the Gangs Matrix over a five-year period, June 2013 to May 2018 (MOPAC, 2018).

In the period June 2017 to May 2018, 82.3% of people on the Matrix were BAME, 99% Male, and 55.6% under 18 years of age. (MOPAC, 2018a: 25). One cannot escape the fact that the Matrix had to an extent become a means of managing and calibrating the criminal punishment of thousands of black teenage boys in London. As such, it is no surprise that in considering the need for particular reforms to the use of the Matrix, the MOPAC report concluded "there is no room for complacency or rashness" (MOPAC, 2018a: 41). It is worth setting out here the scoring and grading system of 'nominals' (individuals) for gang-related offending. Individuals graded 'red' in terms of risk of gang-related offending would see 'daily activity' aimed at them, based on a multi-agency plan put in place for them – while an assessment is made for a judicial order known as a Criminal Behaviour Order. Amber-graded individuals have the same sort of plan drawn up, but 'activity' to disrupt their criminality will be less than daily, and an assessment for the potential for a Criminal Behaviour Order would not be a strict necessity. Finally, green-flagged individuals would receive 'diversion or engagement activities' from primarily just one key agency (MOPAC, 2018a: 21).

In September 2018, 4% of individuals on the Matrix were scored red, 31% Amber and 65% Green (MOPAC, 2018a: 20). MOPAC were concerned that individuals were still maintained as listed on the Matrix when they posed little risk of engagement with gang-related activity, recommending "a thorough reappraisal of the individuals in the Green category, with a focus on: those that currently score 'zero-harm'; those that have never had a harm score or have remained in the Green category for their entire time on the Matrix; and those under the age of 18." (MOPAC, 2018a: 40) There was a serious problem with the Matrix in terms of what is known in European human rights law terms as the 'accessibility' principle, concerning a lack of transparency and thus a shortfall in the publically-available information provided to those included on the Gangs Matrix. This meant that "the MPS' lack of a clear, publicly available policy document specifically setting out how the Matrix operates [was] an important shortcoming" (MOPAC, 2018a: 42).

However, not all legal principles support the idea of greater accountability over how the Matrix operated. In 2017, the High Court had rejected the idea that sporadic or occasional police monitoring of social media accounts containing 'intelligence' made public by an individual could engage the right to respect for private life in European human rights law (under Article 8 of the European Convention on Human Rights). A particular element of this case, brought by Salman Butt, had turned on whether a person who places evidence of their own harmful views or lifestyle online, in a publically-accessible manner, had a 'reasonable expectation of privacy'. The High Court (later supported by a judgment from the Court of Appeal in the same case) found that they would not, where police surveillance of those online expressions was light-touch, irregular or one-off profiling. The *Butt* case will then have ramifications for the use of 'SOCMINT' (social media intelligence), which can be fed into scoring and risk prediction systems such as the Gangs Matrix (Grace, 2017; 2019). As the MOPAC report on the Gangs Matrix explained:

> It has also been suggested that where the police view public profiles and access open source material in order to help inform a decision as to whether an individual should be listed on the Gangs Matrix, then in every case this should require authorisation for directed surveillance under RIPA [the Regulation of Investigatory Powers Act]. It is however doubtful that viewing and considering material that has been placed online by an individual and made publicly available by them would usually constitute surveillance for RIPA purposes. If the viewing was intensive and repeated in relation to a specific target individual, then this might perhaps cross the line into being directed surveillance [requiring more formal authorisation], but it is not easy to define where the border might be.
>
> (MOPAC, 2018a: 46)

In conclusion, the MOPAC report recommended that (MOPAC. 2018a: 55):

> Both the Operating Model and the training should have a particular focus on ensuring:
>
> - that the right people are on the Matrix;
> - that people are added and removed in a standardised, evidence-based manner;
> - that they can be removed and that the 'gang' label will not 'follow' them;
> - that local Matrices are refreshed regularly so that individuals don't stay on any longer than necessary;
> - that the guidance on the use of social media for intelligence purposes is updated;
> - and that the Data Protection principles and legislation are fully applied.

The problem of course, is what we mean by 'the right people': who deserve, we might decide, because of the risk *they* pose (and not because of their family or the estate they grew up on) to be listed for a particular period on the Gangs Matrix. The Gangs Matrix, and any successor system in London, is now regulated as with all data processing by law enforcement bodies in the UK, by the Data Protection Act 2018. The MOPAC Report does not mention S.47 DPA 2018, despite the report being published after the DPA 2018 had come into force. Section 47(3) of the DPA 2018 requires that data processing should be restricted (i.e. not used in an organisation) where "it is not possible to ascertain whether it is accurate or not". And under S.205 DPA 2018, 'inaccurate' data is data which is 'incorrect or misleading'. As a result, incorrect of misleading data should be restricted in its use by a police force. So what about all those 'green'-flagged individuals or 'nominals' with no real risk score at all? Or with zero scores? They are patently not gang members to the best knowledge of the MPS, and their profiles arguably should have been deleted immediately following the publication of the MOPAC report, since the 2018 Act was in force from May 2018.

Timothy Pitt-Payne QC has suggested that the transparency of the Gangs Matrix should be augmented (and in a way that furthers the duty on the MPS under human rights law, following the 'in accordance with the law' criterion) (Pitt-Payne, 2018: 77) with "a public-facing" document covering topics such as the following:

> The purpose of the Gangs Matrix, including: encouraging individuals to divert from gang membership; managing the risks presented by the individuals listed; and managing the risk that those individuals will themselves be victims of violent crime.

- The criteria for inclusion on the Gangs Matrix.
- The basis on which an individual is scored.
- The practical consequences of being listed on the Gangs Matrix with a particular score.
- The circumstances in which an individual's listing will be changed, or in which an individual will be removed from the Gangs Matrix altogether.
- The arrangements for sharing information from the Gangs Matrix on a London-wide level.
- The arrangements for sharing information at borough level.

Shortcomings in transparency around police uses of APIATs are perceived with regularity now. In general, says Yeung (2019), "… a lack of transparency continues to plague the field." Readers will note that the Enforcement Notice from the ICO in relation to the Gangs Matrix led to a commitment by the MPS to operate the Matrix lawfully by the end of 2019, and in line with the recommendations from the MOPAC report. This would include a greater degree of transparency. And yet, this greater transparency has already been missed in relation to the newly-revealed 'Concern Hub' – a predictive analytics tool, purportedly once more set to be used to "safeguard young people at significant risk of becoming involved in violence, drugs, or gang activity" (Yeung, 2019). Crisp (2019), writing in *The Independent* in March 2019, noted that in the drive to replace the Gangs Matrix with a newer system, senior Metropolitan Police Officers were assuring him that "across the board lessons have been learned". And yet confirmation that the recommendations from the MOPAC report on the Gangs Matrix have been progressed has not been forthcoming, nor has the ICO explained any element of progress on the reform of the Matrix (although the ICO has released general guidance to police forces on the operation of gangs databases) (ICO, 2019a).

As the MPS has been set the task of eventual greater transparency over the Gangs Matrix, and rapidly developing the capacity of their new Concern Hub project, the ICO has also been investigating the London Borough of Newham – which it fined £145,000 for unlawful sharing of un-redacted Gangs Matrix content with partner organisations (ICO, 2019b). Some of the details of more than 200 individual profiles on the Matrix were leaked as a result of this breach to gang members on Snapchat. Some of the 200 individuals identifiable in the material, leaked in 2017, went on to become victims of violent gang-related crime.

In the West Midlands, in the last two years, there has been work done by the police, funded by the Home Office through the Police Transformation Fund, in building a true machine learning-based predictive tool, unlike the cruder Gangs Matrix in London, that will be used to identify 'High Harm Offenders'. By way of distinct contrast, this WMP predictive policing project has made efforts, at least in comparison with the older and less sophisticated Gangs Matrix, to be more transparent from the start.

The West Midlands case study

A revealing piece in the *New Scientist* in November 2018 highlighted the way that the National Data Analytics Solution (NDAS) had determined to use its £2m funding from the Home Office Police Transformation Fund to draw on an enormous amount of data from across a number of force areas, to become the largest single UK predictive policing data project to date. According to Baraniuk (2018) the NDAS was designed to draw on:

> Local and national police databases, including records of people being stopped and searched and logs of crimes committed. Around 5 million individuals were identifiable from the data… Looking at this data, the software found nearly 1400 indicators that could help predict crime, including around 30 that were particularly powerful. These included the number of crimes an individual had committed with the help of others and the number of crimes committed by people in that individual's social group… The machine learning component of NDAS will use these indicators to predict which individuals known to the police may be on a trajectory of violence similar to that observed in past cases, but who haven't yet escalated their activity. Such people will be assigned a risk score indicating the likelihood of future offending.

The Alan Turing Institute (2017: 3) and the Independent Digital Ethics Panel for Policing concluded in their *Ethics Advisory Report for West Midlands Police* that the necessarily multi-agency repercussions of adopting a National Data

Analytics Solution that facilitated predictive interventions would see data-driven policing put at the heart of public protection work of that state, a "significant change with profound ethical, institutional and policy implications." The National Analytics Solution Project Team then gave a *Response to the Alan Turing Institute and IDEPP*, explaining that ethical safeguards including data protection impact assessments, proportionality reviews of pilot phases of the work, and independent ethical panel scrutiny would all be implemented. The Project Tem also noted that to "fail to take the opportunity that technology offers is to fail the public we serve by misusing the resources they provide policing with" (National Analytics Solution Project Team, 2017: 4). It was then that the Police and Crime Commissioner for the West Midlands (WMPCC) and WMP jointly established a scrutiny panel and procedure in the form of an independent Data Analytics Ethics Committee, in late 2018 and early 2019 (WMPCC, 2019a). The WMPCC ethics committee can give advice on project, and can urge caution to the extent of rejecting outright those proposals which are flagrantly unethical or distinctly unjustified. The Chief Constable of West Midlands police is as a matter of law not bound by the advice or recommendations of the WMPCC ethics committee – albeit in administrative law terms a chief constable who failed to take into account at all the relevant considerations of ethics committee advice may act unlawfully in taking a decision against such advice.

The first task of the WMPCC ethics committee was to consider a working proposal for an 'Integrated Offender Management' (IOM) tool, which would score more than 8,000 individuals as prospective 'high harm offenders', in order for the resources available to teams of police offender managers to be better targeted (WMPCC, 2019b). This proposal was not rejected entirely (WMPCC, 2019c), but was delayed in its move to an implementation stage, despite some praise from the ethics committee (for a careful weighting of the statistical model underpinning the tool to one that was more statistically *specific* as opposed to statistically *sensitive* (Grace, 2019). During the first design of the IOM tool, WMP had placed emphasis on a number of possible versions of the tool that preferred statistical *specificity*, ensuring a caution around generating 'false positives' for individuals flagged as high risk. The final model chosen had a healthy respect for statistical specificity in this way.

But the ethics committee felt that more could be done to explain the safeguards around possible ethnicity biases against black offenders residents in the West Midlands, arising from using historic data available to the force – concerning the best part of half a million individuals, going back, in some case, 20 years (WMPCC, 2019c). It was also not clear from the first iteration of the model as to whether the data drawn upon would be stronger in terms of criminal process provenance (such as convictions, or charges) or whether records of arrests would also be fed into the algorithm too. Accordingly, the ethics committee required that the police 'Data Lab' working on the IOM tool should clarify and revise their processes around these issues. (The WMP 'Data Lab' later clarified for the ethics committee that the only individuals profiled by the IOM tool were those with convictions and/or charges, but upon whom there might also be police intelligence fed into the model (WMPCC, 2019d).) Tom McNeil, a strategic advisor to the West Midlands Police and Crime Commissioner and driving force behind the establishment of the ethics committee concerned, was quoted in a *Guardian* piece as saying:

> The robust advice and feedback of the ethics committee shows it is doing what it was designed to do. The committee is there to independently scrutinise and challenge West Midlands police and make recommendations to the police and crime commissioner and chief constable… This is an important area of work, that is why it is right that it is properly scrutinised and those details are made public.
>
> (Marsh, 2019)

There are other models of regulation emerging in the United States that local governments in the UK might admire and aspire toward if they were very wary of predictive policing practices, but politically and constitutionally might struggle to develop. The City of Oakland in California has a Privacy Advisory Board (much as if West Midlands Police operated an ethics committee for data analytics in tandem with all local authorities in the West Midlands region) (City of Oakland, 2019), but local government and PCCs do not have the legal power in English law to fetter the discretion of chief constables to purchase something like facial recognition technologies – unlike in San Francisco where expenditure by the police on such tech is now more tightly controlled by local government officials due to privacy concerns (Paul, 2019). Richardson et al. (2019) have also reported how New York City has founded a predictive technology decision-making committee; and that in Vermont an AI task force (and so more like an inquiry panel than an ethics committee) has been established to investigate ethical/unethical practices in the area of predictive policing.

Meanwhile, some actors in the private sector are starting to realise that there might be a place in the market for ethical-only tech. Axon (formerly Taser) have declared publically that their body worn video camera products for law enforcement officers will not be compatible with automated or live facial recognition technology currently used or promoted for law enforcement use by other tech companies. Axon even have an ethics board, established with assistance from academics at US and UK universities, to enhance and define the company's public position on what it seeks to pursue, exactly, by developing ethical tech (Quach, 2019).

Legal points on algorithmic or predictive policing tools

The general common law basis of predictive policing data analysis tools to be used in the UK, such as the 'Concern Hub', can be acknowledged as lawful for the purposes of Article 8 ECHR, given the recent decision in *Catt v UK* (43514/15) (24 January 2019). The decision in *Catt* by the European Court of Human Rights established the idea that while the UK legal framework concerned would tolerate the recording of textual intelligence data about an individual for interim analysis by the police, in order to make predictions operationally about risk, the longer the retention of that intelligence continues where an innocent, or not very harmful, person is concerned, the greater the likelihood that this retention will go on to be seen as disproportionate, and thus unlawful.

Key legal frameworks for predictive policing analytics tools are: the EU Data Protection Directive concerning law enforcement processing (2016), as transposed into Part 3 of the Data Protection Act 2018; the Public Sector Equality Duty (PSED) and the requisite 'due regard' standard for decision-making that must be cognisant of equalities issues, therefore, under the S. 149 Equality Act 2010 (in England and Wales, for example); as well as positive and negative obligations under the ECHR, taking effect through the duty on UK public bodies under S.6 HRA 1998; and the Rehabilitation of Offenders Act 1974, including its section 4 duty to treat a person with a spent conviction/caution 'for all purposes in law' as not committing the offence concerned. Particular challenges for police operators of algorithmic or predictive analytics tools that arise from this legal framework are outlined below.

These particular challenges relate to the legal intricacies of processing certain types of 'sensitive' personal data; the handling of victims' and witnesses' personal data; the exact degree of automation used by a predictive policing tool; the accuracy of a chosen model in terms of its preference for identifying all high risk individuals versus avoiding 'false positives'; the extent of data protection impact assessments as integrated with other impact assessments focusing on human rights and equality issues; the proportionality of decisions taken in an algorithmically-informed way; the extent of the transparency concerning the tool and public engagement and consultation over its development; and the way that spent convictions are, or are not, taken into account and/or processed in the model concerned. These challenges can then be grouped into the following categories: i) data scope issues; ii) process issues; iii) issues of human rights impact.

Data scope issues

The scope of the data retained and that is drawn upon by an algorithmic police intelligence tool (APIAT) must be data processed that is necessary for that purpose. Good practice might then be to determine which pieces of data about an individual 'nominal' are not predictively powerful during the design process for a tool and screen them out. The retention period for items of data drawn on by the tool is another factor to take into consideration. In terms of categories of sensitive personal data: if the use of some sensitive data (caught by section 24 of the Data Protection Act 2018) is implied and so the data cannot be readily removed from the model, then particular care should be taken to justify the necessity of the use of that point of data in the model in the requisite data protection impact assessment (see below), e.g. 'health data' if a person in the model is a victim of violence, or the political beliefs of a person if they are described in arrest data or intelligence as having been arrested at a particular protest.

Importantly, the results or outputs of a tool that draws on intelligence reports, rather than hard legal 'facts' such as records of arrests or charges or convictions will need to be presented to officers that use the tool in such a way that indicates that, in the language of Section 38 of the DPA 2018, these outputs are at least partly based on "personal assessments" of other officers earlier in time. Likewise, the outputs of an APIAT will need to be similarly flagged if they draw upon victims' and witnesses' data as when "processing personal data for … law enforcement purposes, a clear distinction must, where relevant and as far as possible, be made between personal data relating to different categories of data subject".

There are also issues with determining the exact application of the Rehabilitation of Offenders Act 1974, concerning spent convictions and cautions. But in some good news for police forces in the UK, the application of the 1974 Act may not actually be too problematic in the context of working with APIATs, assuming the validity of one judicial interpretation of the 1974 Act. Importantly, the s.4 duty to treat a person with a spent conviction/caution 'for all purposes in law' as though they have not committed a particular offence does not always include public protection purposes as 'legal purposes', following *N v Governor of HMP Dartmoor* [2001] EWHC Admin 93. So an APIAT with clear predictive purposes in the public protection field might benefit from this judge-made exemption from a statutory framework for spent convictions.

Process issues

Section 64 of the Data Protection Act 2018 provides that a data protection impact assessment is undertaken by a body considering deploying an APIAT before any processing of data of 'nominals' takes place, and where "a type of processing is likely to result in a high risk to the rights and freedoms of individuals". In essence, this might mean that an integrated impacts assessment process is required under the combined measures of the DPA 2018, the Human Rights Act 1998 and the Equality Act 2010. (MOPAC produced an 'integrated impact assessment' (MOPAC, 2018b) in addition to its internal review of the operation of the Gangs Matrix over a five-year period, but this did not explicitly incorporate particular human rights as themes in the assessment process in the way that it did with 'protected characteristics' in it equality strand, although human rights-related values of protecting communities from harm while improving their cohesion and health were included.)

In terms of a requisite degree of public engagement and transparency over the inception, development and deployment of an APIAT, the public sector equality duty might require evidence gathering from communities that would disproportionately be engaged through the use of the planned APIAT, and certainly it is the view of notable barrister Timothy Pitt-Payne QC that human rights standards of 'accessibility' of legal information now require that there is public engagement over predictive policing issues, chiefly in the release of information notices to the public concerning the relevant APIAT (Pitt-Payne, 2018). There is an advantage to such an approach, in relation to what is known as the common law 'duty to give reasons', since in this context, the degree of information that has to be provided to those individuals affected by decisions informed by the APIAT should be underpinned, and rendered more clearly lawful, through the notification of communities about the use of the APIAT 'up front'.

A vital consideration in the deployment and use of an APIAT is the extent to which there is automation of police operational decision-making following the onset of the use of the tool concerned, in a particular way. Sections 49 and 50 of the DPA 2018 between them give a particular set of safeguards in connection with a fully automated decisions that would have an impact on the rights of an individual in the criminal justice context – firstly a person is to be informed of the fully-automated decision about them, and secondly, should they then take this opportunity to object, then the automated decision concerned will need to be re-made by a human officer and decision-maker. Automated decision-making is avoided through there being a 'human in the loop' – and so a careful and detailed process map of sorts might really help inform a future and more detailed stance by a police organisation on this issue, when determining the nature of a partial intervention with a 'nominal' individual based on a fully-, partly- or initially-automated decision that draws on the outputs of an APIAT.

Furthermore, a key issue in process terms is the way that an APIAT is developed with a particular emphasis on the 'trade-off' sought between two types of accuracy that can be sought in the chosen predictive model: statistical sensitivity (which *in extremis* would make a tool as strong as possible at predicting high risk offenders, for example, but with a high 'false positive' rate down the line) or statistical specificity (an emphasis in the trade off toward the desire to correctly sort low-, medium- and high-risk offenders, with a correspondingly lower 'false positive' rate for its outputs – albeit with more 'false negatives', or high-risk offenders 'missed'). With regard to the statutory bar on the processing of data in ways that is 'misleading', given the language of S.205 DPA 2018, a careful focus on statistical *specificity* over *sensitivity* is to be applauded, as it will clearly in most instances be less 'misleading' to use a model weighted toward the former (Grace 2019).

Issues of human rights impacts

Issues of human rights impacts typically will boil down to the application of a 'proportionality analysis', in addressing the interference by the processing of data on an individual through a machine learning-based tool on Article 8 ECHR, that is to say, the right to respect for private life under the Convention. Given that the processing of most data by such a tool will be confidential data privy to criminal justice bodies and partner agencies, as opposed to SOCMINT, and so not readily in the public domain, these will be data that if processed, will typically give rise to a 'reasonable expectation of privacy' on the part of an individual or 'nominal'. As such, UK common law in interpreting the Convention requires there is an overall *fair balance* "between the rights of the individual and the interests of the community" (as per *R. (on the application of Quila) v Secretary of State for the Home Department* [2011] UKSC 45). Following the now-standard approach from the UK courts to this proportionality analysis, what will help determine a truly 'fair balance' will be the extent of a rational basis for the processing overall, and whether the processing is 'no more than necessary' to achieve an objective of sufficient importance. Other 'qualified' rights under the ECHR, such as freedom of expression, will also instigate such a proportionality analysis if they are engaged; while the right to freedom from discrimination in the enjoyment of the right to respect for private life (engaged if the decision-making supported by an algorithm leads to indirectly discriminatory outcomes, for example) is violated should there be a pattern of discriminatory data governance practice that is manifestly without reasonable foundation (Grace, 2019; Raine, 2016).

Conclusions

There is clearly an emerging narrative concerning the police practice of developing APIATs across the UK. The public, the media, and certainly human rights NGOs are demanding greater transparency over the concentration and use of such tools. Perhaps a fundamental problem is the common law basis of the creation and operation of (algorithmic) intelligence databases, combined with the generalist underpinning of Part 3 of the Data Protection Act 2018 only. That largely common law basis means that there has yet to be any specific Parliamentary authorisation in statute of machine learning-based APIATs in the field of police practice in the UK, despite the number of forces now wrangling with the legitimacy, both legal and democratic, of these technologies and their ramifications and opportunities.

In their letter to the *Guardian* newspaper in April 2019, Professor Ruth Gilbert and Matthew Jay (2019) argued that

[a] wider public debate needs to be informed by research into how effectively the use of people's data predicts and reduces criminality, who else experiences targeting and privacy intrusion due to prediction errors, and

whether better use of data could reduce such collateral harm… The public has a right to know how data about them is being used.

Public legal education on an issue is well complemented by the deliberation by Parliament over a new statutory framework for a controversial trend in the justice sector. Such a statutory position would be an opportunity to clarification in the law, based on a platform of more public, and more rigorous, discussion of the issues in policy circles.

As such, acknowledgment that a new predictive tool is potentially a new, more intensive form of police 'dataveillance' (Clarke, 1997) in a city or region would be best reflected in the legislature debating a Predictive Policing (Technology) Bill. In many ways, one thing such a Bill could do is set up a regulator/authorisation process via the courts, as per surveillance warrants under the Investigatory Powers Act 2016. The nature of APIATs focused on supporting offender management processes are not particularly secretive, and secrecy only lends them an ominous air that could be reduced (and the ability of citizens to understand and challenge them) if their process of development were also more commonly scrutinised in the open. A statutory authorisation process for such APIATs could then take (the lack of) such transparency into account in the designated method of giving approval for new tech, or new purposes for analytics in data-driven policing.

References

Alan Turing Institute and Independent Digital Ethics Panel for Policing. (2017). *Ethics Advisory Report for West Midlands Police*, 28th July 2017.

Alston, P. (2019). *Visit to the United Kingdom of Great Britain and Northern Ireland: Report of the Special Rapporteur on extreme poverty and human rights*, United National Human Rights Council, 23 April 2019.

Baraniuk, C. (2018). 'EXCLUSIVE: UK police wants AI to stop violent crime before it happens', *New Scientist*, 26th November 2018, from https://institutions.newscientist.com/article/2186512-exclusive-uk-police-wants-ai-to-stop-violent-crime-before-it-happens/.

Boden, M.A. (2018). *Artificial Intelligence: A Very Short Introduction second edition*, OUP: London.

City of Oakland. *Privacy Advisory Commission*, from www.oaklandca.gov/boards-commissions/privacy-advisory-board [accessed 2 September 2019].

Clarke, R. (1997). Introduction to Dataveillance and Information Privacy, and Definitions of Terms, from: www.rogerclarke.com/DV/Intro.html [accessed 25 April 2019].

Crisp, W. (2019). Concern hub: New Metropolitan Police gang database sparks privacy and profiling fears. 13th March 2019, from www.independent.co.uk/news/uk/crime/concern-hub-metropolitan-police-gang-matrix-database-a8812371.html [accessed 1 September 2019].

Gilbert, R. and Jay, M. (2019). We need debate on data-driven policing. *The Guardian*, Tuesday 23rd April 2019, from: www.theguardian.com/uk-news/2019/apr/23/we-need-debate-on-data-driven-policing [accessed 2 September 2019].

Grace, J. (2017). Countering extremism and recording dissent: Intelligence analysis and the Prevent agenda in UK Higher Education (2017). *Journal of Information Rights, Policy and Practice*, Vol. 2(2) (online).

Grace, J. (2019). Algorithmic impropriety in UK policing? *Journal of Information Rights, Policy and Practice*; Vol, 3 Issue 1, from: https://jirpp.winchesteruniversitypress.org/articles/abstract/23/.

Haigh, J. (2012). *Probability: A Very Short Introduction*, OUP: London.

Hildebrandt, M. (2009). Profiling and AI. In: Rannenberg, K., Royer, D. and Deuker, A. (eds.), *The Future of Identity in the Information Society: Challenges and Opportunities*, 2009, Springer.

Holmes, D.E. (2017). *Big Data: A Very Short Introduction*. OUP: London.

Information Commissioner's Office. (2018). *Enforcement Notice – Data Protection Act 1998 – Metropolitan Police Service*, from: https://ico.org.uk/action-weve-taken/enforcement/metropolitan-police-service/.

Information Commissioner's Office (ICO). (2019a). Processing gangs information: a checklist for police forces. Available at: https://ico.org.uk/for-organisations/in-your-sector/police-justice/processing-gangs-information-a-checklist-for-police-forces/.

Information Commissioner's Office (ICO). (2019b). London council fined by the ICO for disclosing sensitive personal data about alleged gang members. Available at: https://ico.org.uk/about-the-ico/news-and-events/news-and-blogs/2019/04/london-council-fined-by-the-ico-for-disclosing-sensitive-personal-data-about-alleged-gang-members/.

Keats Citron, D. and Pasquale, F. (2014). The scored society: due process for automated predictions. *Wash. L. Rev.* 89 (2014): 1.

Marsh, S. (2019). Ethics committee raises alarm over 'predictive policing' tool'. *The Guardian*, Saturday 20th April 2019. Available at: www.theguardian.com/uk-news/2019/apr/20/predictive-policing-tool-could-entrench-bias-ethics-committee-warns [accessed 1 September 2019].

Mayor's Office for Policing and Crime (MOPAC). (2018a). *Review of the Metropolitan Police Service Gangs Matrix*, December 2018, from: www.london.gov.uk/sites/default/files/gangs_matrix_review_-_final.pdf.

Mayor's Office for Policing and Crime (MOPAC). (2018b). *Gangs Matrix Review – Integrated Impact Assessment*, December 2018.

National Analytics Solution Project Team. (2017). *Response to the Alan Turing Institute and IDEPP*.

O'Neil, C. (2009). *Weapons of Maths Destruction: How Big Data Increases Inequality and Threatens Democracy*.

Paul, K. (2019). San Francisco is the first US city to ban police use of facial recognition tech. The Guardian, Wednesday 15th May 2019. Available at: www.theguardian.com/us-news/2019/may/14/san-francisco-facial-recognition-police-ban [accessed at 2 July 2019].

Quach, K. (2019). US cop body cam maker says it won't ship face-recog tech in its kit? Due to ethics? Did we slip into a parallel universe? *The Register*, 28th June 2019. Available at: www.theregister.co.uk/2019/06/28/axon_facial_recognition/ [accessed 2 September 2019].

Richardson, R., Schultz, J. and Crawford, K. (2019). Dirty Data, Bad Predictions: How Civil Rights Violations Impact Police Data, Predictive Policing Systems, and Justice

(February 13, 2019). New York University Law Review Online, Forthcoming. Available at SSRN: https://ssrn.com/abstract=3333423

Pitt-Payne, T. (2018). Appendix 1 – Legal Assessment', from the Mayor's Office for Policing and Crime, *Review of the Metropolitan Police Service Gangs Matrix*, December 2018. Available at: https://www.london.gov.uk/sites/default/files/gangs_matrix_ review_-_final.pdf.

West Midlands Police and Crime Commissioner. (2019a). Ethics Committee, from www.westmidlands-pcc.gov.uk/transparency/ethics-committee.

West Midlands Police and Crime Commissioner. (2019b). Ethics Committee briefing note. Available at: www.westmidlands-pcc.gov.uk/media/514522/Ethics-Committee-03042019-IOM-MODEL.pdf.

West Midlands Police and Crime Commissioner. (2019c). Ethics Committee minutes, April 2019. Available at: www.westmidlands-pcc.gov.uk/archive/april-2019/.

West Midlands Police and Crime Commissioner. (2019d). Ethics Committee minutes, July 2019. Available at: www.westmidlands-pcc.gov.uk/archive/ethics-committee-meeting-july-2019/.

Raine, T. (2016). The Value of Article 14 ECHR: The Supreme Court and the "Bedroom Tax"' U.K. Const. Law Blog, available at https://ukconstitutionallaw.org/) [accessed 28 July 2018].

Winsor, T. (2018). *State of Policing – The Annual Assessment of Policing in England and Wales 2017*. HMICFRS: London.

Yeung, P. (2019). The grim reality of life under Gangs Matrix, London's controversial predictive policing tool. *Wired*, 2nd April 2019. Available at: www.wired.co.uk/article/gangs-matrix-violence-london-predictive-policing.

Chapter 10

Big data policing
Governing the machines?

Michael Rowe and Rick Muir

Introduction

Policing has always been an information business, but the digital revolution has increased by several orders of magnitude the quantity of data that could be used by police agencies to keep citizens safe. Every time the police record a crime or a piece of intelligence they collect information on a range of factors including victims, witnesses, suspects and locations. Every time we type an email, send a text or shop online we are creating new digital traces that could be acquired, analysed and used in the course of a police investigation. It is hard to envisage a crime or incident to which police respond that does not have a 'digital footprint' of some kind given the near ubiquity of smart phones in everyday life.

The police have begun to develop their capability to exploit big data in a number of ways. Most notably we have seen the rise, or perhaps more accurately the anticipated rise, of 'predictive policing' whereby the police use existing crime and related data to anticipate future offending and incident patterns and then deploy officers to prevent future crimes. Police data is also increasingly being used to enable individual risk assessments when officers are attending incidents or making decisions about suspects, such as whether to grant bail or refer a suspect on to a rehabilitative intervention.

Predictive policing has been introduced in US cities using complex algorithms to mine police data and open source information to identify future places where crime will occur and those at risk of victimisation and of becoming offenders. For example, Joh (2014) outlined how artificial intelligence and risk terrain theory underpins predictive policing in New Jersey. Using crime data and information about local highways, the geographic concentration of young men, and the location of hotels and apartment complexes, police have better targeted prevention and detection leading to significant reductions in violent and property crime. Police have used algorithms to profile social networks and identify central and peripheral actors involved in criminal gangs, although as is noted in a section further below this can reinforce disproportionate impacts on marginalised communities.

The availability of big data and its potential use for public and commercial purposes has inevitably raised ethical concerns. The more that is known or knowable about us, the greater the risk that such information could be misused or that organisations that acquire such data could intrude into our private lives. In this chapter we discuss three areas of concern relating to 'big data policing'.

First, we explore how 'machine policing' may pose a challenge to democracy and accountability. In particular we discuss the concern that the more decisions are made 'by machine' the less accountable those decisions become. At a time when Big Data and related technological innovation has the potential to transform police practice and communications with the public there is a concerning lack of development in terms of establishing standards, regulations and mechanisms to govern these emerging systems. To give one example of this, in February 2013 Wisconsin resident Eric Loomis was arrested after being found driving a car that had been used in a shooting. Upon sentencing the court looked at Loomis' risk score according to an algorithmic risk assessment tool called COMPAS. He was sentenced to six years in prison. Loomis appealed the ruling on the grounds that in basing the sentence in part on the workings of a privately owned algorithm whose workings were not transparent the decision violated due process. Although Loomis was unsuccessful in this case the Wisconsin Supreme Court urged caution about the use of such tools (Yong, 2018). While case law plays an important regulatory role in such matters there remains a gap – in Britain at least – in terms of other governance mechanisms. If an increasing number of decisions by police officers or other criminal justice officials are based on algorithms whose inner workings are obscure then there is clearly a danger of an erosion in transparency and accountability. This is particularly the case where an algorithm is privately owned by the company which developed it and not available for public scrutiny.

Second, we look at the problem of privacy. How far is it legitimate for the police to go into a citizen's personal data in the name of public safety? For example, there has been considerable controversy about new consent forms issued to victims of crime in England and Wales. These forms ask victims to consent to handing over their mobile phones, computers and other devices for police examination. Although these can be issued to victims of any crime, they are most likely to be issued to victims of sexual offences. This has raised concerns of an excessive intrusion into the private lives of victims and that such requests are likely to discourage victims from coming forward (BBC News, 2019). A further problem arises since private citizens share information to third parties, through use of apps and websites, without informed consent or knowledge that this might come to inform policing activity.

Third, we look at the problem of bias. This arises because of the biases embedded in police data, which, if acted upon by analytic programmes, can result in unfair and disproportionate outcomes. For example, in 2016 the Human Rights Data Analysis Group artificially reconstructed a predictive policing programme and applied it to drugs offences in the city of Oakland,

California (Lum and Isaac, 2016). Using drugs crime data to direct police resources they found that the software would have sent officers almost exclusively to low-income minority neighbourhoods. This is despite the fact that health data shows drug use to be much more widespread across the city.

Outcomes like this arise because police data is not an objective reflection of crime and harm in society. Many crimes are not reported to the police. Many of the incidents logged on police systems reflect police decisions to prioritise certain types of crime and particular geographic areas. There is a significant risk of a crime data 'feedback loop' whereby people and places disproportionally policed become ever further enmeshed by processes that are objectively neutral (in the sense that they do not reflect the bias of individual officers) but are ultimately based on data that more closely mirrors existing practices, rather than any objective measure of risk or offending. If machine learning is applied to such data then those biases will be reproduced as part of police decision-making.

Each of these themes – governance, privacy and bias – are reviewed in the following sections of the chapter. We raise significant concerns that – we contend – are often sidelined in policy and operational debates that are technically driven. For moral, legal and ethical reasons it is important to consider not just what police 'could' do in a more technologically sophisticated future, but what 'should' police do. The questions we raise are also significant since ultimately, they seem likely to have the potential for a negative impact on public trust, confidence and legitimacy: these are matters of principle but also of operational importance. While we note that 'Big Data' might have some potential benefits and are not unduly negative about its possibilities, the problems we identify are not just abstract concerns. Poor quality or inaccurate data that misidentifies individuals who might be at high-risk of reoffending, for example, has obvious civil liberties and related implications for those concerned but it is also likely to lead to operational failures. While the risk of 'false positives' is problematic, there is also a danger of 'false negatives' that allow for those who are actually high-risk to escape supervision or rehabilitation and to continue to inflict misery on their future victims and all manner of costs to society at large.

The problem of governance

The potential application of Big Data and AI to policing extends across broad areas of political, social and economic life. It is sometimes touted as an approach to regulation and law enforcement that might bring benefits to policing public order, offender management, financial crime and to many other areas of transnational and online activity. Whatever the potential benefits, and we do not dismiss that these might be significant, it is clear that 'machine policing' raises significant concerns about democracy and accountability.

As in other fields, Big Data and AI transforms traditional police activity in terms of gathering and processing information or 'intelligence'. Such 'knowledge work' and communication has been a central feature of policing throughout the modern period (Ericson and Haggerty, 1997) but traditional approaches (described by James, (2016) as 'little data policing') are transformed in the 21st century. Kitchin (2014) identified the distinctive features of contemporary Big Data approaches as being:

- Huge in volume
- High in velocity (created in near real-time)
- Diverse in variety
- Exhaustive in scope (seeking information on the entire population)
- Fine-grained in resolution and indexical
- Relational, with common fields enabling conjoining of different datasets
- Flexible, (new fields can be added) and scalable (can expand in size).

This enhanced capacity offers significant opportunities for policing in relation to routine operational procedures, crime prevention and investigation. Crowd control, for example, can be informed by analysing real-time data generated from information gleaned from apps on smart phones that reveal the location and direction of individuals, as well as their social interactions and communications (see Chen et al., 2016). Meta-data gleaned from smart phone apps reveal information not consciously shared by owners about traffic flow, roadside parking, noise and air pollution, and can be used to sense the mood of gathered crowds (Zhu et al., 2016).

Many of these applications raise concerns about police accountability and democracy. In Britain, and we suggest other liberal democracies, these pose challenges to regulation and oversight mechanisms originally developed to govern policing practices that emerged in the 19th century. The multi-level local, national and regional governance of policing in Britain in general terms often means complex and messy oversight (Rowe, 2020), although these challenges are particularly acute in relation to big data policing. Among the key challenges of accountability are the difficulties of governing private sector companies that have a central role in the gathering and processing of data. Often related to this is the wider challenge of holding to account networks and practices that develop globally and beyond national jurisdictions. Moreover, 'machine policing' is a fast-developing area often opaque and technologically complex. For these and other reasons the governance deficit is particularly worrying given the view cited by Babuta and Oswald (2019: 8) that the current position represents a "patchwork quilt, uncoordinated and delivered to different standards in different settings and for different outcomes".

Concerns about the impact that Big Data might have on relations between police and citizens, and the accountability of the police, relate to the central role that algorithms play in directing emerging strategy and tactics. These concerns are particularly acute in relation to self-learning forms of artificial intelligence, whereby the basis on which the rules and procedures for arriving at predictions about potential criminal or problematic behaviour become ever more difficult to scrutinize. In terms of democratic oversight, these limitations are particularly acute since proponents of big data policing (including the companies selling software and related technology) advocate that the model is more effective and efficient than human decision-making and is an ethically and morally neutral exercise in statistical certainty. There are a number of reasons to doubt such claims. First, the research evidence is clear that the use of algorithms to detect offending behaviour (either past or future) is flawed in terms of the quality and veracity of the information contained in the databases. Quality and veracity are related but separate challenges. The quality of the data might be questionable in the sense that only partial or incomplete information might be provided and that this might mean that subsequent correlations identified by algorithms are 'false positives'. The location of complaints made about antisocial behaviour on a public transport network, for example, might show a spike in reports at a particular terminus, and location details logged in the database. In practice, though, this would be a poor-quality indicator if the greater number of incidents is explained by the nearby presence of a police station, meaning that the reports of experiences elsewhere on the network are made in that location and there is not actually greater prevalence there. Concerns about the veracity of data are subtly different in that they refer to false rather than incomplete information. If prejudiced commuters on the same public transport system are more likely to report concerns about particular groups that they wrongly associate with anti-social or criminal activity, then false information is likely to enter the database and skew subsequent analysis.

Veracity is also a concern when the meaning of data is assumed to be significant in ways that might not bear scrutiny. For example, police sometimes record that an individual of note is present in a particular location and such information can become a 'risk marker' that informs actuarial decision-making even without any detail of what the person was actually doing at that juncture. As Oswald (2018) noted, administrative law requires that public bodies exercise their discretion on the basis of relevant criteria and so the inclusion of irrelevant information within big data policing calculations opens the door to the possibility of legal challenge.

The second related set of concerns refers to the lineage and provenance of data, and the lack of capacity for end-users of machine policing to check how information has been transformed into intelligence and then into data, and by whom. While there are clear rules about continuity of evidence in other forms of criminal justice there may be no parallel in respect of big data policing. This is particularly concerning since research evidence indicates unintentional bias is a core feature of data coding, such that the lack of gender and ethnic representation among computer coders results in errors. This is problematic, for example, for facial recognition software that Garvie and Frankle (2016) noted tends to misidentify or not identify African-Americans compared to other groups. This is a component of the wider problem identified by Harcourt (2007) in his argument against risk-assessment and actuarial prediction. His analysis unravels the conceit that technical statistical analysis is inherently neutral and value-free. Since police data reflects the bias inherent in operational practice, focused as it is disproportionately on certain crime types, particular locations and marginalised sections of the community, it is inevitable that the resulting information inputted into databases is skewed and partial. Harcourt argued that a 'ratchet effect' occurred whereby the over-representation of some groups in police practice leads, through actuarial methods, to a spiral of increasing control and disproportionate police attention in ways that do not reflect crime patterns in society. He noted that (2007: 190):

> The criminal law is by no means a neutral set of rules. It is a moral and political set of rules that codifies social norms, ethical values, political preferences, and class hierarchies. The use of actuarial methods serve only to accentuate the ideological dimensions of the criminal law. It hardens the purported race, class, and power relations between certain offences and certain groups.

While these are problems inherent in actuarialism, they are exacerbated when self-learning algorithms conduct the analysis and identify correlations that reflect bias. If police disproportionally arrest black youths for marijuana use, for example, then the algorithm will identify correlation between ethnicity and offending even if marijuana use is as prevalent among ethnic groups not subject to over-policing (Ferguson, 2017). While one response to this problem has been to remove ethnicity as a field in databases, as for example, Durham Police have done in the UK, there remains the concern that 'proxy' indicators, such as postcode, will effectively continue to embed these disproportionalities into algorithmic policing. There are parallels here with police and media practices in earlier periods, before Big Data arrived, when place names ('Brixton', 'Toxteth' or 'Handsworth' in the UK) were used as synonyms for minority groups and so discussion of crime or social problems could continue to refer to race in coded terms (Keith, 1993).

These problems highlight the wider challenge of developing big data policing in ways consistent with broader principles of democracy. The inherent biases associated with algorithms in policing are associated with disproportionality and the criminalisation of sections of the community. Democratically this is problematic, especially if police practice is contrary to civil rights, privacy and equality legislation. In such circumstances, policing becomes procedurally unjust, which will have a negative impact on public legitimacy (Hough, et al., 2013). As the recent Black Lives Matter movement in the US has demonstrated, the police in such circumstances create and recreate boundaries of community and political inclusion that both reflect and sustain broader patterns of inequality in society.

For those reasons, holding big data policing to account is particularly important, but also especially challenging. First among the problems is that the software and technology that constitute algorithms tends to be created and owned by private IT companies who might be resistant – on commercial grounds – to external analysis of the coding. Kroll et al (2017) proposed a model whereby algorithms are regulated and required to meet certain industry standards, and this could provide safeguards against coding bias, and Carlo and Crawford (2016) propose greater community transparency in shaping the scope of big data policing and the operational outcomes. Engaging citizens alongside external experts and stakeholders at all stages of the development of 'machine policing' can promote accountability through ensuring transparency and openness in the use of algorithms in policing. How this can be achieved, and by whom, is difficult to determine, however. Ferguson (2017) found that legislators are unable to penetrate the working of algorithms and the fast-pace development of technology risks making legislation and post hoc legal challenges redundant. External scrutiny is even more problematic when algorithms are self-learning and relatively autonomous from governance and accountability and when they draw upon multiple streams of data, some of which is open source and some of which is of dubious provenance, the possibility of oversight becomes especially challenging.

There are, however, a few caveats to this review of the negative features of big data policing and the difficulties of holding algorithms to account. First, there is no doubt that many benefits can be accrued from better understanding crime patterns and clearly the appliance of such methods can help tackle crime. Predictive policing has the potential to reduce the social harm, human misery and economic costs associated with crime – costs that often weigh more heavily on those already experiencing marginalisation and relative deprivation. Used well, such approaches might enable the better identification of those at risk of crimes that might otherwise tend to be under-recognised or to help identify patterns and trends that can inform innovative and more effective responses. Recognising patterns in domestic abuse, for example, might allow for better risk profiling and the development of early interventions that prevent recurrence and the escalation of the gravity of the harm done to the victim.

More widely, beyond policing, the need to avoid technological determinism is highlighted by Ziewitz's (2016) critical overview and partial check on debates that algorithms are 'taking over'. He reminds that algorithms should not be 'fetishized' as agential governing entities. For all the debate about the power and dominance of algorithms in diverse areas of contemporary life there remains a stark lack of an agreed definition. On that basis, Ziewitz cautions (2016: 4):

Against this backdrop, claims about governing algorithms deserve some scrutiny and skepticism: how to account for the recent rise of algorithms as both a topic and a resource for understanding a wide range of activities? What challenges do algorithms pose for scholars in science and technology studies ... and in the sociology, history, and anthropology of science and technology? And, yes, what actually is an algorithm?

A final caveat is that for all the limitations and caution about the application of big data to law enforcement and crime investigation, any potential that such approaches might bring in predictive terms could also be applied in ways that further accountability. Internal management and people development techniques are focused, in part, on early identification of officers who might pose a risk in terms of using excessive force, generating citizen complaints, behaving corruptly and so forth. Through identifying patterns of associated behaviour that have been found to correlate with problematic actions, Big Data might help guide interventions that avert problems. In keeping with other models of predictive policing based on analysis of data sets such potential might be partial and should be treated cautiously; nonetheless, algorithms should not be treated solely as a problematic challenge in terms of accountability and governance.

The problem of privacy

In the information age all manner of personal data is potentially available to be collected, processed and used by a whole range of different actors. As the philosopher Luciano Floridi has pointed out, as digital technology has become ubiquitous, the kind of privacy enjoyed in pre-digital times has been eroded (Floridi, 2014). By this he refers mainly to 'informational privacy' or our freedom from intrusion or interference thanks to restrictions on what is known or knowable about ourselves. The leaving of vast digital traces through the execution of everyday tasks creates the potential for that data to be acquired, analysed and used by a whole range of actors, unless otherwise protected by law.

There are of course limits to this exploitation of big data in law intended to protect citizens' privacy. Article 8 of the Human Rights Act states that "everyone has the right to respect for his private or family life." Interference in the private lives of citizens, which may be justified for some societal purpose, must therefore be proportionate. Organisations acquiring and processing the personal data of EU citizens are subject to the General Data Protection Regulation (GDPR) which, among other things, prevents organisations exploiting citizens' personal data without their consent.

Recent controversies about the impact of social media and 'fake news' in both the 2016 US Presidential elections and the UK Brexit referendum illustrate the ways in which corporations, governments and political campaigners can process data harvested from the personal information of millions of citizens. Technically, it might be that individual users of social media permit companies to process and sell their personal data but it is clear that many do not provide informed consent since the scope and extent of this re-use is not understood. Similarly, as Zhu et al. (2016) demonstrated, users of smart phone apps tend inadvertently not to activate privacy controls and so allow access to unknown agencies, companies, criminal or terrorist networks.

Similarly the police are able to use communications data to help identify offenders, although in ways that raise privacy concerns. In the US and the UK legal guarantees of privacy mean that police agencies are restricted (without a specific warrant) to collecting meta-data relating to online and phone activity, rather than monitoring the actual content of communications. However, personal relationships and behaviour might still become apparent. For example, the ability to geo-locate cell phones very precisely, to within a few metres, means that law enforcement agencies have been able to identify and find offenders even where there is no other evidence relating to their behaviour or association with others. Ferguson (2017) cites several examples in which police have used software to identify phones found to be in close proximity to repeat crimes, leading to the apprehension of offenders. That legal provisions to protect privacy are very weak in practice is also illustrated in his analysis, since secondary information gathered from online searches often allow the identification of an individual associated with a particular phone number. Moreover, metadata can reveal interesting patterns of behaviour that might arouse suspicion: for example, an individual calling hydrophonic stores, 'head shops', locksmiths and hardware stores might, Ferguson (2017: 112–113) argued, be preparing to grow marijuana.

Another example of this clash between privacy and big data policing concerns the personal data the police may ask to look through when investigating a crime. In England and Wales, the Crown Prosecution Service and the police now issue a consent form to victims of crime which, if signed, gives the police permission to look through a victim's phone or computer as part of an investigation. These requests have been described by Big Brother Watch as 'digital strip searches of victims' (BBC News, 2019). Although these can be used as part of any criminal investigation, they are most likely to be used in cases of sexual crime. Many organisations and victims groups have raised concerns that victims face a choice between giving the police permission to trawl through their private communications, which many will understandably be reluctant to do, and not pursuing the case at all. Although the Crown Prosecution Service says that digital information will only be looked at where it forms a 'reasonable line of enquiry' and will only be presented in court if it meets stringent criteria, many victims will be reasonably concerned at the prospect of having other people, not least police officers, trawl through their private communications in this way.

These privacy concerns will only increase with the rise of so called 'smart cities' and related 'Internet of Things' (IoT) technologies, such as cameras and sensors, that mean that it will be increasingly difficult to move around towns and cities with any kind of anonymity. Even information generated by the use of IoT devices in the private home will be held by the relevant companies for commercial purposes, but could potentially be accessed for policing purposes. Just because such information exists and can be used does not mean that it should be, and policymakers need to consider the degree to which they are content to allow surveillance and data intrusion on this scale. Indeed the challenge here is not just to regulate privacy concerns about the collection and processing of data by public sector agencies but also the more difficult problem of doing this across transnational private networks.

Public and legal perspectives on data privacy might be subject to change as the expansion of digital culture and interaction continues apace. Bernard (2019) noted that the power and political context that has under-pinned demands for privacy and civil liberties have primarily been connected to concerns to protect the individual from over-powerful states. Resistance on these grounds shifts significantly when the sharing of personal information becomes a matter of belonging, of inclusiveness, and 'togetherness' as individuals pool information on social media platforms as they join communities and circles of friendship and kinship. He noted that US courts have begun to express new approaches in relation to the degree to which there can be a reasonable expectation of privacy in online environments. We suggest that beneficent context of sharing personal data online with private social media companies might become more problematic as such information becomes embedded in AI and machine policing that might have negative and biased outcomes for individuals and communities.

It is increasingly clear that policing needs to think through its approach to these questions carefully, perhaps by putting in place a framework of principles that should govern its approach. It is notable that the Commissioner of the Metropolitan Police, Cressida Dick, in her 2019 Police Foundation lecture, argued that the principles the police deploy to regulate their use of force might also be used as a basis for thinking about data intrusion (Dick, 2019). So, for example, the police service currently works to ten key principles regarding the use of force by police officers, aimed at ensuring the police use minimal force and only when necessary. Dick argued that a similar set of principles could be developed to regulate the use of personal data for policing purposes, ensuring that the degree of intrusion is proportionate given people's right to privacy. While this might be a sensible way forward, it remains a concern if it is left to senior police to establish their own regulations in such an important area. Home Office, Police and Crime Commissioners, the Information Commissioner and a host of civil society groups ought to be more fully engaged in devising mechanisms for governance.

The problem of bias

As has been noted, it is widely argued that actuarial prediction and the use of AI in policing is likely to mean that current 'disproportionalities' in the delivery of policing and criminal justice are likely to be exacerbated. Young people and some minority groups who are already over-policed will become subject to ever-further focus due to what Harcourt (2007) referred to as the 'ratchet' effect. Essentially, the problem of disproportionality is that using prior police (and other agencies) practices as an authoritative source of data that informs future activities means that existing over-representation of some communities and demographics will become ever further entrenched. Considerable and long-standing research data indicates that young males, BAME communities and residents of inner-city districts are more likely than other groups to feature in police stop and search practices (Bradford, 2017). Moreover, it is far from clear that such practices are a direct reflection of underlying crime patterns and might re-produce institutional bias and disproportionality (Harcourt, 2007).

The specific application of AI in the context of social network theory and the identification of gang structures and membership was cited above. Joh (2014: 47) outlined the transformative power this gives to police:

> While traditional police work might easily identify leaders within a criminal organization, social network analysis can identify those with influence or those who transmit information within the group quickly and yet whose roles are not otherwise apparent. The software can even reveal deliberately concealed affiliations. Even if an individual suspected of being part of a criminal organization does not admit his affiliation, social network software can calculate the probability of his membership.

The potential of such approaches in terms of detecting offences might be considerable if hidden associations – among pedophile networks, for example – are revealed. Moreover, the potential to use these techniques as the basis for risk assessment offers the prospect of identifying individuals at heightened risk of crossing thresholds from association to active offending. Joh (2014) noted that law enforcement agencies used results from such models to approach individuals and offer interventions designed to divert them from future, as yet uncommitted, criminal behaviour. However, sociological research demonstrates that the identification of gangs and gang members has often been highly racialised such that some loose connections of individuals become criminalised and labelled as problematic in ways that reflect wider processes of stereotyping and marginalisation. For example, Cockbain's (2013) study of 'Asian sex gang' engaged in the UK in the grooming of children found that understanding the abuse of children in 'ethnic' terms reflects wider racist stereotypes and risks misdirecting investigations. Similarly, in a different context, Gunter (2016) argued that the street gang label is unfairly applied to black youth identified with street-based lifestyles and urban cultures, and that they and their friendship networks become subject to unfair police targeting.

While it might be that Big Data analysis reveals hitherto unknown sets of relationships that disturb established pre-conceptions, it seems more likely (given that resource constraints will limit the application of the software technology) that Big Data will provide an apparently scientific authority to enhance established forms of targeting. Existing disproportionalities would become further entrenched. However, concerns about disproportionality in the context of 'machine policing' reflect that such problems are already firmly embedded in policing and criminal justice practices that have emerged over many decades. On this basis it might be argued that AI can be 'trained' and developed in ways that manage out potential bias and stereotyping. Ludwig and Sunstein (2019) have argued that using AI as a basis for criminal justice decision-making is preferable to the alternative – human judgement – since the latter entails bias and stereotyping. Moreover, they argue, AI can be more easily interrogated to identify false positives or disproportionate outcomes than can human decision-making in which unconscious bias is poorly understood and rarely recognised. Finally, once bias is identified in AI systems lines of software can be written to overcome problems in ways that are much simpler and more effective than 'real world' management efforts to eradicate bias from the decisions made by staff.

Similarly, as touched upon earlier, the development of more effective data and evidence to inform policing and criminal justice activities could provide the basis to tackle criminal and other social harms that impact disproportionally on those already marginalised socially, politically and economically. Sherman (2009) argued that the 'democratic potential' of evidence-based policing rested on the capacity of improved strategic and tactical responses to crime to reduce the negative impact of such problems of the lives of those whose misery is poorly reduced by traditional approaches.

Conclusion

In this chapter we have discussed three areas in which the coming together of policing and big data pose particularly acute ethical dilemmas. First, there is a challenge of democracy and accountability. The innate complexity of the algorithmic tools that are at the heart of big data policing poses a real challenge for policing and criminal justice agencies, whose legitimacy rests on transparent decision-making. What are the prospects for procedural fairness if the rationale for police decisions is incapable of being scrutinised by the lay citizen? This challenge is complicated further by the application of 'machine learning', which means that decision-making tools themselves grow and evolve their thinking in an automated way. Further obscurity is added by the fact that these tools may well be owned by private companies who will not disclose their inner workings for commercial reasons, and by the fact that they may be operating on a transnational basis. It may be that new mechanisms of external scrutiny are required that deploy the kind of technical expertise necessary to bring greater intelligibility to this complex terrain.

Second, there is the challenge of protecting individual privacy in a world where so much more is known or knowable about the average citizen. Even with the limitations on investigatory powers currently in place in countries like the US and the UK, police agencies are already able to know a great deal more about a person from their communications data than was ever routinely possible in the past. Police agencies have to balance their desire to use all means available to prevent harm and keep people safe, with the dangers of expanding the reach of the surveillance state. Victims of crime now face the prospect of disclosing vast swathes of their personal data to the police in order to try to pursue justice, with the risk that many may decide it is not worth the degree of intrusion. It is clear that the police need to think hard about how to embed proportionality in their approach to big data.

Third, we have discussed the challenge of bias. Debates about conscious and unconscious bias in policing are not new, nor are the challenges of policing fairly in a social context that is shaped by unfair structural inequalities. But the use of big data has the potential to reinforce existing biases and result in even more procedurally unfair patterns of law enforcement. This reinforces the importance of transparent decision-making and the need for big data policing to remain accountable, as highlighted above.

In addition to these ethical dilemmas, other challenges limit the practical application of Big Data to policing, at least in Britain. One concerns the institutional fragmentation of policing in England and Wales, which means 43 different police forces being responsible for purchasing their own IT systems. This means that data is very often not shared between police forces, and indeed between police forces and other agencies in ways that may be required if big data is to be utilised to its full potential. Organisational fragmentation also makes it difficult for those developing software to interface with the police and understand their needs as a customer.

There are skills and knowledge challenges too, with police forces competing in a crowded market for data scientists and those with the advanced technical skills required. And in the struggle for precious resources political imperatives generally push police forces to invest in things like additional frontline officers rather than in the back office capabilities upon which big data policing depends. A further challenge will be the 'so what' test: how are outcomes of Big Data practice applied to routine operational police work. Not only might there be serious challenges in terms of training and equipping officers to use the outcomes of AI and other processes but there is also the matter of reconciling this with other factors that shape officer priorities and conduct. The demands of the public, media and politicians have a legitimate role to play in the delivery of policing; the test comes when these stand in contradiction to big data policing outcomes.

None of these barriers, however, are insuperable and the message of this chapter is that if big data policing is to deliver the kind of public value promised, police agencies must also address the ethical challenges it poses, and society more widely needs to develop effective governance mechanisms. Only in these ways can public consent and police legitimacy be secured and the potential of new technology be realised.

References

BBC News. (29 April 2019). Rape victims among those to be asked to hand phones to police. www.bbc.co.uk/news/uk-48086244 [accessed 1 August 2019].

Bernard, A. (2019). *The triumph of profiling: The self in digital culture.* Cambridge: Polity Press.

Bradford, B. (2017). *Stop and search and police legitimacy.* London: Routledge.

Chen, T. Wu, F., Luo, T.T. Wang, M. and Ho, Q. (2016). Big data management and analytics for mobile crowd sensing. *Mobile Information Systems*, doi:10.1155/2016/8731802.

Cockbain, E. (2013). Grooming and the 'Asian Sex Gang Predator': the construction of a racial crime threat. *Race and Class*, 54, 22–32.

Crawford, K. and Calo, R. (2016). There is a blind spot in AI research. *Nature*, 538(7625).

Dick, C. (2019). John Harris Memorial Lecture 2019. www.police-foundation.org.uk/past-event/2019-cressida-dick-cbe-qpm-commissioner-of-the-metropolitan-police/ [accessed 1 December 2019].

Erikson, R. and Haggerty, K. (1997). *Policing the risk society.* Toronto: Toronto University Press.

Fergusson, A.G. (2017). *The rise of big data policing: Surveillance, race and the future of law enforcement.* New York: New York University Press.

Floridi, L. (2014). *The 4th Revolution: How the infosphere is reshaping human reality.* Oxford: Oxford University Press.

Garvie, C. and Frankle, J. (2016). Facial recognition software might have a racial bias problem. *The Atlantic*, 7 April.

Gunter, A. (2016). *Race, gangs and youth violence: Policy, prevention and policing.* Bristol: Policy Press.

Harcourt, B. (2007). *Against prediction – Profiling, policing and punishing in an actuarial age.* Chicago: University of Chicago Press.

Hough, M., Jackson, J., Bradford, B. (2013). The drivers of police legitimacy: Some European research. *Journal of Policing, Intelligence and Counter Terrorism*, 8, 144–165.

James, A. (2016). *Understanding Police Intelligence Work*, Bristol: Policy Press.

Joh, E.E. (2014). Policing by numbers: Big data and the Fourth Amendment. *Washington Law Review*, 89, 35–68.

Keith, M. (1993). *Race, riots and policing – Lore and disorder in a multiracist society.* London: UCL Press.

Kitichin, R. (2014). *The data revolution: Big data, open data, data infrastructures and their consequences.* London: Sage.

Kroll, J.A., Huey, J., Barocas, S., Felten, E.W., Reidenberg, J.R., Robinson, D.G. and Yu, H. (2017). Accountable Algorithms. *University of Pennsylvania Law Review*, 165, 633–705.

Ludwig, J. and Sunstein, C.R. (2019). Discrimination in the age of algorithms. *The Boston Globe*, 24 September, www.bostonglobe.com/opinion/2019/09/24/discrimination-age-algorithms/mfWUxRH8Odm6IRo3PZRLdI/story.html?outputType=amp&__twitter_impression=true [accessed 30 September, 2019].

Lum, K. and Isaac, W. (2016). To predict and serve? *Significance*, 13(5).

Oswald, M. (2018). Algorithm-assisted decision-making in the public sector: Framing the issues using administrative law rules governing discretionary power. *Philosophical Transactions of the Royal Society A*, 376: 1–20.

Oswald, M. and Babuta, A. (2019). *Data analytics and algorithmic bias in policing*. London: Royal United Services Institute.

Rowe, M. (2020). *Policing the police: Challenges of democracy and accountability*. Bristol: Policy Press.

Sherman, L.W. (2009). Evidence and liberty: The promise of experimental criminology. *Criminology & Criminal Justice*, 9, 1, 5–28.

Yong, E. (2018). A Popular Algorithm Is No Better at Predicting Crimes Than Random People. *The Atlantic*, 17th January 2018. www.theatlantic.com/technology/archive/2018/01/equivant-compas-algorithm/550646/ [accessed 2 October 2019].

Zhu, K. He, X., Xiang, B., Zhang, L. and Pattavina, A. (2016). How Dangerous Are Your Smartphones? App Usage Recommendation with Privacy Preserving. *Mobile Information Systems*, doi:10.1155/2016/6804379.

Ziewitz, M. (2016). Governing Algorithms: Myth, Mess and Methods. *Science, Technology and Human Values*, 41(1): 3–16.

Chapter 11

Decision-making

Using technology to enhance learning in police officers

Pamela Richards, Debbie Roberts and Mark Britton

Introduction

In a previous work, the potential of body worn video (BWV) footage to accelerate decision-making skills was explored (Richards, Roberts, Britton and Roberts, 2017). Within this chapter we elaborate on this work. Specifically, we include three examples of embedding technology into scenario-based training, which have proved successful in other professions/domains where complex decision-making is a key attribute for individuals engaging in those naturalistic environments. We outline the importance of the interaction between the creation of a slow, deliberate, reflective conscious training environment (training/educational setting), and the rapid in-action applied setting (naturalistic/vocational setting) (Richards, Collins and Mascarenhas, 2016). Such interplay between educational settings and vocational settings can be integrated into training programmes to accelerate the preparation and decision-making of police officers. In particular, the chapter outlines how the creation of such slow and deliberate reflective environments, in context of various scenario-based learning relevant to policing, can be manufactured to facilitate an individualised learning plan (Richards, 2004) and the formulation of shared mental models (SMMs) within a team context (Richards et al., 2012).

The aim of this chapter is to present an overview of how technology, particularly artificial intelligence (AI), can be incorporated into the naturalistic training setting to enhance individual and collective team decision-making within the police. We will first provide a brief overview of the various definitions of AI and augmented reality and their application to police training and preparation. In the second section, we will present an overview of the current demands of policing and the subsequent changes in the preparation of police officers, including the changing landscape of higher education and its role in supporting the development of future officers. The third section of this chapter will examine scenario-based learning but focus on the integration of technology to develop real-world training environments. Specifically, this third section will consider the use of experiential and immersive learning, which have been used for many years in other practice-based disciplines but, to date, uptake within police forces appears to have been limited.

Artificial intelligence

AI "is a broad, multi-disciplinary field of study that concerns itself with the construction of machines and systems that perform functions commonly associated with cognitive capacities of the human mind" (Dechesne, Dignum, Zardiashvili and Bieger, 2019: 2). Whereas, augmented reality is "an enhanced version of reality created by the use of technology to overlay digital information on an image of something being viewed through a device" (Hitchcock, Holmes and Sundorph, 2017: 20). There are many potential benefits of using this emerging technology, including predictive policing, automated monitoring, managing and pre-processing large amounts of data, image recognition from digital devices, integration of user friendly interactive services for civilians, and enhancing productivity and digital workflow (Dechesne et al., 2019). For example, the advantage of the remote use of large data sets means that officers can be deployed to targeted high-risk areas where crime is predicted (Hitchcock, Holmes and Sundorph, 2017).

Predictive policing involves the utilisation of technological data and information from a variety of disparate sources, which is analysed and interpreted to highlight trends, patterns and key determinants to anticipate criminal action or activity. Such digital processes can be used to inform and shape preventative action resulting in the form of strategic interventions. Such strategic intervention can be designed to prevent crime and/or to respond to crime more effectively. The report from Dechesne et al. (2019) outlines several potential applications for policing but also highlights that whilst technology and specifically AI can excel in converting data into outputs, it operates on formal rules and instructions; thus, making it difficult to automate tasks that rely on tacit knowledge.

Although the emphasis in literature to date has been placed on predictive policing, we would argue that analysis of 'real time' information and data is also central as AI can inform 'real time, in-action' decision-making processes of officers. This process is complex as it requires key data points in the environment to be identified first, before skilled individuals can interpret and make sense of the data points in context of the applied setting (Richard et al., 2009). It is only when experienced officers have engaged in the process of interpretation and sense-making, can they establish connections between the data/information points. Such engagements result in a newly developed understanding of the situation (a higher level of comprehension), which the officer can use to inform future actions. Technology and AI can therefore play a role in both informing 'in-action' policing using 'real time' interfaces (for example, drones, facial recognition) and also in a training context where officers are educated or upskilled using a range of digital synthetic learning environments (for example, augmented reality (AR), virtual reality (VR) and immersive learning environments). Using technology to access such rich information in the form of large data sets, 'real-time' digital evidence, combined with the development of bespoke technological interference (designed to meet the needs of policing) results in the facilitation of more effective training processes and more efficient workflow of officers.

To summarise, technological advancements can identify patterns in the data that would not necessarily be perceptible to humans (Dechesne et al., 2019). For example, video-capturing devices can perform the task of facial recognition and can recognise criminals and key individuals automatically (Hitchcock, Holmes and Sundorph, 2017). AI can also generate new instances of objects/pictures, videos, stories, faces etc., and can be used to generate materials from scratch. All resulting in the design and development of synthetic learning environments. Whilst this clearly presents an opportunity for use as a training aid to generate scenarios; extant AI systems remain somewhat limited. Dechesne et al. (2019) argue that AI systems currently lack what we would call common sense and cannot communicate with people on an emotional level nor make moral judgements (Tong, 2017). The use of intuitive knowledge remains poorly understood in police decision-making (like in many other domains) and further research is required. However, we are beginning to get to grips with the interaction between the psychomotor and psychosocial aspects of decision-making (Richards, et al., 2016) and we would propose such work needs to be expanded further to consider the human and machine (technology) interaction, especially in the context of human-machine decision-making and policing.

The demands of modern-day policing

It has been widely accepted that the number of officers has significantly diminished over recent years (Finnigan, 2017) and that more officers are required to support the increasing complexity and breadth of crime which is being observed in society. In response to this and the recent announcement by the British Prime Minister to recruit 20,000 new police officers in the immediate future (BBC, 2019), discussions are emerging as to how we can rapidly and effectively train a growing police workforce. With increasing attention being directed to the role that technology could play in accelerating the learning profile of police officers who are ready for deployment. It is also relevant and timely to direct our attention to the increasing numbers of police preparation programmes being moved into Higher Education and the emergence of apprenticeship pathways. Such learning pathways, which integrate theory with applied practice, will be responsible for the preparation of our future forces. However, understanding the nature of how this cyclic link from theory to practice can be maximised and accelerated requires a more in-depth understanding of learning and pedagogical processes. The creation of dual processing learning environments (integrating both theoretical and practical settings) which involve embedding scenario-based learning and innovative pedagogical mechanisms, can perhaps be one solution to accelerating the learning capabilities and decision-making in officers. Scenario-based learning facilitates a safe, low risk environment where mistakes can be made and learned from. Equally it is an environment where effective mental models relating to specific situations can be developed (Richards et al., 2012) and one which proves to be cost effective. In 2012, it was estimated that recruiting and training a police officer in England and Wales costs £12,000 per officer (Nottinghamshire Police, 2012).

The advancement in technology combined with enhanced understanding of pedagogical processes enables technology to be more dominantly integrated into the training context to accelerate the decision-making and learning of officers across a range of situations. Depending on the technology used, there is scope within the learning environment itself for information to be layered and to be adapted to meet the needs of the individual learner and context they find themselves in (Richards et al., 2016). In doing so, such an integrated dual training approach can accommodate the training needs of novice officers but is also relevant to the enhancement of expertise in experienced officers and specialised units. Such a layering approach to knowledge development enables the complexity of information to be built upon, resulting in the development and refinement of performance related mental models/shared mental modes relating to situations, and accelerated decision-making capabilities in both individuals and specialist teams.

In England and Wales, the routes to becoming an officer are varied; through an apprentice route, obtaining a higher education degree or through a career change, where previous career experience can be transferred. Regardless of the route individuals choose to enter the force, the training process must capture and develop a range of diverse individual skills. The training will attempt to maximise the attributes that individuals bring to the role, but also refine and shape them in a way that enables future officers to perceive and attend to challenging situations in a similar manner, demonstrating a collective thought process. Such a collective thought process may be force specific, although commonalities across multiple forces can be observed. It is important to acknowledge that there are multiple ways in which a successful incident outcome can be achieved; but the preparation of officers should ensure that similar principles guide the officer's responses. Attention is increasingly being directed towards how officers are prepared to function in complex modern societies. The process of developing shared situational awareness (Klein, 2000) is complex and requires officers to develop a common understanding of roles, policies, procedures and tactical knowledge, which evolves over time as vocational experience is gained. In this chapter we propose that although there is no substitute for experience, training in an environment where technology is integrated with experiential learning could, if designed correctly, support the preparation of police officers' skills to accelerate learning and decision-making.

Over recent years there has been a rapid increase in the number of policing degrees in Higher Education Institutions (HEI) in England and Wales, and the role such establishments play in the creation of probationary constables. As a result, there is an increasing focus on the provision provided by these HEI where classroom learning is combined with applied situated learning experiences, which incorporates elements of real-world experience. The apprenticeship schemes follow a similar, albeit slightly different path. Many UK police services have already embarked upon this journey of hybrid learning where theory-based learning settings are integrated into an applied learning experience. However, the approach to training varies between forces (Finnigan, 2017). Although the mechanisms of hybrid learning are not isolated to the HEI setting and are equally relevant to individuals entering the force from the apprentice route or via a career change, the most effective mechanism to train our next generation of officers are still being explored and examined.

It is essential therefore that all entry routes into the police force enable the individual to experience and be prepared for the appropriate complexities that exists within the policing role. It is recognised that policing is becoming far more complex than ever with new crime classifications emerging (Finnigan, 2017; College of Policing, 2015). More particularly, the demands of policing have recently been re-classified into 'incoming demands' and 'on-going demands' (College of Policing, 2015), each with its own long list of sub-categories. For example, incoming demands include arrests, road traffic collisions, stop and search, missing persons and place of safety orders. Whereas on-going demands include engaging with Multi-Agency Public Protection Arrangements (MAPPA), supporting families enrolled on the 'troubled families programme' and supporting the Child Protection plan, to mention only a few. Moreover, the increased dominance of social media and technology, exploitation of children/vulnerable adults, fraud and mental health related situations, among other occurrences, are adding to the daily demands placed on officers as they respond to societal changes. Although the core role of the police and policing remains the same, there is an increasing need to understand the changing societies in which we live and the current impact of such demands on officers. The changing nature of policing has to consider the level of risk, threat, harm and vulnerability (Finnigan, 2017), further increasing the complexity in which modern police officers and forces function. Such a change in the nature of policing, and the approaches of partner agencies, demands the development of additional policing skills. The impact of developing these sophisticated skills requires training approaches to be realigned. The creation of synthetic learning environments, which integrate theory into applied naturalistic settings, and are adaptable to various settings, is a sensible solution.

Training and upskilling the next generation of officers

Broadly speaking, the initial training schedule for officers has not altered over recent years. Training typically consists of phases of classroom-based learning, on the job tutorship and an initial probation period followed by an extended period of probation over two years before becoming a fully-fledged officer, although it is difficult to garner an exact and accurate picture across all the forces. For example, a Freedom of Information request (FOI) was asked of the Metropolitan Police (and others) by a third party, to release their training catalogues and describe what they were training. This was declined. Although sensitivity is acknowledged in a training context, there is a need for pedagogical and subject experts involved in research and academia to work more closely with organisations such as the emergency services and enter into dialogue where education and training can be supported from a holistic perspective. Such an approach could potentially accelerate the development of skills (and specialist skills) in emergency specialist services, maximising resources and producing cost saving benefits.

The existing recruitment process therefore appears to face two challenges with regard to curriculum content and the integration of technology/AI to support training/development of officers. Firstly, greater clarity is required relating to the current curriculum content for individuals who join the police through the traditional channel (not through the degree route, where the College of Policing curriculum is adhered to). As highlighted above, accessing information with regards to the content of this traditional curriculum is difficult and it appears that the curriculum might vary across different police forces. Without developing an understanding of what is currently delivered it is difficult to support the design and development of synthetic learning environments. Such a synthetic learning environment can be embedded into the training curriculum of police officers, where technological elements and AI can be integrated to enhance the development of both psychomotor and psychosocial skills. Such integration could support the facilitation of modern-day policing skills, and equip officers to function in a complex, dynamic world that is continually changing. We see such synthetic learning environments being a hybrid bridging theory and being utilised in both the traditional entry routes and degree entry routes, in addition to serving the purpose of upskilling of more experienced officers, as part of professional development.

Secondly, current recruitment seems to be based in many forces around values-based recruitment, centring on the Code of Ethics. What this has tended to mean is that values and behavioural approaches deliver a different kind of police officer and is linked to a Code of Ethics. Arguably, police officers are required to be more emotionally intelligent and society aware than in previous times, owing to the complex and continually changing environments in which they work. For many officers, modern day policing requires not only an understanding of the legalities of the incident, but an ability to contextualise and understand the cultural, social and political context in which incidents occur. Softer skills of conflict management (like conflict diffusion) and THRIVE (Smith and Swann, 2019) are considered to be key attributes of current police officers which can be developed through the creation of synthetic learning environments using technology and AI in both the initial training stage and later professional upskilling.

Training in the classroom and tutorship phases appears to remain unchanged (by and large) and consist of role playing, insight from tutors based on their experience and often civilian trainers. Forms of technology such as VR and AR training are being integrated but these appear to be restricted to specialist units such as police firearms weapons and tactics training. Creating a synthetic learning environment, through the integration of technology, for example VR, offers limited or no risk to participants, as the environments are designed to be safe, controlled, and involve realistic scenarios. For example, in a training scenario, officers can engage with a drunk and disorderly incident in a synthetic learning environment. Such a synthetic learning environment (scenario learning in a technology environment) can develop psychomotor skills (e.g. what information should be attended to and when) and psychosocial skills (awareness of situational factors). This would include not only cultural and political issues but also the dynamic of relations with fellow officers, the victim and criminals involved in the incident. In addition, the synthetic environment allows the novice officer (or developing officer) to learn from more experienced officers with regards to the application of legal issues/policing policy.

Tong (2017) explains that the traditional route to becoming a police officer, which has long emphasised the need for legal and procedural knowledge (both of which were gained on the job over time), has served the police force well without the need for a graduate education. Tong further argues that the importance of 'craft skills', described as negotiation, discretion and judgement are under recognised and therefore should be formally accredited in some way, just as they are in other professions such as education, law and medicine. Hitchcock, Holmes and Sundorph (2017) call for more dynamic, technologically based training methods to be used in the preparation of future officers. For example, the 'cyber bungalow', which facilitates learning through carefully created digital crime scenes. Officers can use the virtual environment to collect digital evidence in an instinctive manner within a training setting. Furthermore, AI also has the potential to enhance officer resilience through the development of strategies, as the officers are progressively exposured to crime scenes through a synthetic learning environment. Finally, AI can be used as a training aid, where AR reality glasses formatted with display information relating to a particular context can used warn by officers to help them identify important evidential clues at a crime scene (Hitchcock, Holmes & Sundorph, 2017). AR glasses could be a useful mechanism to accelerate decision-making in officers, as they can be guided to attend to important environmental clues / data points (Richards et al., 2017).

Such technological training can save time and money, while simultaneously accelerating mental models and SMMs of performance in officers when the correct pedagogical process is applied (Richards et al., 2012). Additional benefits of creating synthetic learning environments for officers relate to the development of teamwork and connect thought processes in officers ('connected mindset'). The integration of hybrid technology within training settings can be used to develop team performance between officers through the construction of SMMs with officers (meaning that officers perceive and attend to the situations in the same way). Serfaty et al., (1997: 235) define mental models as "internal representations of the external world ... [which] represent the experts understanding of the situation". The scenarios act as a vehicle to trigger recall from memory, the identification of decision points, the development of critical reflection and problem solving, leadership skills and finally, the development of enhanced individual and team communication skills. The process of individual reflection (which is shared with other officers) is key within this process, as officers can verbally share what information they notice, attended to and how they have prioritised the information. The information captured through verbal reflections is then 'framed' in context of the scenario they are engaging in. This process enables the officers to individually and collectively make sense of the information relating to the incident being explored within the training setting, and in doing so construct SMMs. These models shape future actions in the real world (individual and team), and result in more effective, rapid action decision-making.

Lessons from sports environments indicate that engaging with technology in training environments can enhance individual and team performance levels (Richard, et al., 2012; Richards et al., 2016). Engaging in such scenario-based environments improves retention and recall, enables complex problems/situations to be 'chunked' into phases allowing for a greater level of complex information to be dealt with across multiple individuals/teams. Finally, such environments accommodate multiple learning styles, are innovative and motivationally enjoyable. Recruits are encouraged to learn through and from their experiences using hybrid learning approaches. The integrating of reflection within synthetic learning and hybrid learning environments is a key aspect of the learning/training process and will be examined in later sections of the chapter.

The following sections use exemplars to outline the integration of technology into learning contexts. Owing to the complexity of both range of contexts and complex situations which officers need to be able to respond to, the decision was made to focus on three examples where hybrid/synthetic learning using technology can be used. The identified context used within this chapter will relate to an officer dealing with incidents relating to mental health. To illustrate the application of technology into the hybrid/synthetic learning setting two environments have been identified: individual personal learning environments, and immersive learning environments. Both environments are specifically designed to develop team naturalistic decision-making and shared situational awareness (Richards et al., 2016).

Contextualising learning

Police officers increasingly require awareness and skills to deal with encounters involving mental ill health, in addition to supporting individuals with learning disabilities (Crane et al., 2016; McDaniel, 2019). Neurodiversity is a term used to describe a group of non-related, cognitive disabilities such as Dyslexia, Dyscalculia, Dyspraxia/DCD, Autistic Spectrum disorder, Asperger's Syndrome, Tourette's Syndrome and Attention Deficit Hyperactivity Disorder (ADHD) (Dalton, 2013). Focusing, for example, on autism, Lane and Kelly (2012: 2) highlight that since the 1990's there has been a sharp rise in diagnoses, and therefore, it is reasonable to expect that more individuals with autism will at some point come into contact with police as either perpetrators or victims of crime. Chown (2009) argues that people with autism have a triad of differences when they come into contact with the criminal justice system; they are between 4–20 times more likely to become victims of crime, and 10 times more likely to experience robbery or sexual assault. In addition to increased risk of being a victim, autism itself may be a factor that predisposes individuals to commit criminal acts and that make them more vulnerable when being treated as a suspect by a police officer (Chown, 2009). More importantly, Chown (2009: 60) states:

> Criminal justice system personnel need to be aware of the range of symptoms a person with autism can present with so that they (the police officer etc) have a good chance of identifying autism in a person with whom they are in contact. If they are unable to do this there is a significant risk of the behaviour of the person being misinterpreted (as a refusal to comply with a reasonable request for instance).

A carefully constructed learning synthetic environment can replicate a real-world situation very well, including the sights, sounds and even smells that can be vital cues to guide police practice. The next section of the chapter will explore the learning environment more extensively to highlight how different technologies can be incorporated into the training, to create a safe learning environment that facilitates active experimentations and the formulation of mental models relating to the specific context.

Developing a personalised reflective learning environment for policing using technology

Personalised learning environments aim to encourage reflective, interactive and self-managed learning that incorporates "social, emotional, cultural and deeply intrapersonal" learning experiences (Shaikh and Khoja, 2014: 203). They are more learner-driven, enabling individuals to take control of and manage their own learning in an interconnected, digital world. Individuals use that world to communicate and develop collective know-how (Shaikh and Khoja, 2014). The virtual environment is flexible and can be adapted to individual learner requirements. The technology enables each learner to create their own workspace and in so doing the learner becomes more self-reliant, connected to others and self-aware of their own learning (Ibid). In order to be effective, Syed-Khuzzan, Goulding and Underwood (2008) caution that virtual learning environments must have a robust pedagogy as a foundation. Bringing together subject knowledge and pedagogical expertise produces learning objects. A learning object is any "resource or content object that is supplied to a learner by a provider with the intention of meeting the learner's learning objects" (Vercoustre & McLean, 2005 cited by Syed-Khuzzan et al., 2008). The learning objects are reusable and can be used in different ways by different learners.

Personalised learning environments for policing could include the development of a range of digitally-based scenarios that the learner can enter into, in order to either participate or observe. The scenarios should of course be rooted in the real-world of modern policing, but also have the potential to provide first hand experiential learning and vicarious learning through the experiences of others as performances are shared. The beauty of personalised virtual environments (where the individual wears a headset) is that they can facilitate *Just in time delivery*: being used at the time and place of the learner's requirements; and when combined with wearable technology have the potential to make use of real time assistance to provide feedback on performance. Thus, enabling the mentor or teacher to be virtually present and further accelerate the development of mental models.

Virtual reality uses a range of technologies to enable learners to interact with a virtual environment (Berg and Vance, 2016). It is thought that using virtual reality, the learner can be exposed to a myriad of environments in a short space of time and as such is able to gain valuable experience, knowledge and manual abilities that would otherwise take many years to accrue. It is understandable that practice-based disciplines (such as nursing and the military) use virtual reality to accelerate the development of students.

Policing exemplar #1

The following case study outlines a scenario that was played out by two actors and recorded for use by a single-user VR headset. The student officer wears the headset and experiences the situation first-hand and/or in collaboration with an experienced officer. In either setting, the student officers are able to confirm or refine aspects of their mental model relating to the situations, which can be used to shape and inform future actions.

Example: Samuel is an accountant, he has been a high performer throughout his life; but he finds social situations difficult, so he tends to avoid social gatherings; preferring to stay at home with his partner George. George has periods of low mood and at times gets very frustrated with Samuel over his avoidance of going out with friends. Both Samuel and George can become withdrawn and uncommunicative. Over recent months, the couple have been bickering and their relationship appears to be suffering as a result. The police are called to the couple's flat following a call by a neighbour citing shouting and what appears to be two men fighting and sounds of glass being smashed. On arrival at the scene, both men have facial injuries consistent with fighting and George has a bottle in his hand.

This common scenario can be used by individual learners to personalise their learning in a number of ways:

- Individuals can reflect on their preconceived ideas relating to domestic or intimate partner violence.
- Individuals might consider how they might establish whether either man has any issues that they should be aware of.
- Inexperienced officers might work with more experienced officers to learn to read the cues from the environment in order to ensure personal safety.
- Some learners will focus on their communication and interpersonal skills when approaching both men.

It is acknowledged that personalised learning makes a valuable contribution to training, development and contributes significantly to the development of professional and leadership skills, the development of team cognitive skills (SMMs, shared situational awareness, team metacognitive, application and heuristics processes) and requires an increased level of social interaction (Klein, 2000). Social interaction (soft skills, communication, leadership and negotiation for example) forms the cornerstone of modern policing. Immersive learning environments can be very useful in helping officers to examine social interactions in a range of carefully selected real-world examples where multiple individuals (officers and actors) can engage in the synthetic learning environment simultaneously.

Created immersive learning environments

Using simulated learning enables the students to learn in an environment which Schön (1987) describes as a practicum: a setting designed for the purpose of learning a practice, in a context that approximates a practice world where students learn by doing. Within the practicum there should be the suspension of disbelief in order to both view the scene as an audience member and become an actor as part of the scene (Roberts and Greene, 2011). Roberts and Greene (2011) argue that simulation is an effective method of teaching critical thinking and clinical reasoning skills. Students are able to synthesise the knowledge they obtain in the classroom and gain comfort and confidence in dealing with challenging policing situations. Students can participate as active learners but can also learn vicariously as they observe and consider the experience of others who participate in the scene. The environment itself enables learners to engage in a safe realistic space and enables them to understand the complexities of human relations and interactions. In other words, exposure to realistic policing situations through immersive learning environments, helps the learner to begin to think and act like a police officer; rehearsing and refining communication and social interaction skills.

Experiential learning takes place through personally experienced events; these may be experienced during the reality of the working day or can be artificially but judiciously manufactured as an immersive learning environment. The individual experiences a situation within an environment, is then encouraged to discuss their performance and their learning with tutors and peers and is often asked to reflect or think about that learning in a purposeful way. The final part of the cycle involves the individual considering how this new learning will be incorporated into their practice should they meet a similar situation in the future.

Whilst some training of officers relating to neuro-diverse individuals may be ongoing, it seems there remains a need for training tailored to policing roles (Crane, Maras, Hawkden, Mulcachy and Memon, 2016). The following example will explore how such an incident can be embedded into an immersive learning environment.

Policing exemplar #2

Individuals with autism may be susceptible to persuasion by officers. Again, the police officer can rehearse their interview skills to avoid asking ambiguous questions that may lead to incorrect answers being offered. For example, Chown (2009: 261) explains: "'Were you with your family or John?' The autistic person may respond, 'John' because that was the last choice of the sequence, so the officer should ask a more specific question such as, 'Who were you with?' thus reducing the influence of suggestion to the subject". Similarly, the officer can be alerted to the changes in perceptions of personal space for an individual with autism; as the standardised actor can reproduce appropriate responses.

An immersive environment can be purposefully constructed (using a standardised actor) who can display a range of appropriate responses to a situation; together with a replication of the environment itself using a virtual, digital world. People with autism may become aggressive or try to run away. Chown (2009: 261) describes these options as "fight, flight or fright"; individuals with autism may want to seek a place of safety, which to a novice officer may arouse suspicion. In such situations officers need to practice providing simple, clear and direct instructions. Furthermore, the scene may progress to an immersive environment to include the police station and or police interview.

Autistic individuals can experience sensory overload when faced with busy, noisy custody suites (Crane et al., 2016). In medical immersive learning settings, well-briefed standardised patients are well versed in replicating a range of signs and symptoms experienced by individuals with mental health issues and/or autism and will respond appropriately to the sensory stimulation, perhaps becoming aggressive and anxious. Integrated created immersive learning environments can be used by individual learners to enhance their learning in a number of ways:

- Enhanced communication and team working, as learners can use the scenarios individually or in groups or teams (including inter agency or interprofessional learning).
- Scenarios can be judiciously selected to rehearse particular skills sets or protocols for given situations; for example, interviewing techniques.
- Scenarios can be more flexibly adapted to suit the stage of the learner journey: novice, more experienced officer or expert.

Immersive environments which allow for the type of active experimentation suggested here may provide one solution to helping new or probationary police officers acquire what might be termed as 'softer skills'. For example, using communication as an exemplar skill, officers are able to construct statements using carefully selected language and grammatical terms to 'shape' the desired outcome for the situation. Officers are able to construct such effective communication skills by drawing on SMMs relating to the situation (constructed in the immersive learning setting), which consider all individuals, the context and cultural issues salaciously in the context of what the desired future action would be. Bahreman and Swoboda (2016) quite rightly point out that establishing cultural competence encompasses more than just learning about different cultures. A true emergent experience using standardised patients (victims and criminals, in the context of policing) and scenarios, should highlight the cultural considerations that professionals need to be cognisant of and provide a new way of teaching it.

More specifically, responsive learning environments capture the real-life situations, normally recorded by video footage (e.g. BWV). The footage is used to acquire an expert's mental model ('alpha vision' of performance) (Richards et al., 2009). 'Alpha vision' of performance has been defined by Richards et al. (2009) as:

> The 'alpha' vision of performance contains the knowledge structures and shared perception held by multiple individuals relating to a particular situation, team task or action. The 'alpha vision' is divided into a number of sub components (several shared mental models, which collectively make

the 'alpha vision'). The 'alpha' vision (cluster of shared mental models) shapes and defines what information individuals collectively attended to and priorities within an applied setting, which relates to their own roles and the roles of others, and represent the 'ideal' outcome of what the members are trying to achieve and how best they will approach the task. The 'alpha' vision includes both psychomotor aspects (information, data and decision points) and psychosocial aspects (culture, politics, values and team philosophy etc).

Using Cognitive Task Analysis Shared Mental Models the officer's own role and the roles of other individuals involved in the situation can coalesce into a shared understanding of how to complete the task or deal with the situation (Richards et al., 2016). SMMs, when developed in novice officers can be operationalised within the real world of policing, as knowledge and information stored within the SMM helps to shape what information the probationary officer attends to and influences their future actions and behaviours.

Responsive immersive learning environment: application of the decision-making framework

Our 'decision-making framework' (Richards et al., 2016) proposes that team decision-making is developed by layering information using two dual processes which illustrates the interaction between a reflective learning environment (educational setting) and an in-action naturalistic applied setting (real-world setting). Such real-world settings can be training, competitive or vocational environments. The framework highlights how individual cognitive thought processes can be collectively developed in a progressive manner to establish a collective team mind-set (Weick & Roberts, 1993) and the development of SMMs of performance (Oranasanu & Salas, 1993). Such SMMs are specific to situations and include the roles and responsibility of individuals involved in the context (Richard et al., 2012). The formulation of such knowledge in a progressive and structured manner allows for individuals to develop a shared perception of the situation, resulting in effective communication and action in the applied setting.

The framework enables existing knowledge held by officers (these are referred to as 'passive' SMM, and are based on experience) to be matched/examined with perceived information. The clustering of information into phases and in the context of the situation result in a suitable course of action being taken ('action intelligence'). Existing SMMs ('passive' SMM) contain information which is used to inform the officer's understanding of the situation. New information specific to the situation is added to these 'passive' SMMs (Richards et al., 2009) to contextualise existing knowledge in the milieu of the new situation. This process of matching existing knowledge to new perceived information in the incident enable existing SMMs to become refined and operationalised. It is these new 'active' SMM (those that get refined and operationalised), which is specific to the situation and shapes future behaviour.

The complexity of developing team or collective decision-making is too dynamic and multifactorial to be illustrated singularly, in one simple diagram. Richard et al's (2016) decision-making framework is constructed of two interconnected models (Model 1 and Model 2). They incorporate both psychomotor (individual and team understandings) and psychosocial (team philosophy and performance/applied context in which, the decisions are made) elements of team decision-making. The creation of pedagogical processes which addresses psychomotor and psychosocial mechanisms are outlined in Model 1 and 2 and results in the effective identification, interpretation and communication of key information in complex situations. An overview of the two interconnected models is presented below with the reader being referred to Richards et al. (2016) for a detailed account of the framework and working mechanisms of Models 1 and 2.

Model 1 illustrates the psychomotor processes which are required to develop a shared team cognitive thought process, which itself is positioned within the context of the team's philosophy. Such processes require information to be seen and valued in the same way by all team members, resulting in the construction of SMMs of performance. Model 1 therefore outlines the concepts which necessitate the development of five layers of information which are required to develop team decision-making. Although illustrated separately to provide clarification, the five phases continually interact and define each other. Through the process of individual empowerment, each of the layers addresses the development of SMMs and the contextualisation of these structures in the applied settings.

Model 2 illustrates the psychosocial process involved in co-ordinating individual perceptual representations of situations, so a collective team cognitive thought process can be obtained. Model 2 demonstrates an empirically tested framework that illustrates the interaction between the slow deliberate reflective environment and the rapid applied environment with the focus of developing team decision-making. It is relevant to state that much of what is being proposed here has already been tested empirically in high level elite sport (Richards, 2004, Richards et al., 2009, 2012; Richards, Penrose and Turner, 2015) and within policing (Richards, Roberts and Roberts, 2017). In short, the start of the model has been designed to address and explore a real performance issue of how teams make decisions in highly pressurised naturalistic settings.

The decision-making framework provides practitioners with a structured approach to accelerate team decision-making within the applied vocational setting. Within the context of policing, the framework can be used to accelerate the decision-making capabilities of probationary or junior officers through the capturing and recording of the expert mental model of a situation held by experienced officers. For example, the decision-making framework can be integrated with BWV (Richards et al., 2017) and also with 360 degree dome footage or video capture, and used to help probationary officers develop a SMM of the situation based on the content knowledge articulated by the expert (experienced mentor). The development of a SMM enables the developing officer to attend to information in the same way as an experienced officer and prioritise the information in an effective manner. The formulation of such SMMs in an educational learning setting which integrates technology (e.g. BWV) enables shared mental models to be operationalised and become 'active', in turn shaping the physical actions of officers. Such 'active' shared mental models' incorporate the essential skills required to engage in shared situational awareness with colleagues. The decision-making framework is also relevant to working across multi-agency teams.

Policing exemplar #3

A junior officer is called to attend an incident on a local housing estate. Resident at the property is Donna, a single mother, and her two children: Matthew (aged 16 years) and Robert (12 years). The younger son is outside playing with his friend and is unaware of the situation at home. The older son, Matthew has been caught stealing from his mothers' purse. The call has been received in response to a neighbour's concern of hearing loud voices and things being thrown. This is a regular occurrence, the police have been called many times to the child at home and at the school he attends in address of his disruptive behaviour. Matthew has Asperger's syndrome. When challenged Matthew's behaviour becomes violent and aggressive. The argument started in the kitchen where Donna normally kept her handbag for ease of access. The argument has escalated as Donna had tried to reinforce boundaries by preventing the son, Matthew from going out. The officers (an experienced officer and probation officer) arrive at the scene to find Matthew holding a small kitchen knife and waving it in an aggressive manner at his mother.

The capturing of officer's decision-making in such situations from the first person's perspective (e.g. BWV or the development of a synthetic environment using 3D domes) provides a unique opportunity for officers to engage with experiential learning in a safe and controlled environment when the footage can later be reviewed. BWV footage (either real or manufactured) can be used as the stimulus for learning. The approach outlined in the framework above layers the learning for the developing officer into phases. These layers integrate the individual expert's knowledge, situational factors and the context of the setting in which decisions is being made. Such a process enables the increasing complexity of the situation to be discussed and achieved. Subsequently, slow in-action reflection (review of the BWV) is applied in the training environments to develop SMMs, which can be used by the developing officer to shape and inform future situations. The slow deliberate video-based learning environment empowers individuals to construct specific SMMs of the situations, in the context of their own performance. This process enables visible points, which the experience officers have identified, to be discussed with the probationary officer. These data points (new knowledge points) are added to existing SMMs of probation officers. This results in existing SMMs of developing officers being updated to establish more refined SMMs (SMM increasing in complexity as experience develops), which are then operationalising and used to shape and inform future actions. Within the mechanism advocated here, the probation officer can learn from and have access to the mental model of the more experienced officers as they both watch footage of a situation together. The experienced officer thinks aloud as the video is played; exposing the novice officer to a new mental model or way of thinking and working, based on what data points they attend to and how they are perceived. The two officers can be prompted to engage in deliberate structured discussion to identify key aspects of the footage or cues that were used by the experienced officer in the decision-making process (Richards, et al., 2017).

Officers can use this process to learn in the following ways:

- Individuals can establish and refine SMMs which can be operationalised to information in-action decision-making.
- Probation/developing officers can search from predetermined data points which will help them to operationalise SMMs more effectively.
- Two or more officers working within the same incidents can attend to data points (cues) within the environment, prioritise information and develop a shared situational understanding of the applied setting when SMMs are developed. The development of this shared situational understanding will enhance communication, a shared common language and supports individuals taking collective action within a situation.
- Engagement in the decision-making framework enables multiple SMMs working across different specialist groups to be integrated in a manner to achieve a common objective.

Summary and future directions

Modern day policing is evolving and changing as organisations react and respond to the continual changing landscape in which we live. The nature of society is rapidly changing and officers require an extensive range of knowledge relating to health, mental health and social issues in culturally diverse populations. In order to ensure that probation police officers are prepared to engage with all individuals in society and continue to protect the public, it is important that any preparation to become an officer facilitates the development of effective communication and decision-making skills. In particular, it is recognised that police officers require fast-paced decision-making skills as they work in volatile and rapidly changing situations where not all information may be present.

The ability for officers to engage in effective decision-making is essential as every aspect of their role requires them to assess information, interpret and analyse information and subsequently take intelligent action (action intelligence).

The importance of enhanced decision-making skills as an attribute of officers is further augmented when the complex setting is considered in which officers work. This continually changing, dynamic setting requires officers to contextualise their own action against those of multiple others and often under a time pressure. This chapter explored some of the emerging technologies with AI dimensions and introduces synthetic learning environments, which have been used successfully in other professions and disciplines to facilitate accelerated decision-making in individuals working in a naturalistic setting. We believe that there is a place for the application of these synthetic environments in the preparation of future police officers. Furthermore, we welcome these developments, not least because they offer opportunities to provide a robust evidence-based practice to support their use, but additionally open up conversations between officers, specialist, academic and researchers as to how we can collectively address the challenge of training our next generation of police officers.

References

Babuta. A., Oswald. M. and Rinik. C. (2018). Machine learning algorithms and police decision-making legal, ethical and regulatory challenges, via: https://rusi.org/sites/default/files/201809_whr_3-18_machine_learning_algorithms.pdf [accessed 1 November 2019].

Bahreman, N.T. and Swoboda, S.M. (2016). Honouring diversity: Developing culturally competent communication skills through simulation. *J Nurse Education*, 55(2), 105–108.

BBC News. (2019). Recruitment of 20,000 new police officers to begin 'within weeks'. www.bbc.com/news/uk-49123319 [accessed 26 July 2019].

Berg, L.P. and Vance, J. (2016). Industry use of virtual reality in product design and manufacturing: a survey. Virtual Reality. 1–17. Doi: 10.1007/s10055-016-0293-9.

Chown, N. (2009). 'Do you have any difficulties that I may not be aware of?' A study of autism awareness and understanding in the UK police service. *International Journal of Police Science and Management*, 12(2), 256–273. DOI: 10.1350/ijps.2010.12.2.174.

College of Policing. (2015). Estimating demons on the police service. Informatic. www.college.police.uk/What-we-do/Ethics/Ethics-home/Pages/Code-of-Ethics.aspx [accessed 10 August 2019].

College of Policing. (2019). Code of ethics. www.college.police.uk/What-we-do/Ethics/Ethics-home/Pages/Code-of-Ethics.aspx [accessed 15 August 2019].

College of Policing. (2015). Estimating demand on the Police Service. Internet www.college.police.uk/News/College-news/Documents/Demand%20Report%2023_1_15_noBleed.pdf [accessed 10 August 2019].

Crane, L., Maras. K.L., Hawkden, T., Mulcachy, S. and Memon, A. (2016). Experiences of Autism Spectrum Disorder and Policing in England and Wales: Surveying Police and the Autism Community. *Journal of Autism Dev Disorders*, 46, 2028–2041. DOI 10.1007/s10803-016-2729-1.

Dalton, N.S. (2013). Neurodiversity HCI. Interactions. 20(2), 72–75. Open Research Online http://dx.doi.org/doi:10.1145/2427076.2427091 [accessed on 15 December].

Dechesne. F., Dignum. V., Zardiashvili. L. and Bieger. J. (2019). AI and ethics at the Police: Towards responsible use of Artificial Intelligence in the Dutch Police. (Version 1.2. March 2019). www.universiteitleiden.nl/binaries/content/assets/rechtsgeleerdheid/instituut-voor-metajuridica/artificiele-intelligentie-en-ethiek-bij-de-politie/ai-and-ethics-at-the-police-towards-responsible-use-of-artificial-intelligence-at-the-dutch-police-2019.pdf [accessed 1 November 2019].

Finnigan, S. (2017). Better understanding demand – Policing the future. NPCC Performance Management Coordination Committee. www.npcc.police.uk/2017%20FOI/CO/078%2017%20CCC%20April%202017%2024%20Better%20Understanding%20Demand%20Policing%20the%20Future.pdf [accessed 10 August 2019].

Higher Education Funding Council for England (HEFCE). (2011). Collaborate to compete: seizing the opportunity of on-line learning for UK higher education: Report to the Higher Education Funding Council for England (HEFCE) by the online learning task force. www.aoc.co.uk/sites/default/files/Collaborate_to_Compete.pdf [accessed 10 August 2019].

Hitchcock. A., Holmes. R. and Sundorph. E. (2017). Bobbies on the net: a police workforce for the digital age. Reform Research Trust. https://bluelightsdigital.com/wp-content/uploads/2017/09/Bobbies-on-the-net.pdf [accessed 1 November 2019].

Klein, G. (2000). Cognitive task analysis of teams. In: Schraagen, J.M.C., Chipman, S.F. & Shalin. V.J. (eds.) Cognitive task analysis. Mahwah, NJ, Erlbaum, pp. 417–429.

Lane, J. and Kelly, R. (2012). Autism and Asperger's Syndrome in the Law Student – Making Accommodations in Academic Assessments. In 47th Annual Conference (Re)assessing Legal Education, 1st April – 3rd April 2012, Lady Margaret Hall Oxford, UK.

McDaniel, J.L.M. (2019). Reconciling public policing, mental health and police accountability. Police Journal: Theory, Practice and Principles, 92(1), pp. 72–94. https://doi.org/10.1177/0032258X18766372.

Nottinghamshire Police, Freedom of information request. (2019). www.nottingham-shire.police.uk/sites/default/files/documents/files/FOI%20005829%2012%20Costs%20of%20recruiting%20and%20training%20a%20Police%20Officer%20and%20a%20Police%20Community%20Support%20Officer.pdf [accessed 12th August 2019].

Orasanu, J. and Salas, E. (1993). Team decision making in complex environments. In: Klein, G., Orasanu, J., Calderwood, R. & Zsambok, C. (eds.) Decision making in action: Models and methods. Norwood, NJ, Ablex, pp. 327–345.

Patterson, C., Stephens, M., Chiang, V., Price, A.M., Work, F., and Snelgrove-Clarke, E. (2017). The significance of personal learning environments (PLE's) in nursing education: Extending current conceptualisations. Nurse Education Today, 48, 99–105.

Pearsall. B. (2010). Predictive policing: The future of law enforcement? National Institute of Justice Journal, (No. 266, May 2010) cited by Babuta. A., Oswald. M. & Rinik. C. 2018. Machine Learning Algorithms and Police Decision-Making Legal, Ethical and Regulatory Challenges. https://rusi.org/sites/default/files/201809_whr_3-18_machine_learning_algorithms.pdf.pdf [accessed 1 November 2019].

Richards, P. and Ghaye, T. (2004). Thinking teamwork: Being the best through reflective practices. Sport and Exercise Scientist. 2, 24–25.

Richards, P. (2005). *Empowering the decision-making process in the competitive sport environment through using reflective practice. Can performance intelligence be taught?* 4th Carfax International Conference on Reflective Practice. Gloucester, UK, June 2005.

Richards, P., Collins, D. and Mascarenhas, D.R.D. (2012). Developing rapid high-pressure team decision-making skills. The integration of slow deliberate reflective learning within the competitive performance environment: A case study of elite netball. *International Journal of Reflective Practice.* Special Olympic Edition, 1–18.

Richards, P., Collins, D. and Mascarenhas, D.R.D. (2016). Developing team decision making: A holistic framework integrating both on-field and off-field pedagogical coaching processes. *Sports Coaching Review*, 6(1), pp. 57–75.

Richards, P., Mascarenhas, D.R.D. and Collins, D. (2009). Implementing reflective practice approaches with elite team athletes: parameters of success. *International Journal of Reflective Practice.* 10(3), 353–363.

Richards, P., Penrose, S. and Turner, M. (2015). *Developing team decision making capabilities in elite football youth academy players.* Cluster for Research into Coaching: International Coaching Conference, 9–10 September 2015, Manchester Metropolitan University, Crewe, UK.

Richards, P., Roberts, D., Britton, M. and Roberts, N. (2017). The exploration of body-worn video to accelerate the decision-making skills of police officers within an experiential learning environment. *Policing: A Journal of Policy and Practice.* Available from: DOI: 10.1093/police/pax017 [accessed 29 March 2017].

Roberts, D. & Greene, L. (2011). The theatre of high-fidelity clinical simulation. *Nurse Education Today*, 31(7), 694–698.

Schön, D. (1987). *Educating the Reflective Practitioner.* Jossey-Bass, San Francisco.

Serfaty, D. et al. (1997). The decision-making expertise of battle commanders. In: Zsambok, E. and Klein, G., *Naturalistic Decision Making.* East Sussex: Psychology Press. p. 235.

Shaikh, Z.A., and Khoja, S.A. (2014). Personal learning environments and university teacher roles explored using Delphi. *Australas. J. Educ. Technol*, 30, 202–226.

Shimmin, A. (Inspector). (2019). Qualitative interview with Staff Development Manager Isle of Man. (27th June 2019).

Syed-Khuzzan, S.M., Goulding, J.S., and Underwood, J. (2008). Personalised learning environments– Part 1: Core development issues for construction. *Industrial and Commercial Training*, 40(6), 310–319.

Smith, W and Swann, J (2019). *Vulnerability Conference Presentation*, College of Policing.

Tong. S. (2017). Professionalising policing: seeking viable and sustainable approaches to police education and learning. *European Police Science and research Bulletin- Special Conference Edition*, Summer (2017), 171–178. ISN 1831–1857.

Weick, K.E. and Roberts, K.H. (1993). Collective mind in organizations: Heedful inter-relating on flight decks. *Administrative Science Quarterly*, 38, 357–381.

Wood, D. and Tong, S. (2009). The future of initial police training: a university perspective. *International Journal of Police Science and Management*, 11(3), pp. 294–305. ISSN 1461–3557.

Conclusion

John L.M. McDaniel and Ken G. Pease

The combination of big data and the ability of algorithms to identify patterns has led to new and complex inferences being drawn about people who are liable to experience (or commit) crime, places likely to host it, and variables associated with its solvability. The possibility that police officers could be informed in advance that there is a high risk that a particular person is preparing to commit a crime, engage in violence or thinking of carrying out an act of terrorism is impossible to ignore. It could potentially allow police forces to put the right resources in place at the right time to prevent crime and harm. The riskiest people and places could become the focus of police efforts, while reducing the possibility of innocent citizens being caught up in the criminal justice system. Turned inwards, these processes could even help to uncover patterns in police behaviour, including systematic stereotyping, racist motives, flawed heuristics and common sources of input errors and misclassifications.

The development and utilisation of predictive and AI technologies sounds progressive and an antidote to some current policing approaches that have garnered public opprobrium. In the recent past, the strategies advocated most often to militate against substandard policing included the drawing up of a more prescriptive code of conduct, the improved supervision of police conduct and the establishment of effective systems of complaint and inquiry; today attention has turned to the introduction of predictive algorithms and AI systems to solve problems. The potential uses and benefits of these systems is so varied that our contributors could write volumes on all kinds of desirable futures that are possible and plausible. It is why the text started with Chan's discussion of socio-technical imaginaries in Chapter 1.

Policing, though, is not conducted in our imaginations. One of the reasons why we compiled this edited collection was to go some way towards bridging the gap between what is imaginary and what is real at the nexus of policing, predictive algorithms and AI. The reader may have found the reality sobering. Extant technologies are often uncertain, error-prone and biased, which we addressed in Section I of the text. Although most software packages and machine learning systems have the capability to process a lot more data than human police officers or analysts, they run a substantial risk of pointing police officers and organisations in the same directions and towards the same general populations that they would have focused on anyway. Over or under representing particular demographics in datasets can seriously affect model accuracy, from individual risk scores to hotspots and facial recognition. Due to greater scale, they may even serve to amplify problematic police activities in the same old areas.

Their propensity for uncertainty and error may lead to more innocent individuals being misidentified or improperly risk assessed and subjected to police powers and interference. Individuals, who should be thought of as complex beings with a rich history and a unique character, are instead risk scored according to how similar they are to an aggregate population. The idea that a person's trajectory in life can be predetermined according to what other people (who are similar to them in some ways) did months or years earlier, sounds a little like a belief in predestination. The use of algorithms to predict crimes (which is what most of them do) and predicting individual criminality is chalk and cheese.

Setting predictive algorithms and AI systems loose on big data can also see a resurgence of lazy stereotyping. Simply 'liking' a post by someone calculated to be a high-risk offender or a top crime 'influencer' (someone who is known to persuade people to 'co-offend' with them), or being friends with several such people, should not amount to a reasonable suspicion of criminality. Similarly, a person's proximity to crime hotspots or gang hangouts, whether they live there or are visiting for the evening, is not sufficient for a stop and search at least without other corroborating evidence. Innocent civilians, including journalists and activists, should not be subjected to surveillance (even through the installation of tracking 'cookies' onto their computers, which some people might not consider to be invasive) simply for exercising their civil liberties.

The reality facing many police services that purchase or develop predictive and AI technologies in partnership with commercial providers is that they may not always know what they are buying into. The tech industry now accumulates far more personal and aggregated data than police services, much of it concerns what people do online (Royal Society, 2017). Tech companies have a vested interest in gathering a broad range of data to identify all sorts of patterns. Whoever can develop the best insights, predictions and products can use their competitive advantage to secure highly lucrative contracts from advertisers, police services, governments and others. A significant volume of work in the AI field is being undertaken by a select few high-profile companies which gather their own data, purchase large datasets from data brokers and regularly acquire smaller start-ups once they develop novel AI systems and algorithms (Royal Society, 2017). Big data has been described as the 'new oil' and the 'new gold' to reflect the amount of behavioural 'bio-prospecting' that they are engaging in (Royal Society, 2017; HLAI, 2018).

It is worth noting that the emergence of this new data-driven 'surveillance society' is not solely the work of police services but largely the result of corporate prospecting and 'surveillance capitalism' (Zuboff, 2015). The commercial prospectors are not limited by the same constitutional constraints as police forces and their financial resources are usually far superior to those of a single force. As both data collectors and data consumers, police forces are in danger of being swept along by the fast flowing undercurrent. This, however, does not mean that they are passive bystanders. Many police departments are already using online platforms to conduct their own overt and covert investigations and social network analysis of particular people and places, which is commonly referred to as Open Source Intelligence (OSI).

Human rights exist because the citizens of liberal, constitutional democracies do not afford police officers unfettered powers to conduct surveillance nor allow them to go to any lengths to interfere in people's lives in an attempt to reduce crime and disorder. Human rights have a rich history, many of our judicable rights have been hard won. Jurisprudence has helped to enshrine key legal standards that should govern legitimate and justified uses of police powers, not least the principles of necessity and proportionality. Laws exist around the collection, retention and minimisation of police data for good reason. Whatever potential big data and AI technologies have to positively help police officers enhance public safety and prevent crime, they arguably have an equal if not greater potential to negatively affect human rights and people's lives and life chances. Most predictive and AI technologies are 'dual use' i.e. each tool can be put toward beneficial or harmful ends, and can be used by police officers and civilians alike in an array of different configurations and contexts (Brundage et al., 2018). For example, a technology labelled as an AI may prove to be accurate more often than it is inaccurate (so one of the better ones) but a police officer may still use it in an unsafe manner. Similarly, one observer may argue that the predictive or AI 'revolution' offers a 'new clarity of purpose' for policing organisations (Deloitte, 2018) whereas another could argue that it offers police leaders a convenient, yet flawed, evidence-base to continue with their go-to traditional approaches.

Every police-related predictive algorithm and AI system discussed within the text is different. Each one can be applied in a multitude of ways and raises unique and complex problems and trade-offs. They each demand a comprehensive risk assessment and equality impact assessment before they are used on real people (with real criminal justice consequences) and the results should be aired and debated in public in advance (unfortunately, this rarely happens). Citizens may be willing to accept some level of error and bias in the use of these systems, affecting some number of victims of algorithmic error, if more people can be kept safe. In such circumstances, for those people who are wrongly targeted, they should be able to appeal easily and should expect full transparency, especially those who are not computer literature and those who are already disproportionately targeted by police forces. Although some algorithms, particularly machine learning systems, are often unintelligible even to computer scientists and are referred to as 'black boxes' as a result, police officers and forces must be accountable for their actions. The democratic ideal is that all aspects of police work should be made available for scrutiny unless it is specifically in the public's best interest for relevant information to be withheld (Patten Commission, 1999). Police officers and the organisational hierarchy may not know exactly how a hand-crafted algorithm or AI system generated a risk score but they will know what they did with it and why.

Police activities and their decision-making processes are not an unintelligible black box. Police officers must be able to justify why they used their police powers in every case, up and down the organisational hierarchy. As a matter of principle, algorithms and AI should not be used by police officers as cover to do what they wouldn't do (or shouldn't do) if the same information had come from a non-algorithmic source or without further corroborating information. In reality, this should be the easy part. Harder questions can be asked upstream, not least whether the person(s) who provided the data should be accountable for any harms and to what extent, and the culpability of the person(s) who built the AI, the person who validated it, the company that sold it, and the agency that bought it, among others. Some AI systems could even be bestowed their own legal personalities in future.

The burden of accountability arguably lies predominantly on the policing side at present. Computer scientists who are responsible for developing AI systems are not routinely schooled in human rights law and the constitutional standards surrounding, *inter alia*, privacy and the presumption of innocence. Some of the most popular undergraduate texts, such as Russell and Norvig's *Artificial Intelligence* (2014), contain no distinct chapters on human rights, structural violence or social justice. Their focus is predominantly on creating complex codes that work, not the various ways they may be used to infringe on civil liberties in an array of policing contexts. For example, in one notorious case of functionality trumping ethics, instead of fixing one visual identification algorithm which was unable to distinguish between black people and gorillas, Google reportedly sought a quick fix by disabling the ability to search for gorillas in related products rather than fixing the underlying data sets and code (HLAI, 2018). Much of what we refer to as AI is actually machine learning that is influenced and supervised by human scientists who select particular features for it. Such is the concern for achieving computational performance over ethics, Big Tech companies have been described as 'data cartels', and the environment that they have created as a 'race to the bottom' on AI safety (Ibid, Valentine, 2019).

It is partially for these reasons that trade-offs and broader political and societal considerations cannot be left to AI developers (or police forces) to determine in isolation. If predictive and AI technologies are to help solve some long-standing policing problems, then it is imperative that these realities are recognised and addressed from the outset. Police forces have a responsibility to the public to address concerns and help develop a good understanding of the capabilities and limitations of the technologies that they utilise, including hand-crafted algorithms and AI systems. This can be exceptionally difficult, requiring regular reform and adaptation commensurate to the speed of innovation and technological change. It should, nevertheless, be a price worth paying for police services whose first job is to protect the public from harm (including harm caused by police officers). As the Law Society (2019: 5) observes, police forces and other agents of criminal justice should be "trusted to use technology well, with a social licence to operate and in line with the values and human rights underpinning criminal justice ..." It adds that if the nature of policing and the justice system are to change because of scientific and technological innovation, then this change should be 'a conscious one, understood and meticulously stewarded, rather than a transformation beyond clear societal control and with unclear implications' (Ibid: 12). Technology companies are well used to innovating within boundaries, so police forces, legislatures and civil society should not be afraid to set them (they can debate the degree of 'stifling' that this may cause).

A lack of evaluation of developers' claims and testing of algorithmic systems in real-world settings (as opposed to the development of them in artificial micro-worlds) was a regular source of concern throughout the edited collection. Stevenson (2018: 306) has remarked elsewhere that it is a little unnerving that some algorithmic systems have acquired a "sheen of scientific credibility" and "somehow ... gained the near-universal reputation of being an evidence-based practice despite the fact that there is virtually no research" showing that they have been effective in criminal justice settings. Even those police leaders with the most rudimentary knowledge of police history should appreciate that miscarriages of justice are often the result of an over-reliance on technologies and techniques that are poorly understood, inadequately evaluated or accepted on face value.

Another cause for concern is the omnipresent trope traded by developers, politicians, consultants and police leaders that predictive and AI technologies will inevitably enable police services to realise cost savings and 'do more with less'. On the contrary, it is more likely that they will be expected to 'do more with more'. The imaginaries that we readily associate with predictive and AI policing involve the recruitment of more police officers and civilian staff to respond to all of the additional insights and leads that would be generated. Officers already spend a significant amount of time on public protection work, managing high-risk offenders and protecting vulnerable people. Taking a problem-oriented policing approach to identify and address the causes of crime and other policing problems would require significant resources and thought. Whole departments engaged in multi-agency partnerships and the design of public health approaches could be needed. The comprehensive realisation of data quality, AI safety and police accountability is not cheap either. Teams of analysts, computer scientists and researchers should be employed to examine how accurate systems are in reality and how they are shaping police activities on the ground. Some of the skills needed for the future, including data science qualifications, are among the most in demand in the labour market at present (Deloitte, 2018). A chief data scientist could, for example, command a much higher salary in the private sector than a chief constable would receive from her police organisation (Ibid). Bridging this gap and building a technologically savvy and fully accountable police organisation will not be cheap. Train rank-and-file police officers to the highest standards and they may leave police services for more lucrative private sector positions, leaving an under-qualified workforce interacting with complex, intimidating and uncertain algorithm outputs on a daily basis.

Since predictive and AI systems carry a degree of uncertainty, police officers will continue to detain and target some proportion of innocent people. This creates financial, societal, individual and opportunity costs. Moreover, attempts by defendants to cast a reasonable doubt over the probity of police actions may lead to more acquittals, while innocent people may increasingly pursue civil cases for compensation where their civil liberties have been unlawfully infringed upon. Predictive policing cannot be cost free. Expect too much from hard-working police officers without providing them with the proper support and they too may seek remedies from their police organisation for the stress it causes. The full range of costs that surround predictive policing and AI technologies are far more complex and inter-dependent than many observers realise.

Reliance on predictive and AI tools may also see a return of centralising tendencies which have long been resisted in many jurisdictions. Since pattern-matching algorithms often thrive on larger volumes of data, the linking of databases and the creation of regional or national hubs to manage them sounds attractive. In 2019, for example, the Home Office in the UK provided £4.5m in funding for a National Data Analytics Solution (NDAS) to pool together information held by a number of different police services and use machine-learning techniques to calculate risk scores. Within a year, the NDAS was crunching data on millions of people, drawing information from incident logs, stop and search records, custody records and conviction histories, among other sources (Dearden, 2019). The funding to set up such hubs is attractive to police services, many of whom have borne the brunt of a decade of austerity. Centralisation, though, does not come without its risks. Immediate issues that would need to be resolved include: the amplification of bias and error as information arrives from an even greater number of imperfect sources; the difficulty of scrutinising the quality and provenance of bulk data; the prevalence of 'group-think' if the expertise of scientists is too intimidating for non-specialists to challenge; the tendency for remote police leaders to assume they know what citizens and communities need, want and think without actually asking them; and many other common occurrences associated with centralisation such as function creep and regulatory capture.

A fully decentralised system is not ideal either, as one Police and Crime Commissioner (PCC) recently observed: 'the public would be outraged or scared if they knew how hard it was for us to share data and how we struggle with it' (Deloitte, 2018: 21). Issues of system inter-operability and differing legal and data standards at the local, national and international levels remain problematic, leading not least to the evolution of the National Crime Agency (NCA) in the UK and Europol at the EU level, among other institutions and frameworks. The police service that isn't seen to be investing in harmonised data systems, AI and algorithmic technologies, cloud computing, biometrics, drones and virtual personal assistants may quickly become the subject of public opprobrium and professional criticism for relying on 'outdated' techniques and for failing to take crime and public safety seriously enough.

What is currently happening at the nexus of policing and AI is reminiscent of the boom and bust cycles that have long been associated with AI development. Relatively short periods of heightened excitement in the progress of AI have been followed by more prolonged periods of disappointment and disillusionment, known as 'AI winters', once researchers were unable to deliver on the full scale of their promises in the short-term (HLAI, 2018). We would appear to be in a similar period of heightened excitement around AI in policing. Technologies are being piloted and adopted by police services around the world based on the promises of predictive accuracy and future cost savings rather than on sound evidence that they work. Many police services have procured predictive and AI tools without commissioning independent evaluations of how they perform in practice or how predictions might impact ordinary lives on the ground. Many of them have also done so secretly, piloting predictive and machine learning technologies, occasionally for years, without ever revealing it to the public, to police oversight bodies or to local or national parliaments. The Law Society (2019: 70), for example, found 'a general and concerning lack of openness or transparency about the use of algorithmic systems in criminal justice across England and Wales'. There are, however, some indicators to suggest that this period of initial excitement may be ending. After five years of working with PredPol's predictive software, Kent Police ended the partnership in 2018 (Ibid), while Black Lives Matter activists called upon Amazon in 2020 to abandon its contracts to provide facial recognition and cloud computing services to various US police forces (Paul, 2020). To avoid associations with human rights concerns, some police services have even started to use euphemisms in this space, with some referring to them as 'explanatory' models rather than predictive tools.

We would caution against the use of the terms 'predictive', 'intelligent' or 'science' in many contexts because it is arguable whether many of the systems that are labelled as such are actually good at predicting events or are similar in any substantive way to human-like intelligence. We cannot think of any real benefits of equating the capabilities of predictive and AI systems with the intelligence of police officers or other humans, particularly when the gaps between them seem so great. Like the Wright brothers who succeeded in their quest for artificial flight by *not* trying to imitate birds, we could do with bringing an end to these comparisons and attempts at emulation, at least during this early stage of police-AI development. We could focus instead on the development and functioning of each technology, how they are used in the hands of police officers and organisations in practice, how they are affected by the distinct environments in which they are used, and their impact on people's day-to-day lives.

There are many issues that we were unable to address in this text. For example, some 'deep fakes' and other kinds of digital forgery which can replicate people's faces and voices in synthetic images and footage are now so good that they are nearly indistinguishable from the authentic kind (Brundage et al., 2018). Investigating cases where these technologies are used to scam people out of money or make it appear that a person has committed a crime is likely to be challenging for police investigators. Other kinds of malicious uses of AI include the weaponisation of driverless cars and drones for the purposes of terrorism, or the coordination of large scale cyberattacks to breach digital security systems (Ibid). Disinformation is likely to be a particular problem for police forces in future. Vulnerable people could be targeted with extremist propaganda in an attempt to persuade them to carry out attacks, or disinformation campaigns could be waged against police forces and other state actors involving the use of deep fakes and propaganda to sway public opinion and cause unrest. AI systems could even be used to intentionally poison police databases with large quantities of misleading data in order to interfere with police intelligence systems and operations. Counter-AI strategies may also become popular, for example by simply wearing sunglasses with someone else's face on them in order to confuse facial recognition systems, or flashing a picture of a stop sign in front of a driverless car to cause a collision. The risks are considered to be so serious, and transnational in nature, that the United Nations recently set up a Centre for Artificial Intelligence and Robotics within its Interregional Crime and Justice Research Institute (UNICRI) in The Hague.

In many of these cases, police organisations and local and national legislatures will need to co-produce solutions in partnership with a range of commercial entities. Partners will include Big Tech companies and banks that will have resources that are often vastly superior to police services, and smaller partners like independent retailers who want to use facial recognition technologies to identify shoplifters. If police organisations leave key issues untended because they are inconvenient, overly complicated or expensive, then AI-related societal transformations may take place without a functioning policing system in place. We may even see a rise in vigilantism as pattern recognition and online surveillance tools become more widely available to ordinary citizens. The rapid evolution of predictive and AI technologies, many of which remain far from perfect, has led very quickly to a significant blurring of boundaries that have long helped to define and constrain modern policing, at least in principle (the functions of modern police forces have always been the subject of debate). Perhaps this is the best opportunity yet for people to define what they want and what they do not want from their police forces.

As for the future of predictive policing and AI, we have not come across any clear, official roadmaps outlining the direction of travel in the UK, the US or Australia. This is worrying. Police forces will likely use an array of different predictive and AI technologies from a patchwork of sources and providers, utilising datasets of varying quality, and each one will raise its own distinct set of issues (which may or may not be addressed). It is not acceptable to say that the current suite of tools are experimental and that they should simply be acquiesced to until society better understands their forms, full range of uses and consequences. Even during their design stages, important trade-offs are made. Algorithm and AI safety should become a key concern of the police and the public.

References

Bostrom, N. (2017). *Superintelligence: Paths, Dangers, Strategies*. Oxford: OUP.

Brundage, M. et al. (2018). *The Malicious Use of Artificial Intelligence: Forecasting, Prevention and Mitigation*, Future of Humanity Institute, University of Oxford.

Dearden, L. (2019). Police testing technology to 'assess the risk of someone committing a crime' in UK. The Independent. 17 July 2019.

Deloitte. (2018). Policing 4.0: Deciding the Future of Policing in the UK.

Ferguson, A.G. (2017). *The Rise of Big Data Policing: Surveillance, Race and the Future of Law Enforcement*. New York: NYU Press.

House of Lords Select Committee on Artificial Intelligence (HLAI) (2018). AI in the UK: ready, willing and able? Report of Session 2017–19, HL Paper 100.

Law Society Commission. (2019). Algorithms in the criminal justice system. *The Law Society of England and Wales*, June 2019. Available at: www.lawsociety.org.uk/en/topics/research/algorithm-use-in-the-criminal-justice-system-report [accessed 1 August 2019].

Patten Commission. (1999). A New Beginning: Policing in Northern Ireland. The Report of the Independent Commission on Policing for Northern Ireland.

Paul, K. (2020). Amazon says 'Black Lives Matter' but the company has deep ties to policing. The Guardian. 9 June 2020.

Perry, W.L., McInnis, B., Price, C.C., Smith, S.C. and Hollywood, J.S. (2013). *Predictive Policing: The Role of Crime Forecasting in Law Enforcement Operations*. Santa Monica: RAND Safety and Justice Program.

Royal Society. (2017). *Machine Learning: the Power and Promise of Computers that Learn by Example*, The Royal Society, April 2017 DES4702.

Russell, S. and Norvig, P. (2014). *Artificial Intelligence: A Modern Approach*, 3rd Edition, Harlow: Pearson Education Limited.

Stevenson, M. (2018). Assessing Risk Assessment in Action, Minnesota Law Review, 103, 303 to 378.

Valentine, S. (2019). Impoverished algorithms: Misguided governments, flawed technologies and social control. *Forham Urb L.J.*, 364–427.

Zuboff, S. (2015). Big other: surveillance capitalism and the prospects of an information civilization. *J Inf Technol*, 30, 75–89.

Index

Printed in the United States
By Bookmasters